THIS IS BOP

Popular Music History

Series Editor: Alyn Shipton, Royal Academy of Music, London.

This series publishes books that challenge established orthodoxies in popular music studies, examine the formation and dissolution of canons, interrogate histories of genres, focus on previously neglected forms, or engage in archaeologies of popular music.

Published

An Unholy Row: Jazz in Britain and its Audience, 1945–1960
Dave Gelly

Being Prez: The Life and Music of Lester Young
Dave Gelly

Bill Russell and the New Orleans Jazz Revival
Ray Smith and Mike Pointon

Chasin' the Bird: The Life and Legacy of Charlie Parker
Brian Priestley

Handful of Keys: Conversations with Thirty Jazz Pianists
Alyn Shipton

Jazz Me Blues: The Autobiography of Chris Barber
Chris Barber with Alyn Shipton

Jazz Visions: Lennie Tristano and His Legacy
Peter Ind

Lee Morgan: His Life, Music and Culture
Tom Perchard

Lionel Richie: Hello
Sharon Davis

Mosaics: The Life and Works of Graham Collier
Duncan Heining

Mr P.C.: The Life and Music of Paul Chambers
Rob Palmer

Out of the Long Dark: The Life of Ian Carr
Alyn Shipton

Rufus Wainwright
Katherine Williams

Scouse Pop
Paul Skillen

Soul Unsung: Reflections on the Band in Black Popular Music
Kevin Le Gendre

The Godfather of British Jazz: The Life and Music of Stan Tracey
Clark Tracey

The History of European Jazz: The Music, Musicians and Audience in Context
Edited by Francesco Martinelli

The Last Miles: The Music of Miles Davis, 1980–1991
George Cole

The Long Shadow of the Little Giant (second edition): The Life, Work and Legacy of Tubby Hayes
Simon Spillett

The Ultimate Guide to Great Reggae: The Complete Story of Reggae Told through its Greatest Songs, Famous and Forgotten
Michael Garnice

This is Hip: The Life of Mark Murphy
Peter Jones

Trad Dads, Dirty Boppers and Free Fusioneers: A History of British Jazz, 1960–1975
Duncan Heining

This is Bop

Jon Hendricks and the Art of Vocal Jazz

Peter Jones

equinox

SHEFFIELD UK   BRISTOL CT

Published by Equinox Publishing Ltd

UK: Office 415, The Workstation, 15 Paternoster Row, Sheffield, South Yorkshire, S1 2BX

USA: ISD, 70 Enterprise Drive, Bristol, CT 06010

www.equinoxpub.com

First published 2020

British Library Cataloguing-in-Publication Data

A catalogue record for this book is available from the British Library.

ISBN-13 978 1 78179 874 4   (hardback)
           978 1 78179 875 1   (ePDF)

Library of Congress Cataloging-in-Publication Data

Names: Jones, Peter (Peter Douglas) author.
Title: This is bop : Jon Hendricks and the art of vocal jazz / Peter Jones.
Description: Bristol : Equinox Publishing Ltd, 2020. | Series: Popular music history | Includes bibliographical references and index. | Summary: "Biography of Jon Hendricks: hipster, bopster, comic and raconteur, a wordsmith par excellence, and a fearless improviser who took the arts of scatting and vocalese to new heights"-- Provided by publisher.
Identifiers: LCCN 2020019606 (print) | LCCN 2020019607 (ebook) | ISBN 9781781798744 (hardcover) | ISBN 9781781798751 (ebook)
Subjects: LCSH: Hendricks, Jon, 1921-2017. | Jazz singers--United States--Biography. | LCGFT: Biographies.
Classification: LCC ML420.H3729 J66 2020 (print) | LCC ML420.H3729 (ebook) | DDC 782.42165092 [B]--dc23
LC record available at https://lccn.loc.gov/2020019606
LC ebook record available at https://lccn.loc.gov/2020019607

Typeset by S.J.I. Services, New Delhi, India

In memory of Holli Ross, 1956–2020

Contents

Introduction: The Verge of Impossibility   1

1   You've Got Something Money Can't Buy   8

2   Mitigating Circumstances   25

3   We Don't Want No Singers, Man   33

4   The Most Beautiful Thing   48

5   A Mouthful of Hot Rice   65

6   Everybody Got Tired   82

7   The Mistakes Are the Only Part That's Jazz   99

8   No Chord is Better Than the Wrong Chord   117

9   We Need You to Control Him   133

10   Keep Smiling   152

Appendix A: The Voice, the Scat, the Vocalese   167

Appendix B: The Lyrics   175

Appendix C: The Wisdom and Philosophy   183

Discography   200

Notes   222

Bibliography   243

Index   249

Note from the Publisher

Every effort has been made to establish the identity of photographers/copyright holders. Anyone not credited may please get in touch with the publisher.

Introduction: The Verge of Impossibility

In February 2017, nine months before jazz singer Jon Hendricks died, a concert was staged in his honor at St. Peter's Church in midtown Manhattan. It was to feature the first-ever performance of a musical suite—a vocal version of the 1957 Miles Davis/Gil Evans album *Miles Ahead*—which Hendricks had been working on for half his life. A twenty-two-voice choir, who had spent months learning the entire work by ear, had flown in from London and Jon's daughter Michele had come over from Paris. Close to a hundred years old at the time, Jon Hendricks was not in the best of health. Just before the performers arrived he was taken into hospital, and it seemed likely he would never come out again. Although the immediate cause was a skin condition, his main issue was cognitive decline due to dementia: in recent months he had become largely unresponsive to everyone around him except his younger daughter Aria. To anyone who had known the man, the idea of him shutting down to the outside world was shocking—Jon Hendricks had always possessed the energy of ten men. He was a singing, joke-cracking, storytelling musical genius; a man who had known and worked with just about everyone of significance in the history of jazz; a man whose charisma lit up whatever room he was in.

By Friday 17, the day of the concert, Jon was still in the hospital and—as far as his doctors were concerned—he was going to stay there for at least two more days. The church, meanwhile, had been rigged with sound equipment and cameras. The band and the choir were rehearsed and New York jazz notables including singers Jay Clayton, Annie Ross, Veronica Swift, her mother Stephanie Nakasian, and Sheila Jordan were expected. But it now looked as if the real star of the show would not be there. It was too late to organize a live video feed of the gig to the hospital. In desperation, the choir's director toyed with the idea of performing *Miles Ahead* at Jon's bedside.

At noon, after much persuasion, the doctors reluctantly agreed to let Hendricks go. He was helped out of bed and taken home to get dressed for the concert. Yet, as the clock ticked ever closer to seven o'clock, there was still no sign of him. This was typical; Jon's lateness was legendary. Then—at the last possible moment—he appeared at the door with Aria and a nurse. They made their way inside the church, the guest of honor walking largely unaided. After stooping to embrace Annie Ross, who was sitting in the front row, he took off his tweed overcoat to reveal a snappy black striped suit with a bright red shirt, red tie with white spots, and white pocket handkerchief. Aria sat on one side of him, the nurse on the other. Once he had acknowledged the audience's standing ovation, the concert began with a selection of tunes that Hendricks had sung throughout his career. And as the first notes of "It's Sand, Man" emerged from the choir, the old man's face registered sheer joy. He mouthed the words, conducted with his hands, and occasionally even rose from his seat. After the concert he made a brief speech and scatted a chorus on "The Preacher" as Michele held the mic for him. Back home, later on, he was still thinking about the concert. "It was beautiful," he kept repeating, "I was knocked out."

The final triumph of *Miles Ahead* was the icing on the cake, the last hurrah of a life and career that no screenwriter would dare send to a movie producer. Jon Hendricks was born at the beginning of the Jazz Age; was schooled in jazz by bebop pioneer Art Tatum, a family friend; was shot at by his own side in World War II before deserting the army and going on the run; was persuaded to leave his hometown and come to New York by none other than Charlie "Bird" Parker; wrote songs for Louis Jordan; recorded with King Pleasure; was

Jon and Aria Hendricks at St Peter's Church, February 2017 (courtesy Pete Churchill)

divorced, broke, starving, addicted to heroin and alcohol five years later; and became a jazz superstar at the tender age of thirty-six with the singing trio Lambert, Hendricks & Ross. He sang with Louis Armstrong, Duke Ellington, Charlie Parker, Count Basie, Thelonious Monk, and Antonio Carlos Jobim, and knew them all well. He wrote and performed in the long-running, highly successful stage production *Evolution of the Blues*. He won two Grammys and was nominated for five more. He met presidents (three of them). He was presented with the Legion d'honneur by the French government. Any one of these achievements would have been the highlight of anyone's life; Hendricks lived several lifetimes, all at once.

Over the course of his ninety-six years, he rose from extreme poverty in small-town Ohio to become one of the greatest figures in jazz. There may have been better singers, but he was unmatched when it came to

Jon Hendricks meets Ronald Reagan (courtesy Aria Hendricks)

scatting and vocalese, writing lyrics, or fronting a band. In the course of researching this book I heard him variously described as a wide-eyed elf, a street hustler, a genius wordsmith, and a charming, erudite, swinging hipster—the greatest swinging hipster you ever came across, with the greatest stories ever told. "When I heard that Jon was coming to the University of Toledo to teach a course called The History of Jazz," recalled Jon Richardson, ex-president of the Toledo Jazz Society, "I thought, that's almost laughable—because all Jon has to do is stand up at the front of the room, and that *is* the history of jazz."

Post-war, that history really began with Charlie "Bird" Parker. And if you listen to Parker's 1952 recording of the Jerome Kern/Oscar Hammerstein tune "The Song Is You," you will hear something close to what Hendricks had heard at a concert at the Civic Auditorium in Toledo, Ohio, two years before. For Bird the gig was just a routine one-nighter, but for Hendricks that night in 1950 turned his life through ninety degrees: he sat in with the band, scatting several choruses. Bird instantly recognized that here was no ordinary singer. As the pianist and singer Ben Sidran put it:

> When [Jon] would scat sing, he was as fluent in the idiom of bebop—and I mean the grammar that went back to Bird and Bud Powell and all those guys—that was like a native tongue of his. And I don't think he was ever motivated to move beyond that. He said ... that bebop was the most elegant way of speaking ever invented. And I think that's very much who he was ... The idea of getting immersed in that harmony was really important to him.

Today, to observe the raw power and awesome vocal facility of Jon Hendricks in his prime, you have to seek out the scratchy monochrome videos floating around the internet. One of these features the singing group that made him famous—Lambert, Hendricks & Ross—on some unnamed TV show, possibly Dutch, performing Sonny Rollins's "Airegin." On it, Hendricks contributes his trademark saxophone scat solo, fingers twiddling the air in front of his chest, pouring out chorus after chorus at an impossibly fast tempo—his energy, note choice, and all-round execution as good as any saxophonist who ever lived.

The sheer difficulty of what Hendricks was able to do with his voice was masked, in some ways, by the apparent effortlessness of his delivery. The jazz writer Gene Lees compared watching the trio perform with watching great gymnasts at work:

> The human voice has its own limitations. The material Lambert, Hendricks and Ross adapted and tackled comprised complex, humorous, often scintillating lyrics by Hendricks and Ross, set to 'existing' ensemble and solo 'instrumental' passages, and was

implicitly anti-vocal. The tensions of bebop chromaticism and odd intervallic leaps create almost insuperable problems for a singer. What Lambert, Hendricks and Ross did was difficult to the verge of impossibility. Indeed, the only thing that proved it possible at all is that they actually did it.

Hendricks became a master of jazz, the only American art form, despite his inability to read music or to understand even the most basic tenets of music theory. Far from regarding his musical illiteracy as a drawback, he argued against the whole idea of music being written down: writing it down stopped you listening to it, and listening was the only proper way to learn it, in his opinion, because music starts to die as soon as you write it down. Whenever he had to teach a pianist a new song he would sing the chords one by one, note by note, badgering the poor guy until he finally hit the right chord. ("Drives them crazy," he chuckled.) Whenever he signed an autograph for a fan, Hendricks would add: "I wrote the shortest jazz poem ever heard. Nothing about lovin' 'n' kissin' ... one word ... listen!" They were lines he had written and performed on George Russell's *New York, NY* album in 1958.

His influence on jazz singers can hardly be overestimated. Kurt Elling maintained:

> [Without Hendricks] I wouldn't have half of my material. I don't know what I would have done. I wouldn't have even thought I could write a tune ... There is vocalese from the classic era of Lester Young, as well as Dexter Gordon or John Coltrane solos that are still there to be tackled, and that's only possible because of Jon. I love him for the innovation in lyricism that he brought to the table.

To Hendricks, a lyric wasn't just a lyric—it was a poem and, as such, oral literature. He loved England and English writers, particularly Shakespeare, and he enjoyed being part of the literary tradition. "I saw him as somebody who was interested in taking the tenets of literature, the classic narrative, and bringing it into bebop," said Ben Sidran. "His lyrics were always so unbelievably literate." His influence spread beyond jazz: another consummate wordsmith, Joni Mitchell, fell under the spell of Lambert, Hendricks & Ross as a teenager, learning every song on their album *The Hottest New Group in Jazz*.

Hendricks was not only a singer but a showman, an entertainer. He had learned the artistry of stagecraft, understood how to carry himself on stage, what to say between songs. Today, according to Kurt Elling, these techniques of presentation have almost disappeared from live jazz performances because Jon Hendricks's generation has gone—there is almost no-one left to show people how it should be done. Said Elling, "You need to be able to address an audience, and to communicate with them even when the music's not playing. And that is as important as any other example that he set, for me." Stagecraft is much more than entertainment; it's how you make everyone in the room feel welcome. It's also what ensures they don't get bored or feel awkward. "The lack of venues today deprives young singers of the chance to learn that aspect of their craft," he added. "Jon not only understood this, but executed it night after night, even when he was sick as a dog."

Humor played a large part in Jon Hendricks's life and in his art. The jokes he told on stage were always the same, but he always made them sound as if he was telling them for the first time. "An actor has to say the same thing every night, and Jon could do that, he was a great entertainer," said his long-time pianist David Leonhardt. "He would shape the concert set from beginning to end. It was like a work of art."

It has been said that biography consists of holes tied together with string. I have tried to fill as many of the holes in the Jon Hendricks story as possible, but some remain—one or two are still quite large. However, many people helped by supplying the string, while others provided essential support. My sincere thanks are therefore due to the Hendricks family—his children Jon Jr. (in Uruguay), Michele (Paris) and Aria (New York), and their cousin Bonnie Hopkins and her daughter Priscilla Florence in Toledo, Ohio. I am also most grateful to Amy London for her hospitality and kindness in New York, to Kevin Fitzgerald Burke for granting access to his Brooklyn basement, to Gunnar Mossblad in Toledo for his warm friendship and invaluable help, and to Gerry Sahagian who kindly drove me to Detroit; likewise to Vincent Pelote at the Dana Library jazz collection in Newark, New Jersey, and staff at the New York Public Library in the Lincoln Center and at the Schomburg Center in Harlem. In London I was greatly aided by David Nathan at the National Jazz Archive and by the staff at the British Library. I am also eternally grateful to all those others who helped by offering possible leads, by agreeing to be interviewed, or by providing photographs: Yolande Bavan, Claude Carrière, Renato Chicco, Pete Churchill, Les Cirkel, Kurt Elling, Larry Goldings, Dave Green, Frank Griffith, Bob Gurland, Martin Hone, Noel Jewkes, Eric G. Johnson, Audrey Lasbleiz, Anne Legrand, David Leonhardt, Paul Meyers, Stephanie Nakasian, Eghosa Osarabo (a.k.a. Clarence Becton), Dean Pratt, John Richardson, the late Holli Ross, Daryl Runswick, Janis Seigel, Don Sickler, Ben Sidran, Roseanna Vitro, Larry Vuckovich, Andy Watson, Val Wilmer, Norma Winstone, and James K. Zimmerman. In researching this book I have relied extensively on three detailed interviews conducted with Jon Hendricks: James Zimmerman's two-day marathon in 1995 for the Smithsonian National Museum of American History, Marc Myers's 2009 interview for his JazzWax blog, and Lee Ellen Martin's 2010 interview conducted for her BA thesis. Her 2016 PhD dissertation also proved a valuable resource.

My gratitude is due also to those who read the manuscript and whose comments and suggestions improved it no end: Bridget Jones, Amy London,

Gunnar Mossblad, and Jim Trimmer. I would also like to thank my commissioning editor Alyn Shipton, copyeditor Dave Doyle, and Valerie Hall and Janet Joyce at Equinox. Any errors that remain in the book are my responsibility alone: readers are welcome to send corrections, clarifications, comments, and additional information to thisisbop@icloud.com.

Peter Jones, London, July 2020

1 You've Got Something Money Can't Buy

A tiny speck on the map near the middle of Ohio marks the birthplace of John Carl Hendricks. It's a small town called Newark, known to archaeologists for its mysterious prehistoric earthworks, but not for much else. Jon Hendricks (he dropped the *h* from his first name when he went into show business) was born there on September 16, 1921. Back then, Newark was a railroad switch town with a dirt road running through the center. The trains ran north towards Lake Erie, east to Pittsburgh, and west to Columbus.

Jon was the ninth child and the seventh son born to Alexander Brooks Hendricks and his wife, the former Willie Mae Carrington. Jon's father never talked about his life before he met Willie Mae, apart from saying that he was a runaway. All Jon knew about Alexander Brooks was that he came from Richmond, Virginia, and as young man moved to Huntington, West Virginia, to work as a coal miner. While there he stayed in the boarding house where Willie worked and before long he had decided that she would be the perfect Mrs. Hendricks.

Her ancestry was a microcosm of America's tangled racial history. She was five-eighths African American, a quarter Cherokee, and one-eighth European. Her great-grandmother, an African American slave, married James McGaffick Sr. of Wythe County, son of a substantial white Virginia slave owner. When they had a son, McGaffick developed a great regard for the boy and arranged for him to be educated. According to Jon Hendricks, McGaffick afterwards sold his wife, which made the boy so angry that he ran away from the plantation and married the daughter of a Cherokee chief. This was Jon's great-grandmother. Her daughter, Jon's grandmother, lived in West Virginia and married his grandfather, a freed slave called John Carrington. Jon (or John) was named after him. The Carringtons had six daughters, one of whom was Jon's mother.

At the time of his developing interest in Willie Mae, Alexander Hendricks did not appear the ideal son-in-law, being a casual laborer and a drunk to boot. Willie's mother refused to let her daughter see him, but Alexander persisted. He carried on working in Huntington and, as soon as he had saved enough money to buy a covered wagon so that they could elope, he asked Willie to marry him. She agreed, and they took off for Newark. Almost immediately, Willie discovered she was pregnant—a condition she remained in almost permanently for the next twenty years.

At first, Alexander's new family responsibilities seemed to have no effect on his love for the bottle. As children arrived in endless succession, he

Wille Mae Carrington (courtesy Bonnie Hopkins)

continued to drink. Soused to the gills one wintry night, he slipped on the ice and banged his head, lying unconscious on the frozen ground in front of the house for two hours. Willie Mae knew he was there, but by this time she was so sick and tired of his drunken behavior that she decided leave him there. The children pleaded with her to drag their father indoors but she was adamant, explaining that it was time he took responsibility for his own actions. Later, waking up in the freezing cold, Alexander couldn't believe that he was still alive. In later life he described it as an out-of-body experience, a revelation. He felt that God had saved him for a reason: at that moment he resolved not only to change his ways, but to devote his life to God.

A drunkard's promise doesn't usually amount to much, but Alexander Hendricks was truly a changed man. From then on, alcohol was banned from the house, and he refused even to set foot in any establishment that sold liquor. Together with his good friend Edward Waller from Richmond, he enrolled in a Methodist seminary in Virginia, completing the training course back in Ohio at Payne Theological Seminary. Payne was part of Wilberforce University (named after the British abolitionist William Wilberforce) and the first college to be owned and run by African Americans through the African Methodist Episcopal Church (AME). It quickly became apparent that Hendricks had not only embraced Christianity wholeheartedly, but was a natural-born preacher with a gift for energizing congregations. As a result, he was given the job of recruiting new members throughout the Midwest. The head of the Church in Ohio, Bishop R. C. Ransom, would post Rev. Hendricks to small towns like Kenton, where the congregation was somewhat run down, and put him to work reinvigorating it. For the first six years of his ministry, every time the job was done, he would have to uproot his growing family and move to another town; Jon Hendricks claimed that as a child he went to thirteen different schools. The church paid for their relocation and there was always a parsonage that went with the job, so they were assured of a place to live. But his ever-expanding brood had to sleep three to a bed.

The Hendricks children were, in chronological order: Norman Stanley (known as Stanley), William Brooks (W. B.), Florence Missouri (Zuttie), Charles Lancel, Stuart Devon, Vivian Christina, Edward Alan, then came John/Jon, followed by James, Clifford Jiles, Robert, and Lola Mae. Interviewed in 1995, Jon forgot to mention Bela (named after a local Hungarian butcher who was generous to the family in the matter of credit), Donald, and Arthur. Two more children died in infancy. Yet another member of the family was Jon's niece Bonnie Hopkins, daughter of Zuttie (who was aged only thirteen when she gave birth). During the Great Depression, as Jon was growing up, his father would occasionally cut people's hair to supplement his meager income. Once he was known in an area, he would call at local farms and bring home whatever small surpluses of corn or potatoes they could spare. Jon remembered being about nine years old and standing in line with him to collect government food, often cans of beef stew, which would last them about a week. Things improved with Franklin D. Roosevelt's New Deal, but—like so many of their friends and neighbors—the Hendrickses were still desperately poor, relying partly on a vegetable garden to put food on the table. On one occasion, Jon and five of his brothers stole a gun then stole, killed, and butchered a cow—something none of them had a clue how to do. After this bloodbath there was the problem of keeping the meat fresh, so they stole some ice. Then they had to find a way of hiding the dismembered animal from their father. Wisely, Rev. Hendricks turned a blind eye—something he found himself doing almost constantly as the kids grew up. The scarcity of food in the Hendricks household largely explains Jon's many lyrics on the subject in later life.

At least playmates were plentiful, with so many children around the house. What the brothers didn't have was money; going to the movies cost a dime each, plus a nickel for popcorn, so they would go "junking"—wandering through the alleys, picking up whatever the neighbors had thrown out. If they were lucky enough to come across a broken lamp, they could take it to the junkyard and get a few cents for it. Jon also discovered that he could make a nickel by hanging around public toilets, offering to crawl under the door to open it for people, who would then give him the nickel it would have cost them anyway. Despite the poverty, it seems to have been a relatively orderly life in a loving and tight-knit family. And although by nature a loud and boisterous man, Rev. Hendricks was (by Jon's account) no grim, distant patriarch but a kind and affectionate father. He told the kids that being broke was not the same as being poor. Jon recalled:

> My father said, "When you're poor, you're poor in spirit, but when you're broke, you're just out of money. If you're rich in spirit, you might be broke, but you've got something money can't buy, so you're never poor as long as you know the spirit of God is in you." And that's the way it's been with my life. I'm never poor, I've been broke but I've never felt poor.

Each day began at six o'clock with prayer. The Hendricks children were expected to kneel next to a chair or a table and listen while their father addressed the Lord. The length of this address would vary according to whatever he thought needed to be done that day that might involve God. There would be more prayers before every meal. In the morning, task number two was to line up to go to the bathroom. This complex process was organized by age with the youngest going first, helped by the older ones, who would wash last. In this home of traditional family values, the sisters were given the household chores: as soon as Zuttie and Vivian were old enough to stand on chairs, they wiped the dishes. They also swept the rooms in the house, helped eventually by Bonnie, who was tasked with getting the boys out of their rooms so that she could clean and tidy. Having imposed this regime, there wasn't

Alexander Brooks Hendricks
(courtesy Bonnie Hopkins)

much else for Rev. Hendricks to do to keep them in order. "We were just exhorted to love one another," recalled Jon:

> We had no problem with that. We got down on our knees to suppli-
> cate to a power that was bigger than us. Every morning he prayed
> for good and for the safety of all the world. And he exhorted us
> every morning to know—not to believe, to know—that we were
> alive by the grace of God. He told us that there's nothing living that
> we can dislike … He warned us that outside our front door, nobody
> believed that. So he said our task was to take that knowledge with
> us when we went outside, so that we behaved that way whenever
> we met someone. The problem was the real world didn't always
> work that way or respond in turn to kindness and love. My father
> taught me to fight for the right things, not the wrong ones. My
> father's way of looking at life gave all of us a strong humane-ness.
> Everybody to this day likes my brothers and sisters.

His father's version of Christianity seems to have been pantheistic, almost Buddhist in scope:

He would tell us, you are children of the living God, and every living thing is your relative. If it's alive you love it and you're responsible for it. If it's a bug on the sidewalk you don't step on it, you step over it or walk around it. You have respect for what's alive because all the life comes from the same place ... it's from God. As children of the living God you respect all life.

The issue of race was also one that Alexander Hendricks had thought about carefully. "To be a racist," Jon explained, "you have to be a person who does not believe in God, because if you believe in God, then you must know that God is no respecter of persons." By this he meant that race, rank, power, or wealth were irrelevant. "So if God is no respecter of persons, how can a person created by God be a respecter of persons? It's impossible. So that makes that remark that my father made even more cogent and more right to the point ... So when people ask me about race, I say, 'What time does it start?'" Another story further illustrates the point. When Jon was sixteen Rev. Hendricks was posted to a church in Greenup, Kentucky, and the family moved out of Toledo. After Hendricks Sr. got to know the local white preacher, the latter would come by each evening for coffee, and the two of them would sit on the porch and talk. One night the subject came around to race. The white preacher had never mentioned racial superiority before, but it seemed some of his parishioners had expressed their disapproval of him spending his evenings with a black man. "Reverend, you know I like you," the preacher said, "but I just can't help feeling that my people are superior to your people."

"Brother, do you believe in God?" asked Rev. Hendricks.

"Reverend, you know I do," replied his companion.

"Then what's your problem?" asked Rev. Hendricks. The rest of the evening passed in silence apart from the creaking of their respective rocking chairs, until the preacher finally stood up, said goodnight and went home. Their meetings continued, and the subject was never raised again.

Alexander Hendricks's views were more than merely theoretical. Jon told the story that, on another occasion, the family were visiting relatives in Kentucky—in the days when blacks were being lynched on a regular basis in the South. He and one of his brothers were crossing two planks over a patch of mud and stood aside to let a white couple go by. The man told them to get *all* the way off the planks.

"Why?" Jon asked, "There's room for you to pass."

"Oh, you one of them smart niggers," said the man, and went off to fetch the sheriff. When the sheriff arrived, he shoved the boys into the mud. Hearing about this, the Rev. Hendricks took them down to the lawman's office.

"Sheriff, I want to talk to you," he said.

"Yeah, Reverend, just a minute," said the sheriff, and carried on writing for several minutes while the preacher stood waiting.

"Sheriff, I want to talk to you," he repeated.

"I heard you, Reverend, just wait a minute."

The pastor—who was a large man—reached down, pulled the sheriff from his chair, and stood him upright. The boys froze, expecting him to reach for his gun.

"All right, what is it, Reverend?" he said.

"Don't ever put your hands on my children," said Hendricks Sr.

"All right, Reverend," said the lawman.

The significance in folklore of the seventh son was not lost on the Hendricks parents, Jon believed. Early on in life, he was picked out from his brothers to succeed his father as a man of the cloth and therefore ended up spending a lot of time with him. Although the lure of entering the ministry was never quite strong enough ("I said to myself, I would have been a disgrace to my father if I came into the ministry"), Jon's lifelong self-belief—the feeling that he was somehow special and carried with him some kind of destiny—appears to have begun around this time. At school he was already earning A grades in English and soon he became his father's secretary, tasked with selecting verses from the King James Bible which would form the basis of Rev. Hendricks's next sermon. Jon noticed the book's spare, economical use of language: saying as much as possible with as few words as possible became his own approach to lyric writing.

Willie Mae exerted as great an influence on him as his father. On one occasion a local ne'er-do-well known as Whitman Red shot and killed a man down by the railroad tracks, which ran right by the Hendricks house. The local women were making the expected comments about what a terrible person Red was but, once they had left, Willie Mae said to herself, "Poor Red." Explained Jon, "My mother had compassion for the murderer. I've since understood that that is a very high spiritual thing to do." Wherever the family ended up, she would lead the church choir. When Jon was six or seven years old she would hold his hand, squeezing it when she wanted him to sing. In the days before amplification, a powerful voice was needed in church. It was Willie Mae who taught him the spirituals that he always said were the source of the blues. And Willie not only sang ("Nearer My God to Thee," "Joshua Fit the Battle of Jericho"), but wrote lyrics too. Jon's father, by contrast, "had a voice like a wounded bull elephant" and was once awarded a coconut cake out of sympathy when the preachers held a singing contest amongst themselves.

Eventually, Alexander Hendricks began to chafe against his allotted role in the AME of always being the one who did the grunt work, only to be moved on after a year or two and see someone else take over the thriving church community he had established from the sweat of his brow. The frequent relocations became increasingly stressful on the family, so it was a relief when, in 1932, they were finally allowed to stay in Toledo for several years. Rev. Hendricks had taken over as pastor of the Warren AME church on Collingwood Boulevard. Like Newark, Toledo was a railroad switch town, with connections east to Cleveland and west to Chicago. The train journey between the east and west coasts took four or five days and, since Toledo was a station at which passengers would often change trains, it was a convenient point at which to break a long trip. Among the most regular travelers were black jazz musicians moving between engagements. Typically these would be members of territory bands: groups of between eight and twelve players who would go from town to town, playing dance music to communities that were often remote and desperate for entertainment. In Ohio these included McKinney's Cotton Pickers, Andy Kirk and his Twelve Clouds of Joy, and Luis Russell's Orchestra. Being black, the musicians were barred from staying in white hotels, which meant they had to take whatever lodgings they could find in black neighborhoods. City Park Avenue, where the Hendricks family lived, was a respectable, middle-class street at the time, occupied by both black and white families.

There was no space for visitors to sleep in the overcrowded Hendricks household but bands would come over for dinner, attracted partly by Willie's reputation as a cook and partly by the presence in the house of two good-looking young women—Zuttie and Vivian. Rev. Hendricks's friend Edward Waller had a son, Thomas—better-known as Fats—who would often come through Toledo, as did the Virginian folk singer Josh White, who used to "ride the blinds" on the train because he had no money for a ticket. The Hendrickses had a piano in the living room and visiting musicians like Ben Webster and Duke Ellington's trombonist Lawrence Brown would play it. Knowing the minister would not allow liquor, tobacco, or drugs to be consumed in his house, they would arrive as close to dinnertime as possible and leave as soon as possible afterwards. Fats, however, worked out how to get around the ban on intoxicants. He would play a few hymns on the piano then settle into a chair next to the window and talk with Alexander Hendricks. In order to maintain his daily regime of a fifth of gin, he would pay one of Jon's friends fifty cents to hold the bottle just outside the window. Every so often he would say "just a minute, Reverend" and lean out to take a swig from the bottle, while the pastor would look down in his lap. Fats once asked if he could take Jon out on the road to sing with him; the request was turned down. Jon was warned not to spend time with musicians who, like Fats and Ben Webster, were known for their heroic intake of booze.

Jon realized he could turn his talent for church singing into some much-needed spare change. He began touring the local bars, whose clientele were often from specific ethnicities. When he walked into an Irish saloon, he would sing:

> Sure, I love the dear silver,
> That shines in your hair,
> And the brow that's all furrowed,
> And wrinkled with care.

I kiss the dear fingers,
So toil-worn for me,
Oh, God bless you and keep you,
Mother Machree.

It worked like a charm. The men would start sobbing into their beer and toss him a quarter. If the place was Italian, it would be "*Guarda il mare com 'e belle! Spira tanto sentimente*"—a song he had learned at school. At Stanley's, the local hamburger joint on Indiana Avenue, he worked a variation on his crawling-under-the-toilet-door technique. Hanging around the jukebox, he would learn the songs—including all the instrumental solos. When someone approached, and before they had put their nickel in, he would ask them what they were going to play. He would then offer to sing it himself, and he would get the nickel. He explained in later life that his ability to imitate instruments while scatting stemmed from these experiences, as did his vocalese compositions.

As music became an increasing source of fascination, Jon began listening to singers like Gene Austin, Bing Crosby, and Russ Columbo on the radio. Among the popular songs of the day that formed the early Hendricks repertoire were "Love Letters in the Sand," "Mighty like a Rose," and "I Cover the Waterfront." And if he didn't like the lyric, he would change it:

> When I was small I was singing popular songs and I used to like the song "It's the Same Old Dream": "I can see a steeple surrounded by people," and I said, "Wait a minute—what, are they on stilts?" And so I changed it: "I can see a steeple, a church full of people."

At school he also learned some songs from the operas and *Hava Nagila*, and began spending time with other children who liked music, loitering outside the bars along Indiana Avenue and listening to Muddy Waters, Lightnin' Hopkins, Speckled Red, or Memphis Slim. Sometimes, when he had nothing better to do, he would go downtown to spend an afternoon in the music departments at Lamson's or Tiedtke's, where they hired musicians to demonstrate the latest sheet music for customers. Hendricks was never going to buy anything, but he was already adept at learning by listening. When visiting bands played at the Trianon Ballroom, he and his friends would climb the fire escape to the roof and watch the band through a skylight.

Soon Jon was being asked to sing at banquets and other functions—for money. He did filler spots at the Rivoli Theatre. While waiting to go on, he would shoot marbles with the other kids in the alley behind the theatre. On one occasion the manager came looking for him. Jon's hair was standing on end, and his trouser knees and shoes were dirty. "These people have paid good money to be entertained and they don't wanna see no little ragamuffin coming out there on that stage," said the manager, thwacking him twice around the chops. This forcefully impressed upon Hendricks the importance of being well turned out. He noticed that when the Jimmie Lunceford band came to the Paramount Theatre they had three different tuxedo outfits (white, orange, and black) that they changed into during the show. Later in life, when Jon complimented Duke Ellington on his elegant appearance, the great composer said, "Well, Jon, one should always look better than one's audience."

By the age of eleven or twelve, Hendricks was beginning to be noticed. Ted Lewis, who had popularized the song "Me and My Shadow," had an act that included a young black boy who copied everything he did and offered the part to Jon. As with Fats, his mother vetoed the idea.

Five doors down City Park Avenue, at number 1123, lived the Tatum family—friends of the Hendrickses. Jon would go there to play on their front porch, yelling and clowning about on the swing with Karl and Arline Tatum, while inside their older brother Arthur would be practicing the piano. Arthur's mother would come out of the kitchen and say, "Stop that noise. Can't you see Art is practicing?" In time, Jon started listening to what he was playing.

Before he took up the piano, Arthur Tatum was a violin prodigy and played in amateur contests in which Hendricks also participated. His mother, who scrubbed floors in a downtown bank, decided it would help her son's musical career if he had a piano, so she bought him a pianola and some paper music rolls to go with it. Particularly liking one of the pieces, she set her son the task of learning it by the time she came home from work the next evening. What neither of them realized was that the roll had been cut by two pianists playing together. Recalled Hendricks:

> She came home the next day and she asked him, "How are you coming along with that?" He said, "I'm ready!" And he played it! I said "Whoooo, look at that!" Then I whispered in her ear, and told her it was two guys playing. She said, "It is?" I said, "Yeah!" She was so surprised. He not only played it, he learned it by ear and played it in a day. To this day, I'll never forget that.

From then on, Art devoted himself to the piano. As Jon and Art played in amateur shows around Toledo, Jon found the pianist to be an excellent accompanist, in part because he avoided the melody. These early learning experiences with Art Tatum defined the rest of his life. He would stop by the house on his way home from Robinson Junior High School. Reluctant at first to take any kind of music lesson, Jon would have to listen while Art played passages with different chords and their extensions and Jon would have to sing them back, note by note. It was the most rigorous ear training imaginable. Tatum was blind in his left eye and had very limited vision in his right, allowing him to see little more than outlines and shapes. But according to Sweets Edison, his ear was so good he could "hear a gnat pee on cotton". He could "hear around corners"— something Hendricks himself also claimed he could do. "He was very intelligent and he could hear," said Jon:

Art Tatum, Vogue Room, New York, late 1940s (William P. Gottlieb/public domain)

Boy could he hear. You know, if you asked him about the song so and so, he would say, "How does it go?" And [you'd] sing it. He played it perfectly with the right chords and everything. He heard the chords amazingly. He was a reincarnation of Blind Tom. They say Blind Tom was a slave that could play anything on the piano. He could hear an opera once and play it on the piano and his masters thought very highly of him, kept him in the house and he entertained at parties and things.

Although initially influenced by Fats Waller, Tatum rapidly outpaced him, and during the 1930s pianists would converge on Toledo from all parts of the country to hear him play. Among them—from Detroit, just fifty miles to the north—were Tommy Flanagan, Hank Jones, and Barry Harris. From Chicago, meanwhile, came Nat King Cole. It is impossible to overstate the awe with which Tatum was regarded by the biggest names of the day in jazz. On his first visit to New York in 1930 he was greeted by a welcoming committee consisting of Fats, Willie "the Lion" Smith, and James P. Johnson—all of them masters of stride piano. At a Harlem bar called Morgan's, they staged a battle of the pianists; by the end of the evening, Tatum had emerged as the undisputed king. "That Tatum, he was just too good," admitted Fats. "He had too much technique. When that man turns on the powerhouse, don't no-one play him down. He sounds like a brass band."

One writer admired "the note-perfect clarity of Tatum's runs, the hardly believable leaps to the outer registers of the piano ... his deep-in-the-keys full piano sonority, the tone and touch control in pyrotechnical passages clearly beyond the abilities of the vast majority of pianists," describing them as "miracles of performance." Wrote another:

> Tatum's style was notable for its touch, its speed and accuracy, and its harmonic and rhythmic imagination. No pianist has ever hit notes more beautifully. Each one—no matter how fast the tempo— was light and complete and resonant ... His speed and precision were almost shocking. Flawless sixteenth note runs poured up and down the keyboard, each note perfectly accented, and the chords and figures in the left hand sometimes sounded two-handed.

While most singers learn melody in a linear way, working with Tatum trained Hendricks to think vertically, in terms of the harmonic possibilities of a tune; he would hear and sing the chords, as opposed to merely learning the melody. This, he believed, was what gained him acceptance from instrumental players, who also learn far more about harmony than do most singers. Anyone who witnessed him in his pomp—eyes closed, head back, scat soloing at incredible velocity whilst still hitting the chord changes—was experiencing the influence of Art Tatum. According to Hendricks, Tatum was also the jazz musician who mostly deeply influenced Charlie Parker:

> What Bird did when he got back to Kansas City was ... he realized, hearing Art play, that ... if he was to be said to know any song, he would have to know how to play it in any key, so he started by

going back over his whole repertoire and playing it in all the keys and playing it accurately in every key.

As well as shedding useful light on both Tatum and his own early training in jazz harmony, these comments also raise an issue which loomed large in Hendricks's later dealings with jazz musicians, namely his supposed total ignorance of music theory. He claimed that the reason he never learned to read music was that, during his sessions with Tatum, he found he could hear more clearly with his eyes closed. Later he would ask questions, such as whether a certain key was louder than another. But in conversation with James Zimmerman in 1995 he was able to discuss Tatum's "substitute chord structures." Whatever the truth of his actual level of understanding, Hendricks's conception of singing was to approach it like an instrumentalist:

> I always tried to sing as though I were a saxophone, for example, 'cos that was near enough to the timbre of my voice ... When I spent those two years with Art, he would make me learn these fast phrases. It became simple for me—by the time I was seventeen I could scat anything. I could scat any song I could sing. I could take two or three choruses on that song.

In the twenties and early thirties, Prohibition created a huge, lucrative market for mobsters across the USA: they were the ones who ran the roadhouses and supplied them with illegal whiskey. Toledo's location made it the center for much of this activity and, as an accidental by-product, had turned it into a hip, entertainment-oriented town. The two main gangs were the local Italian Licavoli mob and the Detroit-based Purple Gang, most of whom were Jewish. The Purple Gang operated in Ohio and part of Illinois and the southern Michigan and Detroit area, running liquor down to Ohio from Michigan. At around this time (Hendricks was always extremely vague about dates), he and Tatum were working in a Purple-operated nightclub called the Chateau le France. "I would come home after school, eat an early supper, and go to bed," said Hendricks. "Then my mother would wake me up at eight and I would get ready to go to work from nine until about one thirty in the morning. We did it because the family needed the money and I loved to sing." The mobsters would cruise around the back of the Chateau le France in Packard trucks, each truck protected by two men carrying sawn-off shotguns, and park under the trees. Clad in heavy overcoats and Borsalino hats, once inside the building they would take the shotguns out from under their coats and deposit them in a barrel next to the back door, as if they were umbrellas. Being black, and therefore not permitted to enter the front area of the club, Hendricks and Tatum had to hang around in the kitchen before they went on stage:

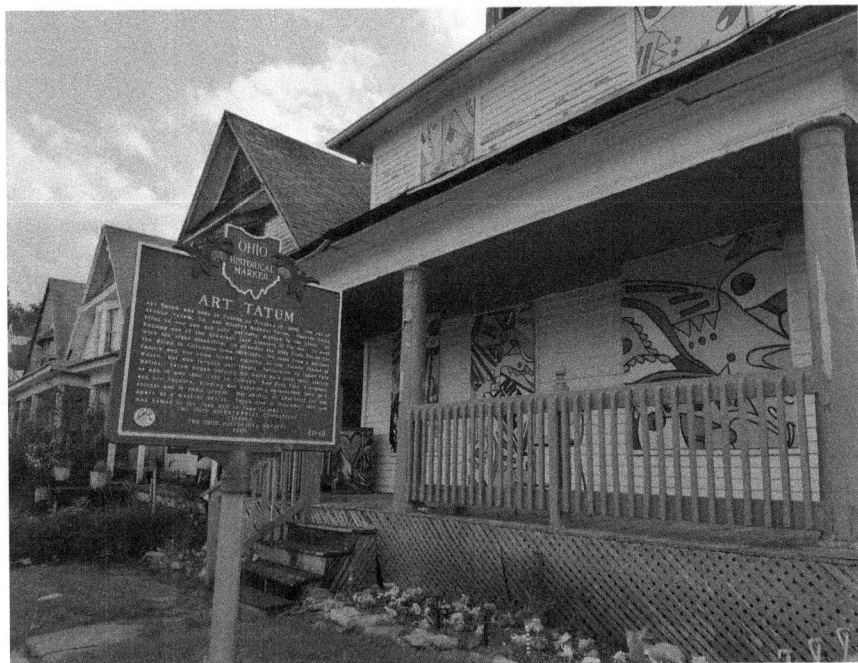
Art Tatum historical marker, Toledo, Ohio (author photo)

They'd say, "Hi kid," and rub my head and put something in my palm. I'd get mad because I knew white people considered it good luck to rub a little nigger's head ... Then I'd look in my hand and there would be a twenty-dollar bill, and my anger would subside somewhat. I was bringing home between fifty and seventy-five dollars a night. My mother would be sitting by the coal stove, asleep, still wearing her apron. The way I used to wake her up was I would start pouring this change into her apron and the weight of it, you know it gets sort of heavy, she'd wake up. And she'd save my supper: if she had a pie, she'd always save me the last corner and I would eat that.

At around the age of fourteen, while he was attending Scott High School, Hendricks found steady work at Toledo's Waiters and Bellmen's Club as the opening act for headlining artists like Louis Armstrong, Duke Ellington, Sweets Edison, Count Basie, and Teddy Wilson. (The place was named in recognition of the two best jobs any black man could hope to get, since they conferred some degree of dignity and a decent income.) The after-hours club opened up at midnight: they would turn the lights off at the front of the building and draw the curtain, with customers filing in through the side door. Unusually for the time, the Waiters and Bellmen's attracted both black and white patrons. "It was what they called Black and Tan in those days," said Hendricks. "Lester Young used to say, 'The place is full of grays.' That's what he called white people that came over to hang out with black people." The club was owned by Johnny Crockett, who was not actually a member of the Mafia, but had to do business with them as there was no alternative at the time if you needed normal restaurant supplies—anything from tablecloths to liquor. Those who passed through the house band included Ahmad Jamal, Linton Garner, and his brother Erroll. The Waiters and Bellmen's put on a full variety show: It would open with a band, followed by a line of dancing girls. An emcee would then introduce the main act which was usually a featured singer; sometimes this would be Jon Hendricks, who would sing three or four numbers, followed by a tap dancer.

Downstairs were two dressing rooms—one for the dancing girls and one for the musicians. At first Jon used the musicians' dressing room, but the air was so thick with marijuana smoke that it was decided he would be better off with the girls. And whenever they saw him, they would give him affectionate hugs (according to Aria Hendricks, the Waiters and Bellmen's was actually a strip club):

> They would come in between acts to change costumes and rip off their blouses and their brassieres, and bare breasts would be flopping everywhere. They would say, "Oh, Jonny, come here! Come here, Jonny!" They would take my head and bring it to their bosoms and press. I'd be like, "Hey, bus driver! Open the door!" Yes, these ladies would get me in trouble.

Jon also found time to devise and direct shows at high school, including an annual event called Scott's-a-Poppin'. At some point in his early to mid-teens (he never seemed sure whether it was when he was eleven, fifteen, or sixteen), Jon began singing on the local radio station WSPD, performing with The Swing Buddies. The group was made up of four singers and a guitar player. Jon was asked to join because their lead singer had recently quit in hopes of making it big in New York as a solo artist; it was Art Tatum's suggestion that they take Hendricks on as his replacement. The Swing Buddies were contracted to WSPD for three years, performing three evenings a week for a fee of $125—a small fortune. The gig brought financial stability to the entire Hendricks family.

Jon had long since realized that jazz shared the same melodic and rhythmic elements he grew up hearing in the church. As an adolescent in Toledo he formed his own jazz quartet, but found that the group did not understand the swing feel that he heard every week in his father's gospel church choir. Swing came to him naturally after being exposed to it from infancy but, realizing that not everyone had experienced the same musical education, he took his bandmates to church. "Everything started in the church," Hendricks told Lee Ellen Martin:

> The church was swinging before anybody else ... [The quartet] weren't swingin' to my idea of swing. I was playing drums and ... I had to make them sound like they were swingin'. Five houses down from mine became a sanctified church and they had a piano, bass, drums, and guitar. Man, they swung like dogs. They swung those spirituals man with that back beat you know and the guitar player (sings) "wang dang" and the drummer "bap bap bap." So I took my quartet on a warm summer night, I said, "let's go in and stand by the door," and we stood against the wall. I just let them listen to these guys do a couple tunes then I said, "Let's go." I said, "Now that's the way we should swing."

The years after the Hendricks family's move to Greenup, Kentucky—when his father was finally assigned to a new church—are frustratingly obscure for anyone wanting to follow the Jon Hendricks story. In interviews he had surprisingly little to say about this period, his narrative usually jumping from the Swing Buddies to World War II, with little to say about the years in between. Certainly by this time Art Tatum had moved on, consolidating his reputation in New York, then visiting California and England. We know that Jon did not accompany his parents to Greenup, but stayed behind in Toledo with the older brothers and sisters, since it was important that he kept his lucrative job at the radio station. He worked as a full-time musician in both Toledo and Detroit.

Aged sixteen and still in high school, Jon established a long-term relationship with a girl called Thelma and fathered a child, Dwight, whom he would visit whenever he was in town. After his contract with the Swing Buddies expired and he finished high school, Jon moved to Detroit for two years where he sang with his brother-in-law in a group called the Jesse Jones Band. Jesse, who played violin and trumpet while Jon sang, was a well-known drunk—popularly known as Juice Jones. They would perform the popular jazz songs of the day, like "Nagasaki":

> Hot ginger and dynamite,
> That's all they serve at night,
> Back in Nagasaki,
> Where the fellers chew tobaccy,
> And the women wicky wacky woo.

Jon's niece Bonnie Hopkins thought it quite likely that Jon lived with his sister Vivian when he was in Detroit. And he played with the likes of Hank Jones, Barry Harris (at the Bluebird), Tommy Flanagan, Wardell Gray, Billy Mitchell, and Doug Watkins. It was also in Detroit that Hendricks met Dizzy Gillespie for the first time. In Toledo he worked with Harold Lindsay, Mozart Perry, and other Toledo jazz greats at the Jeep Club, the Waiters and Bellmen's Club, and C&L on Indiana Avenue. He continued singing in and around Toledo and Detroit until 1942, when he was drafted into the army to fight in World War II. The experience turned out to be the strangest and most terrifying of his life.

2 Mitigating Circumstances

While the portion of Jon Hendricks's life immediately before he was conscripted to fight in World War II is shrouded in mystery, the war years are not only known about in some detail but have been the subject of two European film documentaries—*Tell Me the Truth* (France) and *Blues March* (Germany).

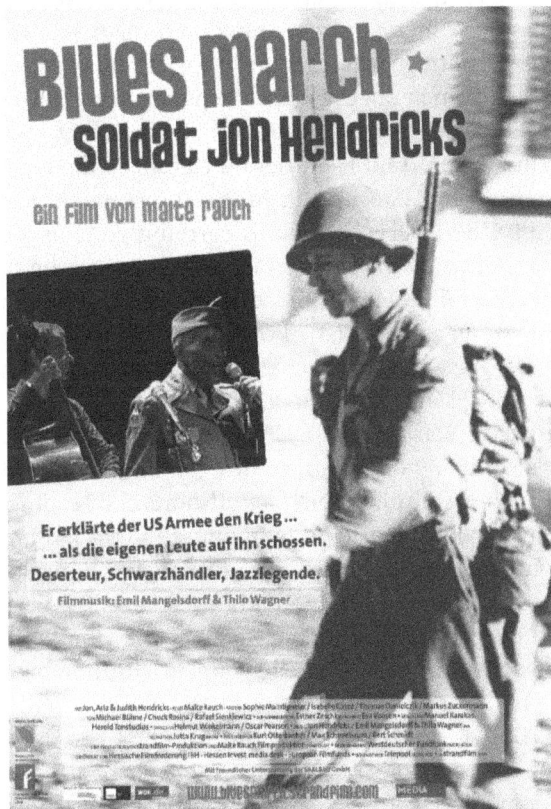

Poster for the German-produced Blues March (Strandfilm gmbH, 2010)

Hendricks was one of over half a million black Americans to be conscripted into the US Army when America entered the war. In 1942—after he completed basic training, first at Camp Shelby in Missouri and then at Camp Rucker, Alabama—he and his brothers Edward and Charles were sent to an air base in Kettering, England, via Scotland and Wales; brother Clifford entered the navy. Jon's first assignment was to load bombs on to US Army Air Forces planes that were being sent on raids over France and Germany. But, having enjoyed an early life that was relatively free from racial prejudice, from his earliest days in Europe the US Army treated him and the other black soldiers like slaves. As soon as they arrived in Kettering, they were confined to barracks for three days without explanation. On release, they learned that their white colleagues had spent the three days spreading rumors among the English townspeople that the black Americans were riddled with venereal diseases and unfit to fraternize with. In response, Hendricks encouraged the other black soldiers to give their chocolate, sugar, and coffee rations to the appreciative English townsfolk. "They thought we were absolutely charming," Hendricks reported, having discovered that local white girls were amenable to dating him and his buddies after all. This, of course, was what the whites had been trying to prevent from the outset—and it caused constant racial strife. At the time there were almost no black people in the UK. No matter that the Americans were now on foreign soil; to the whites, miscegenation was an outrage wherever it took place and black soldiers who fraternized with white women ran the risk of being beaten or shot. "It was so bad to be serving in the army of a country that hates you that much. Just awful. So demoralizing for us," said Hendricks. Protests to the local commander were in vain, and would merely result in the complainant getting transferred to another unit. The black GIs took to carrying guns on dates. "In other words," said Hendricks, "we were veterans at fighting by the time we met the Germans."

Once his high school experience of producing shows became known, he was given the task of organizing them for the USO—wrangling the jugglers, singers, and dancing girls sent over from the US. But the fun came to an abrupt end at five o'clock on the morning of June 18, 1944—a few days after the start of the D-Day landings in northern France—as Hendricks and his company disembarked at Utah Beach under fire from German soldiers. Having deposited them just offshore, the landing ships turned back to fetch more men. Hendricks found himself in the sea up to his waist, under fire and without a weapon with which to defend himself. Men on both sides of him were shot immediately—and he felt certain he was going to be next. He took off his pack and carried it, wading on his knees through the water in order to present the smallest possible target to the gun batteries. Once on shore he ran as far inland as he could, as men continued to drop all around him.

But by now the D-Day invasion had been going on for twelve days and, for the remnants of the exhausted German army, the odds were worsening; somehow Hendricks survived. Wearing his full eighteen-pound field pack and heavy steel helmet, he and his group marched eighteen miles, unloaded their kit, erected their tents, and fell asleep. The next morning they walked to a nearby farmhouse, where they were greeted warmly by the farmer and his wife. The couple dug up some bottles of calvados they had buried to avoid it falling into the hands of the Germans. From then on Hendricks developed a deep fondness for the French who, he found, did not practice discrimination and treated him as an equal. He was now attached to the 548th Quartermaster's Headquarters. The American military command believed that blacks were inferior physically, mentally, and emotionally to whites and therefore unfit for combat. By the same logic, this meant they didn't need to be armed. Initially Hendricks's skin color restricted him to physical labor, but his obvious intelligence and gift of the gab led to him being promoted to the position of battalion clerk. His duties now included keeping track of food and fuel rations, as well as liaising with other infantry divisions in France and Belgium. Reporting to a major, he maintained the records of all the companies that made up the battalion. It was his job to organize forms and passes as well as requisitions for food, drugs, guns, and ammunition. The Articles of War—essentially the army's rulebook—was another area of responsibility and, as new instructions arrived in the office, Hendricks was required to read, memorize, and then file them. Whenever the major needed to quote one of the articles, or wanted to know what it covered, he would ask Hendricks. This inside knowledge of military procedures and laws soon came in more useful than he could have imagined.

Even with more responsibility, Hendricks continued to experience racism. At the beginning of 1945 his battalion was ordered to Épernay in northeastern France, the country's Champagne region. Around two hundred Italian prisoners of war had been put to work in the vineyards and some had managed to inveigle their way into the affections of the local young women, both in Épernay and in nearby Reims. They introduced them to Hendricks and his black colleagues. "The Italians are not fighters," explained Hendricks in later years, "they're very passive, they like to sing and drink wine, make love—very similar to us!" Enraged by the sight of black soldiers consorting with the local women, a detachment of white American military police began shouting at the women, "What are you doing with these niggers? Can't you do better than that?" They broke the soldiers' wine glasses and poured the wine over their heads. Hendricks understood that they were trying to provoke a violent response, urging the men to stay calm and not retaliate. The next morning, back in camp, they were working on an abandoned rifle range when bullets began pinging off the concrete all around them—the MPs were not finished. Hendricks ran to the office to find the captain, telling him they needed guns. The captain refused to give them any; instead he picked up the phone and called for another detachment of MPs to come and stop the shooting. Hendricks tried to explain that they would all be dead by the time the reinforcements arrived, and quoted from the Articles of War. "I don't need you to tell me a damn thing, Hendricks," replied the officer, "I am not giving you the guns to shoot at American soldiers."

Hendricks asked, "What are we?"

The captain replied, "I don't care what you are, I'm not giving you guns."

"Yes sir," said Hendricks, and saluted. "I hereby resign from the US army."

Waiting outside the office were four of his fellow black soldiers. Hendricks told them to go and pack their bags, and be back in fifteen minutes. He hurried over to the stores and grabbed handfuls of papers—travel passes of various durations; passports; requisitions for sugar, salt, eggs, and gasoline—and stuffed them into his duffel bag. He scribbled out requisitions for four carbines, two forty-five caliber automatic pistols, ammunition, two giant trucks, and a jeep out of the motor pool, signing it all with the captain's name. ("That was my personal declaration of war," he said.) With the paperwork complete, they took off into the French countryside, knowing very well that the penalty for desertion was hanging—it was one of the Articles of War. Jon chose an alias for himself: Eric Douglas. (A decade later he gave the name to his second-born son, Eric Douglas Hendricks.) Accompanied by a white Frenchman named Roger, whom they disguised as a US Army captain, they drove south to Besançon, not far from the Swiss border. There they commandeered a hotel and hid, avoiding other soldiers and doing their best to blend in with the local population. To survive, they sold gasoline back to the US Army, sometimes dressing in civilian clothing when they went out to make the sale. Their other clients were often well-to-do locals with enough money to buy a truckload of gas costing perhaps thirty-five thousand dollars. Soon, the runaway soldiers were making more money than they knew what to do with; what they hadn't bargained for was all the requisition paperwork finding its way back to the Supreme Headquarters of the Allied Expeditionary Force (SHAEF) at Versailles. Inevitably, it was only a matter of time before someone started questioning why a small battalion like the 548th Quartermasters in Épernay had ordered such a vast quantity of food and gasoline. Hendricks claimed that, by the time he and his fellow deserters were captured, he had accumulated over a million dollars in cash.

His account of what happened next became increasingly cinematic: "So one morning I woke," he said. "I dreamed I was coming back into New York through the Lincoln Tunnel, and I could see through the tunnel it was very black; it seemed like the tunnel wasn't getting lighter. Because this tunnel I was looking through was a forty-five automatic pointed right at my forehead." As he opened his eyes, a voice told him, "With your left hand, take the covers back and get up slowly or you're going to get killed now." It was a member of the US Army Criminal Investigation Division (CID). Hendricks did as he was told.

The CID man fetched the other soldiers from their rooms.

"You sons of bitches, you been making a lot of money on United States Army goods—you know you're gonna hang, don't you?" he said.

"No, what are we gonna hang for?" said Hendricks. "I didn't kill anybody."

"Desertion in the face of the enemy."

"What enemy?" Hendricks asked. "You mean the white military police firing on us? Yeah, we deserted in the face of that enemy. But when we tell the court, I don't think we'll get hanged."

"Never mind, just get dressed."

Once they were dressed, he lined them up and walked along the line, looking at each face, and stopping when he came to Dave Tinsely—the biggest of them. "Selling cans of gas, you son of a bitch."

"Shit," said Tinseley, "I'll sell cans if you put wheels on it so I can roll it up to a Frenchman's house." The CID man smashed Tinseley in the teeth. He came next to Hendricks, who simply said guilty, and Mr. CID passed along to the next man. The five were arrested and taken to the stockade at the US Army headquarters for the Champagne territory, Reims—right opposite the medieval cathedral. There was no need for bars on the windows; the room they were put in was six floors up. After a while a defense counselor from Kentucky arrived.

"Well, you boys know what you did," he said.

Hendricks said, "Let me tell you something—there ain't no boys in here. We're soldiers in the United States Army. You know what that is? You should, you look like one yourself."

"You don't speak to me like that," said the counselor.

"You're talking to an officer in the United States Army," said Hendricks. "You are here to save our lives, not to harass us. So if you're going to do your job get to it. If you're not, get going."

The counselor's face flushed crimson. "You know you deserted in the face of the enemy, and so this is a capital offense."

"We did not desert in the face of an enemy; we deserted in the face of racist white soldiers who liked to kill niggers. So it looks like you are not the defense counsel that we need."

"I'm the one you got."

"We had a race riot," Hendricks reminded him.

"Oh, we don't want that known, the Army doesn't want that."

"Do you mean to tell me we have to hang because the Army doesn't want to be embarrassed?" asked Hendricks.

"Put it any way you want."

"Did you ever read my record?"

"No," said the counselor.

"You should read my record," said Hendricks. "I was battalion clerk and my duties were to know everything that went on in the battalion. So what you're talking about has nothing to do with the truth. The truth is white American soldiers ... came out shootin' at us, that's the truth and we ain't deserted in the face of no enemy. So you don't sound like the kind of defense counsel we want. So you're fired."

"You can't fire me," said the counselor.

Hendricks quoted him the relevant Articles of War. "If you are involved in a capital case—and this is a capital case—and you are dissatisfied with the defense counsel, you have the right to dismiss them. Now you are dismissed."

"I'm not leaving here, you have no authority to dismiss me," insisted the counselor.

Hendricks turned to Dave Tinsely. "So, Dave, what do you think we ought to do to this cat?"

"Throw the motherfucker out the window," advised Tinsely.

The counselor bolted from the room, stuffing his papers back in his briefcase.

Among his friends, Hendricks was known as "Professor." Now one asked him, "Well, Professor, what's going to happen now?"

"Well, it's a capital case. We have to have defense, so it's just a matter of time. I don't know if it will be this week, or next week, or a month, or two months—I don't know when they are going to do it, but they are going to send us another counsel."

Two or three weeks passed and then, sure enough, another lawyer appeared. This one was Jewish and from the Bronx. Hendricks had previously told the CID captain that there were mitigating circumstances to their case.

"What do you know about mitigating?" the captain had asked.

"Mitigating. *M-i-t-i-g-a-t-i-n-g*, mitigating," said Hendricks, staring at him, enraged. Now he told the new counselor about the mitigating circumstances.

"Oh no," said the new man, "You are not going to hang if I can help it. This is not a hanging offense."

He was right. At the court martial on November 9, 1945 Hendricks was sentenced to three years in the US Army stockade in Marseilles, where he spent his days drilling on the quad and doing manual labor: digging ditches or helping local farmers, which he enjoyed, since the food was better than the prison diet of lumpy oatmeal and eggs boiled to the consistency of bullets. The regime was unrelenting—unless a soldier was being hanged or shot, in which case they were given the day off. The following October, after serving eleven months of his sentence, Hendricks was reinstated and given all his back pay. However, two of his fellow runaways fared less well: big Dave Tinsely and a soldier they called Cannonball had previous criminal records and were sent to Fort Leavenworth in Kansas, home to the army's maximum security prison.

The war in Europe was already over, having ended before Hendricks's court martial. After his reinstatement he was posted to Bremerhaven in Germany, the port for the city of Bremen. Once the authorities learned about his experience as a clerk in his battalion, they arranged for him to be examined by a Viennese psychiatrist called Dr. Jacobs, who had studied under Sigmund Freud. After establishing that Hendricks spoke French and a little German, Jacobs appointed him as his clerk. Over the next few months, Hendricks at

Hendricks, _____ Jon C. _____ 35557682
(Last name) _____ (First name and middle initial) _____ (Army serial No.)

Private _____ 4406th Quartermaster Service Company
(Grade) _____ (Organization)

_____ Dijon, France _____
(Station)

By

GENERAL COURT MARTIAL

Appointed by the Commanding ~~Officer~~ GENERAL

OISE INTERMEDIATE SECTION
Theater Service Forces, European Theater

Tried at

Reims, France _____ 9 November _____, 19 45

CHECKED AND PASSED:

last had the chance to recover from the ordeals of the previous two years—until one morning he woke up and found he couldn't speak. He wrote a note and showed it to the other soldiers: "I've lost my power of speech, not my voice but my power of speech." Not knowing what else to do, they took him to the hospital, where he wrote another note asking to see Dr. Jacobs.

Jacobs arrived and said to his patient, "When I talk with you, you write to me the answer to this question."

Okay, wrote Hendricks.

Jacobs asked how he felt physically, whether any part of his body felt bad.

No, wrote Hendricks.

"All right," said Dr. Jacobs. He left the room, returning a few minutes later with a gallon jug and a rubber hose attached to a hypodermic needle. He pushed the needle into Hendricks's arm and blood began running out through the tube into the jug.

As the blood began to pool in the bottom, Hendricks yelled, "Hey this is my blood. *Hold it!*"

"Ah," said Dr. Jacobs, "you are all right physically. You can come back to work tomorrow and you will be fine." It was probably a mild case of PTSD, although the term was not yet in use. Jacobs's questions about his family and his early life—the reminiscing and sudden return to normal ways of thinking—had unleashed all the emotions that Hendricks had suppressed during the war, when his mind had been entirely focused on survival. Over the following months, Jacobs worked closely with Hendricks to help him come to terms with his harrowing experiences. Once again, Hendricks was reminded that black Americans were treated with respect in Europe; he was rapidly losing any desire to return to the USA:

> I wanted to stay. I was engaged to marry a German girl and when [the US Army] found that out, they broke that up, and put me on a ship with chains on … And I had to get on the ship and sail three days before they took the chains off. So then I knew. So I said to myself that I would look out over the rail at the water and I made a vow to myself. I said when I get back to that rotten country, I am going to live within its laws and do anything that is legal … I have always lived at the top of the heap. I wasn't going to live in the ghetto or in the slums and nobody was going to degrade me.

Notwithstanding his reluctance to return to America, it was on board ship that music re-entered Jon Hendricks's life. He had just won three hundred dollars shooting craps and was lounging on his bunk when he heard a hot jazz tune coming over the ship's radio. It sounded new and thrilling, yet also somehow familiar—it reminded him of Art Tatum. Hendricks leapt up and ran to the control room where the disc jockey was sitting.

"What was that?" he asked.

"What?" said the DJ.

"That last song you just played."

"I don't know."

"Where is it?" Hendricks demanded.

"It's down there, on the floor."

Hendricks looked down and saw that the floor was covered with discarded seventy-eights. "What color was the label?"

"It's a red label," confirmed the DJ.

Hendricks began rifling through all the discs with red labels, holding up each one in turn until finally the DJ recognized the one he had just played. It was on the Guild label and the title was "Salt Peanuts." The artists were Charlie Parker and Dizzy Gillespie.

Hendricks handed the DJ thirty dollars and said, "Play this for the next hour." The DJ did as instructed, no doubt to the profound annoyance of his other listeners. But Hendricks was in ecstasy. He couldn't believe that he was actually hearing the musical ideas he had been carrying around in his head since working with Art Tatum. As soon as he got off the boat in New York he headed for a record store and bought all the Parker/Gillespie records he could find, spending the next two months listening to them—it was like being in heaven.

But, once he returned to Earth, he also recognized that he would have his work cut out settling back into civilian life. If he was ever to make something of himself, he would have to find a job.

3 We Don't Want No Singers, Man

After his arrival in New York, Hendricks seems to have returned initially to Detroit before moving to Rochester, New York, where two of his brothers were living. Stuart Hendricks was part of the management of The Pythodd, a private club in an old three-story house that was jointly owned by the Oddfellows and the Knights of Pythias of North and South America, Europe, Asia, and Africa (KPNSAEAA, a masonic organization with a black membership). With nothing more than a high school diploma to his name, Hendricks was well aware that his job options were limited. He applied to study medicine at the University of Rochester, using funds from the recently passed GI Bill. However, the school told him that they had already met their quota: what they meant was that they allowed only a limited number of black students to apply for medicine in any academic year, and he was too late.

So, with "Salt Peanuts" still ringing in his ears, Hendricks decided to form a bebop band; a quintet with the same instrumental line-up as Gillespie's, plus himself. He found an alto player and a young trumpet player—both influenced by Bird and Dizzy—and a good young bassist who played in the Curly Russell style. But to Hendricks's mind, the drummer didn't know how to swing:

> So one day at rehearsal I said, "No man, it goes like this," and I sat down and I played. So all the other guys said, "Man you should play. Why don't you just play?" So I started playing. I never had any lessons or anything like that. I had it in my ear, so I just played what I had in my ear what the drums should do.

The group was called Jon Hendricks and his Beboppers and they worked in Rochester for the next two years, their leader both singing and playing drums. Unbeknown to him, he said, Dizzy Gillespie had gone looking for him in Toledo during that time, as he was putting a big band together and needed a singer. When he played in Detroit, Gillespie had called Hendricks and asked him to sing with them. Afterwards, he told Jon the gig was his, if he wanted it. But once Hendricks had made his move to Rochester, Diz couldn't find him—so Joe Carroll got the job instead.

Having experienced extreme racial violence during the war at the hands of the armed forces of his own country, Hendricks had developed a keen sense of social justice. His father had imbued him with a clear understanding of right and wrong, and he still believed that the Bible held the key to doing the right thing and keeping out of trouble. He now began to notice the prevalence of racism at home, which was growing as vast numbers of black people migrated from the South during the forties, in what became known as the Second Great Migration. As a child he had taken *de facto* racial segregation for granted:

> When I was little, I knew that when we went to the movies, we had to sit upstairs because the white people sat downstairs. We sat upstairs and accepted it as a matter of course. We didn't have any idea that it was discriminatory against us, because we still saw the movie. We didn't have that kind of social consciousness about it. Everything was happy. We were treated well. There was never any overt action taken against any of us. Nobody was beaten or whipped or insulted directly.

In 1949, Hendricks decided to make another attempt to get himself on to a university course. This time, rather than medicine, he thought he would try for pre-law at the University of Toledo—which in his case meant majoring in English with a minor in history. This time he was accepted. For a while, he envisaged a future for himself working for the NAACP, helping to fight the increased number of race-based legal actions coming before the courts. But it wasn't just about the law; racism was an insidious process, which was accepted as normal by blacks and whites alike. In the student canteen, Hendricks was struck by the sight of the black students huddling together in one corner while the whites sat anywhere they liked. While at UT he was also elected president of a student branch of the United World Federalists. "It means that the countries of the world should federate and be the United States of the World," he explained, "and whenever a fight broke out between two countries it would immediately be arbitrated and there would be no killing. It would be the United States of the World."

While studying he continued to work as a musician with a quartet called The Mainstemmers—in which he again sang and played drums—along with Harold Jackson (who had played bass with Duke Ellington), left-handed guitarist Bill Jennings, and pianist Buster Hawkins. Late for a job one day, he was fined ten dollars by the group's leader. Since he couldn't afford to pay, he agreed to write an original song for their next gig instead. The song he came up with—the first he had ever written—was titled "Just Because I Kissed the Bride." After that, he said, he wrote a new song every week.

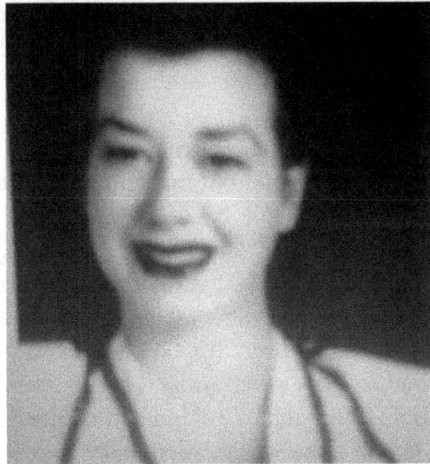

Colleen "Connie" Hendricks
(courtesy Jon Hendricks Jr)

At one gig, at the Gay Nineties club in Toledo, he encountered a young Irish-descended singer and cocktail waitress called Colleen Jean Moore—named after a silent movie star—although most people called her Connie. Hendricks took to her straight away, and let her sit in with the band. They began dating, and in short order they were married. In Ohio in the late 1940s the sight of a black man with a white woman was a rarity, to say the least, and they were stared at in the street. She and Jon teamed up to sing around the Toledo area until mid-1949, when she became pregnant. The idea of a black man married to a white woman, he found, caused deep offense to most white people. One night he was arrested and jailed for no reason he could discern, although he knew perfectly well what it was. Since there seemed to be no sense of urgency about dealing with his case, he eventually resorted to having a note smuggled out of jail by a newly released prisoner. In the note, which was hidden in the sole of the prisoner's shoe, he asked Connie to write to the authorities and say she was divorcing him. In a later variation on this tale, he said he told her to write *him* a letter to say she was divorcing him, knowing the sheriffs would intercept it. Even after his release, the marriage continued to be a source of problems and the birth in February 1950 of the Hendrickses' son Jon Jr. made matters worse.

Having achieved the highest overall grade in his final year at the university, Jon Sr. had high hopes of being appointed the state's Juvenile Probation Officer. The job would involve socializing with police court and juvenile court judges, and therein lay the embarrassment: he and Connie were an interracial couple. On the other hand, it was going to be difficult for the authorities to turn down a man with the grades he had achieved, which had traditionally made the appointment automatic—but the authorities came up with a stratagem. Again, Hendricks told slightly different versions of the story, but the most coherent account runs as follows: As a probation officer, Hendricks would be reporting to another young black man who had a wife and two children. This man was sent to Hendricks's house to threaten him and tell him to leave town.

"They told me," the man said, "that if you don't withdraw your name they're going to fire me. I'm not going to do that. I'm just going to leave it in your hands."

"Okay," Hendricks replied, "Withdraw my name. I don't want to deal with people that are that stupid." By this time his enthusiasm for righteous causes and a straight, respectable job in the law had understandably begun to wane. At the same time, his GI benefits ran out just as he was about to enter the graduate law program and he realized he would have to find something else to do. Studying at Toledo had clarified in his mind where his true talents lay. He had done well academically, had written poems for the student newspaper, and was very proud of the fact that he received the first student A grades in speech and creative writing in several years. He was first and foremost a creative soul. But he could no longer see a future for himself and his family in Toledo.

Meanwhile, Charlie Parker came through town to play a one-nighter at the Civic Auditorium in Toledo. Jon had been a fan of Bird ever since his epiphany aboard the troop ship some four years earlier, and had bought many of his records, so the opportunity to hear Parker perform live was thrilling. At the gig, he expected to see Miles Davis and Bud Powell on the bandstand—not realizing that Kenny Dorham and Al Haig had recently replaced them. On drums was Max Roach, with Tommy Potter on bass. Knowing Hendricks as a scat singer, the locals asked him whether he was going to sit in and scat with the great man. Hendricks said he would be prepared to do it, but was paralyzed with fear at the thought of approaching Parker. Connie, however, had no such inhibitions. She walked up to Parker and told him that her husband was a great bebop singer and a big fan of his, and would like to sit in.

"Bebop singer?" said Bird.

"Yeah," said Connie.

"Heck yeah," said Bird, "Tell him to come on up." The band launched into "The Song Is You," and Parker motioned to Hendricks to join them on stage. As Hendricks began to sing, it must have been immediately obvious to Parker that this newcomer not only knew the song but was hitting the changes in his vocal solo, as he had learned to back in the days of Art Tatum. "After I was through, my knees were knocking," Hendricks confessed. "I was so nervous, I thought I was going to faint. All I wanted to do was get off that stage." Having scatted several choruses, and as Kenny Dorham started his trumpet solo, Hendricks got up to leave the bandstand, but felt someone tugging at his jacket. He turned around and saw Bird beckoning to him and patting Dorham's chair next to him. He sat down again, and Bird asked him, "What are you doing in this town?"

"I'm in school," said Hendricks, "This is my hometown."

"Oh," said Parker, "What are you studying?"

"I'm studying law."

"You ain't no lawyer," said Parker.

"What am I then?" Hendricks enquired.

"You a bebop singer, just like your wife said."

"What do I do about that?"

"Well," said Bird, "You got to come to New York."

"I don't know anybody in New York," said Hendricks.

"You know me."

"Where will I find you?" New York was, after all, a city of ten million people, with another million passing through every day.

"Just ask anybody," said Bird.

That's ridiculous, thought Hendricks. "Well," he said, "If I get there I will get in touch with you."

A couple of years later—tired of the endless hassles and frustrations they experienced daily due to their mixed marriage—Jon and Connie decided to move to Canada, where racism seemed less prevalent. They packed up their possessions, including Jon's drum kit, and headed north with $350 in cash. But when they reached the border at Buffalo, the immigration officer told them they would need at least a thousand dollars to be allowed into Canada, to show that they would not immediately become a burden on the country's welfare system. Jon said he could go back and fetch more money, but it was no dice: if he didn't have the funds right now, he could forget it. So forget it they did, and drove to Rochester instead. On the way, Jon changed his mind yet again and soon he, Connie, and Jon Jr. were on their way to New York in a belated take-up of Charlie Parker's suggestion. Shortly afterwards, the carburetor fell out of their car. The highway patrol helped them move the ailing vehicle off the road and gave the Hendrickses, their luggage, and Jon's drum kit a ride back to Buffalo. From there they caught a Greyhound bus into New York. Once it arrived at the terminal, they found a restaurant. Connie and the baby sat at the counter while Jon went to look for a telephone. The only person he knew in New York (apart from Charlie Parker) was Joe Carroll, the singer who had taken the job with Dizzy Gillespie. Joe recommended they stay at the Claremont Hotel on 110th Street, near Columbia University. It was neat and clean, he reported, only $18.50 a week and all the musicians stayed there. Then, remembering what Charlie Parker had said to him back in Toledo, Jon asked Joe where the great man could be found; the answer was The Apollo Bar, on 125th Street and Seventh Avenue. It was exactly as Bird had said about finding him: "Ask anybody."

Hendricks returned to the hotel, where there was a folding crib for the baby, and told Connie he was going to look for Charlie Parker. To save money he walked the fifteen blocks to 125th Street. As he approached the Apollo, he felt his confidence draining away—after all, the brief encounter with Bird had been more than a year ago in an obscure Midwest town. Realizing the foolishness of just strolling in and expecting Bird to remember him, he turned around to walk back to the hotel. Maybe by tomorrow he would have come up with a better idea. And yet, what would be the point in delaying? Parker was the only musician who knew who he was and what he could do. There was nothing else for it: he would have to brazen the thing out and hope for the best. Once again he turned and carried on walking until he reached the Apollo.

When he opened the door, he found himself next to the bandstand. There was a narrow aisle next to the wall. He edged his way in, noticing Bird himself with Gerry Mulligan playing baritone, Roy Haynes on drums, Curly Russell on the bass, and Bud Powell playing piano. "Hey Jon," called Bird, "How are you doing? You want to sing something?" Hendricks grabbed the wall for support—how was it possible that Parker remembered him after all this time? Shortly after, the band came off for a break and only Roy Haynes stayed behind, talking to a girl at the bar. Hendricks went to sit at a table by himself. As the band returned to play the final set, they gathered around Hendricks's table and Bird introduced him to everybody. He had met Bud Powell once before, but doubted whether Bud would recall the occasion since he was usually high on drugs. He had seen Haynes play, but never met him. Just before they went back on stage, Bird said, "Okay Jon we'll play one number and then we'll call you up to sing something."

Haynes was not impressed: "No, Bird, this is the last set—we don't want no singers. We don't want no singers, man." Hendricks's heart sank.

"Look, Roy," said Bird, "You don't know what you're talking about. I'm telling you this is okay, so just cool it."

After the first tune, Bird said to Hendricks, "Do something else."

"Well," said Hendricks, "You all just play, and I'll join in."

He took solos on the next two numbers and it seemed to go down well with the audience, because he was truly soloing when he scatted—hitting the changes, just like he had back in Toledo. Bird and Mulligan were delighted, while Haynes came up and apologized for his earlier comments. It had gone better than Hendricks had dreamed possible. Was this the start of a whole new singing career in New York?

"I'll see what I can get for you," promised Bird. Hendricks went back to the hotel and a couple of nights later Bird had got him a decent bebop gig that paid twenty-five dollars.

To earn a steadier income he found himself a day job as a clerk at a newsprint company, typing invoices in an office. Once he had earned a little money the Hendrickses moved into an apartment in the Bronx, at 201st Street and Gun Hill Road, near White Plains. ("It was quite a nice place to live in those days," Hendricks recalled later.) His thoughts now returned to songwriting—having written several tunes for The Mainstemmers, he saw this as another way to raise his profile in the music business and also make some money.

Long before the pop hegemony of composers like Leiber and Stoller, and Goffin and King, the center of music publishing and songwriting was the Brill Building near Times Square. Most black writers were refused membership of the American Society of Composers, Authors and Publishers (ASCAP), the organization which collected (and still collects) fees due to the creators of music. However, those who got the credit—and the royalties—were not always the actual creators. Hendricks used to maintain that the real composer of "Stardust" was not Hoagy Carmichael but a West Indian-born stride pianist called Lucky Roberts, who sold the song to Hoagy for twenty-five dollars. Although he did not identify Fats Waller by name, he also claimed that the real composer of "I Can't Give You Anything But Love, Baby" was not Jimmy McHugh (who got the credit) but Fats, who is alleged to have sold it (including its lyrics by Andy Razaf) to McHugh for five hundred dollars. It was, in short, common practice for famous songwriters like Frank Loesser and Irving Berlin to employ other writers to compose tunes which they themselves would then put their own names to.

Loesser had offices on the fifth floor of the Brill Building. Two men who wrote material for him were the lyricist Richard Adler and the composer Jerry Ross. As they emerged from the building for lunch, Hendricks and the others who hung out on the corner would say, "Here come Adler and Ross: the two evils of Loesser." Despite the jokes, it was a cruel and unfair system as far as black writers were concerned. Churchill Kohlman—the prolific songsmith who wrote Johnny Ray's 1951 number one hit "Cry"—worked as a night watchman at a dry-cleaning factory in Pittsburgh. The song's publisher, Perry Alexander of Mellow Music, had told him there were no royalties. Hendricks remembered seeing Kohlman outside the Brill Building and giving him the two bucks he needed to get home to Pittsburgh. (The dispute was finally settled in 1953, when Alexander was ordered to pay Kohlman $15,331.24.) Hendricks would hang out on the corner with Quincy Jones, with whom he briefly shared an apartment. At first, Hendricks claimed, the white songwriters stole his ideas. They would ask him what he was working on and he would sing his pieces for them. Shortly after, he would hear his song on the radio with someone else's name on it. Because most black writers were not members of ASCAP, it was difficult for them to assert the copyright to music they had written. Hendricks and Jones eventually started going from floor to floor in the Brill Building, selling the same song multiple times. Hendricks, who would be doing this in his lunch hour from the print factory, had negotiated an extra-long break with his manager, in return for which he worked later in the evening. This meant that he was spending even less time at home than before and sleep was becoming a luxury.

During this period he heard another tune that rivaled "Salt Peanuts" for the lightning-bolt effect it had on him. It was a record called "Moody [sic] Mood for Love," by the singer King Pleasure (a.k.a. Clarence Beeks). Since this tune is the ur-text for vocalese as an art form, it's worth telling the full story of the recording. In 1949, the tenor saxophonist James Moody was recording in a studio in Sweden and realized he needed one more song for the session than he had planned for. He decided on "I'm in the Mood for Love," the standard by Jimmy McHugh and Dorothy Fields. For some reason he played an alto saxophone on this cut, an instrument he was less comfortable with than the tenor. Despite this, his solo on the recording was one of the best he ever recorded. Modestly, he claimed that the haunting notes he produced were not pure melodic inspiration but actually a result of groping his way around an unfamiliar horn.

A couple of years later, the then-unknown King Pleasure was bracing himself to take part in the fear-inspiring Amateur Hour at Harlem's Apollo Theatre. Wondering how he could make an impact on the famously hard crowd that attended these events, he decided to steal an idea from another singer, Eddie Jefferson. For over a decade, Eddie had been entertaining friends and fellow musicians at private gatherings by putting words to recorded instrumental solos. One of these was Moody's solo on "I'm in the Mood for Love." Pleasure had been planning to sing his own lyricized version of Lester Young's solo on "DB Blues" for his Apollo debut. But late in the day he changed his mind and decided to go with the Moody/Jefferson tune instead, which Pleasure had heard Jefferson perform in Cincinnati. It was a brave, even foolhardy decision: this was a solo known, note for note, to every member of the toughest audience in jazz and he would have to memorize it with perfect accuracy. But the performance caused a sensation and King Pleasure found his moment of fame. In 1953 his rendition of what was renamed "Moody Mood for Love" became a hit record that won a *DownBeat* award.

The first time Jon Hendricks heard it, he was having lunch in Washington Square Park before returning to his desk at the newsprint company. It had a profound impact on him. He had been writing songs for years, but "Moody Mood" opened up exciting new possibilities—there was potentially more to songwriting than the thirty-two bars that had been the norm in jazz tunes for decades. His first effort in this new direction was a vocalese version of Jimmy Giuffre's 1947 tune "Four Brothers," which Giuffre had written for the saxophone section of Woody Herman's Big Band (the so-called Second Herd) when he was their arranger.

As he worked at his songwriting, Hendricks also realized that the best way to sell his compositions was to tailor them to specific artists. He had heard several of Louis Jordan's recordings on the radio and thought he could write songs for him. This is how he came up with his celebrated comic song "Gimme That Wine," with lyrics inspired by the conversations of the bums in Washington Square Park. Now all he had to do was to track down Louis Jordan. Fortunately he knew someone at Decca Records, Jordan's label, who told him that the jump blues star had a session scheduled in Decca studio B the next day.

"What'cha got?" Jordan asked Hendricks, after the Decca man had introduced them. Hendricks sang him his new "Gimme That Wine" song.

"I just did another drinking song, 'Drinking Wine Spo-Dee-O-Dee,'" said Jordan, "You got anything else?"

"Yeah, I got a song called 'I Want You to be My Baby.'"

"How does it go?"

Hendricks sang it, and Jordan asked him to write it out for him. Although Jordan had enjoyed an impressive run of jump blues hits during the forties, by the fifties they had dried up. Trying to keep up with the changing times, he moved to more of a rock 'n' roll sound and the feel of "I Want You To Be My Baby" is akin to Bill Haley's "Rock Around the Clock." In retrospect, the style is also quintessential Jon Hendricks: clever and entertaining, with a lot of words sung very fast, the main lyric building up as words are added bit by bit. But Louis Jordan's "I Want You To Be My Baby" didn't hit the top ten in 1953, nor when it was re-released in 1954. "I'll Die Happy" (co-written by Jon and Connie Hendricks) and "Messy Bessie" (both 1954) were similarly unsuccessful. Jordan's mistake on "I Want You To Be My Baby," as Hendricks correctly pointed out, was to begin with twelve bars of boogie-woogie followed by three full choruses of saxophone, before the vocal finally kicked in—by then, no disc jockey would be listening.

Despite the lack of hits, the Jordan-Hendricks collaboration succeeded in giving Jon some credibility as a songwriter—particularly when Lillian Briggs, a former laundry truck driver, recorded her own version of "I Want You To Be My Baby" in 1955 and it finally became a hit, selling over a million copies and reaching number eighteen in the Billboard Hot 100. A rival version, recorded by Georgia Gibbs, charted at number fourteen, although it sold fewer copies. And—by a curious coincidence—in the UK a young singer called Annie Ross released it as a single, with Tony Crombie and his Orchestra. There have been several other versions in different countries over the years, including a great live TV recording by Keely Smith and Louis Prima, and another sung partially in Chinese for the 2018 film *Crazy Rich Asians*. It ended up as Hendricks's most popular composition, with thirty-three recorded versions. There was more belated recompense for Hendricks's efforts with Louis Jordan when "Messy Bessie" featured in the musical stage show *Five Guys Named Moe*, which played first in England in 1990 and then on Broadway in 1992. Hendricks said he saw the show in London:

> So I went backstage and I said, "Hey, 'Messy Bessie' is my composition but I'm not getting any royalties." He [presumably the producer] got a paper and he says, "Yeah well we send it to Ray Charles." I said, "Ray Charles didn't write that, I wrote that." He says, "Well somebody wrote down Ray Charles." I said, "Just because they put it down there, that's my tune." So I had to get that money

back and that was good. I was able to get it back because Ray didn't even know about it.

Nineteen fifty-three was an important year for Jon Hendricks. Michele, his second child with Connie, was born on September 27. And although the exact chronology is far from clear, it was also in 1953 that he met both King Pleasure and Dave Lambert.

The initial encounter with King Pleasure took place in the Turf Bar at Fifty-second and Broadway, a well-known hang-out for songwriters and performers. Someone introduced them and Hendricks was immediately taken with the handsome, urbane, well-spoken Pleasure. He told him that "Moody Mood" had changed his whole approach to songwriting. Pleasure then told him about a tune that Stan Getz had recorded in Sweden a couple of years earlier with his Swedish All-Stars group, which included the baritone saxophonist Lars Gullin, called "Don't Be Afraid." The idea was to record a vocalese version, retitled "Don't Get Scared," with an arrangement by Quincy Jones. Pleasure handed Hendricks the lyrics he had written to the melody and the Getz solo, but there was no sign of any words for Gullin's solo—which was the part Hendricks was expected to vocalize. When Hendricks questioned this, Pleasure told him, "You write them yourself." Far from feeling put-upon, Hendricks was pleased and impressed: it wasn't his project, so he considered Pleasure's invitation to contribute lyrics to be an act of generosity. On the recording of "Don't Get Scared," the head and the first four solo choruses are Pleasure's and the last three choruses are by Hendricks. Since vinyl 45 rpm singles were then replacing the old shellac seventy-eights, Prestige released it in both formats.

"Don't Get Scared" is a blues. It begins with the same strange, deep horn riff that bookends the Getz original. The singers do the head together, an octave apart, then comes the vocalese. Mostly there's just a trio backing—brushes, bass, and a distant-sounding piano, punctuated by horn stabs at intervals—then a one-chorus saxophone solo. Hendricks sounds relaxed but the key pitches him lower than feels comfortable. The recording ends with the same odd riff.

Jon Hendricks told several conflicting versions of the story of how he and Dave Lambert met. In one of these, Jon was contacted by the young black pianist and entrepreneur George "Teacho" Wiltshire, who owned a small record label called Avalon. Wiltshire had heard "Don't Get Scared," and had since learned that Jon had also written a lyric to the Jimmy Giuffre/Woody Herman tune "Four Brothers." After Jon had come to his office to sing it for him, Teacho asked who he would like to record it with. Jon's choice was a singer called Dave Lambert who, together with his partner Buddy Stewart, had been a pioneer of bop singing in the late forties, recording for the Keynote label. Teacho duly did some asking around, found Dave's number and told him he had someone he thought he ought to meet. He then set up an appointment for Jon to go over to 22 Cornelia Street in Greenwich Village, where Dave had an apartment. When he got there, Dave was with an arranger called George Handy and both of them were stoned on marijuana. Dave asked Jon what he had, so Hendricks told him about the "Four Brothers" lyric. Skeptical at first, they asked him to sing it. More interested now, they asked him to sing it again and Dave started writing out a vocal arrangement on the spot. Twenty minutes later he had it scored for six male and two female singers.

"When I went to Dave's house," Hendricks recalled in another interview, "he was sitting there with John Benson Brooks and George Handy, who were pianists and composers. Handy spoke in groans and grunts. I was from Ohio and I had studied law and I was very prim and proper in my three-piece suit. These cats were looking at me very funny." In yet another variant on the tale, the Lambert-Hendricks meeting took place soon after Jon's arrival in New York. Having admired Lambert for years, Hendricks actually went looking for him—first by writing him a letter, according to some sources, and proposing a partnership, since the two had been working on the same idea individually.

Despite these conflicting versions of events, what we know for sure is that Dave Lambert was four years older than Jon, born in Boston in 1917. His claim to fame at the time he and Jon Hendricks met was for trailblazing the nascent art of scat singing and vocal harmonies; for this he had become something of a cult figure in the world of jazz. Apart from a year of drum lessons when he was ten years old, Dave had received no formal musical education. He worked as a tree surgeon in Westchester, New York, before serving in World War II as paratrooper. It was while in the army that he became entranced by vocal group singing and began listening to the Merry Macs and The Modernaires. In 1944 he joined Gene Krupa's orchestra, singing with Krupa's vocal group the G-Noters, and becoming close friends with their front man Buddy Stewart. In January 1945 he came up with an original song called "What's This," which he recorded together with Stewart, and then again with Krupa for Columbia Records. Unusually, at a time when one might have expected the head to be played by Krupa's instrumentalists, Lambert and Stewart scatted the melody themselves. This was a novel idea: only Ella Fitzgerald was then using scat in a non-comedic way. The Lambert/Stewart partnership proved a success and, in 1946, they left Krupa to launch a new career as a vocal duo.

They were doing well until February 1950, when Buddy was killed in a car accident in Deming, New Mexico. Dave carried on working, assembling a five-voice choir which he called The Dave Lambert Singers—in truth just the working name for whatever loose assemblage of vocal talent was needed for a particular project. They provided the backing for two tracks on the 1953 record *King Pleasure Sings*, a vocalese album for Prestige which also featured "Don't Get Scared." In May of that year the Dave Lambert Singers were an important part of what is considered by critics to have been a debacle involving Charlie Parker. In a foreshadowing of his work with Miles Davis, Gil Evans was hired by Bird to create some jazz arrangements with a choir and orchestral instruments (French horn, flute, oboe, and bassoon) to create a sound more like twentieth-century classical music than jazz. Dave Lambert wrote the arrangements for a ten- or twelve-strong vocal group that included Annie Ross and Butch Birdsall, but the vocal arrangements were too complicated and difficult; at the recording session in May, producer Norman Granz so disliked what he was hearing that he pulled the plug before they had even finished all the tunes. The Lamberts—Dave, his wife Hortense, and their young daughter Dee—had become friends with Gil some years earlier, when the latter was renting a basement room at the Gotham Hotel on W. Fifty-fifth Street, behind a Chinese laundry. The room was a regular haunt of musicians including Miles Davis, Gerry Mulligan, and Charlie Parker, who would take turns sleeping in Gil's bed when they had nowhere else to spend the night.

From this point on, times were hard and Dave had to resort to scuffling. Sometimes the only way to survive was to steal food from a supermarket. The technique he devised was to dress little Dee in his old army field jacket and wheel her up and down the aisles in a shopping cart, filling the jacket pockets with necessary food items, while he would put a couple of small items in the cart for the sake of appearances. At the checkout he would pay for these and wheel the cart outside. When Dave lifted her out, Dee would be so loaded down with canned goods that she could barely stand. Dave later quipped that he was too poor to steal butter, so he stole margarine instead. On one occasion he offered his services to the King of Thailand, whom he had heard was an amateur clarinetist and jazz fan. Perhaps, Dave surmised, the king would fly him out to Thailand and pay him a salary. Dave persuaded Hortense to write a letter to that effect. His royal highness replied, on royal stationery, along the lines of, "If you're ever in town, look me up." It came as no surprise—with the failure of such desperate strategies—that he and Hortense separated and eventually divorced.

Now that Lambert and Hendricks had met, the "Four Brothers" project began to move forward. Teacho Wiltshire provided the backing with his trio, adding singers Butch Birdsall and Harry Clark to the mix. Dave arranged for the quartet to sing the ensemble orchestral sections of "Four Brothers" and the singers split the tenor saxophonists' solos between them (to be specific, Hendricks sang Al Cohn and Stan Getz; Birdsall, Serge Chaloff; Lambert, Zoot Sims; and Clark, the Woody Herman parts). Hendricks's lyrics established a scenario explaining the relationship between each of the brothers.

Today the recording, made in late 1953, sounds a little uptight compared with the wild, confident sound of Lambert, Hendricks & Ross. Hendricks takes the first solo, followed by Dave Lambert. You can hear everything they later perfected with Lambert, Hendricks & Ross, but one miscalculation—in hindsight—was the decision (which Hendricks pinned on Wiltshire) to slow the song down so that the lyrics would be easier to follow. What had originally been a three-minute instrumental therefore turned into a five-minute vocal track, split in half over two sides of a single. Hendricks later said he'd had his doubts about the idea, but lacked the confidence so early in his New York

career to contest it. "Jon Hendricks's lyrics aren't the wittiest," commented the *DownBeat* reviewer, "but they give Lambert a chance to score them incisively for this crazy madrigal club." *Metronome* described it as "a wonderful idea that doesn't quite come off ... The words make sense, nearly always fit, and permit the singers to get a beat."

Nothing much happened to "Four Brothers" commercially, but Decca's Milt Gabler heard it and approached Hendricks and Lambert about recording it again for his label. This time they decided to do it at the original (faster) Woody Herman tempo. On the flip side was another upswing tune, Leroy Kirkland's blues "Cloudburst." Lambert and Hendricks were backed on both sides of their single by a piano trio, with the drummer playing brushes. "Four Brothers" isn't particularly strong on melody—the arrangement is all about rhythm and recreating the Basie sound with voices. On "Cloudburst" the women sound like Julie Andrews and her twin sister, the high soprano anticipating the kind of bat-squeaks that Annie Ross and Judith Hendricks achieved many years later. After the opening chorus, Hendricks vocaleses at dazzling speed. More enthusiastic this time, *DownBeat* said, "No-one can hip a vocal group more expertly than Dave, and he and Jon are both a gas as soloists." Again, the record didn't sell, but a little money came Hendricks's way when

British trombonist and singer Don Lang released his own scat vocal version of "Cloudburst" in the UK, where it made number sixteen on the singles chart.

Amidst all the excitement of Jon's burgeoning musical career, he still had a wife and children at home in the Bronx apartment. On February 21, 1955, their second son Eric was born, followed by a second daughter Colleen the following year. For a while Jon's mother-in-law came up from Texas to stay

Jon Hendricks Jr in Uruguay, 2020 (courtesy Jon Hendricks Jr)

with them, helping to look after the children, but proved to be a harsh child-minder. Jon continued performing every night, but there were now more mouths to feed as well as rent and bills to pay. This busy schedule resulted in him spending even less time with the family, which made Connie increasingly unhappy, since she now hardly saw her husband at all. In search of solace, she hit the bottle. There were bitter clashes over who was going to look after the children, their hours, their competing careers and—perhaps most of all—Jon's frequent absences. Jon did not (perhaps could not) take care of his obligations as a father. Connie was working two jobs as a waitress and singing at nightclubs at night, leaving Jon Jr. at home to be the babysitter for Michele, and then Eric, when Junior was himself only eight or nine years old.

Sometimes Jon would take his eldest son with him. Junior said:

> He would blow in and grab me, and tell my mom, "OK I'm taking Junior with me, we're going on a tour, we'll be gone six weeks" … So I would go on these tours with him, and I would have people like Dizzy Gillespie as a roommate, and various assorted other people. So I got to meet a lot of the guys when I was young. But that was only for a few weeks, and he'd bring me back and drop me off, and I wouldn't see him again. There was a lot of mixed emotions.

In later years, Junior would room with Dizzy because the latter was known—unusually in those days—for being clean of drugs, and a vegetarian to boot. "He would eat one huge salad a day," said Junior. "He would walk around in his boxer shorts and his tank-top t-shirts and his house slippers. That's all he ever wore in the room." The only problem was that Diz practiced for six to eight hours a day—and played for six to eight hours a night. "He was always blowing his horn when he wasn't eating or sleeping," Junior said.

Meanwhile, Connie was not coping with the pressure of bringing up four children by herself. Her drinking increased to the point where she eventually succumbed to alcoholism and could no longer look after the children herself. The Hendrickses split up, and Connie moved back to Toledo, leaving the kids in the not-so-tender care of Jon's relatives.

4 The Most Beautiful Thing

After the breakdown of his marriage, Hendricks left the apartment and moved into the Alvin Hotel on Fifty-second and Broadway. It was located right in the center of the New York jazz scene—just across the street from Birdland—and was the gathering point for the Andy Kirk, Jimmie Lunceford, Basie, and Ellington bands. At various times Hendricks named numerous other hotels he had lived in, including the Eros ("I was paying seventeen to eighteen dollars a week and it was hard to come by that"), the Earl ("a little alcove with a bed in it"), and the Cecil at 117th Street in Harlem.

Dave helped Jon get gigs, sometimes with the tap dancer Bunny Briggs, and would always give Jon the sheet music to take with him to make it look as if he could read. Jon recalled:

> I just sang whatever someone next to me was singing. If I was sup-posed to be singing a third I would go a third above. We were pros, we knew what to do, but I didn't know anything about reading. It looked like I knew how to read but I did it because these guys would fire me if they knew.

When Dizzy Gillespie booked him for a week, Hendricks once again hid his musical illiteracy by asking Diz for the lead sheets, then taking them to a friend who could read and getting him to sing the tunes for him.

In February 1956, *DownBeat* announced that Jon Hendricks was "cutting three new sides, with Quincy Jones writing and directing." This may have been the obscure rhythm and blues single "Crazy, Crazy, Crazy Boutcha Baby"—released on Pleasure Records that year, written by George Barnes—backed with "You Baby," written by Hendricks himself. After his divorce from Hortense came through, Dave suggested Jon move in with him at Cornelia Street, since he had a spare room. "Instead of scuffling for two rents we only have to scuffle for one," he told Hendricks. With funds running perilously low,

Hendricks needed no second invitation. Dave Lambert was a past master not just at scuffling, but what he termed "honorable scuffling," and had devised four rules for it. They reveal much about the kind of man he was: Firstly, be ready and willing to do any kind of work. Second, scrupulously keep track of all your debts and repay as soon as you can; don't go to the same well too often. Thirdly, if you borrow anything—a car, a tool, an article of clothing, an instrument—always return it when you promised, in better condition than when you got it, so the owner will be happy to loan it to you again. (Hence a borrowed car would always be washed and gassed up, tools sharpened and cleaned, and a borrowed tux would have been to the cleaner before it was returned.) Fourth, give fair exchange to anyone who feeds you. Make a party for them however you can. Make music, sing songs, tell stories, let the good times roll.

On the day agreed for Hendricks to move into Dave Lambert's apartment, he dragged his few possessions over to the fifth-floor walk-up, which had a toilet in the kitchen. Standing outside, he knocked on the door—but there was no answer. He left his stuff at the top and walked all the way back down in search of a phone.

"Where are you?" asked Dave, when he answered.

"I'm here. I knocked on your door but there was no answer."

22 Cornelia Street, New York City

"Well," said Dave, "You didn't call and let me know you were coming. You gotta call first."

"Okay," said Jon, "I'll be right back up." The Mafia were rife in the neighborhood and used Cornelia Street to drop off the corpses of people who had annoyed them in some way. The mobsters would initially store the bodies in tunnels underneath the Copacabana nightclub on Forty-seventh Street, then drive them down Seventh Avenue to dump them in Cornelia Street—hence Dave's cautiousness concerning visitors.

Despite their shared living arrangement, paid singing work remained elusive for Dave and Jon; the pair would often go hungry for days at a time. Always the soul of generosity, when Dave found a gig for himself, he would sometimes ask if he could "bring a friend" who didn't need to get paid. They would do the gig together and Dave would then split his fee with Jon. A bit of part-time teaching helped. In May 1956 Jon told *DownBeat* that he had "been giving high school kids a chance to learn more about jazz in a series of weekly lecture-demonstrations." In September it was announced that Jon had been elected to ASCAP, but still he and Dave were close to starvation. Dave had an account at Joe's Dinette, where the two would go to eat every night—their only meal of the day, unless somebody invited them out to dinner. This just about kept them alive. For a while, Joe allowed them to run a generous tab, but when it reached three hundred dollars he had no option but to cut them off; they simply weren't getting enough gigs to pay off the mounting debt. It was at this dark, desperate time that Dave made a suggestion.

"Well look, you love Basie, I love Basie—why don't we do a Basie album? Why don't you write lyrics to three or four Basie tunes and we'll take 'em uptown and try and sell them to a record company."

"Well," said Jon, "It takes a long time to write words to everything going on in those arrangements, you know, with all the horns."

"You got anything else to do?" Jon hadn't, so he started work. Dave's idea for the project was to use a twelve-voice choir, as he had at Capitol in 1949 and, less happily, with Charlie Parker in 1953. Aided by prodigious quantities of marijuana, Jon began his vocalese writing with "Down for the Count" and "Blues Backstage." By the time these were finished, plus a couple more, they began looking for a buyer. For four days—being without money for the subway, never mind a taxi—they walked forty-six blocks uptown to Fiftieth and Broadway, going from one record company to the next. There were no takers. The problem was that they hadn't the funds to record a demo of their idea—something that, then as now, record companies regarded as *de rigeur*.

One of those they approached was radio producer Bob Bach, who also ran a tiny record label. On the afternoon they called him at his house, a jazz singer and actress friend of Bach's wife happened to be visiting, "a silent, beautiful, red-haired girl" by the name of Annie Ross. Bach asked her if she would like to stick around and hear Dave and Jon performing their idea. When they arrived, they put on a Basie record and sang the solos. Having recorded vocalese versions of "Twisted" and "Farmer's Market," Annie was intrigued.

Nothing came of it on this occasion—at least, not in the way Dave and Jon were hoping. Eventually, they heard about a new company called ABC-Paramount Ampar that had hired a young A&R man fresh out of university. His name was Creed Taylor and he had made a good start at the company, recording Quincy Jones and Kenny Dorham. Creed already knew Dave slightly from the carpentry work Dave did in Greenwich Village to make ends meet. With no demo, the two singers once again performed the tunes live, this time in Creed's office. Unlike the others, this A&R man liked what he heard and promised to recommend their project to the company. Jon said he asked them to come and sing to the board. There was quite a contrast between the singers and the ABC-Paramount board, the latter stiff in their three-piece business suits and the singers clad in what were little better than rags. But when they sang there were some stirrings of interest. When they had finished, they were asked to wait outside. Half an hour later, Creed emerged from the boardroom and gave them the sort-of good news. "We got an OK, but we have to do it in three dates. They won't go overtime and they just barely gave us enough to do it." He suggested they wait until the Basie band was in town so they could use their rhythm section on the recording: Freddie Green on guitar, Eddie Jones on bass, and Sonny Payne on drums—along with pianist Nat Pierce, a close Basie associate.

In a version of the story that Jon told Ben Sidran, four days after they approached Creed Taylor, he said they could have one record date to see how it turned out. If it went well and sounded good, ABC-Paramount would pay for the whole album. "Dave and I danced around the room, 'coz it means we would have five hundred dollars apiece in our pockets 'coz he said as soon as they accepted we'd get an advance of a thousand dollars, so we were going to be able to pay the rent ... buy some food, maybe even have a ball and get high," he said.

Creed Taylor

Writing the whole album took them around six months. The first session took place at Beltone Studios at number 4 W. Thirty-first Street. Dave had hired twelve singers—six men and six women—all studio professionals and all white, most of them from *The Perry Como Show* and *Your Hit Parade*. One was the young Mark Murphy; another was Georgia Brown. For a jazz singer, swing requires singing fractionally behind the beat, not on it. But, half an hour in, it became clear that these singers didn't know how to swing like the Basie band. Experts in singing advertising jingles, in a jazz context they sounded stiff; the subtle phrasings and nuances of jazz were outside their experience. Eddie Jones, the bassist, tried to help. "Look, this is the way the band plays it. It's got to be laid back." Met with blank looks, he tried to explain the difference between laying back and slowing down. Years later, Hendricks recalled:

> They [were] not of or in the culture, so these words didn't mean anything to them. Because "laying back," to a person who doesn't know the subtlety of laying back, *is* slowing down! The way it becomes laying back, in lieu of slowing down, is that what you lose on the three beats, you catch up with on the fourth one or the seventh one or the ninth one.

On and on went the rehearsal, eating up valuable studio time, but it was all to no avail. The women seemed even more clueless than the men so, in desperation and with only a couple of hours left in the session, Dave called Annie Ross. She had been somewhat put out that Dave and Jon hadn't asked her to be a part of their project in the first place, and now Dave was asking if she could come over to Beltone and give the women singers the Basie feel. "Well that was a laugh in itself," she said, years later. "I mean you can't teach that to anybody, you have to be born with it, be brought up with it." But she went along anyway—for all the good it did. What they had in the can was terrible. Dave said unhappily, "It sounds like Walter Schumann sings Count Basie." Eventually Jon said, "I think we'd better get some Negroes. No offense, but these people couldn't swing if you hung 'em." They sent the choir home. Creed Taylor was by now sweating bullets, having just burned through $1,250 of his new employers' cash with nothing to show for it. But outwardly he kept his cool. "He's the kind of guy that's always calm," Hendricks said of him. "He could be standing in a building that's burning, and he'd say, 'Seems a little hot in here.'" The older men were touched by this seeming *naiveté*; Jon described his impression of Creed at the time as "fresh-faced, green, and innocent as a baby lamb."

As it happened, the combination of talents required to make the project a success was now assembled in the room. Annie Ross had recently arrived in New York to do cabaret at a place called The Upstairs at the Downstairs. Unlike Lambert and Hendricks, she wasn't starving because in the daytime for a couple of years she'd had a small walk-on and dancing job on ABC's *Patrice Munsel* TV show, and in the evenings was being expensively wined and dined by the various Mafiosi who ran the clubs. More importantly, she had form in the business of jazz and vocalese. She had also had a remarkably strange upbringing. Born Annabelle Short in south London, England—on July 25, 1930, to the vaudeville performers Jack and Mary Short—she spent her early life in Glasgow, Scotland. When she was four, her parents took a holiday to New York, where they entered her in a children's radio competition. The prize was a movie contract with MGM, and Annie won it. Her parents returned home, leaving her in the care of Mary's sister Ella Logan, a singer, who raised Annie in Hollywood. It may have been this that gave rise to the rumor that her aunt Ella Logan, who subsequently raised her, was her real mother. At any rate, show business was in her DNA and by the age of eight she had already become a Hollywood child star, playing a Scotsman in the Little Rascals short *Our Gang Follies of 1938*. At twelve she appeared as Judy Garland's kid sister in *Presenting Lily Mars* and, when she was fourteen, she won a songwriting contest, judged by Johnny Mercer and Dinah Shore, with the song "Let's Fly."

Still in her teens—and after arguing with Aunt Ella—she flew to Scotland, argued with her family there, and moved to London, finding work as an actress in the West End and as a singer in jazz clubs. She moved to Paris and spent the next five years singing and acting (but mostly consorting with expatriate American jazz musicians, revelling in all the sex and drugs). It was there that she made her first recording, in February 1950, for Prestige, with a Franco-American jazz group that included James Moody and Jack Dieval. Briefly returning to the States in late March of 1952, she made *The Voice of Annie Ross*—her first session under her own name—in New York. Six months later she made the recordings that made her name as a jazz musician, writing and singing her famous vocalese version of Wardell Gray's "Twisted," as well as Art Farmer's "Farmer's Market"—with none other than Teacho Wiltshire at the piano. It was the idea of Bob Weinstock at Prestige, who was anxious to cash in on the success of the recent hit "Moody Mood for Love," and it won her *DownBeat's* New Star award. In December 1955, after a stint with Lionel Hampton back in Europe, she enjoyed her first big theatrical hit in the London revue *Cranks*. The following year it opened at The Bijou on Broadway, where it did less well, closing after three weeks. But this meant that, in 1957, Annie Ross was in the right place at the right time.

Meanwhile, back at Beltone Studios, someone came up with the idea of overdubbing. Jon always credited the suggestion to Dave Lambert, who was a bit of a technical whiz; the kind of man who knew how to build radio sets. Don Elliott had recently created an artificial vocal quartet album for ABC-Paramount by laying down four tracks of his own voice; if Don Elliott could turn one voice into four, couldn't they turn three into twelve? Neither Jon nor Creed knew what was meant by multitracking but Dave suggested that if

Annie could sing the trumpet and the alto saxophone parts, he and Jon would do the tenor and baritone saxes and the trombones. Creed Taylor wanted to know where the money was going to come from, now that they had blown ABC-Paramount's $1,250. Dave asked him what time the studio opened and closed, to be told that it usually operated from seven in the morning until eight in the evening. "Dave said, 'Well we'll come at eight thirty and we'll stay 'til six thirty in the morning and nobody will know what we are doing,'" Jon recalled. They would also need an engineer; Creed suggested Irv Greenbaum, who had worked for Columbia Records.

Ever after, Hendricks seemed to believe that he, Lambert and Ross were the people who invented multitracking. In fact, aside from Don Elliott, it had been done first by Patti Page a decade earlier and developed further in the early fifties by guitarist, composer, and technician Les Paul, who lent his name to Gibson's first solid-body electric guitar and made some pioneering records with his then-wife, singer Mary Ford. But even if Lambert, Hendricks, Ross, Taylor, and Greenbaum were merely reinventing the wheel, they certainly created their own version of overdubbing.

They started work on September 16, 1957—Jon's thirty-sixth birthday. The first job was to record the Basie rhythm section, which they could then listen to while singing. Since all three voices were recorded simultaneously around one microphone, if anyone made a mistake it would have to be done again. Irv Greenbaum followed Dave Lambert's suggested method, capturing each track on a quarter-inch Ampex recorder. But in those long-ago analog days, whenever you added music to music, you were also adding tape hiss to tape hiss. And that wasn't all: with only four tracks available to record on, each recording of their three voices would be added to another tape of the three voices, until they had twelve in total. After several weeks of this, the recordings had degenerated into a weird cacophony ("eee wa wa ah woah wow," as Jon later characterized it), like something out of a horror film. Their mistake had been to record the lead voices first. In these primitive studio conditions, the leads had been gradually buried under a pile of subsequent, less important vocal parts. After the failure of the choir, the dreadful sound quality was a further hammer blow to their ambitions. No-one knew how to rescue the situation; there was nothing for it but to rerecord it all from scratch and rebalance the recording. However, with a more logical sequence—laying down the harmonies first and the lead voices last—Taylor and Greenbaum finally worked out how to crack the hiss problem by rolling off the high, ten-to-twelve-kilohertz frequencies that were causing it; one can only assume they also found ways of correcting the accumulated wow and flutter.

For three months they worked like this, spending all night at the studio then heading off at dawn to do their day jobs—in Hendricks's case, long hours at the newsprint factory. "When it was over," he said, "and we heard it back, all four of us just sat down on the floor and cried like babies ... I never heard anything that beautiful in my whole life." As the project came to a close,

Hendricks collapsed from exhaustion. He took a taxi to Bellevue Hospital, where he had an operation. "I almost died from my heart ... I was very sick from self-abuse," he said. "A lot of marijuana smoking, liquor drinking, general debauchery of all kinds ... We stayed up forty-eight hours at a time and worked day and night, non-stop." But what they had at the end of it all was a completed album entitled *Sing a Song of Basie*, which would soon be hailed as a masterpiece. When Annie Ross got home, she called Miles Davis and played him a tape copied from the final mix. "What do you think of this?" she asked. Miles said, "Wait a minute. Mingus, Mingus, get on the phone." Charles Mingus listened in too; both of them loved it.

In January 1958, an ad from ABC-Paramount appeared in *DownBeat*, listing ten imminent releases from the new label. *Sing a Song of Basie* was at the top of the list. In February, the album finally emerged into daylight. Dom Cerulli's *DownBeat* review appeared rather late in the day (on April 17, to be exact). There is a suggestion in the opening line that the album had lain untouched on the reviewing shelf for quite a while. But Cerulli was awestruck:

> Here, without a doubt, is the sleeper of the year. The three voices were multitaped singing the section parts to Basie's big band scores. All the words, except "Every Day," were written by Hendricks. The results are fantastic. I'm not sure whether this is properly reviewed under Jazz or Recommended, but it's ***** in either category. The words alone are amazing. In writing to the nuances of the tunes, Hendricks has pulled off the seemingly impossible. The words make sense, even unto the alternating riffs of the sections and the occasional solo comments by the horns. My words can't properly describe the effect. This should draw airplay on the shorter tracks. It should also draw considerable interest among all fans of Basie. If you flip as high as I did on first hearing "[It's] Sand, Man" or "Little Pony" or "Down for Double," this should sell on a par with its artistry. And dig particularly Miss Ross'[s] trumpet sectioning, and her just-right solo at the start of "One O'Clock Jump." A second set is in the works, I'm told, and it's long overdue already. Don't pass this one by, or you'll miss one of the outstanding listening experiences of the year.

The monthly *Metronome* was also positive, although more cautiously so. And in a review of Prestige's *King Pleasure Sings/Annie Ross Sings* compilation in the same issue, the writer noted that both Pleasure and Hendricks were great interpreters of "what the soloist may well have been thinking." There was an even more belated review in the November 1958 issue of the UK's *Jazz Journal*: "I don't normally believe in gimmicks, but this is one that succeeds in a remarkable way," opined Gerald Lascelles:

Take three voices, a three-piece rhythm section, multi-tape the voices to take the place of the various instruments in the Basie big band entourage, and the answer is anything but the proverbial lemon. Where the gimmick takes off for fun is that Jon Hendricks'[s] arrangements [sic] are not just the old "voo-dee-da" sounds one associates with this sort of thing; nor are the deliberate vocal copies of instruments as practiced by the Mills Brothers. Every line, be it brass, reed or solo, is given a part, with words sung to that part in such a way that the blended result sounds like a phonetic immitation [sic] of the real thing. What comes out of the groove has movement and life, even if it does not come up to the high standards we expect of the Basie product. I doubt whether it is a repeatable gimmick, but I like what I hear for its entertainment value.

In three months of blood, sweat, and tears, Dave, Jon, and Annie had ground out barely half an hour of music. Yet the astounding thing about *Sing a Song of Basie* is how relaxed, fresh, and enthusiastic it sounds. Memphis Slim's "Every Day I Have the Blues" had been a big hit for Joe Williams and the Basie band a couple of years earlier. The lyricized version is here titled simply "Everyday." And it sounds terrific—high-spirited, spontaneous fun. Among the album's other highlights are Annie Ross hitting the first of many super-high notes in "It's Sand, Man!" and in "Two for the Blues" she even includes the trumpet shake in her contribution to the section, plus multitracked soli in "Down for the Count." "Little Pony" features some high-speed Jon Hendricks vocalese on Wardell Gray's tenor solo. Many of the numbers not only became staples of the trio's live show, but featured in Jon Hendricks's set for the rest of his singing career: "Down for Double," "Goin' to Chicago," "Blues Backstage," "Avenue C," and "Fiesta in Blue." On the cover, the album is credited not to Lambert, Hendricks & Ross, but as follows: "Dave Lambert and his Singers, Jon Hendricks and his Lyrics, featuring Annie Ross and the Basie Rhythm Section." This was intended, after all, as a one-off collaboration. According to Hendricks, it was Creed Taylor's suggestion that ABC-Paramount print all of his lyrics on the back of the liner. They are prefaced with:

These are lyricized versions of actual Basie band arrangements, as the arranger wrote them. Only words have been added. Parts marked "Brass" include Trumpets and Trombones. Parts are marked by the instruments that were used, as Trumpets etc, Rhythm is Piano (Nat Pierce), Bass (Eddie Jones), Guitar (Freddie Green) and Drums (Sonny Payne). The use of only three voices entailed a multiple-taping process. All the parts are sung by Dave Lambert, Jon Hendricks and Annie Ross. All the words (except the vocal on Everyday) were written by Jon Hendricks.

Gradually word got around that this was a great record. One day Jon picked up a copy of *DownBeat* and saw that *Sing a Song of Basie* was number thirteen on the jazz album chart. Meanwhile, Creed Taylor—who not so long ago had feared for his job with ABC-Paramount—was more than relieved that the album had not only been delivered as promised, but achieved its sales target. Incredibly, given the headaches and heartaches of the whole process, Dave, Jon, and Annie had hit the big time—at least, in theory: six months after the release, Jon and Dave still had not a penny to their names. Jon in particular was desperate to get out on the road and capitalize on the album's success; Dave and Annie less so, with good reason. As Jon explained later to Les Tomkins:

> At that time there hadn't been so much talk of integration, or the freedom rides and all the things that have happened to divide people and bring to the fore this idea of different races and all that. I wasn't thinking in terms of social life, but in terms of music and art. They didn't say anything; they just laughed. But I kept badgering them: "Why shouldn't we sing together?" Finally, after about an hour, Dave says: "Well, look—if you can get us a gig, we'll make it." I called a friend of Dave's, as a matter of fact. He had a club in West New York, New Jersey, called the Bankers Club. It had been a bank before it was converted to a nightclub. And he offered us twenty-five dollars a night for a weekend—Friday, Saturday, Sunday.

Al Haig played piano, Zoot Sims was on tenor and, in the event, the gig went so well that the owner doubled their fee. Soon after, they took a Greyhound bus to Pittsburgh and did it all again. These initial outings proved they could make the whole vocal harmony shtick work in a live context by keeping it simple. There was no prospect of recreating the studio sound of twelve over-dubbed voices, so why not simply go out and gig as a vocal trio, backed by an instrumental trio? They contacted Monte Kay, manager of The Modern Jazz Quartet, and sang some of their vocalizations for him in the Cornelia Street apartment. Kay then got them an audition with Willard Alexander, who had been managing Basie since 1936, and who also booked tours for Harry James, Woody Herman, and other big bands. "Willard *literally* fell off his chair when we sang 'It's Sand, Man,' you know, the Basie tune," said Jon. "He leaned back to laugh and the chair fell over." The deal was sealed, but Dave was now faced with the task of rearranging the twelve-voice arrangements for three voices. Thanks to Annie's wide vocal range, her parts were not too difficult to score—although, like Jon, she couldn't read music, so Dave wrote her parts out in *do-re-mi*. But it was a different matter for Dave's own parts, which he had to write in a higher register than was comfortable simply to get the voicings right. The rearrangements put more strain on him in live performances than he'd previously had in groups of four or five singers. Jon carried on writing lyrics, which he would bring to their meetings along with his daily crossword puzzle; Annie would arrive with a pile of newspapers to read. Meanwhile, Dave would be scribbling charts. After about an hour and a half, they would try out the arrangement—then it would be a matter of reproducing it on stage.

By the spring they were back in the studio, this time with Joe Williams and the Count Basie Orchestra: Basie's record label Roulette had contracted Lambert, Hendricks & Ross to record *Sing Along with Basie*, a sort-of sequel to *Sing a Song*. It was recorded over five dates in May, September and October of 1958 and, according to Hendricks, it was "the best time of my whole life, singing-wise, to have Dave, Annie and Joe, that was a perfect group, to have Joe's beautiful, rich syrupy baritone at the bottom, it was just what it needed … We still talk about that, Joe and I." While not arousing quite the same level of enthusiasm as the first album, *Sing Along* was another hit with *DownBeat*'s reviewer. "Hendricks is incredible," wrote Dom Cerulli. "His lyrics here continue to be as bright and unexpected as they were on the earlier set … The bulk of the solo-to-words singing is done by Hendricks, whose labial dexterity is beyond description." He pointed out that without all the overdubs, the album gave you the chance to hear how the trio (augmented by Williams) swung in a club setting. For Cerulli, the only let down was Neal Hefti's "Li'l Darlin'," which he found too fuzzy and played too slow. He added that the track was in danger of being pulled off the album because of a dispute with Neal Hefti. Had Hendricks neglected to ask permission from the composer to add his lyrics to the tune? If so, this would not be the last time it happened. *Metronome*, less enthusiastic, described the album as "clever, swinging, fun," and noted that Hendricks had assumed command of the combo. Basie himself found them impressive. "They had to do a lot of tongue twisting to make those words get some of the licks and runs in those solos by Lester and Dicky and Sweets and Herschel and Tate and so on," he observed, "But that was all part of the excitement that was already their trademark." Not everyone was enthused. When former Basie trombonist and arranger Johnny Mandel took *DownBeat*'s Blindfold Test in another edition of the magazine, his reactions were mixed. They played him "Ev'ry Tub" from *Sing Along*. As on the first Lambert-Hendricks recording of "Four Brothers," the original tempo had been slowed down to allow for the coherent delivery of lyrics. "The rhythm section sounds terribly mushy on account of it," he said. "A lot of that is in the recording, too … Again it sound[s] like it's in a barrel." After heaping praise on the singers—particularly Ross, whom he describes as the best singer he has ever heard—he added:

> To hear this group even through one tune gives me the jitters. I
> don't know how to rate this record. It's got more talent on it and yet
> I can't say I like the sum total at all … I just don't like the group as
> a group. I love them all as individuals, musically, but I can't stand

to listen to a whole side of this. It was very well handled both by Jon and Annie. I guess I'll give this three stars and an E for effort.

The album is certainly far from perfect, with some poorly mixed cuts. Often there's simply too much going on. Some of Hendricks's lyrics illustrate the problem of lyricizing instrumentals without having anything much to say other than how great the musicians are (see lyrics chapter). On Lester Young's "Tickle Toe," an old-style swing tune, the lyrics are about how great the Basie band is. On "The King," the lyric praises Duke (Ellington), Earl (Hines), and Count (Basie).

On August 1, 1958, Lambert and Hendricks played Long Island's Great South Bay Jazz Festival, with Flo Handy singing the parts written for the temporarily absent Ross, together with Kenny Burrell, Addison Farmer, Osie Johnson, and Nat Pierce. *DownBeat* reported:

> They did several of the *Song of Basie* LP things; Mrs. Handy and her husband George's torch song "Leaving Town" effectively, and there were new numbers—"Doodlin'," "Air Mail Special," "I Remember Clifford," "Spirit Feel." It seemed an extremely clever, delightfully entertaining vaudeville turn.

That "vaudeville turn" was the sting in the tail: it was still looked like a novelty act as far as the jazz press were concerned. On the same day, with the same band, they cut a single for United Artists (with Ross rather than Handy this time) consisting of Horace Silver's "Doodlin'" and "Spirit Feel" by the Modern Jazz Quartet's vibes player Milt "Bags" Jackson, both with Hendricks lyrics. Three weeks later, the trio caused a sensation at the Randall's Island Jazz Festival in New York, earning another rave from *DownBeat*.

Not all areas of the music press welcomed the multi-racial group with open arms. *Billboard* reviews in 1958 and 1959 referred to them as the "Dave Lambert Singers," or as the "Dave Lambert Singers: featuring Annie Ross," leaving Jon Hendricks's name out altogether. But Jon Hendricks was on a roll. Having written lyrics to Benny Golson's "I Remember Clifford" that year, he continued with Gigi Gryce's "Social Call" and Randy Weston's "Little Niles," among others. And over three widely-spaced dates, starting in September 1958, he also took part in the star-studded recording of George Russell's *New York, NY* album in the company of Max Roach, Bill Evans, Al Cohn, Benny Golson, Art Farmer, John Coltrane, Phil Woods, and Bob Brookmeyer. Hendricks wasn't singing this time: his brief was to narrate between the cuts, but because it all rhymed and was delivered in such a hip, rhythm-conscious manner, it now sounds closer to the yet-to-be-invented genre of rap. The quality of the recording is immaculate and the style of music far more contemporary—more Bernstein-like (*West Side Story* had come out two years earlier)—than *Sing Along with Basie*. All the tracks except "A Helluva Town" clock in at over eight minutes, giving musical themes the chance to develop. After Bill Evans plays the intro to "Big City Blues," Hendricks raps about the struggle faced by musicians—"But lack of acceptance is less like somethin' to hide from and more like somethin' Bird died from." On "Manhattan-Rico," his theme is immigration from San Juan, Puerto Rico, with just Don Lamond's drums backing him—this time more Latin-sounding, with a lot of rim shots. It's an edgy piece, with a great trombone solo from Bob Brookmeyer.

On November 26, Jon emceed the Carnegie Hall and Town Hall *DownBeat* Critics Poll winners' event. The Modern Jazz Quartet, Ray Charles, and Thelonious Monk all featured, with Lambert, Hendricks & Ross doing "all the introducing musically." Jon and Dave's rise from starvation to Carnegie Hall and the open arms of the establishment in a few short months was nothing short of staggering. On November 23 they made their debut TV appearance, on Steve Allen's NBC show. It was a little late in the day to get on TV, considering the attention that had been lavished on them up to now .... until, that is, you factor in the race problem. Then (as now, in some parts of the USA) the idea of a black man standing in close proximity to a white woman was liable to give many white folks an attack of the vapors. Even so, *Ebony* magazine reported that following the Steve Allen appearance, the trio's weekly pay had risen from $750 to a "respectable" $1,250. Their virtuosity had been noticed. *Ebony* explained:

> Vocally, Hendricks's range starts at low F and climbs to B flat to reproduce an alto or tenor sax, and muted trumpet. Annie Ross, the group's distaff member, spans more than three octaves, capturing vocally solos originally played by trumpet, tenor and alto sax. Dave Lambert, the third singer, cleverly uses his voice to sound like a trumpet, clarinet or trombone.

The trio rounded off their *annus mirabilis* with an early December week at the Village Vanguard, then moved to Boston's Storyville for two more weeks. By now the group had settled into a set onstage routine: while each member would be featured at different times, it was Jon and Dave who did the scatting while Annie kept time in the background.

Lambert, Hendricks & Ross were still not billed as such. *Sing a Song of Basie* had been credited primarily to the Dave Lambert Singers; *Sing Along with Basie* to "Joe Williams, Dave Lambert, Jon Hendricks and Annie Ross, Plus The Basie Band." On Christmas Day, *DownBeat* announced that the Dave Lambert Singers with Jon Hendricks and Annie Ross had been voted the third-best vocal group behind the Four Freshmen and the Hi-Lo's. Hendricks was only the nineteenth best male singer; Sinatra won that category by a country mile. The following February the same magazine published a photo of the trio clustered around a microphone, with the caption:

Currently the hottest vocal group in jazz, the Lambert, Hendricks and Ross group popped into the pop field with a single, Horace Silver's "Doodlin'," for United Artists. Dave Lambert, Jon Hendricks and Annie Ross, shown at the UA cutting session, may tour England and the continent early this Spring.

Not long afterwards, Leonard Feather issued a ponderous assessment of Hendricks, beginning with the words, "The term genius is not something to be thrown around indiscriminately." Ellington, Armstrong, Tatum, Gillespie, and Parker, he thought, were probably worthy of that description—but it was too early, suggested Feather, to include Jon Hendricks among them. Yet the article makes clear that, for Feather, it was only a matter of time before he was.

The next four years became a blur of recording studios, concert stages, airports, and hotels. With variations from time to time, the regular band consisted of Lester Young's one-time pianist Gildo Mahones, Ike Isaacs on bass, and Jimmy Wormsworth on drums. Hendricks had now moved out of Dave's Cornelia Street place and relocated to apartment 16, 316 E. Sixth Street. He found personal representation with ABC (not the record label but Joe Glaser's Associated Booking Corp), who represented a large number of jazz acts. The trio appeared with Basie at Birdland, at the Apollo Theater in Harlem, and the Red Hill Inn in Camden, New Jersey. Dates were also planned at the Crescendo, a live jazz venue on Hollywood's Sunset Boulevard that had once been owned by Billy Eckstine. It was there, on March 21 and 24, 1959, that the group recorded *The Swingers!* When the album was released later that year, they were credited officially as Lambert, Hendricks & Ross for the first time. On this occasion they were backed by Zoot Sims, pianist Russ Freeman (prominent through his work with Chet Baker), Eddie Jones (bass), and Sonny Payne (drums), with Freddie Green then Jim Hall on guitar. Most of Ralph Gleason's liner notes are devoted to the genius of Jon Hendricks's lyrics, comparing him with James Joyce and T. S. Eliot. In Gleason's opinion, he was a better lyricist than Johnny Mercer, and Gleason went on to compare the group to Gilbert and Sullivan. It's certainly a good album, which makes a concerted effort to sound different to the preceding Basie recordings, and each singer is given some individual tracks. On Sonny Rollins's "Airegin," Zoot's cool-school contribution modernizes the trio's sound. Dave's vocal on "Dark Cloud," a Randy Weston composition, sounds less accurate than the other two, and he relies more on vibrato to get near the required pitch. "Jackie," a breakneck blues with lyrics by Annie, was originally written by Hampton Hawes, but it is Wardell Gray's solo that she turns into vocalese. Annie's one-word questions are interpolated by the other two, and she rhymes "Coca Cola" with "Gorgonzola." On "Swingin' Till the Girls Come Home," Oscar Pettiford's tune with Jon Hendricks lyrics, the latter scats brilliantly, capturing Pettiford's bass sound. "Where," another by Randy Weston, reveals Jon as a balladeer for the first time in a slow lament that sounds like a spiritual, backed only with piano, bass, and brushes. And there's a vocalese version of "Now's the Time" as Charlie Parker had recorded it in 1945, with Miles Davis on trumpet. Here, Jon sings Bird's solo and Annie follows it with the trumpet solo by Miles. This got Jon into trouble with the irascible trumpeter. Annie, in Jon's opinion, had sung the solo in a "limp and fatuous" manner. About eight months later, he was in Toronto working in a steakhouse that put on live jazz. He had just ordered his steak, and was getting ready to eat it, when Miles walked in. "How ya doin," he said, grabbing Jon's knife and fork, and shoving him to one side. He then ate the whole steak. "Man, you ate my steak," Jon pointed out. "You fuck with my solos, I fuck with your food," explained Miles.

Four weeks after recording *The Swingers!*, Lambert, Hendricks & Ross played a gig at the Crescendo, with the George Shearing Quintet and the Basie band. And when Mort Sahl pulled out of his engagement at San Francisco's hungry i, the club brought the trio in for a couple of weeks as replacement. During this engagement a call came in from their slave-driving agent, Willard Alexander, telling them to skip over to London for a one-off charity performance at the Royal Festival Hall one Saturday. It was a benefit gig in aid of Christian Action, who were raising money for anti-apartheid campaigners under arrest in South Africa. The weary trio duly flew out on the Wednesday and were back the following Monday to resume the hungry i residency. The London concert was underpublicized, and many people were not even aware that the trio were in town. But the critic Benny Green was there, and he was impressed: "Their performance that night was a technical *tour de force*. Their harmonies were note-perfect, their phrasing faultless, and their stage presence highly exciting," he wrote. On May 4, the group was a nominee in the newly-instituted Grammy Awards in the category Pop: Best Performance by a Vocal Group, but were beaten by Keely Smith and Louis Prima for their recording of "That Old Black Magic." (Oddly, the Four Freshmen were nominated in the category Best Group Jazz Performance.) On July 2, the first night of the Newport Jazz Festival, what *DownBeat* called "the Dave Lambert-John [sic] Hendricks-Annie Ross singing group" were featured with Count Basie. It was the closing slot of the evening, and didn't get started until well past midnight. After a few instrumentals by the band, Joe Williams came out and sang "Shake Rattle and Roll" and "Well Alright, Okay, You Win."

Even in the context of Basie's glittering career, this was a high point for him. In his autobiography he wrote:

> [Joe Williams] left the crowd all sparked up ... and that's when Lambert, Hendricks and Ross joined us ... with "It's Sand, Man," and there was no letdown in the audience at all. They were a hit by the time they finished the first couple of numbers, and when they got through their thing on a cool tune by Horace Silver called "Doodlin,'" that crowd wanted to keep them out there. But it was

time for the wrap-up then, so we brought Joe Williams, and the four of them took off on "Every Day" and from that we made a fast segue right on into the outchorus of "One O'Clock Jump."

Observed *DownBeat*'s reviewer:

> The crowd booed when Joe Williams vacated the stage to make way for Jon, Dave and Annie. The subsequent excitement over the trio suggested that most of the audience never had heard of them. The loudest booers were later the loudest cheerers. One of the memorable moments of the evening was provided by Jon Hendricks. In a framework provided by the trio's eerie vocal settings of great band arrangements, he took off on a scat solo that continued for countless choruses. Standing like a tenor man, Hendricks blew ... and blew ... and kept building his line with absolute logic and relentless swing. Considering the usual tedium of scat singing, this was a remarkable performance. And so the crowd found it, and so it continued to be when Joe Williams joined the group to take the evening to a bashing conclusion.

In the same issue of *DownBeat*, Hendricks topped the category of New Star Male Singer in the International Jazz Critics' Poll, beating Ray Charles into second place.

At the end of the month they played French Lick Jazz Festival near Indianapolis, which attracted a crowd of twenty thousand. Another reviewer remarked that they were the most talked-about act on the bill, and picked out Jon's scatted impression of a tenor sax, which was

> as incisive and hard-biting as any tenor you have heard. The vowels he used, and the intonation of them, evoked almost an actual reed sound from his larynx. After what seemed an interminable solo, he was joined by Lambert, who soloed with Hendricks, and then took off on a solo of his own, equally driven and exciting. Annie Ross jigged and marked time in the background.

In short, they were enjoying themselves. Once, playing at the Apollo Theater in Harlem, Jon did his usual bebop scat solo, ending with screaming vocal saxophone which sent the knowledgeable and highly vocal audience wild. Then it was Dave's turn. He went up to the mic, opened his mouth wide—but didn't make a sound, and fell backwards in a massive pratfall. The crowd loved it even more than Jon's solo. The plaudits continued to pour in: in an ad announcing the poll winners represented by Willard Alexander, Annie Ross was voted number two New Female Singer, and in a jazz DJ poll published in *Billboard*, the trio were named number three Favorite Jazz Vocal Group.

And one night, during a Birdland residency, the recently-divorced, thirty-eight-year-old Hendricks, father of four (and at least two more) spotted the young woman who was to become his second and final wife.

5 A Mouthful of Hot Rice

Twenty-one-year-old Judith Dickstein was the daughter of Max Dickstein and Maida Dickstein Laffstein. She was born on July 4, 1937, at the same New York City hospital where she later died. At the time she met Jon Hendricks, in March 1959, she had hopes of becoming a professional ballerina and was meanwhile earning a living as a cigarette girl at Birdland in the evenings. The moment Hendricks clapped eyes on her, he began his pursuit. "[At] Birdland, everybody hits on you that comes through," Judith said, describing their first encounter. "When I met Jon, I said, 'This guy can never talk to me, because I know this is trouble.' So he'd talk to me, and I'd run like hell." It was an understandable reaction: Hendricks was black and Christian; Judith Dickstein was white and Jewish. Although some of her friends had dated people of different races to their own, she herself never had. The US Supreme Court had recently declared school segregation unconstitutional, but laws forbidding interracial marriage still existed in around half of all states. And though it was legal for mixed couples to marry in New York, that didn't mean it was easy: the stigma was as marked as it had been when Jon married Connie. Social attitudes had not changed since the previous century: a Gallup poll conducted in 1958 revealed that only four percent of Americans approved of "marriages between white and colored people." Nonetheless, Judith's resistance to Jon's charm offensive soon crumbled. As Lambert, Hendricks & Ross played their final night at the club, she realized that she might never see Jon again. At that moment, he came down the stairs with Percy Heath and asked her if she wanted to go for a cup of coffee. She did, so they stepped across to the street to Lindy's. Unlike Judith, Jon had firsthand experience of the public reaction to mixed-race couples—first with Connie, then with his singing partner Annie Ross. It therefore came as no surprise when the other diners fell silent as Judith walked in on the arm of the dapper black singer. "If we walked down the street together, parents and children would pass us. They'd hide their children so they couldn't see us," Judith said. "I mean you didn't get racial couples unless it was the pimp and the whore generally." At Lindy's, Judith ordered apple pancakes; Jon had the borscht with boiled potato. They returned every night for the next two weeks.

At around the same time, Annie Ross also found romance, although of a different kind—with the taboo-busting comic and notorious junkie Lenny Bruce. In his book about Bruce, Albert Grossman describes how Ross (whom he thinly veils as "Francie") had always been attracted by lowlife types: "Involving herself with a whole succession of often nasty drummers, she got hooked on drugs, dragged into bad scenes and seemed destined for the tragic fate of a Billie Holiday when she made a lucky strike by joining a highly original trio that became famous overnight by vocalizing instrumental jazz." Grossman describes her as a sort of Scottish *femme fatale*, with her "pale, translucent skin and authentic red hair." While she was quiet and self-contained, he revealed, her low voice and relaxed demeanor was no more than a veneer, masking a volcanic lust for sex and drugs. "Lenny's engagement ring was a hypodermic needle," Grossman confided. "Francie was off drugs when Lenny met her. He turned her right back on again. That was one of his tricks with women." Bruce would inject heroin as casually as others drank coffee, using old and dirty works, which he would leave lying on top of a cupboard, frequently sharing this apparatus with his nearest and dearest. But that wasn't all. Street smack sometimes contained lumps of pure heroin that were enough to kill a man, and it was only a matter of time before Annie overdosed. On one occasion, she shoved the needle into her leg, squeezed the bulb and turned an alarming shade of blue-white, gasping and sliding off her chair and on to the floor. Lenny rushed to apply mouth-to-mouth resuscitation while his friend Kenny massaged the area around her heart. After a few moments she regained consciousness and the two men spent the next hour walking her up and down the room. Lenny and Annie later spent a week in Florida with the idea of not shooting any more heroin, at least for the time being. Shortly afterwards they split up: despite the drugs, both their careers were blooming.

Lambert, Hendricks & Ross generally avoided the South. According to Annie, the only racial problem they experienced in the North was in Philadelphia, where the police tried to arrest Jon for being with Judith. Dave was the one who stepped in to rescue him. On another occasion, they were planning to play in a boxing ring in El Paso, Texas. Hearing of this, Basie took Annie aside and warned her not to do it, because there could be trouble from the crowd. They went anyway and nothing untoward happened. But even in the North, not everyone subscribed to racial equality. In Chicago, in November 1960, Jon was refused a room at a hotel in the mostly white Gold Coast neighborhood when the management realized not only that he was black, but that his wife was white. Lambert, Hendricks & Ross often played at fundraising events for liberal causes including the Chicago Urban League, the NAACP and, in August 1960, a jazz festival held inside Lorton Reformatory, a prison in Laurel Hill, Virginia. The following year, Jon took part in a syndicated telethon organized by the Congress of Racial Equality (CORE) to raise funds for the desegregation of buses in the Southern states.

In August, 1959—back in New York—Dave, Jon, and Annie cut five tracks for yet another album. Five more went down in early November, with Jimmy Wormsworth replacing Walter Bolden on drums. In between, *DownBeat* published an issue with the trio on the cover under the strapline "The Hottest New Group in Jazz," which handily provided a title for the album.

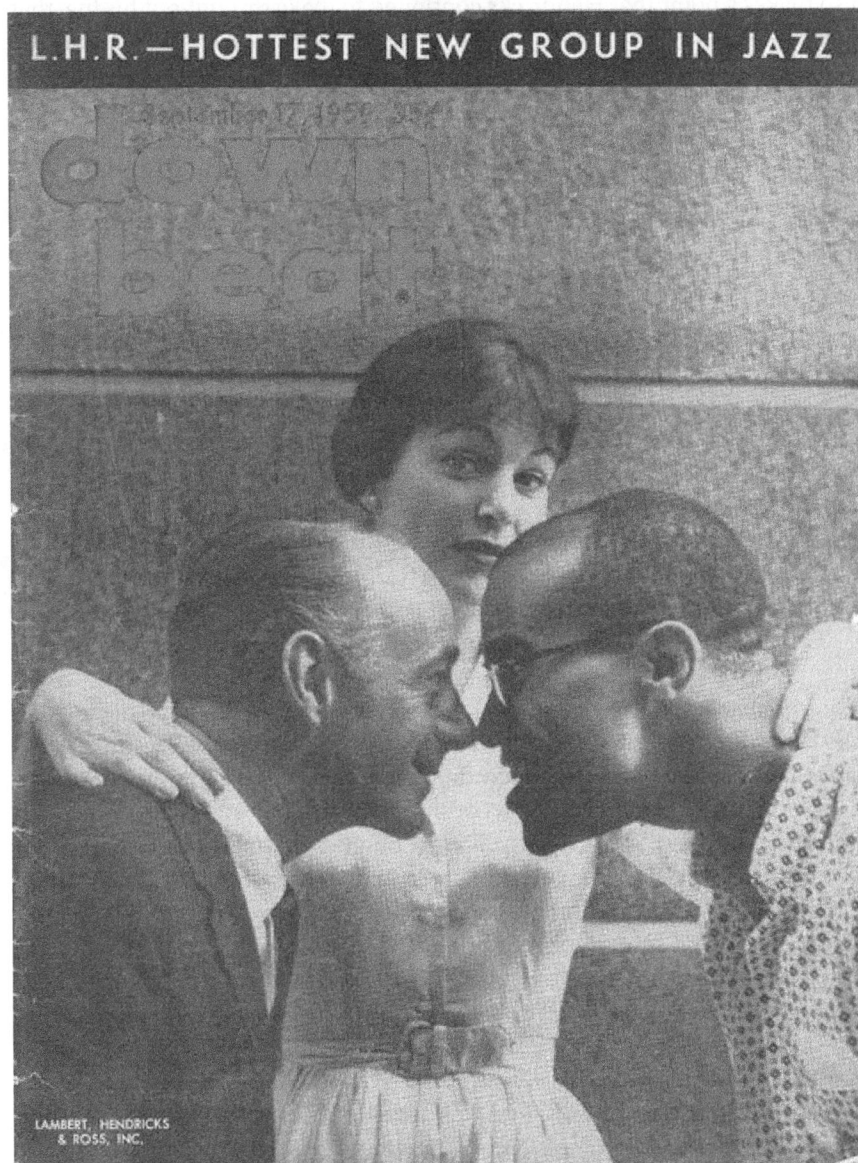

The accompanying article was written by Jon Hendricks, prefaced by a somewhat dazzled Gene Lees, who was then *DownBeat*'s editor. He had approached Hendricks at Newport earlier in the year and the idea had developed over subsequent months. When the piece arrived, it turned out to be partly in rhyme ("As to dates, times, names and places," Hendricks begins, "my accuracy ain't apt to be too outstanding. Data's too demanding.") He revealed that the group were currently planning yet another album—*Sing Ellington*—and that they were now being managed by Jon's brother Jimmy. The article also makes a point that Hendricks continued to make throughout his life, that

> opera houses dedicated to European musical culture are *not* the American norm. Jazz is America's cultural art form ... America's real opera houses ... are the Howard Theater in Washington DC, the Regal Theater in Chicago, and Harlem's Apollo. And our divas are ... Billie and Ella and Sarah, and they sing jazz!

As for *The Hottest New Group in Jazz* (the album), the title is amply justified by the contents. Backed by Ike Isaacs's trio, plus Sweets Edison on trumpet, Lambert, Hendricks & Ross sound better than ever. The album—their first for Columbia—is justifiably regarded by most (including Hendricks) as the high point of the trio's career. A small backing group was a better context for them than a big band. The sheer brilliance of the arrangements and the singing might have been off-putting in a show-offy kind of way, but the humor of both Jon and Annie's lyrics defuses any such criticism. You may not like it, but you can never accuse it of being po-faced. And the album title was no idle boast: *DownBeat* was no longer dubbing them the hottest *vocal* group in jazz, note, but the hottest *group* in jazz—period.

"Charleston Alley" is a terrific mid-tempo opener, a cool and swinging tune credited on the label to guitarist/arranger Leroy Kirkland and pianist Horace Henderson (brother of Fletcher). This was also the first time anyone had heard Jon's lyrics to "Moanin'," a call-and-response Bobby Timmons slow blues. Reprising her Prestige recording of six years earlier, Annie performs her own words to "Twisted." (According to Dave, the message of the song was, "Anybody who goes to a psychiatrist ought to have his head examined.") "Bijou," originally subtitled "Rhumba à la Jazz," was written by Ralph Burns for the Woody Herman orchestra in 1945. It's stunningly good, a strange and sophisticated tune, with many different sections; Dave takes most of the lead. The first side ends with a dusted-off and polished-up "Cloudburst." Jon's breakneck vocalese is enough to scare off any other singer thinking of giving it a try. It's just dazzling at three hundred beats per minute, especially when compared with the slightly slower, earlier version in which he sounds less energetic and the recording quality is inferior. (Annie said years later that performing "Cloudburst" live had by now become a question of, "How fast can we sing it, and they still understand the words?") While your head is still spinning from "Cloudburst," the second-side opener "Centerpiece" comes as slow swing relief. The first twelve bars are sung in unison, then they split into three parts. The tune is credited to Sweets Edison, who plays a muted trumpet solo on this version. It is one of the trio's most iconic recordings, with subsequent versions recorded by many others—most notably Joni Mitchell. "Gimme That Wine," the tune Jon had intended for Louis Jordan, is a brilliant slice of manic comedy, particularly his asides at the end of each verse. "Sermonette," a slow swinger written by Cannonball Adderley in 1956, and now given the Jon Hendricks lyric treatment, reaches back to that ol' time religion he constantly returned to later in his career. The very brief (one minute and forty-three seconds) "Summertime" is based on Gil Evans's Miles Davis arrangement; it required Jon to adjust the original DuBose Heyward lyric somewhat to fit the melody Miles played: "And the livin' is easy" becomes "And the livin' ain't bad," with the answering horn lines sung by Dave and Annie. "Everybody's Boppin'," another Hendricks tune at a lunatic tempo (even faster than "Cloudburst," at about 320 bpm), becomes a pure bop-fest with not much time to contemplate melody. By the end, before the final head, they're all scatting like lunatics with Annie adding tiny mouse squeaks—it's exhilarating.

Hendricks had formed a company, Hendricks Music Inc., through which all his lyrics were published. Today, most writers know that when they put a lyric to an existing tune they must change the title. This is essential, because using a different title enables the organizations that administer copyright (principally ASCAP and BMI in the United States) to distinguish between the writer of the music and the writer of the lyric, ensuring that royalties are paid accordingly. But in the early days, when Hendricks wrote his lyrics, he would retain the original title of the song. This meant that when the time came for royalties to be paid, confusion would arise. Hendricks would exploit the fact that Hendricks Music Inc. was registered with ASCAP, whereas most of the musicians whose work he was lyricizing were with BMI. He would claim the song for Hendricks Music Inc., then attempt to collect royalties not only on the version with his lyrics but on the instrumental version too, since it had the same title. He justified this practice on the grounds that once he had written a lyric, his contribution made the song so important that he *deserved* to collect on the instrumental. This got him into hot water with many composers—including Sweets Edison, writer of "Centerpiece." Despite his friendly-sounding moniker, Sweets was not the sort of man to be trifled with and routinely carried a gun. After the recording of *The Hottest New Group in Jazz*, Sweets became so enraged by Hendricks's purloining of his tune that one day he went out looking for him. "If I'd have found Jon Hendricks," he said, "I would have blown him away and there would be no Jon Hendricks." Ironically, Sweets had himself stolen "Centerpiece" from Johnny Mandel, whose original title was "Keester Parade," recorded in December 1955—with Sweets himself on trumpet.

The group's busy recording schedule may give the impression that Lambert, Hendricks & Ross were permanently in each other's pockets, but all three of them were also working on solo projects: Annie Ross recorded two albums for World Pacific with Gerry Mulligan's Quartet, in December 1957 and September 1958, and two more in 1959: *A Gasser*, with the Russ Freeman Quartet, and *Gypsy*, with Buddy Bregman and his Orchestra. Dave Lambert recorded a solo album—*Dave Lambert Sings and Swings Alone*—with a piano trio for United Artists during 1958 and 1959. Jon Hendricks also found time to record a solo album that same year at Fugazi Hall, a small theater and night-club in North Beach, San Francisco. As well as the usual suspects (Mahones, Wormsworth, *et al.*), *A Good Git Together* features at different times two Adderleys (Nat and Cannonball) and three Montgomerys (Wes, Monk, and Buddy). As was now the norm, all the lyrics on the album were penned by Jon Hendricks. The tunes range from the spiritual ("Everything Started in the House of the Lord"), through upswingers like Gigi Gryce's "Music in the Air" (with a nice light, hip solo by Cannonball), and ballads like Randy Weston's dark "Pretty Strange."

Now at the peak of their career as a trio, Lambert, Hendricks & Ross were starting to feel the strain. "We had a lot of fun," recalled Annie Ross:

> Relationships were good. When we started getting a little bit of a name, things began to change. My motto was, don't believe your own publicity, because you'll be in big trouble. Unfortunately, that didn't seem to be the rule for certain people. If you tell yourself something enough times, I suppose you get to believe it. But it wasn't right, all the time. Jon had a very annoying habit of telling any woman that he wanted to be with, "I'll make you a singer." It was awful. I'd have these hostile women saying, "I can sing. Jon Hendricks told me." I'm sorry. I cut that. "I was told that I could sing, and I will replace you," which I thought was pretty lousy. It was usually when alcohol had been prevalent.

In October they made a TV appearance for the syndicated television series *Playboy's Penthouse*, taped at WBKB-TV in Chicago, with Count Basie and his rhythm section. It started with Annie chatting with Hugh Hefner and Tony Bennett, and then the group are invited to sing "Spirit Feel" in front of the studio's blazing log fire. After Jon's wild voice-saxophone scat, Dave follows him up with great energy, after which the two of them trade fours. Annie does "Twisted," and later in the show they are joined by the looming figure of Joe Williams for "Every Day" and "The King." And later still there's a fine rendition of "Doodlin'."

Sing Ellington, their fifth recording together, was a less happy experience. Backed by their road trio (Mahones, Isaacs, and Wormsworth) they began on May 9, 1960, with four cuts and got another four down on the twelfth, with additional dates on June 2 and August 18. (One tune, "What Am I Here For," was never issued.) Jon was disgruntled with Dave from the start for his refusal to use multitracking as they had on the original Basie album. He took the view that it was disrespectful to Ellington not to employ the method that had made *Sing a Song of Basie* so successful. "But Dave Lambert was not of the culture, so he didn't even have any sense of what I was really talking about," Jon said later, "so that made me angry, that that happened." Not of the culture? Since Dave was steeped in jazz to his fingertips, this reads like pretty obvious code for "because he was white." Duke had asked Jon, "When are you going to do an album of my things?" and Jon felt it was their sacred duty to complete the project with same degree of energy and care that they had committed to the original Basie sides. "I was very angry at Dave, because he at that time had gotten jaded and tired and didn't want to multitrack Duke Ellington."

For the first time, when the album came out, there were no Jon Hendricks lyrics on the liner. Its front depicts a rather glum-looking trio, the tuxedoed men posing with chins on fists, and Annie Ross looking less than enthused. The visuals were an accurate reflection of the music, which lacks the vim and madcap inventiveness of their earlier work. On "Cottontail" (originally two words) Hendricks relates a childhood story about a rabbit with a carrot habit, and himself plays the rabbit. It is surely not too fanciful to imagine a reference to Ross's recently-acquired heroin addiction—not to mention Hendricks's own. At any rate, we are in the world of Warner Bros cartoons, as the rabbit hears the farmer's bullets zinging through the air. "All Too Soon" is a rare Lambert, Hendricks & Ross ballad, with lyrics by Carl Sigman. Ross's voice takes on the quality of a musical saw as Lambert sings the lead, Hendricks adding street corner bass, creating a somewhat parodic effect. "I Don't Know What Kind of Blues I Got" is a slow blues led off by the close-miked Annie Ross, with answering phrases from Dave Lambert. It sounds very old-school, and Lambert is off-key as he takes over in the second part. "Caravan" finishes off the album, which at last shows some signs of life, but we could have done with more than two and a half minutes of it.

They kept the bad vibes well hidden at their appearance on July 2 at the Newport Jazz Festival, backed by the same trio. After their triumphant debut with Basie the previous year, expectations were sky-high—and they did not disappoint. The set kicked off with a fine, swinging "Jumpin' at the Woodside," Ross soloing first, vocalizing Buck Clayton's stratospheric trumpet solo. Hendricks was next up, shoehorning his hip lyrics into Prez's tenor solo. Then "Doodlin'," a showcase for Ross's range and flexibility, followed by "Happy Anatomy" from the new Ellington collection, an adaptation of Duke's score for the recent Otto Preminger film *Anatomy of a Murder*. "Airegin" was next, a number which Hendricks had by now turned into a blazing vehicle for his own multi-chorus scatting, ending with a fiery exchange of scat lines between him and Dave Lambert. The fireworks were temporarily doused with Jimmy Mundy's mellow "Fiesta in Blue," featuring Ross's seductive vocal, Hendricks and Lambert supporting her with horn-like choruses. On "Swingin' Till the Girls Come Home" Lambert soloed first, followed by Hendricks, whose scat solo quoted freely from the Oscar Pettiford *oeuvre*, before going on to summon up vocally a succession of famous bassists: Percy Heath, Paul Chambers, Ray Brown, Charles Mingus—just as he had on the *The Swingers!* After "Rusty Dusty Blues," "Gimme That Wine," "Cottontail," and "Cloudburst," they closed a scintillating set with "Every Day," Hendricks doing a creditable impression of Joe Williams's deep-toned bluesy style.

When they played a morning show at the Flamingo Hotel, Las Vegas, the stars came out to see them: Frank Sinatra, Dean Martin, Jerry Lewis, Don Rickles, Redd Foxx, Jack E. Leonard, Peggy Lee, Pearl Bailey, and Lena Horne. The presence of Judith did not go unnoticed. Willard Alexander had warned Hendricks not to take her, but he ignored the agent's advice:

> I took her to dinner in the restaurant of the hotel, and I saw people looking at me from behind pillars. And the waiters would stand still and hardly approach my table until I waved at them. I still didn't understand what the hell was going on. After about a week or so I finally got the message—the rest of my group told me. I haven't been back to Vegas since.

On August 8 they played the Playboy Jazz Festival at Chicago Stadium, performing "Doodlin'" and "Spirit Feel" with Basie, and were joined by Joe Williams for "Every Day." This appearance was the setting for an onstage racial incident, as *Ebony* journalist John Johnson noted:

> Pretty Annie Ross of the jazz trio of Lambert, Hendricks and Ross was "riffing" with Count Basie vocalist Joe Williams. At the conclusion of their number they impulsively embraced. "Oops!" gasped Big Joe, clamping his hand over his mouth, and Annie darted from the stage.

There's a YouTube video, which may have been taken from this concert, of the trio singing "Avenue C" with the Basie band. And at the second-ever Monterey Jazz Festival held in the beginning of October, 1959 the trio were the collective emcee, introducing each act by singing a few lines of their best-known number, with words by Jon Hendricks.

His extraordinary creativity did not end with his lyric-writing or his fertility and energy as a scat soloist. At Monterey the following year he created and starred in a stage musical he called *Evolution of the Blues Song* (soon afterwards abbreviated to *Evolution of the Blues*). The festival's founder Jimmy Lyons had asked him to come up with a Sunday afternoon entertainment that should be "something about the blues." Hendricks later said: "I thought about it for a long time and went into my own family history. I got a lot of historical information and I realized that was probably the story for every Negro person in America, so I began to really get into it." He liked the possibilities for a project on this scale and staged it—and attempted to stage it—in various forms for years afterwards. To help him write it, he took on board the advice of his English teacher at the University of Toledo, to "write about what you know," and also returned to his models of literary excellence: the King James Bible and the *New Yorker* magazine. But first he wrote about his own family:

> I wrote about my people, my great-grandmother who came from Guinea, Gold Coast, West Africa; about my father Alexander Brooks Hendricks, who ran away from the master who sold his father, mother, and sister separately, came into West Virginia, married my mother Willie "Sweet Will" Carrington and moved to Ohio by covered wagon where he became a minister, known as a circuit rider.

Hendricks said that he wrote *Evolution of the Blues* primarily for children:

> I know that children are born into this earthly life with all knowledge, that the devil is an adult, that children are corrupted by adults [who are] too adult to realize that childhood is the kingdom of heaven, so I wrote my history for children, because they will understand.

And so whatever Jimmy Lyons originally had in mind, *Evolution of the Blues* was about far more than the blues, representing Hendricks's political/educational credo at a time when slavery was never talked about. It depicted the whole American black experience: all the way from Africa to modern American jazz, via drums and chants, field hollers, spirituals, the blues, and the birth of jazz in New Orleans. On the final day of the jazz festival—on Sunday afternoon, two minutes before the curtain went up—Hendricks was still scribbling. On stage with him were Miriam Makeba from South Africa, the folk singer Odetta, Jimmy Witherspoon, Big Miller, Hannah Dean, the Andrews Sisters Gospel Singers from Oakland, and the Gildo Mahones Trio. Hendricks himself was seated in a child's chair facing a group of children whose backs were to the Monterey audience. He told the audience that "the spirituals are the mother of the blues and the blues are the mother of jazz." Over the next fifty minutes, the cast illustrated these ideas through songs, and in between Jon narrated the story in rhyme, emphasizing the links between childhood, slavery, song, dance, community, and the Bible. Backstage, J. J. Johnson commented, "They're hearing the truth now!" Ralph Gleason wrote afterwards:

There have been few moments in this writer's lifetime of listening to jazz that have been as good (and none better) than [*sic*] the afternoon's sessions at the Monterey Jazz Festival, out in the beautiful Autumn sunshine in a picture-book setting listening to good music.

Writer Frank Kofsky summed up the general reaction of Jon's audience that day by saying, "If in its three years, the Monterey Jazz Festival had done nothing other than present this program, it would have justified its existence."

The week after its first presentation in Monterey, *Evolution of the Blues* was recorded for Columbia Records in Hollywood, with most of the original cast present and only minor changes in script. This time the accompanying gospel singers were from Hannah Dean's church in Los Angeles rather than from San Francisco, as they had been in Monterey. Ben Webster was added to the Ike Isaacs Trio for the recording, as was guitarist Bobby Gibbons, and there were some new songs—"Amo," "Some Stopped on de Way," and "Aw, Gal." We are fortunate that most of the original version of the production was recorded in sound. There's a lot more talk than music on side one: its introduction is a mini-sermon, asserting that adults "have their minds made up, don't confuse 'em with facts," and refers to musicians as "metaphysicians." The chorus hums a simple two-note backing vocal as Hendricks delivers the Christian message of "becoming as a child," an idea reflected in the messianic cover image of him surrounded by children of all races. As soon as he starts talking about rhythm, the backing cuts out, and we hear "Amo," a brief African chant with just drums and voices in some African language. With "Some Stopped on de Way," the hums are now harmonized, and Hendricks talks about slaves being brought from Africa and stopping off in the Caribbean. This gives him the opportunity to sing a brief calypso in the style made famous by Harry Belafonte. Hannah Dean and the chorus sing "Swing Low Sweet Chariot" to illustrate how music helped slavery to be bearable after the slave owners' methodical destruction of African families and traditions and the gradual erosion of collective cultural memory. Christianity was a lifeline for them, as it helped the slaves to reassert their identity, the preacher replacing the tribal leader. With "New Orleans" the narrative jumps to the post-Civil War period and freedom, to a slow blues backing. After an extended lecture from Hendricks, Pony Poindexter (from New Orleans) briefly starts talking about how Buddy Bolden, Joe "King" Oliver, and Louis Armstrong were the originators of jazz, and how Louis ("the first Messiah") and Lester Young (the second) subsequently made their way to Chicago. The musical connection that Hendricks always talked about, between gospel music and blues, is made with "I Had My Share," sung by Big Miller: the church calls women "sister," and the music is gospel; outside the church, they're called "baby" and the music is the blues. Big Miller sings his own fast blues, with Ben Webster soloing. Hendricks wonders aloud why they're called "the blues," whimsically speculating that the word came from the colors of the sky and the sea. The first side of the album concludes with Jimmy Witherspoon's belting rendition of Percy Mayfield's classic "Please Send Me Someone to Love."

Side two kicks off with Miller's "Sufferin' Blues," featuring another Ben Webster solo. Hendricks makes the point that everyone understands the blues (quoting a "great American philosopher"). This is followed by Hendricks's field holler "Aw, Gal," simply harmonized voices with handclaps, and Witherspoon's "See See Rider," a song credited to Ma Rainey about the circuit riders who, like Jon's father, wandered the country spreading the word of the gospel. Pony Poindexter returns on "Jumpin' With Symphony Sid," which includes references to Lester Young. The program ends with Witherspoon's brilliant rendition of Big Bill Broonzy's "Sun Gonna Shine in My Door," Hendricks's lugubrious "WPA Blues," and Big Miller's "Sometimes I Feel Like a Motherless Child." Hendricks expresses regret that the blues has fallen out of favor, then restates the linked themes of his opening chat, with hums coming back in towards the end, talking over Miller and chorus's slow *a cappella* rendition. It's a somber ending.

At one point during the height of their success, Lambert, Hendricks & Ross took part in a tour called Jazz for Moderns, featuring six racially integrated groups. "We asked for and received non-segregated clauses in all the contracts," Hendricks told Sanford Josephson. "This was the sixties, but well before civil rights. But we were the number one jazz vocal group in the world. If they wanted us, that's what they had to do to get us." But the cracks within the trio were widening by the time they recorded *High Flying* in Chicago on March 13 and 14, 1961, with the same musicians as *Sing Ellington*. It was their sixth and final album as a singing group and another excellent collection, with a satisfying quotient of zany numbers, as well as indications of a deeper, less frenetic repertoire. Ross's "Farmer's Market" is dusted off and performed punishingly fast; "Cookin' at the Continental" shoots along at an equally manic tempo. There's something almost Beach Boyish in the slow, sweet, harmonized hymn-like "With Malice Towards None." "Home Cookin'," another Horace Silver tune, provides Hendricks with a good excuse to slurp nostalgically about soul food, with risqué (and frankly sexist) lyrics reminiscent of Wynonie Harris's "I Like My Baby's Pudding." The enjoyable nuttiness that Lambert, Hendricks & Ross brought to vocal jazz is on full display in "Halloween Spooks," in which the trio compete to see who can make the silliest noises. Slim Gaillard's "Popity Pop" is a rhythm changes number with more nonsense lyrics, pure rhythm really, and Hendricks scats a well-known patriotic song. "Blue," written by Gildo Mahones, is slow, beautiful, and somber to the point of gothic, with celeste and bowed bass, and Ross's singing is deep and bluesy. "High Flying" justifiably won a Grammy for Best Performance by a Vocal Group.

But gig-wise, Annie Ross had become unreliable—missing live dates—and Dave and Jon had to look around for possible substitutes. This was not unconnected with her destructive affair with Lenny Bruce. At a jazz festival in Pittsburgh in 1960, where virtually all of the acts were clients of the Willard Alexander agency, the unknown Carol Sloane was put in as the first act on a Friday night. Afterwards Jon told her he liked her singing and asked whether she would be willing to sub for Annie Ross when she couldn't make club dates. He pointed out that it would involve learning enough of the Lambert, Hendricks & Ross songbook to jump in at short notice. Carol told him she would give it a try. She had all the Lambert, Hendricks & Ross albums at home, so when she returned to New York, she came home every night from her secretarial job and put them on; it was convenient that all the lyrics were printed on the back. One day Jon called to say Annie wasn't able to sing with the group at Pep's Lounge in Philadelphia. Without even giving two weeks' notice, Carol told her boss that she had to quit; unfortunately for her, it didn't last. Another short-lived Ross substitute was Canadian-born Anne-Marie Moss, who had been singing with Maynard Ferguson's big band.

It was in Philly—and probably at Pep's—that Hendricks first met the young Bill Cosby, who became a close friend until he stabbed Hendricks in the back (see chapter 7). Lambert, Hendricks & Ross often played at Pep's, and tours would include comedians like Lenny Bruce and Woody Allen. Cosby worked there as a bartender and used to have them cracking up in the dressing room. Hendricks urged him to take his comedic talent on stage.

Nineteen sixty-one was the year Jon married his girlfriend Judith. It was amazing that he could spare the time: he made two more solo albums that year—*Salud! João Gilberto* in Los Angeles and *Fast Livin' Blues* in New York. *Salud!* came about after music publisher Howie Richmond asked him to write an English lyric for Antonio Carlos Jobim's "Desafinado." Hendricks was fourth choice for the job: it had already been turned down by Johnny Mercer, Ned Washington, and Hugh Martin. In the course of his research, Hendricks came across an album of João Gilberto singing Brazilian songs accompanied by and arranged by Jobim. And having heard it, he was hooked:

> I found this album. I was transfixed by this album … I played it all the time. It was so beautiful to me, and it was so hip. It had all the swing and the creativity of jazz music, and all the excitement, but yet it had the gentleness and the brilliance of a symphonic string section and that incredible bossa nova rhythm that I think is one of the world's great art forms. So I just fell in love with it.

In fact, it was Hendricks's theory that young Brazilians had invented bossa nova, an update on bossa antiqua, after hearing American bebop. At any rate, the bossa nova craze was well under way in the US. Four arrangers are credited on *Salud!*, including Johnny Mandel and Jobim himself. Leonard Feather's liner notes remind us that Hendricks had already written lyrics for "Desafinado" and "One Note Samba." Strangely, although guitar is heard prominently throughout the album, no-one is credited with playing it. Perhaps the guitarist could not be named because he was under exclusive contract to another record label. It may have been Gilberto himself, who was featured in a bossa concert at Carnegie Hall in 1962. In his own liner notes, Hendricks writes: "I met João Gilberto in New York. He is Gemini. He is very sensitive, very gentle, very shy, and more than a little afraid of this country. Listening to Gilberto has been one of the greatest singing lessons I've ever had." Laurindo Almeida, who had made a couple of Brazilian-themed albums with Bud Shank, is another candidate for the mystery guitarist. Feather mentions that in order to develop suitable English versions of the Portuguese lyrics, Hendricks spent many hours at Almeida's home, listening to the original João Gilberto recordings while the guitarist translated the words for him. At the end, Feather adds, "It is clear Jon Hendricks will never sing a season at the Met: his vocal equipment makes an unpretentiously suitable vehicle for the transmission of his unique talents as a lyricist."

Whatever the shortcomings of his vocal equipment, *Salud!* turned out well, revealing a softer side of Hendricks that had not been heard up to now. "O Pato (The Duck)" and "Voce e Eu (Me and You)" find him in sweet and gentle voice, a contrast to all the manic bebop of the fifties. ("What a pleasure to sing softly, gently after years of so much volume. It's a relief and a pleasure.") However, expressing the kind of melancholy found in Brazilian lyrics was not really in Hendricks's nature, as in his performance of Dorimel Caymmi's "Saudade da Bahia (Longing for Bahia)." On "Trem de Ferro (Little Train of Iron)" he is noticeably off-key. "Chega de Saudade (No More Blues)" became one of the best-known tunes in the Hendricks repertoire, but again the vocal is less than accurate. Written by Vinicius de Moraes, the tune's lyrics are credited on the record label to Hendricks and Jesse Cavanaugh (the *nom de plume* of Howie Richmond). This American version dispenses with the sadness of Moraes's original words, which include the lines, "There is no peace, There is no beauty, It's just sadness and melancholy." The English lyrics make no attempt to translate the original, instead making the song about the narrator's optimism about returning to his hometown, where he will settle down and be happy. *Salud!* also includes Hendricks's lyricized version of Nat Adderley's "Jive Samba." It demonstrates yet again how good he was at finding singable words for the flimsiest concept—in this case, simply talking about what kind of beat the song is written to.

Fast Livin' Blues, also recorded that year, came out in 1962. Here, Hendricks shows himself to be an accomplished and professional songwriter, albeit in this case a rather conventional and not especially memorable one, although he is well served by his excellent band. "Fast Livin' Blues" itself, contrary to the title, is a slow-draggin' number, with interjections from Joe Newman's muted trumpet. "Saturday Night Fish Fry" had been a hit for Louis Jordan, who co-wrote it with Ellis Walsh. The Hendricks version is very fast, revealing once again his ability to get a lot of words out in a short space of time, and hollering with terrific energy. "I'll Die Happy," also dating from the Louis Jordan era, features another torrent of words, a cheerful self-assertive lyric along the comic lines of "Gimme That Wine." "Contemporary Blues" is a slow one, with deliberations about the kind of woman Jon Hendricks likes—namely the good-hearted type who'll keep him well fed (both qualities he had found in Judith).

On September 12 and 19 of the same busy year, Lambert, Hendricks & Ross worked together on an intriguing and almost-forgotten stage musical with Dave Brubeck and Louis Armstrong called *The Real Ambassadors*. Produced by Teo Macero, the soundtrack album was recorded in September and December of 1961 in the Columbia Records studio on Thirtieth Street in New York, and was released the following year. The history of *The Real Ambassadors* is a fascinating one. Back in September 1957, Louis Armstrong—not previously known for speaking out on race and civil rights issues—had indeed spoken out against President Dwight Eisenhower and Arkansas Governor Orval Faubus for their handling of that year's Little Rock Central High School integration crisis. Inspired by Satchmo's intervention, the socially aware Brubeck and his wife Iola wrote a script and the score for what they intended as a Broadway musical to be titled *World, Take a Holiday*. Set in a fictional African nation, its narrative encompassed the civil rights movement, the music business, the Cold War, the nature of God, and a number of other large themes. Armstrong, who had done his patriotic duty as a cultural ambassador on overseas tours sponsored by the State Department, was the leading character. Carmen McRae was also on the recording session, and the band included Satchmo's trombonist Trummy Young and Brubeck's drummer Joe Morello. Lambert, Hendricks & Ross appear on only three tracks, and as background singers, at that. Armstrong was intrigued by them. "Y'all sound like you have a mouthful of hot rice," he chuckled. But the entire premise of *The Real Ambassadors* was unwelcome in 1962, running counter to the prevailing conservatism of the USA. "You weren't supposed to have a message," commented Brubeck. "I forget the word they used, but it meant you weren't entertaining. We couldn't lecture the American public on the subject of race."

Lambert, Hendricks & Ross recorded their final sessions as a unit in New York on February 19, cutting the tracks "Walkin'," "This Here" (retitled "Dis Hyunh"), and another version of "Swingin' Till the Girls Come Home"; on March 9, they jumped aboard the latest dance craze with "Twist City" and "Just a Little Bit of Twist," and added a vocal take on Dizzy's "A Night in Tunisia." Both sessions featured Pony Poindexter and Gildo Mahones, with Ron Carter on bass and Stu Martin on drums. At the end of the following month they toured the UK with Count Basie's orchestra, with fourteen dates from Portsmouth to Glasgow. A printed program from the tour states that Lambert, Hendricks & Ross would select their repertoire for each evening from:

The Real Ambassadors session – Hendricks, Brubeck, Armstrong

Every Day, Down for the Count, Sandman, Blues Backstage, Doodlin', Goin' to Chicago, Rusty Dusty, Little Pony, Twist City, Gimme That Wine, The Preacher, Sermonette, Just a Little Bit of Twist I Say, Swingin' Till the Girls Come Home, Come on Home, Home Cookin', Etc Etc.

Benny Green, the often acerbic UK jazz critic, was a big fan of Annie Ross, marveling at her confidence, dramatic stage presence and ability to project—as well as her fine ear for modern harmony. Despite his rather sententious manner, Green was a formidable analyst of jazz and his thoughts are worth quoting at length:

> Broadly speaking, there are three ways in which it is possible to sing jazz. Either you can stick to the written melody and put what expression you can into a conventional reading. Or you can bend the melody round, in which case you will find yourself being obliged to put vowel sounds on the rack of protraction and keep going "Ooh-ahh, ahh" in order to make your new phrases for the old time values. Or, if you have the patience of Job, you can choose your improvised line first and then write your own lyrics. All three methods are terribly difficult, and all three can sound wonderful or execrable, depending on who is doing the singing. Billie Holiday belongs at least partly in category one, because although she bent the melody she stuck to the time values of most of the words. Ella

Fitzgerald and Sarah Vaughan have both made themselves complete mistresses of the second method, and have almost the facility of an instrumentalist in flitting through the chord changes. But the third method is comparatively new and has seen only a handful of practitioners.

The Lambert-Hendricks-Ross team is easily the most outstanding instance of the third method by which the singers select an already created solo and transform it into a vocal performance. One has only to think about the problems involved in this method to realize why so few people have ever pulled it off. First, and perhaps most important, the singer has to have so well developed a sense of jazz that he, or she, must be able to sing through an intricate instrumental solo without a single error. Second, and just as vital in its way, somebody in the group must be so talented at lyric-writing that he, or she, must be able to work out a coherent rhyme scheme in the face of the highly complex lines played by the jazz soloists on whom they rely. It is very rarely that you get one person capable of these two things. To find three who can do it together is so remarkable that from their conception the L-H-R combination flashed to the forefront of the jazz world almost from the first.

The trio broke up shortly afterwards. According to Annie Ross, it was after they finished a date in London in May 1962 that she made up her mind to stay there and try to throw the monkey off her back:

> We played LA and then difficulties began to arise, because I had a very bad habit of heroin, cocaine, anything I could get my hands on. We went to Europe, to tour with Basie. We went to England. I knew that if I went back to America, I felt I would die, because I was a terrible junkie. I didn't know one thing from the other. So I used to mix all kinds of stuff.

Jon Hendricks told a different version of what happened. At a concert in Frankfurt (possibly as part of that year's German Jazz Festival), he said that Annie collapsed half an hour before they were due to go on stage and had to be flown back to London. The promoter was terrified that the audience would tear up the seats if the concert was cancelled at such short notice. Dave and Jon assured him that the concert could go ahead with just the two of them. They announced that Annie had been taken ill, and then faked the gig, dividing Annie's parts between them as best they could. Afterwards, when they too went back to London, they found their erstwhile colleague had been given a year to live.

Whatever the precise details of her departure, she had gone, and it was big news for people who cared about jazz. "Annie Ross blows the lid off the jazz world," yelled *Melody Maker*, accompanied by an exclusive interview with the burned-out star. Apart from its failure to mention heroin addiction, the piece was remarkably frank by the standards of the day and made clear that Annie had been unhappy in the trio for quite some time:

> I realize that I have a certain loyalty to the boys. We've been through a lot together. But I owe a lot to myself too. Jazz singing in the States is the most awful soul-destroying rat-race on earth. It's nothing but a grinding succession of one-night stands, traveling and recording. The last things you get time for are sleep or decent feeding. You get so wound up on the merry-go-round you don't even know what time it is.

She told the interviewer that she had been ordered into a nursing home by her doctor immediately she returned from the Continental tour, describing her abrupt departure from the trio as a breakdown:

> All I want to do now is rest and get well ... The doctor warned me that if I didn't submit to the proper treatment and rest, then he couldn't be held responsible for what might happen to me later ... I talked it over with Jon and Dave before I went into the nursing home. They realized it was going to be for the best for all of us in the long run. They assured me that when I'm ready to go back, they'll be ready to receive me. But... oh I don't know if I'll ever go back really.

6 Everybody Got Tired

If neither Jon Hendricks nor Dave Lambert achieved anything again as good as they did as two-thirds of Lambert, Hendricks & Ross, it wasn't through lack of trying. No other singer possessed the sophistication, zany humor, and jaw-dropping vocal technique of Annie Ross. Having already tried to replace her with Carol Sloane and Ann-Marie Moss (which for a brief time made them Lambert, Hendricks & Moss), they finally settled on Yolande Bavan. As usual, there are variations in the story of how Yolande joined the trio, but its essence is remarkable enough: Jon Hendricks took Judith with him for the 1962 Lambert, Hendricks & Ross/Basie UK tour. (On the plane, the Basie band's Frank Foster had asked him, "Why do you bring a sandwich on a picnic?") Instead of partying late into the night with the others, the couple went out sightseeing during the day, visiting the British Museum and the Tate Gallery— as well as more out-of-the-way places like the Theosophical Society—and Jon conducted some research into his pet theory that Francis Bacon had written Shakespeare's plays (see p. 187). And while the Hendrickses headed for bed, Dave Lambert went out to a lavish party at the home of London jazz socialites Don and Sandra Luck.

Yolande Bavan was a fan of Lambert, Hendricks & Ross. She, like Annie Ross, had spent time in Paris and became close friends with Billie Holiday. (By chance, as an actress and singer, she had recreated Annie Ross's role in the 1960 stage revue *New Cranks*—an update on the 1956 *Cranks*.) Yolande was a friend of the Lucks; one day, early in 1962, they took her to hear Count Basie and Lambert, Hendricks & Ross in London. Afterwards they went backstage, and Yolande met Annie for the first time. Two nights later Sandra and Don threw their party, which was full of jazz musicians—including the entire Basie band. A Dizzy Gillespie album was playing as Yolande helped Sandra clear ashtrays and serve drinks, singing along with the record as she did so. As Dizzy hit a high note at the end of one of the tunes, Yolande hit the same note. Immediately, a man she didn't know whirled around and asked, "Who did that?" She told him it was her, he introduced himself as Dave Lambert and they chatted for a while, before going their separate ways. A few days later she heard from the Lucks that Annie had quit the group. She thought no more about it until a few weeks later, when she was woken up at three in the morning by a ringing telephone. The voice at the other end said, "This is Jon Hendricks."

Yolande was too dazed to recognize the name.

"I'm calling from New York. We want you to come to New York," said Jon.

"To New York? To do what?" she asked.

"To sing," said Jon. "Annie Ross has left the group and we want you to come over."

Yolande told him it was impossible, but Jon said there was a plane ticket and a work visa waiting for her at the American embassy, and that she would be leaving London on Wednesday. Again Yolande protested, but Jon had done his homework. "Joe Williams and Sarah Vaughan recommended you," he said, "and so did Dave Brubeck." In the end she gave in, but said it would have to be Saturday, not Wednesday. Jon told her to get hold of the group's albums and memorize their songs. Her friend, the *Melody Maker* jazz writer Max Jones lent her some Lambert, Hendricks & Ross records and she started listening to them for hours at a time, singing along with them—but it was difficult to work out how she was going to sing Annie Ross's parts.

On the following Saturday she flew to New York with one suitcase. She told herself, "I'll rehearse, they'll realize they've made a big mistake. I'll see the Statue of Liberty and return home." In the meantime, Dave and Jon had been battling with the American immigration authorities to allow Yolande—who was born in Sri Lanka—to enter the country to work. The 1952 McCarran-Walter Immigration Act dictated which ethnic groups were "desirable immigrants," and was biased towards the white races. In practice this meant that anyone from Ireland (for example) would face little difficulty, but there was a strict quota system for Asian countries. Quotas of a hundred immigrants per

Dave Lambert, Yolande
Bavan, Jon Hendricks
(1962)

country were established for individual Asian countries, and two thousand per year was the cap for all of them combined. But once Dave and Jon had certified that they had gainful employment for Yolande Bavan, the way was cleared.

She arrived on the morning of May 5, 1962. Dave Lambert was there to meet her, and told her they had to hurry to catch another plane to Schenectady in upstate New York. When they arrived, a car was waiting to take them to Union College, where a concert was already in progress with an audience of two or three thousand students. Tom Paxton, the folk singer and guitarist, had played in the first half, and it was now the intermission. Dave and Yolande got out of the car, and went backstage to meet Jon. She was still wearing a plaid sari and had her Pan Am bag over her shoulder. When were they going to rehearse? she asked Jon. "Oh, the concert is already on," he said. Yolande was pleased, looking forward to sitting in the audience and listening to the trio sing. At this point she heard the announcer introduce Lambert, Hendricks & Ross. The audience cheered, and the band started to play the intro to "One O'Clock Jump." To her astonishment, Jon and Dave rushed her on stage, where the usual rhythm section plus Pony Poindexter were waiting. Not knowing what else to do, she started to sing along with them. Dave kept nudging her to go an octave higher, to get into the trumpet range. After three nights of trying to learn lyrics, followed by a long day, a transatlantic flight, jet lag, and more travel at the other end, she felt like a zombie, but somehow managed to hit a high note at the end of the tune—the audience reaction was enthusiastic (they had been restless up to now, as Dave and Yolande's late arrival had delayed the start of the second set). They continued the concert with "Little Pony," "Four," and "It's Sand, Man." Still not sure of the lyrics, she stuck to vowel sounds.

The next day—again, without rehearsal—they played Rhode Island and then went into Manhattan. Yolande found they had booked her into a small, dark hotel room with a tiny kitchen on Forty-seventh Street, off Broadway. Shortly afterwards they performed in a midnight jazz concert at Carnegie Hall, a benefit for a drug rehabilitation program named after Billie Holiday. ("All I could think was, if Billie were alive and could see me there, she would have flipped," Yolande later said.) Backstage, she saw many of the musicians she had met in Paris and London—the Basie band, Art Blakey, Bobby Timmons, and others. All of them wanted to know what she was doing there. Lambert, Hendricks & Bavan eventually went on at around one in the morning, and were a big hit with the audience.

Jon and Dave gave her a record player and a set of song lyrics. In the hotel room she listened to the records over and over again, as she had in London. But rehearsals were a rarity. One night, having been told to learn Horace Silver's piano solo for "Come On Home," for which Hendricks had just written lyrics, she found she was expected to sing them in a club in Chicago without rehearsal. It was the same pattern as in the Annie Ross days: Jon would come up with some lyrics, they would run through them quickly, and then they would be out on stage performing them in front of an audience. Yolande had never toured before and felt very much alone, one woman traveling with seven male singers and musicians plus manager and roadie. At first, while they were out on the road, she thought she would be going out and doing things in the daytime—but soon realized that no-one else got out of bed before five in the afternoon. She was now a member of the most famous singing group in the world and there were lines around the block to see them, but once they arrived at the gig she would still have to wrap her sari in a kitchen smelling of bacon fat.

Three nights of shows on September 6–8, 1962, were recorded by RCA for the album *Lambert, Hendricks & Bavan: Live at Basin Street East*. Those who dismiss the Bavan years might pause to consider how they would have reacted to these recordings if they had never heard Annie Ross. "This Could Be The Start of Something" is played fast and furious, with very tight harmonies throughout the head, while on "Shiny Stockings" Yolande gets to do some vocalese. Her accent adds charm, and she soon proves she can hit the same terrifyingly high notes as Annie. The album also includes Jobim's "Desafinado" with Hendricks's lyrics. His lead vocal is faultless, although Brazilian music purists might take issue with the changes he made to Newton Mendonça's rather ambivalent, metaphysical original, in which the line "If you say I defy love, Know that this causes me immense pain" is jettisoned in favor of the more upbeat, and indeed cheesy, "Love is like a never-ending melody." In places ("April in Paris" and "One Note Samba") the vocal strays off-key, reminding us both that it was recorded live, and that pitch correction software was not then available. The Hendricks tune "Feed Me," recently recorded for *A Good Git Together*, appears again, complete with impromptu sexist comments—"I don't care how you look as long as you can cook." And the old Lambert, Hendricks & Ross standby "Swingin' Till the Girls Come Home" completes the set, sounding lively and fun. But the critics were regretful about Annie's departure. Commented *Jazz Journal*: "Miss Bavan hasn't quite got Annie's fantastic control, nor is her voice quite as jazz tinged, but these are early days, and for a debut this was extraordinarily successful." In truth, the album rather lacks the wackiness and energy of Lambert, Hendricks & Ross. This was not necessarily Yolande Bavan's fault—the Basin Street recording was five years on from *Sing a Song of Basie*, and Dave and Jon were that bit older now. A few days later the group appeared on Jack Paar's *Tonight* show, and a few days after that—as Lambert, Hendricks and Yolande—at the Monterey Jazz Festival, where they performed in a cut-down version of *The Real Ambassadors* with Carmen McRae and Louis Armstrong.

Despite the terrifying roller-coaster ride she'd been on ever since leaving London, Yolande found a welcome degree of support and respect from the musicians who were protective of her quiet dignity, elegance, and youth (she was barely out of her teens). Even Mingus would warn the others, "No

SUNDAY EVENING, SEPT. 23

Early Starting Time
at 7:15 P.M. Sharp

1. *DIZZY GILLESPIE and the MONTEREY BRASS ENSEMBLE*

Trummy Young
Joe Darensbourg
Billy Cronk
Danny Barcelona
Joe Morello
Eugene Wright

2. *JEANNE LEE and RAN BLAKE*
Entr'acte
In keeping with the Monterey Jazz Festival's policy of introducing new talent, this unusual duo is making its West coast debut at the Festival.

3. *"THE REAL AMBASSADORS" (excerpts)*
An original musical production with music and lyrics by Dave and Iola Brubeck, featuring . . .
   Louis Armstrong
   Carmen McRae
   Dave Brubeck
   Lambert, Hendricks and Yolande
   with . . .
   Billy Kyle

4. *JEANNE LEE and RAN BLAKE*
Entr'acte

5. *LOUIS ARMSTRONG AND HIS ALL-STARS*
With . . .
   Jewel Brown, vocal
   Trummy Young, trombone and vocal
   Joe Darensbourg, clarinet
   Billy Kyle, piano
   Bill Cronk, bass
   Danny Barcelona, drums
And . . .
   LOUIS ARMSTRONG

1962 Monterey Jazz festival program

swearing around Bavan." And although Dave and Jon seemingly threw her in at the deep end at every opportunity, they put the others on notice that sellers and users of drugs were neither to speak to her nor contact her. Yolande exuded a certain bird-like fragility, as well as a whiff of the exotic. The saris seemed to be part of it—although, raised as a Catholic, she wore them not for religious reasons but simply because she found them comfortable, plus they were part of her culture. She and Dave got on well, but Jon was never entirely happy with her. He would say, with apparent gratitude, "You saved us!" But behind her back he frequently contrasted her with Annie, once telling the *Village Voice*: "Annie was the cream, and Yolande is like skimmed milk." Years later he told the *New York Times* that working with Dave and Annie was the peak:

> When you work with someone like Annie and you write a part for her and she sings it right back to you and it's tremendous, you didn't have to worry about how it was going to sound. It was just extraordinary. But after Annie left, I found it was hard to get the sound that I wanted. I guess everybody got tired. There wasn't the fire that I felt ought to be in it.

Yolande soldiered on into 1963. On February 22 the trio made an appearance on Ralph Gleason's *Jazz Casual* for KQED San Francisco, on which Jon was interviewed by the host. After a couple of instrumentals featuring Pony Poindexter they sang selections from the recent live album—"This Could Be the Start of Something Big," "Melba's Blues," "Shiny Stockings," "Cousin Mary," and "Cloudburst." Lambert, Hendricks & Ross had never been able to get on to the major TV shows—apart from Steve Allen, and despite winning so many awards—because Annie Ross was white and stood next to a black man. It is very revealing about American social attitudes that all this changed with the arrival of Yolande Bavan, who was dark-skinned and could therefore stand next to a black man without making white people feel uncomfortable.

Early that year Jon recorded his lyrics to Herbie Hancock's "Watermelon Man" for Reprise, with Sonny Burke producing, and later complaining that Hancock had never paid him. On May 20 the trio appeared at the Civic Opera House in Chicago for a televised show called *International Hour: American Jazz*. But it is their Newport Jazz Festival appearance on July 5 that has survived, since it was recorded for their second album *Lambert, Hendricks & Bavan: At Newport '63*. Clark Terry and Coleman Hawkins joined the rhythm section, which now consisted of Gildo Mahones, George Tucker on bass, and Jimmy Smith on drums. Although the performance is fun and full of energy, one gets the feeling that the group is treading water. "One O'Clock Jump," already recorded for *Sing a Song of Basie*, had also appeared on the *Basin Street East* album. "Gimme That Wine," from *The Hottest New Group in Jazz*, also turns up again, complete with Jon's well-worn gag name-checking "Sammy Davis Johnson" and "Nat King Wilson." And why not? It provokes laughter from the audience—some still hadn't heard it. And even if they had, it was still funny. The comedy continues with Big Nick Nicholas's uptempo blues "Deedle-Lee, Deedle-Lum." Jon pretends to instruct the crowd in singing along, while deliberately confusing them. It's an enjoyably silly song in the vein of Louis Jordan. "Walkin'" is another uptempo blues, recorded by Lambert, Hendricks & Ross for the compilation album *Giants of Jazz* the previous year. As the longest track on *Newport '63* by far, clocking in at eight and a half minutes, it gives us the chance to hear Clark Terry soloing—followed by a storming vocal solo from Dave Lambert that makes you realize he seemed to feature less often these days. The final track, its third recorded outing, is "Cloudburst," with Jon still on volcanic form, scatting at incredible velocity—straight through, no solos—to a wild audience reaction. The recording is also notable for Jon's newly lyricized version of Mongo Santamaria's boogaloo tune "Yeh Yeh." It was its first recording in this form, and the vocal performance sounds a little uncertain. But this was this version that Georgie Fame heard before he recorded it himself in England and had a UK number one hit with it in January 1965.

When Dizzy Gillespie recorded his live *Dizzy for President* album at that year's Monterey Jazz Festival, it included a version of "Salt Peanuts" with vocals (and new lyrics) by Jon Hendricks:

> Your politics ought to be a groovier thing,
> Vote Dizzy! Vote Dizzy!
> So get a good president who's willing to swing,
> Vote Dizzy! Vote Dizzy!

The joke caught on, and Ralph Gleason started using his *San Francisco Chronicle* column to promote Dizzy's "campaign." Diz promised, if elected, to rename The White House "The Blues House," and had already planned his cabinet: Duke Ellington would be Secretary of State; Miles Davis, Director of the CIA; Max Roach, Secretary of Defense; Malcolm X, Attorney General ("because he's one cat we definitely want to have on our side"); and Charles Mingus, Secretary of Peace ("because he'll take a piece of your head faster than anyone I know"). He advocated US withdrawal from Vietnam, promised free education and health care, and pledged to put an African American astronaut on the moon. If there were no volunteers, Gillespie said he would make the trip himself.

Family life briefly intruded when Jon's last child Aria (his first with Judith), was born on November 22 in Montreal, where Lambert, Hendricks & Bavan were playing a gig. But the joy of the event was overshadowed by the murder of John F. Kennedy on that same day. Without saying anything to Dave, Yolande or any of the musicians, Jon simply disappeared and went to the hospital to be with Judith at the birth.

The third and final trio album was *Havin' a Ball at the Village Gate*, again recorded live—this time in New York, a couple of days before Christmas—with Thad Jones on cornet and flugelhorn, Booker Ervin on tenor, and the same rhythm section as before. All the touring had by now given the trio a tightness and energy not previously evident, and Ervin in particular is on terrific form. That said, half the tunes had been released before: "Jumpin' at the Woodside," the Basie number with Jon Hendricks lyrics, had been on the *Sing Along* album and here it's a relaxed, swinging opener. Yolande effortlessly delivers the vocalese on Benny Carter's gospel-style "Meetin' Time," while the slow and emotional "Days of Wine and Roses"—with lovely Thad Jones cornet—leaves you wondering why they didn't do more of this sweeter material, given the quality of her voice. There's some stage business on "Three Blind Mice," which is introduced as a folk song, sung straight by Yolande before being interrupted by Jon, with some new lyrics about the mice being blind from drinking wine, and then they swing it. The comedy continues: "With 'er 'ead Tucked Underneath 'er Arm" is a song about the ghost of Ann Boleyn, delivered by Dave Lambert in an almost convincing Cockney accent. (Written in 1934, it was originally performed by Stanley Holloway in his vaudeville days.) Lambert and Hendricks might have got the idea from Bobby Clancy (from the Irish folk group The Clancy Brothers and Tommy Makem), who recorded it twice. *Havin' a Ball* is the best of the three Lambert, Hendricks & Bavan albums, and all the lyrics are printed on the back of the sleeve, just like in the old days. What Yolande Bavan did not realize while the trio was under contract to RCA was that, paid a one-off fee of $350 for each album, she was being cheated out of a lot of money. By the time the truth dawned on her, the statute of limitations had kicked in and it was too late to take legal steps.

Dave quit the group in February 1964 after a concert in Washington. Jon tried Don Chastain as a replacement, but it didn't work out. Yolande then left in June, to be replaced by Pat Harris. (Aria Hendricks recalled seeing some rare footage of her father singing with Don Chastain and an unidentified glamorous blond woman, and being shocked at how bad the two of them were.) For several months Jon tried to maintain the original format, but the fresh spirit of 1958 could not be recaptured. On September 10 he went into the studio and cut versions of "Sister Sadie," "River's Invitation," and "The Comeback," but none of these has ever seen the light of day.

For years, Jon had toured the world while all the children except Aria had simply been farmed out to relatives. Michele had seen almost nothing of either parent since their divorce and had been shuttled between Rochester, Toledo, and finally Detroit, where her Aunt Vivian lived. Aunt Vivian was married to Uncle Kurt, the pastor of their local church; Michele and her siblings endured five long years of religious fervor and corporal punishment. When they were mischievous, it was the Devil at work, and Vivian would have to beat it out of them. She locked them in the basement or in the closet. Every night before they went to bed she beat them anyway because, after all, they *might* have done something she didn't know about.

Meanwhile, Jon was finally facing the truth: the dream was over. He had been on the road constantly for seven years, but a change of direction was now needed—and that included finally taking responsibility for his own

Jon and Judith (right) with (front row) Eric, Colleen and Michele (courtesy Bonnie Hopkins)

children, whom he had effectively abandoned in his quest for glory with Lambert, Hendricks & Ross. Jon Jr. was aged fifteen, Michele was twelve, Eric ten, and Colleen nine; Aria was eighteen months. Every September for the last five years, Jon had appeared at the Monterey Jazz Festival and afterwards he and Judith would usually take a month's vacation, renting a house in the Big Sur area and always commenting on how beautiful it was. Judith, a girl from a middle-class Jewish family, thought that if there was now to be a lull in Jon's singing career, it was the ideal time for him to start being a father to his children. So in the fall of 1964 they rounded up the Hendricks offspring, left New York, and for a year rented a houseboat in Sausalito, Marin County—just across the Golden Gate Bridge from San Francisco—where they found local schools for the kids.

At that time Sausalito was a quaint hill town with a Mediterranean feel to it, once described as "Portofino with autos." Looking for a local music venue, Jon discovered that the former manager of New York's Village Vanguard, Lou Ganapoler, was now running a waterside restaurant called The Trident on behalf of its owner, Frank Werber—manager of the hugely successful Kingston Trio. The setting was magnificent, with big picture windows looking out across the bay to San Francisco, luxury yachts in the harbor and in the restaurant a Steinway baby grand that no-one ever played. Jon started going in for lunch, and one day suggested to Ganapoler that he put on some live music. "Whadda we need music for?" grumbled Frank, "We got the best food around, we're doing plenty business." Knowing that Ganapoler had a social conscience, Hendricks told him it was his civic duty to provide music for the people and work for the musicians. The emotional blackmail succeeded. Frank booked a local trio for Hendricks to sing with: pianist Flip Nunes, bass player Fred Marshall, and drummer Jerry Granelli. This allowed Jon to pursue his current enthusiasm, which was the music of Miles—"Bye Bye Blackbird," "All Blues"—although he remained in thrall to Wardell Gray for his phrasing.

And at gigs he was still as spontaneous as ever, departing from the agreed set list at the drop of a hat, if the mood took him.

The Trident engagement lasted six weeks, with two shows per night, and resulted in the excellent album *Live at the Trident*, recorded with the trio plus tenor saxophonist Noel Jewkes. Many of the tracks are familiar: the album starts with "This Could Be the Start of Something"—a hip, energetic take on the tune Lambert, Hendricks & Bavan had recorded at Basin Street East, with some of the lines doubled by voice and sax, and Jewkes takes a cool solo. It feels properly live: on "Watermelon Man," which previously appeared on *Newport '63*, Marshall and Granelli don't quite pick up the cue for the ending. The old favorite "Gimme That Wine" appears again, with perfect comic timing from Hendricks amid the audience laughter. The sad Gildo Mahones ballad "One Rose" shows Jon's mastery of the slower form. No album of his was complete without yet another version of "Cloudburst": this one clatters along at a terrifying tempo, which they not only manage with ease, but Jon somehow makes the lyrics comprehensible. It's impossible to tell where he's breathing. "Shiny Stockings," also recorded on *Basin Street East*, is here titled "Shiny Silk Stockings," and "Yeh Yeh" appears for a second time after its recent outing on *Newport '63*. Clark Terry's "Mumbles" becomes "Jon's Mumbles," a hopping funk-blues comedy number with nonsense syllables.

It was at the Trident that Jon first met Al Jarreau, who told him he wanted to be a jazz singer, although it took some persuading from Jon to get him to sit in. With the continuing bossa nova craze at the time, San Francisco was full of Brazilian musicians—many of whom played at the Trident—so it may have been here that Jon first heard and fell in love with the music of Edu Lobo, recording his songs "Upa Neguinho," "Reza," and "Arrastão" in later years.

When Jon and Judith went to hear Thelonious Monk playing in San Francisco, the great man came over to them at the bar and Monk told Jon he was the only "motherfucker" he would be happy to have writing lyrics to his tunes. Next morning, the couple picked him up in the car and drove him to the houseboat, where they had a piano. Monk sat down and started playing "Pannonica," and Jon instantly started writing down words. Monk got to the end of the tune, and Jon said, "Okay, Thelonious, I got a lot of this, but could you go back and play the bridge again?" Monk didn't reply, but went back to the start and played the tune again. Jon waited until he reached the bridge and tried writing something for it, but still hadn't heard enough of it. "Thelonious, I didn't get everything, could you please play the bridge again?" By now Monk was seething. Once again he started at the beginning, and meanwhile Jon could hear him muttering, "You write those lyrics too fast. *It took me six months to write this tune!*" Ultimately, the Monk project proved to be one of many that Jon left uncompleted. He was still talking about it in 1982: for years it was going to be his next album. He had written lyrics to "Round Midnight," "Well You Needn't," and "Crepuscule with Nellie." But although he loved Monk, and wrote a lot of lyrics to his tunes, he complained that the family wouldn't give him permission to publish them after the pianist's death, in 1982. Curiously, others used his lyrics without any apparent problem including Carmen McRae, whose 1990 album *Carmen Sings Monk* includes no fewer than eight Monk compositions with lyrics by Jon Hendricks (see p. 136).

One day in 1965 Jon was astonished to receive a call from Duke Ellington, asking him to perform in the premiere of a religious suite he had written called *A Concert of Sacred Music*. He asked Duke why him rather than any number of singers he sincerely believed were better than him, such as Frank Sinatra, Billy Eckstine, or Joe Williams. Duke replied, "Too many people sing about God without authority. I want someone to sing about God *with authority*." The authority, it turned out, derived from Jon being the son of a minister. He went to Lake Tahoe to rehearse his contribution, a segment called "In the Beginning, God." During preparations, Duke asked him to come to his hotel to run through some of the material. "What's your high note?" he asked Jon, who of course had no idea. It was the same answer to the question, "Well, what's your low note?" Duke was baffled. "Well, how do you sing?" To which Jon replied, "I don't know, I just sing." The premiere took place at San Francisco's Grace Cathedral, on top of the city's Nob Hill, on September 16 (coincidentally Hendricks's birthday) and was recorded for the local public TV station KQED. The producer was Jon's old friend and *San Francisco Chronicle* jazz critic Ralph Gleason. "In the Beginning, God" starts out in solemn and operatic style, then the swing groove kicks in and Jon goes into a rap about all the things that didn't exist before God: "No mountains, no valleys, no main streets, no back alleys ... no aspirin, no headaches ..." This informality—this modernity—was of course highly controversial in a place where white people worshipped, particularly when tap dancer Bunny Briggs came on at the climax. Yet the overall consensus deemed it a triumph. "It was successful beyond my wildest dreams," reported Duke, "both in San Francisco and at a subsequent performance in ... New York ... I think what registered most with many people was the dancing of Bunny Briggs."

Meanwhile, the counterculture was already in full swing in the Bay Area. On December 5, 1965, with a band then known as The Warlocks, Jon recorded the song "Fire in the City"—a fast acoustic guitar tune with a rock backing—for the documentary film *Sons and Daughters*. On the flip side was the film's title song, a slow blues written and produced by Hendricks. Shortly afterwards The Warlocks changed their name to The Grateful Dead. It was no more than a brief excursion into the rock genre, but in this era Hendricks did sometimes play benefit shows alongside rock performers. One such show, in September 1966, took place at the Fillmore on behalf of San Francisco's Both And Jazz Club, with Elvin Jones, Joe Henderson, and Jefferson Airplane on the bill.

On the domestic front, after a year on the houseboat, Judith Hendricks realized that the rent they had so far paid was equivalent to the down payment

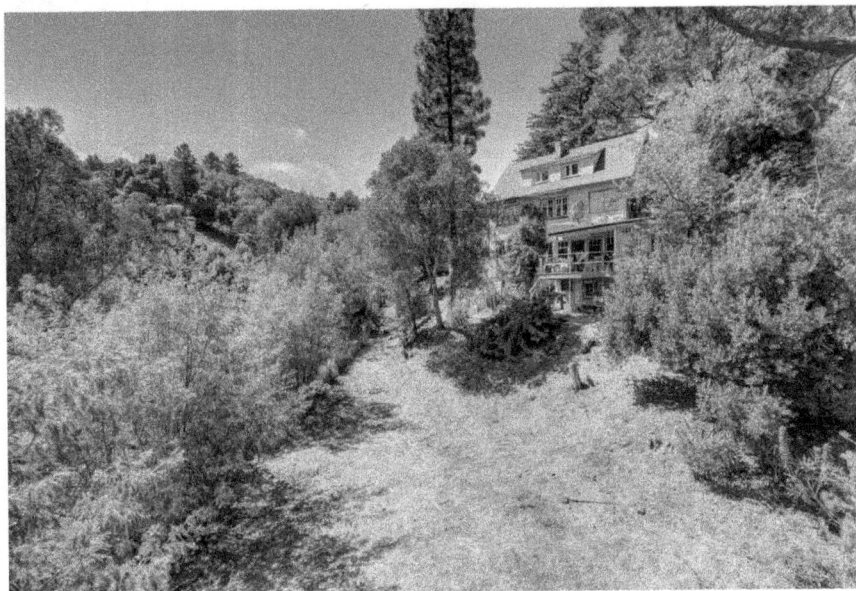

The house in Mill Valley

on a house. Not only that, but—with five children on board, and Colleen and Michele sharing a bedroom—space was at a premium. So she and Jon started looking for a larger and more permanent home nearby. They eventually found a big, sprawling, wood-framed house at 328 Ridgewood Avenue, Mill Valley, built in 1905. It was old-fashioned and no-one else seemed to want it, but for them it was perfect.

With the housing issue settled, Jon once again began to feel the call of the road. The success of *Evolution of the Blues* at Monterey had made him think there was plenty more mileage in the project: its material could form the basis for gigs, or it could be staged in its entirety. But Flip Nunes didn't want to go on tour, so Jon needed a new pianist. Flip recommended a sharp, versatile bebop player called Larry Vuckovich whose family had fled Montenegro in 1951 and arrived in the US as asylum seekers. Larry had subsequently been trained by Vince Guaraldi who taught him that, when working with singers, less is more: "The idea was to lay down a beautiful harmonic palette," said Larry. "On the faster tunes you do some rhythmic punches to enhance riffs and things. And you don't noodle. Too much noodling is no good." Before meeting Jon, Larry had gained a reputation for his work with Mel Tormé (whom he'd been backing on and off since 1963), as well as subbing for Guaraldi with Irene Kral and June Christy. After one rehearsal with him, Hendricks was sold. They toured major clubs in Vancouver, Toronto, Pittsburgh, Detroit, and elsewhere. Noel Jewkes joined them and Jimmy Witherspoon was also part of the show, along with Clarence Becton on drums and Bob Maize on bass. After Vancouver they gigged around the Bay area, including Stamford and UC Berkeley. In the middle of winter they went up to Denver, the mile-high city. Noel rode with the family—Judith, Colleen, Michele, and Aria—and they all had to cuddle up to keep warm. There was a lot of singing in the car and Jon would play Miles Davis tunes on his portable record player, mostly to teach Judith the parts he wanted her to sing. Noel would ply him with questions, which Jon found irksome. "You know, I like you, Noel," he said. "The duller you are, the more I like you." But the main thing Noel learned from Jon was to be "in the moment" musically. He taught him to listen closely—particularly to the harmonies within the chord, finding the voice that would complement the lead— and urged him to listen to Wardell Gray and other players who had negotiated the transition from swing to bebop.

Since the break-up of Lambert, Hendricks & Bavan, Jon had stayed in touch with Dave, who had now got himself a radio show on WBAI and found some other freelance work back in New York. One of his projects was a vocal combo called Lambert & Co.—essentially a revival of the Dave Lambert Singers. This multiracial group consisted of Dave plus four younger vocalists and in 1964 he had taken them to RCA Records' studio to perform a few of his own compositions for producer George Avakian. Documentary filmmaker D. A. Pennebaker—later famed for his documentaries about Bob Dylan and the sixties counterculture—filmed the recording session in a fifteen-minute black and white documentary called *Audition at RCA*. It was the last appearance of Dave Lambert on film and the only extant recording of these songs; by then the Beatles had arrived, demand for vocal jazz was on the wane, and Avakian declined to take them on.

In a phone call Dave told Jon he was doing a solo gig up in Cape Cod, suggesting they get together when he returned and maybe think about finding another female singer. On October 2, 1966, he drove up to a Connecticut theater to pick up his girlfriend, an actress. In the early hours of the following morning they were driving along the Connecticut Turnpike, near Westport, when they saw a motorist waving a white handkerchief at the side of the road, trying to flag down someone to help him with a flat tire. Being what Jon termed "a compulsive do-gooder," Dave stopped. While his girlfriend waved the handkerchief to warn off traffic, he and the motorist, Richard Hillman, worked on the tire. It was then that they were hit by a tractor-trailer driven by a man called Floyd H. Demby; both were killed instantly. At the inquest, the coroner ruled that Demby was not at fault because the disabled vehicle was not fully off the roadway, its lights were turned off, and Lambert and Hillman were in the road when they were struck. Dave Lambert was forty-nine years old. At the funeral Zoot Sims played one simple chorus of "Pennies from Heaven," a favorite tune of Dave's. It seemed to distill his sunny spirit. Three weeks later there was a packed memorial concert at the Village Gate attended by Dizzy Gillespie, Tony Bennett, Clark Terry, Bob Brookmeyer, George Wein's Newport All-Stars, Horace Silver, Jimmy Rushing, Yolande Bavan, Al Cohn, and Zoot Sims.

Jon was asked whether Dave's death had affected him:

> Oh yeah, very much. I still think of him … because when I start to try to find young jazz singers who can scat, I realize what an important presence he was, because he was one of the founders of the bebop school of scatting. In fact he was the one responsible for taking it into that area, the area of Bird, and he did work with Bird at the Royal Roost, and he recorded with Bird: "Old Folks" and "In the Still of the Night," with arrangements by Gil Evans. So he was the quintessential bebop scat singer. When I try to search for people today, I realize what a great treasure this guy was … You didn't have to show him anything. He'd show you.

It was an oddly businesslike tribute to a man he had shared his life with for the best part of a decade. Interviewed by Marc Myers, Dave's daughter Dee painted a more vivid picture of a happy and multitalented man:

> His toys were a long Flexible Flyer sled, snorkel and fins and a collection of flutes, a penny whistle and a kazoo. When I asked him if I should be a singer, dad said, "You should be whatever you want to be, but when you know what that is, be it all the time. If you want to be a dancer, dance all the time; if you want to be a singer, sing all the time." Dad sang all the time. When he walked down the street, he would scat or "*ch-ch-ch*" rhythms. He never went up … the five-flight tenement stairs to our apartment one step at a time. He remembered phone numbers not by the number but by what part of *do-re-mi* the number represented. Consequently, everybody's phone number was a seven-note tune. He was a daredevil diver. When we went to Leroy Street pool, he would go off the high board in a jack knife dive. He read the Sunday *New York Times* in a couple of hours. He had close to one hundred percent retention of everything he read, and he was a speed-reader. Dad's words of wisdom: "When sick, drink lots of water and think kind thoughts," "When you talk about somebody who has hurt you, you give them power over your life," "If you don't have anything good to say about someone, don't say anything at all," "If your friends won't pay to see you, who will?" And he always signed off on phone calls or in letters with "Happy Days."

Yolande Bavan said:

> Dave was always helping people, and jazz musicians loved him. Even Miles Davis was crazy about Dave. I remember when we were in Philadelphia in 1963. Miles was playing around the corner. I

begged Dave to take me to see him. The moment Miles saw Dave, his face lit up and he put his arms around him and sent us a bottle of champagne.

"Do you think of Dave a lot?" Gene Lees asked Jon Hendricks in 1999. "Every day of my life," Jon said, "and especially every night when we're singing."

Having his children back with him and in school in California might have seemed like the perfect end to a long and difficult period in the Hendricks family history, but it turned out to be only the beginning of a new set of problems. All four of Jon's children with his former wife Connie had felt the pain of abandonment by their parents, as well as emotional and physical pain at the hands of their aunts and uncles. After all this time, it was not going to be a simple matter of letting bygones be bygones—especially in an era when drugs were plentiful and seemed an attractive way of helping you forget your troubles. The Hendrickses were not the only parents to find themselves battling with their offspring's self-medication. Jon and Judith decided to take Michele out of high school because, as far as they could see, the girls in her year were all obsessed with sex and drugs. Hendricks blamed the parents, because these were the children of "stars whose means of showing them love was to buy them a Mercedes XL or a BMW or a new wardrobe from Holsten ... It's not enough for a child." This moral decay, as he saw it, meant that the Hendricks children were often left with babysitters who were themselves of questionable responsibility. A large part of the problem was their father's peripatetic lifestyle as a professional jazz musician: he simply was not a nine-to-five guy, and the Hendricks kids were often left to their own devices. Even Aria, who had spent her life in the company of her parents, felt neglected. Her early life was one in which "I was constantly kissed and cuddled and told how loved I was, then they would get up and leave me in the care of some total stranger," she later said. The rituals that mark the progress of each year in most families were not observed: there was no tradition of celebrating birthdays and holidays in the Hendricks family. Aria remembered a party being organized for her sixth birthday, but it was the only one; gifts were not given. There would be the occasional Christmas or Thanksgiving, and at such times her parents might throw a huge party, but otherwise these annual events were totally ignored. Ever after, once she had her independence and a family of her own, Michele became a fervent devotee of these seasonal traditions.

The broader social upheavals of the 1960s left few American families unscathed. While Jon was on tour across the country in 1967, long-term urban rage and desperation sparked by poverty, unemployment, and crime boiled over in a number of East Coast and Midwestern cities. There were riots in Detroit, Newark, Milwaukee, Buffalo, Tampa, and Cincinnati, resulting in dozens of burned-out neighborhoods—some of which never recovered. And while San Francisco bathed blissfully in flower power, it was also full of drugs, which had inevitably made their way into schools. Hendricks began finding hypodermic needles in his own house. The children's new friends were smoking pot and more and, one morning in November, he overheard someone calling his son Eric, who was then aged twelve. On the line was another local twelve-year-old, who told Eric he had just stolen five dollars from his mother's purse and wanted Eric to go with him to buy a bag of weed. Hendricks hung up the phone and woke his wife to tell her what had happened, and that he was going to follow Eric to school. Shortly afterwards he watched his son buy a five-dollar bag from a sixteen-year-old. Hendricks marched up to them, grabbed the bag and emptied its contents on the ground, telling the older boy, "Don't be selling no drugs to my children."

"I'll do anything I want to," replied the youth.

Hendricks lifted him up by the shirt and said, "If I ever see you around my children again, I'll kill you!" The boy was visibly shocked, and Hendricks realized he would have to go and speak to his mother, whom he knew. By the time he reached her house, it was eleven o'clock. The mother came to the door, a cigarette in one hand and a drink in the other. "Oh, Jon," she said, "it's about time you came to see me," and walked him into the living room and then into the bedroom. Ignoring the invitation, Hendricks told her what had happened, expecting her to be horrified. "Oh that's nothing," she said. "Sit down, relax." According to his own account, Hendricks then made his excuses and left. Talking it over at length back home, he and Judith agreed that something had to be done. Hendricks went to see the local chief of police and told him everything. To his amazement, the chief said he couldn't do anything about it. "Why not?" asked Hendricks, "You're the chief of police!"

"These are the children of the people who pay me," said the chief, "We know everything about it, we know where they get it, who brings it in, and we can't touch 'em because we'll all get fired."

Hendricks had had enough. Making a typically dramatic and spontaneous decision, he began making arrangements to leave the country, taking the whole family with him. His first move was to put in a call to Ronnie Scott in London, asking for a gig. Scott said he had a month free in February. "I'll be there," said Hendricks, "Send the papers, the contracts and everything." The deal was done. Hendricks went to the bank, took out a large sum of money, and bought air tickets for them all—minus seventeen-year-old Jon Jr. who refused to go, saying he wanted to stay behind and get re-acquainted with his birth mother Connie.

One of the last things Hendricks did before leaving the USA was to appear on a February 14 Thelonious Monk session at Thirtieth Street Studios in New York. "Thelonious Monk used to come up to me and say things like, 'Two is one,' and 'it's always night, or we wouldn't need light.' Then he would just walk away," said Hendricks. "I couldn't figure out what the heck that cat was talking about. I thought about what he said for a long time before I understood what he was saying." His lyrics for "In Walked Bud" were written when (he said) he was recording with Cuban percussionist Mongo Santamaria. Hearing that

Monk was recording on another floor of the same building, he went and found the band sitting around waiting for saxophonist Charlie Rouse, whose father had just died, unbeknown to them. Producer Teo Macero suggested Hendricks sing something. Hendricks picked up his legal pad and asked Monk what he'd had in mind when he wrote "In Walked Bud." Monk told him he was thinking about when he used to play on Fifty-second Street in New York with the Gillespie/Pettiford band, with Don Byas and Max Roach. The nineteen-year-old Bud Powell would come along and sit in. The two pianists liked each other, but the rest of the band hated the way Bud played. Monk got his way and would always cede the piano chair to Powell but the others would grumble, talking about how much fun they were having, *until* all of a sudden in walked Bud. Always preferring the upbeat approach, Hendricks decided to reverse the actual mood of these occasions so that instead of slumping, the joint started jumping. After fifteen minutes Hendricks had scribbled out the lyric and sang it while the band played, not realizing that the engineer was recording it. The cut appeared on Monk's 1968 album *Underground.*

A few days later, the Hendricks family flew to London.

7 The Mistakes Are the Only Part That's Jazz

The initial plan was for the Hendricks family to stay in the house of the pop singer Donovan while he was away in India (with the Beatles, Mike Love of the Beach Boys, and actress Mia Farrow), learning the techniques of transcendental meditation from the Maharishi Mahesh Yogi. At the airport, Michele and Aria became separated from the rest of the family, until a kindly stranger helped to reunite them. Somehow he ended up getting into the car with them on the way to Donovan's. Jon thought Judith had invited him; Judith thought Jon had invited him. But, since he seemed to be a pleasant and well-meaning individual, he ended up being the children's babysitter. The parents left them in his care while they flew to Germany for a gig. That evening the babysitter said he was going to a nearby pub and asked whether either of them wanted anything. Michele asked him to bring back some peanuts. The next morning there was no sign of him and his bed had not been slept in. When Michele mentioned this during a phone conversation with her stepmother in Germany, Judith said, "Oh my God, go into the bedroom and look in the bottom drawer under Dad's pajamas." This was where they kept all their cash. Sure enough, it was gone; in its place was a bag of peanuts. A few days later the culprit was apprehended back at the airport with a suitcase full of Donovan's possessions, including fur coats and jewelry.

Jon's month-long Ronnie Scott's booking began on February 26. He was backed by a quintet consisting of Ronnie himself on tenor, Kenny Wheeler on trumpet, Dave Holland on bass, and Tony Oxley on drums—plus Larry Vuckovich on piano, whom Jon had persuaded to come to London. They played opposite Johnny Griffin and the Stan Tracey Trio. The gigs sold so well that the booking was extended for a further month, this time opposite Phil Woods. Curiously, Jon always used to tell people that, during the second month of the residency, a *Melody Maker* poll voted him the number one male jazz singer in the world. In fact, this was entirely untrue: in the international (i.e. non-British) category, readers voted for Mel Tormé, Mark Murphy, and

Frank Sinatra in that order. In the critics' poll Louis Armstrong was number one, with Joe Williams and Jimmy Witherspoon sharing second place; Jon's name appeared nowhere on either list.

Rather than head back to the States once he had finished at Ronnie's, Hendricks began to see advantages to a longer stint in London. He knew plenty of people there and in mainland Europe from visits with Lambert, Hendricks & Ross. His new plan, insofar as he had one, was to book some UK and European tours using some of his American band members—particularly Larry Vuckovich and drummer Clarence Becton, although the latter declined on this occasion. They started a tour, reaching Birmingham and Manchester, with the great Puerto Rican conga player Jose Mangual and drummer Jimmy Smith; then Jon received an angry letter from the British Musicians' Union, who exerted an iron grip on the jazz scene at the time, telling him he had to hire British players. This put an end to Larry Vuckovich's stint in the UK. Mainland Europe was a different matter, however, and they played at jazz festivals in Norway (Molde) and Köln before doing dates in Poland and Switzerland. While they were appearing at the Berlin Jazz Festival, the owner of Munich's Domicile club offered Larry a steady house band gig backing visiting American jazz stars. After a while, Clarence Becton (who later changed his name to Eghosa Osarabo) joined him. Jon's live album *Cloudburst* was recorded at the club.

The Hendrickses initially lived in a rented property in Regent's Park, later moving to a number of other London addresses—including West Hampstead and Primrose Hill—before finally settling on a house near Marble Arch at 8 Stanhope Place. Soon after arriving in London, Jon had made contact with the popular UK singer and organist Georgie Fame, who had knocked the Beatles off the top of the singles chart in January 1965 with his Tubby Hayes-arranged version of "Yeh Yeh," featuring Jon's lyrics. Jon told Max Jones of the *Melody Maker* that he was excited about the possibility of working with Georgie Fame. His idea was for the two of them to get together with Annie Ross and make a record. There would be more Basie and Ellington tunes, plus some new songs which he and Georgie would write. "As soon as I get the word I'm going to start writing," he said. The word never came, in this instance. But, after only a couple of months in the UK, Jon was talking about establishing a career in London "as a singer, writer, music publisher and recording artist." To get himself on a business footing in the UK—and to satisfy UK immigration rules—he had transferred his ASCAP royalties.

"I feel there is a demand here for songwriters just now," he said. "It exists everywhere of course, but particularly in this country. Britain has become the center of the pop music world, and it's extended to dress and oh, a whole new sub-culture." Far from resenting the "British invasion," which his jazz compatriots blamed for hammering nails into the coffins of their careers, he said he was full of admiration for the way the Brits had acquainted "the mass of the people [in the US] with negro music in general, which had been overlooked." It was hard, he said, to be an artist there and make a living.

In another interview, he said that Donovan was going to record him for CBS. And he had conceived a new idea: to write a song, sing it on tape, scat on it, and then write lyrics to his own scat solo. It was an interesting notion, but it came to nothing, and in 1968 all he recorded was a single for Verve—flutist Hubert Laws's "No More" (credited on the label solely to Jon Hendricks), backed with the Gildo Mahones tune "Rainbow's End."

Except for Aria (who was still too young), the children were placed in a variety of private English boarding schools specializing in music and art. It was Michele's ambition to perform in musical theatre—dancing as well as singing—with the ultimate dream of playing Maria in *West Side Story*. She and Colleen attended Grandison College in Croydon as weekly boarders, Michele studying dance. This arrangement meant they could go home to their parents on weekends. Eric—a young man for whom following rules was anathema—was in constant trouble in UK schools and, to make matters worse, had recently developed diabetes. Having played no part in family life while he toured the world with Lambert, Hendricks & Ross/Bavan, Jon was now determined never to let the children out of his sight again. No matter that he had only just got them settled in schools, he took them out again so they could all be together while he toured. Aria was desperate to go to boarding school like the others; denied any kind of stability in her early life she grew up craving structure, order, and discipline: "It was not easy to be a passenger on that ride," she said. Much of her childhood was spent out on the road with

Michele aged 16

her parents, which affected both her early schooling and her opportunities to make friends. For her, no school year ever started at the proper time or lasted until the end. The one she attended the longest was King Alfred School in Golders Green, where all she remembered learning was how to be a proper young lady with correct table manners and use of cutlery.

Meanwhile their father was having a whale of a time getting gigs and tours, including the Jazz Am Rhein festival in Köln at the end of August, and making TV and radio appearances. It was a happy time—the best time of his life, he said afterwards. He loved London and he loved the house they lived in. Not long after his arrival in the UK, he secured a guest slot on the BBC Radio 1 show *The Jazz Scene* and later made several appearances on the prime time Simon Dee TV show (*Dee Time*), with a Maynard Ferguson-led orchestra as studio band. The BBC also booked him as a guest on *Happening for Lulu*, singing a duet with his arm around the bubbly hostess. "That was the difference in the racial climate in London as opposed to the United States. So that made it very acceptable as a place to live," he said. These were not obscure local TV stations but mainstream national television networks. People in the UK, Jon felt, were more open-minded about music and the arts in general than his compatriots, and didn't feel the need to put everything into watertight compartments. Artists from different disciplines hung out with each other: Hendricks met Peter O'Toole, Rudolph Nureyev, and Margot Fonteyn in Ronnie Scott's, and was proud that actor Nicol Williamson came to see him for five nights at the club. In the same inclusive spirit he was happy to appear at the pocket-sized Marquee Club in Soho on the same bill as Welsh prog rockers Man and future rock superstars Yes.

But he didn't like the way jazz was going. The "low state of music" he complained about to Moody was typified, for him, when Miles Davis visited London in November 1969 and Jon shared the bill with him at Hammersmith Odeon, alongside Mary Lou Williams. There, and later at Ronnie Scott's, Miles played selections from his recently recorded album *Bitches Brew*. Hendricks was angry, not only that his bebop hero was playing this new electric stuff, but that he was now denigrating the music he had made in the fifties. "He's lost his mind!" growled Hendricks.

He was becoming a familiar face in London and with the wider British public. Shortly after their move, Martin Luther King was murdered back in the US; Jon made a speech about him at a memorial concert on the steps of St. Paul's Cathedral in front of thousands of people, along with Dakota Staton and Philly Jo Jones, both of whom were also then living in the UK. In March 1969 he was the featured artist in an episode of BBC2's *Jazz at the Maltings* TV series alongside Ronnie Scott and his band. Jazz critic Benny Green wrote:

> Tonight's programme brings together two of the wittiest men in jazz—Ronnie Scott, club owner, saxophonist and bandleader, and Jon Hendricks, singer and lyricist. The TV debut of Scott's

new band, combined with the salty professionalism of Hendricks's vocal delivery makes the programme one of the most intriguing in the whole series.

And in June, Jon's reputation as a funny man was given added weight as he was interviewed for Marty Feldman's TV documentary *One Pair of Eyes* (also on BBC2), a relatively serious look at what makes people laugh.

That same year, bass player Daryl Runswick had a regular gig with the Reg Powell Trio at the Pickwick Club in Great Newport Street, near Leicester Square. Powell was the pianist and the drummer was Mike Travis. They played from eleven in the evening to three in the morning, which paid thirty pounds a week, plus a free meal. (It was enough of an income back then for Daryl to marry his girlfriend Elaine and furnish a flat.) Musicians used to drop into the Pickwick frequently, especially those who were working just up the road at Ronnie Scott's—including Jon Hendricks. Having sat in a few times, Jon started sweet-talking the management and suddenly the billing changed to "Jon Hendricks with the Reg Powell Trio." Jon didn't get on with Travis and fired him, replacing him with American drummer Bill Moody. He also brought in a conga player with the unlikely name of Reebop Kwakubaah. Jon's presence attracted many visiting Americans, including Jimmy Cobb. The gig lasted several months, Tuesdays to Saturdays. During that time they also played a couple of one-night stands in France and Belgium.

Jon had by this time acquired a car, a black Austin Princess: a stately vehicle which, at a casual glance, could easily be mistaken for a Rolls Royce. It became Jon and Judith's preferred mode of transportation to gigs. Michele, Eric, and Aria would sometimes be in tow and Jon would get them up on stage to do a number each—in Eric's case "Feed Me" ("'cos the way to my heart is through my stomach"). One day, Jon told the band he had lined up a gig for them in Stockholm. As they crossed the Swedish frontier in convoy, with Jon himself at the wheel of the magnificent Austin Princess, hordes of people turned out to watch the motorcade pass through towns and villages en route to Stockholm; he didn't understand why until he learned that the only car like it in Sweden belonged to King Gustav VI. The Runswicks travelled to Stockholm separately. On arrival, it transpired that Jon had only been half-offered the job and was now negotiating with the club owner, while everyone else had to sit around kicking their heels and rapidly running out of money—since Stockholm then, as now, was hideously expensive. Daryl Runswick realized he would soon be too broke to pay for the return journey, so he and Elaine cut their losses and returned to England. In the end, the gig did come through and Daryl accepted that he had effectively resigned from the band. Jon replaced him with Red Mitchell, who happened to be in Stockholm at the time. But it was Jon who got Daryl his first gig at Ronnie Scott's; one or two sit-ins there led to Ronnie's manager Pete King booking Daryl to play a season with Annie Ross—and many more gigs thereafter. Annie had been clean of heroin for several years by now, and for a few years had run her own Covent Garden jazz club known as Annie's Room. Seeing Jon with her, it seemed to Daryl that they weren't very close—affable but distant. They didn't hobnob like old friends, didn't even sit together on the same sofa.

During his time with Hendricks, Daryl also played on the album *Jon Hendricks Live*. In fact, "Live" was stretching things a little: there were no more than a dozen people present apart from the band, most of them friends of producer Johnny Franz. It was recorded over three sessions at Philips Studios in Stanhope Place, the same street that Jon lived on. Bassist Dave Green replaced Daryl on one of the sessions, and whoever else was around at the time was invited to come along and play. Jon's approach was inclusive: any time he spotted one of his American musician friends in the audience, they would be invited up.

The money was Judith's department. Jon might say yes to a band member's request for a pay rise, then come back the next day and say no, because he'd run it past Judith and she had vetoed it. He deferred to her on all executive decisions. It was in London that she first started singing with the band, initially contributing one song to the act. Later, when Michele had finished school, she too was added to the group. "Michele's always been very hip," her father said. "She sang 'Shiny Stockings,' one of the Basie songs, when she was seven." For a while, when Eric was also singing with them, the group became a quartet. In fact it was an unspoken understanding that each of the kids would become part of the Hendricks family act by the age of seven; it was something they all enjoyed. Aria was even younger when she first went on stage with her father. At first, it didn't faze her at all: "I always felt that as long as I was with him, on his lap or holding on to his legs, the audience couldn't see me," she said. But by the time they got to Europe, it had dawned on her that she was indeed visible; after that, her parents had a hard time getting her on stage. On one occasion, aged seven, she sang at Ronnie's with the other three kids as back-up singers. It was a Les McCann song to which Jon had written lyrics about Jack Sprat, especially for her. She was so terrified that her mother had to physically push her on stage.

For Jon, however, there was never any separation between offstage and on. Outside the house he always dressed as flamboyantly as he would on a gig. He and Judith were so focused on getting and playing gigs in those days that life was permanent chaos. Sometimes they would go somewhere for a gig and never come back, leaving all their stuff behind. Not even illness or death mattered when it came to *the gig*. Jon would perform even if he had a temperature of 104 degrees, with pus in his throat. He would perform a two-and-a-half hour concert even when he was unable to speak or eat. Gigs were everything, and everything else came a distant second. Aria was constantly pulled out of school to go on tour with them: "I was a piece of luggage," she said, "except when I was carrying luggage. They never considered me a separate person." When traveling with Jon, various combinations of children would come along—often Michele and Colleen, sometimes Eric—and all of them sang at some point. The family would stay in a different hotel from the band, so the musicians wouldn't see much of them during the day. That same year the singer Norma Winstone received a phone call from Jon, whom she had never met or spoken to before. He was eager to come over and talk to her about an idea he'd had for Miles Davis's 1957 album *Miles Ahead*. He planned to write lyrics to all of Miles's solos on the album, and re-record the whole thing with voices instead of horns. Norma liked the sound of it and, when Jon asked her if she would like to be involved, she was enthusiastic; for the next forty-eight years she heard no more about it. Like the Monk project, it was an idea that hung around for decades.

Jon and Annie were on hand in early January 1970 to sing at a major television showcase for the Buddy Rich Orchestra at the Talk of the Town, a large, glitzy London nightclub. That year Jon was featured half a dozen more times on various Radio 2 jazz shows, and once more on BBC2 in May, with Dusty Springfield and Paco Pena, on *The Young Generation*. In 1971 he contributed to the soundtrack of the British film *Jazz Is Our Religion*, which focused on the work of iconic British jazz photographer Val Wilmer, and the French film *Hommage à Cole Porter*. With the help of expat American actor-director George Margo, Jon also staged *Evolution of the Blues* in various venues over the next couple of years—principally Hampstead Theatre Club in north London. Given the subject matter, it was essential to cast black performers—but he said he had difficulty locating any, complaining that some very good West Indian jazz musicians never got to play in top end clubs like Ronnie's:

> It's not that I didn't expect to find prejudice here, because I know it's a condition of humanity existing everywhere in the world. Nonetheless, it's still distressing, especially in a music like jazz, which is relatively free of it in the States. Sure, they have plenty of American Negro musicians playing for London audiences, but they ought to pay attention to their own, too, you see.

Hendricks's assertion did not bear close scrutiny: "Total rubbish," was the reaction of bass player Dave Green in 2019. He went on to name several West Indian-born musicians who played at Ronnie's at the time including guitarist Ernest Ranglin, tenorman Wilton "Bogey" Gaynair, alto player Joe Harriott, and trumpeters Dizzy Reece and Shake Keane. Hendricks's concern for his fellow musicians did not always extend to financial matters. Green remembers Hendricks paying him five pounds for a gig—which was stingy even then, much as Green enjoyed playing with him. After Bill Moody was forced to return to the US, not having a work permit for the UK, Les Cirkel took over on drums both in the UK and in Europe. He too remembers Hendricks being a cheapskate: "I was doing function gigs for seven or eight pounds at the time," he said.

Evolution of the Blues at the Blackie, March 1972, with Jon and Michele Hendricks, centre and right (Black-E archive)

"Jon was paying five pounds, and he expected us to rehearse." This was Jon's *modus operandi* for much of his career. As he once confided to saxophonist-arranger Frank Griffith, "I love working in Britain because I get some of the finest jazz musicians in the world and don't have to pay them very much." Instructed to turn up at the house at 8 Stanhope Place, Cirkel and pianist Alan Berry would often find that Hendricks was either in bed or not there at all. During these long waits Judith would be the perfect hostess, plying them with cups of tea and showing off the new guard dog she had acquired. It was a Basenji—a strange choice for a guard dog, the most notable feature of this African breed being its inability to bark.

One day Hendricks took a call from a young composer called Andrew Lloyd Webber, who was planning a new stage production called *Jesus Christ Superstar* in which, he hoped, the singer would play Pontius Pilate. But Hendricks turned it down, huffing about "sacrilege." Was it sacrilege, or was it that he didn't want to play the hand-washing villain of the piece? Or perhaps he preferred to limit his theatrical ambitions to *Evolution of the Blues*.

Another of his overseas dates was a weeklong run at a plush nightclub near Zurich. On the way—with Jon, Judith, Aria, Les Cirkel, and pianist Hywel Thomas on board—the Austin Princess developed an exhaust problem and toxic fumes began to flood the inside of the car. Les Cirkel noticed that Aria was slowly turning green and told Jon to pull over. He grabbed Aria and walked her up and down until she had inhaled enough oxygen to continue. At the gig both Lionel Hampton and Charlie Shavers turned up and sat in. Despite the poor financial rewards, Les loved working with Jon and learned a great deal from him—not least a lifelong appreciation of singers. Jon was the first he had come across who took the trouble to tune his air saxophone or air bass before scatting with it. He was also a masterful bandleader, sometimes telling the drummer, "Don't follow me," meaning "Don't repeat on drums or refer to what I just played." He wanted Les to keep playing time.

In 1971 Jon cut two sides for a Philips single release—"I Got Soul" backed with "Slow Train"—produced by Wally Stott who, the following year, was also involved in one of Jon's most interesting albums: *Times of Love*. This featured tenor saxophonists Ronnie Scott and Bob Efford, with an orchestra directed by Stott and again produced by Johnny Franz. It's refreshing to listen to a Jon Hendricks studio album, with no scat or vocalese, that features a full orchestra. As Benny Green's ever-insightful liner notes explain, it was the first time Jon had appeared on record as a ballad singer—although he had always sung ballads live. It's an album of slow, dreamy, and often melancholy tunes. Only some of the songs on *Salud!* had hinted at this side of him. His voice is not always up to the task, but Stott's orchestral arrangements are rich and lush. Throughout, the tracks are linked by a few bars of an uncredited folk song:

> My love and I, we two are one
> Our very souls entwine.

There's no question we're in England here, although two tunes—the title track and "Where?"—were written by the French-Lebanese singer Cyril Azzam. "Times of Love," the title track, had already been released on the 1970 *Live* album. It's a sweet song, with a great sax break by Ronnie Scott and some tasteful (though uncredited) vibraphone. "Where?" a slow, bluesy lament, is not to be confused with the Randy Weston tune of the same name that appeared on *The Swingers!* Here Jon's vocal is reminiscent of Johnny Mathis. The standard "It Could Happen to You," usually rendered as mid-tempo swing, is given the slow treatment, and it's fascinating to hear a version of "Nature Boy" by someone other than Nat King Cole, with a completely different orchestral arrangement. But Jon was now past fifty and, here and on some other cuts, his vibrato not only sounds off-puttingly old-school for 1972 but suggests that he didn't always find it easy to sing in the relaxed and contemplative manner demanded by the ballad form. Cole Porter's "I Concentrate on You," arranged with a gentle Latin beat, is a case in point and on the album's weakest cut— "Li'l Darlin'"—he harmonizes his own voice and is not completely in tune. The vibrato also causes problems with these overdubbed harmonies since, as most singers know, harmonies don't work unless they are sung without vibrato. It was three years before the disc received a US release, when it was finally put out by Rod McKuen's Los Angeles-based Stanyan label. In 1994, Jon said it was his favorite of all the albums he had recorded.

In July, Judith told Jon she wanted to go back to the US for the birth of her niece. This meant that the four Hendricks kids also had to go. Jon called Max Gordon at the Village Vanguard and secured a good enough booking to pay for them all to travel. Soon afterwards they decided to stay in the US, and Jon was looking back fondly at his sojourn in the UK:

Naturally, living in Britain with my family for four-and-a-half years left me with quite a few impressions. Really, the thing that makes me the happiest is that it gave me the opportunity to bring my children into a fairly stable society. We came over here at the time of the riots in America. My daughters have had the four-and-a-half years of schooling in England; if you had known them before and see them now, you see the difference it made in their personalities and their characters. For the rest of my life I will be grateful for the hospitality that I've been shown in this country.

No-one thought to inform Aria's school that she wasn't coming back.

The Hendricks family settled back in Mill Valley, California, where Jon immediately went about finding work for himself. Jan Wenner of *Rolling Stone* was so desperate to get him to write for his magazine that he gave

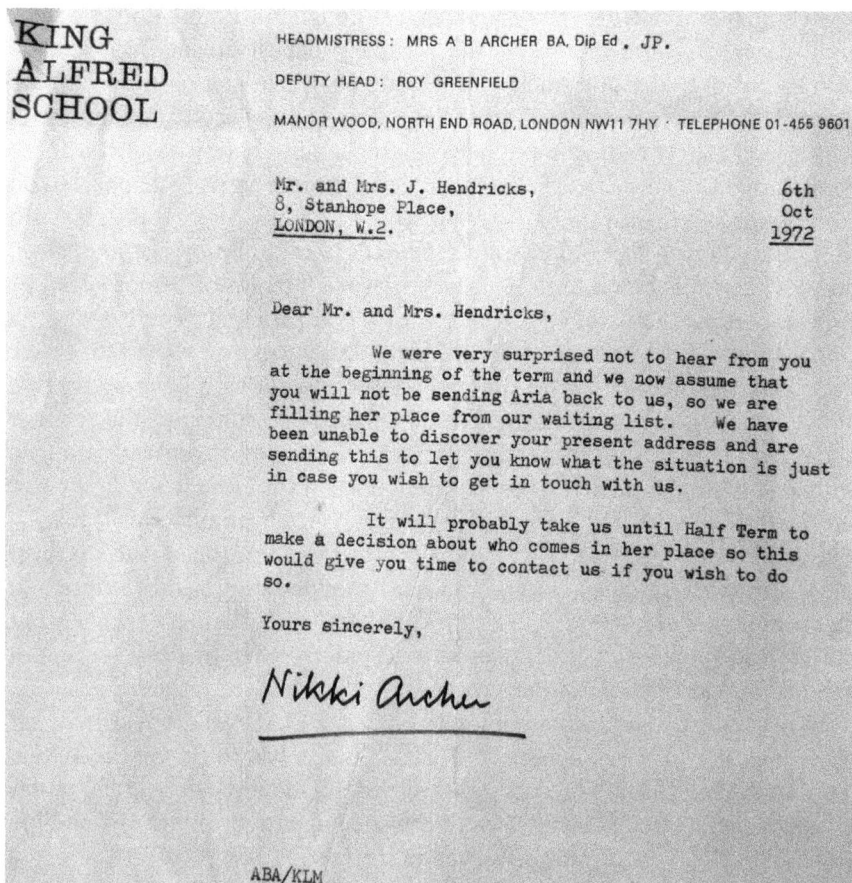

KING ALFRED SCHOOL

HEADMISTRESS: MRS A B ARCHER BA, Dip Ed . JP.

DEPUTY HEAD: ROY GREENFIELD

MANOR WOOD, NORTH END ROAD, LONDON NW11 7HY · TELEPHONE 01-455 9601

Mr. and Mrs. J. Hendricks,
8, Stanhope Place,
LONDON, W.2.

6th
Oct
1972

Dear Mr. and Mrs. Hendricks,

We were very surprised not to hear from you at the beginning of the term and we now assume that you will not be sending Aria back to us, so we are filling her place from our waiting list. We have been unable to discover your present address and are sending this to let you know what the situation is just in case you wish to get in touch with us.

It will probably take us until Half Term to make a decision about who comes in her place so this would give you time to contact us if you wish to do so.

Yours sincerely,

Nikki Archer

ABA/KLM

Letter from Aria's school in London (courtesy Aria Hendricks) him a typewriter. Jon kept the typewriter but never wrote a word for *Rolling Stone*. But when his old friend Ralph Gleason retired as jazz critic for the *San Francisco Chronicle* in 1973, he took over the job and, among many articles, wrote a long piece on Billie Holiday for the Sunday supplement. He also found some work teaching jazz history classes at California State University at Sonoma and the University of California at Berkeley. And as before, he continued to rub shoulders with musicians outside jazz. In October 1972 Jon Hendricks & Family appeared at a concert at San Francisco's Winterland Ballroom to promote voter registration, sharing the bill with Kris Kristofferson and Country Joe MacDonald.

Jon had a habit of dropping in on other people's recording sessions. One of them was an Art Blakey date at Fantasy Records in Berkeley. Pressed into service to sing his lyrics for "Moanin'" on the session, Hendricks was then asked if he had any other Blakey lyrics that could go on the B side of a putative single. He hadn't. What he suggested was not an Art Blakey tune but Benny Golson's "Along Came Betty." This was March 1973 and the album was Blakey's *Buhaina*.

One of the first things Jon had done on returning to the USA was to call CBS in search of a record deal, but it was not ideal timing: the label was going through an internal investigation following the firing of several executives for various payola and cocaine scandals. One of them was its head, Clive Davis, who was alleged to have paid for his son's lavish bar mitzvah by making phony expenses claims amounting to ninety-four thousand dollars. Davis went on to found Arista and this was the label on which Jon's next album appeared. In mid-1975 Steve Backer, director of jazz A&R at Arista, called the pianist and producer Ben Sidran to offer him what he described as "a simple gig." Clive Davis had handed Jon a budget of twenty thousand dollars to make an album called *Tell Me The Truth* but now Arista were nervous because, so far, there was no sign of anything being recorded. Backer wanted Ben Sidran to go to San Francisco and take over the production. When he arrived at Wally Heider's studio the band was in place, the engineer was in place, but Jon Hendricks was nowhere to be seen. After two hours he came running up the stairs and said to Ben, "Hey man, nice to meet you. Say, lend me some bread, I got a cab waiting." Ben dug out some cash, Jon clattered back down the stairs, and that was the last they saw of him that day.

Once the recordings were finally under way, Jon and Ben were alone in the studio and Jon was showing him the song "Old Folks." As Ben described it:

> We went over to the piano where he sketched out some chords to me and then started singing. I followed him as best I could. Jon, being the great jazz musician that he is, completely gave it up on the vocal, throwing back his head and letting the anguish and the nostalgia of the song soar into the room. When it was over, the

A Legend? Just Smile Silly

By Jon Hendricks

("Lady Sings the Blues," a film biography of Billie Holiday, starring Diana Ross, is currently playing at the Coronet Theater. Jazz singer and Chronicle critic Jon Hendricks here registers some memories of the great singer.)

THE FIRST thing I noticed was her dignity. Simple, human dignity. The kind that is innate, within a person, not dependent on outside forces, not that haughtiness of manner that's supposed to be "dignified." Any bum can act "dignified," but not everybody has dignity. That Lady had it. I saw it.

Annie Ross had taken Dave Lambert and me to Birdland "to meet a friend," she said. She led us to a front table, where Oscar Pettiford, one of the greatest bassists who ever lived, was sitting with a cat whose name I have forgotten, and a quite beautiful lady who was all made up to look like Billie Holiday, right down to the white gardenia in her hair. Annie introduced Dave and me to her and, sure enough, she was the legendary Miss Billie Holliday, white gardenia and all.

How do you act when you meet a legend?

Me, I just mumbled "What a great pleasure it is to meet you," touched the soft, warm hand, even held it for a fleeting instant, sat down, and went into silent shock, hoping no one would notice that the silly smile frozen on my face was really a case of lockjaw. And trying not to look at the Lady, yet quite unable to take my eyes off her.

Lester Young had dubbed her "Lady Day," and forever after that was to be her name. She and Pres had got tight, as they say, during a tour with the Basie band. Some say they had become lovers. And if so, then why not? That two such beautiful souls should mate is as old as "Romeo and Juliet," and every bit as romantic.

They say she adopted her style from the way Pres played. "How can you play a song when you don't know the words?" he used to say. I've also heard it said that Bird — Charles Parker Jr. Kansas City, Missouri, alto saxophonist — wrote "Billie's Bounce" for the Lady. The tempo of "Billie's Bounce" was the one she liked to sing the most. It's the tempo of "Miss Brown To You," of "Me, Myself and I," of "I Cried For You," "Ooh, What A Little Moonlight Can Do," and the ever - popular "Many Others." So both those saxophone players. Lester Young, called Pres, and Charlie Parker, called Bird, matriculated in Kansas City, home of Moten Swing like Basie's. Both set styles of playing that inspired generations of musicians beyond their own time. Both were born in the sign of Virgo. And both loved that lady.

Duke Ellington and his orchestra were appearing at Birdland that night, and Jimmy Woode was on bass, with Sam Woodyard on drums. Duke came over to the table and showered his magic upon the Lady and all the rest of us. He hugged and kissed everybody and we all knew that he really did love us madly, and it was marvelous. Jimmy Woode asked Oscar Pettiford to sit in with the band while he sat with us and the Lady, and O. P. got up on the stand and played as though he were giving a special concert for her. That rascal turned that fiddle

The Blue Stars, with Blossom Dearie, and had seen it all come back home when some of the Blue Stars, after digging Lambert, Hendricks and Ross, formed The Double-Six of Paris, some of whom left to join expatriate American Ward Swingle in his Swingle Singers, among them being Christiane Legrand, sister of Michel, and a member of the Swingles to this day. Yolande Bavan, who was later to replace Annie Ross, had also known the Lady in Paris.

Thinking back on it now, I saw Mal Waldron, Lady's accompanist in the final days, in Munich, where he now lives. We played together there in a little jazz club called Club Domicile. It had been a reunion for us, be-

BILLIE HOLIDAY
She was dubbed "Lady Day"

cause I have known Mal since he was just a kid in the Bronx, and had never dreamed that he would ever accompany the Lady, but he was with her right down to the wire, so he knows all those tales that would make spicy copy, but I never got around to asking him about her, nor did he ever mention it. That's how important it is to him. I imagine he moved away because after spending so much time with Lady, and her gone, nothin' looks good anymore.

I didn't see her anymore after that night at Birdland until her final concert at the Phoenix Theater in New York city in the spring of 1959. She was tired. The spirit was about to leave the body down here where it found it and go back home, where every woman is a lady. But we still hear you, Lady. And we will tell your story to the coming generations. Why, even at this moment our children are lining up at theaters across the country to see Diana Ross and Berry Gordy make their motion picture debuts by paying their respects to you.

San Francisco Chronicle article (courtesy Andy Watson)

engineer in the control room said, "Would you guys like to hear that?" We hadn't known it was being recorded.

Jon was so enthused by what he heard he wanted it to go on the record. But Ben was concerned that he himself had still been learning the tune and had made some mistakes. Because they were recorded by the same mic there was no separation between the piano and the voice, so re-recording the piano while keeping the vocal performance was impossible.

"No," said Jon, "That's as good as I can ever sing that song. It's great. We've got to use it."

With his responsibility to Arista in mind, Ben said, "Jon, I think it's a great song, but that take really isn't good enough. Let's recut it."

"Ben," said Jon, "Sometimes the mistakes are the only part that's jazz." Needless to say, the take ended up on the record. But Jon's recorded output over the rest of his long career became ever more patchy. He became curiously resistant to the whole idea of recording. Perhaps this is why so many of his albums were live. A dyed-in-the-wool improviser, he appeared uneasy with the whole idea of a fixed performance. That said, *Tell Me The Truth* sounds slicker than many of his recordings, thanks largely to Ben Sidran. Like *Times of Love*, the album features less of the usual blues and scat and only "Old Folks" has lyrics by someone other than Jon himself. The Pointer Sisters, who had recorded "Cloudburst" for their debut album and "Little Pony" for their second, make a guest appearance on the opening track, Slim Gaillard's nonsense song "Flat Foot Floogie" (with added Hendricks lyrics). It establishes a feel-good vibe as Jon sings Jack McVea's tenor solo from Gaillard's 1945 recording, Judith sings Dizzy Gillespie's, then it's Jon again with Charlie Parker's, and finally June Pointer with Slim's own. The Pointer Sisters as a group sing a transcription of the original piano part. Another interesting choice on the album is "On the Trail," a drifting ballad by American neo-classical composer Ferde Grofé from his 1931 *Grand Canyon Suite*. Over eight minutes the Hendricks version moves from ballad to upswing scat, reverting to ballad at the end. Jon's own composition "Tell Me the Truth" starts as a slinky Latin shuffle. It's a great song, rendered initially with a certain melancholic restraint and with a lyric as relevant to the Trump era as it was to the seventies. When Jon starts ranting about hypocrisy and injustice the backing becomes fast and funky, before reverting to Latin. The only disappointment on the album is "Blues for Pablo," a dramatic rendition of Gil Evans's arrangement for *Miles Ahead* with remarkably off-key singing by everyone involved—Judith, the four ensemble singers, and Jon himself. Ben Sidran turns the reverb up to eleven, but it can't hide this blemish on an otherwise highly polished album.

In July, Jon gave an interview to *Billboard* to promote *Tell Me the Truth*, as well as his forthcoming three-night stint at the Bottom Line with Judith, Michele, and Beverley Getz (wife of Stan). He revealed that he was planning to record all of the tunes on *Miles Ahead*, creating his own unique lyrics for

Miles's solos. Several of them were already in the can, he said, and would appear on his second Arista LP. In the event, *Tell Me the Truth* was the only album Jon ever recorded for Arista; Aria didn't remember what the issue was, but clearly recalled her father talking on the phone with Clive Davis:

> He was pacing back and forth, his body language when he was angry. His voice started raising. He didn't get angry that often, but when he did, you couldn't stop him. Nothing could. And it was getting louder and louder and louder and louder and finally he said, "Clive—fuck *you!*" Even at the age of ten, I thought that was probably not a good idea. There went all the album promotion.

For a man with such strong opinions about everything, Hendricks seemed unusually diffident in his *Billboard* interview, saying he was waiting for some reaction from broadcasters and the public as to what style they might prefer so he would have a clearer direction for himself. "I can only think in terms of what I love," he said. "I can't perform only what is considered marketable." In the same interview he was typically ambivalent about rock and fusion, saying he found a lot of contemporary jazz to be dishonest because its practitioners were only doing it to make money, "so they water down their art." But he also called the fusion of jazz with rock an "honest attempt" by young players to create a communications vehicle.

In early October 1976, wearing a bright orange suit, he appeared with Annie Ross, Eddie Jefferson, and Leon Thomas—with Larry Vuckovich on piano—for an hour-long TV show called *Sing Me A Jazz Song* for WTTW Chicago, an educational television station. Part of the *Soundstage* series, the show was the brainchild of Ben Sidran, and Jon did all the announcements, as well as hogging most of the limelight. After a couple of ensemble tunes he performed an extract from *Evolution of the Blues* relating to Louis Armstrong. After an out-of-tune Annie Ross performed "Farmer's Market," she and Jon (who had now changed into a brown velvet double-breasted suit) essayed "Li'l Darlin'" as a duet. Leon Thomas sang the Dave Lambert part in "Centerpiece" with Hendricks & Ross, and on "Cloudburst" it was Eddie Jefferson's turn to play third banana. Next it was time for "Tell Me The Truth," and all of a sudden, in the R&B section of the tune, the act finally caught fire. The four singers took their bow on "Everybody's Boppin'." The following year Jon contributed to the Jimmy Rowles/Stan Getz album-length collaboration *The Peacocks*, singing his own lyrics to Wayne Shorter's "The Chess Players." He had heard a tape of the session and was so taken with the interpretation of the tune that he scribbled out some lyrics and, without a word to Getz, brought Judith, Michele, and Beverly into the studio to overdub them. When Stan came home after a gig in London, Jon innocently asked him to listen to the tape. Fortunately Stan was amused as well as surprised, and called Shorter to okay the lyric.

Annie Ross and Jon Hendricks on Sing Me a Jazz Song (courtesy Ben Sidran)

The teaching, the journalism, and the gigs kept Jon busy through the seventies, as did a new attempt to find a long-term home for *Evolution of the Blues*. After its first appearance at Monterey in 1960, Jon had gone back to working with Lambert, Hendricks & Ross, before mounting it again at Newport and Carnegie Hall with Joe Williams and Jimmy Witherspoon, followed by a university tour with Jimmy Rushing and around nine other cast members. They kept the show on the road for seven months before the Hendrickses decamped to London. On their return to California they put it on at the Paul Masson winery in Saratoga, with its stunning amphitheater and mountain setting. This raised enough money to produce it in San Francisco, where it eventually opened on August 28, 1974, at the On Broadway Theater, produced by PR man and manager Dean Jennings. Although most of the singers he worked with came and went over the years, for Jon there was no such problem with members of his own family—and he needed them now. Michele, aged twenty-one, had left California a couple of years earlier to live in New York, where she formed a vocal group with Buddy Rich's daughter Cathy and Stan Getz's daughter Beverley. They called themselves (optimistically, perhaps) Hendricks Getz Rich, and enjoyed some modest success, putting out a single. But when Jon wanted Michele to be in *Evolution of the Blues*, back she came to California. Aria was also dragooned into the cast, playing a slave girl, and Jon Jr. made some appearances during the early part of the show's run. Otherwise he rarely saw his father, from whom he was effectively estranged— despite Judith's best efforts to keep him within the family orbit. Away from *Evolution*, Junior (who, some thought, bore a remarkable resemblance to Joe Williams), would occasionally sit in on guitar with Jon's trio, which he preferred to singing, despite his excellent voice. An interesting family detail came to light in the show's printed program. Without any undue concern for accuracy, this stated that Judith was "the mother of five of [Hendricks's] seven children." Adding together his four with Connie and the one child (Aria) with Judith, this still left two unaccounted for. Dwight was presumably one of them; the identity of the other was probably another child of Jon's called Jacques, later renamed Edward.

The show also featured Larry Vuckovich on piano, Melvin Seals playing gospel organ and piano and arranging the choir, Vernon Alley on bass, and Lenny McBrowne on drums. Bob Maize, who by then had been Jon's bassist in concert for some years, played the part of Dave Lambert, and Judith—who also designed the costumes—played Annie Ross. Jon and Dean Jennings were worried how Larry might feel about being the only white musician in the band. But Larry himself was not unduly concerned, telling Jon, "This music is about everybody—you know that yourself." Jon saw his point. Having grown up with the minor scales and flatted fifths of Balkan music, Larry Vuckovich was also well equipped to handle the blues. Jon told the audience, "If you're wondering what Brother Vuckovich is doing here, he comes from that part of Yugoslavia called Monte*negro*." He liked the joke so much that he continued making it even after Larry had left the production and his place had been taken by a black pianist. *Evolution* became a major hit, running in San Francisco for five years, and Jon began to entertain serious hopes of taking the show to Broadway.

In 1978 the production moved to Los Angeles, where it was directed and choreographed by Donald McKayle. In his autobiography *My Dancing Life*, McKayle is highly critical of Jon Hendricks, saying that although the show was great entertainment, it was somewhat spoiled by Jon's intrusive ego: the production skated too quickly through blues and jazz history and lingered far too long on the work of Lambert, Hendricks & Ross. He was also unimpressed by the involvement of Judith and the children in the show—billed as Hendricks, Hendricks, Hendricks, and Hendricks. McKayle had flown up from Los Angeles to see *Evolution* in San Francisco at the request of Hal Grossman and Mark Green, who wanted to bring it to Los Angeles and hoped to develop it into a full theatrical production. Although Jon retained his credit as co-director, McKayle found him adopting a strangely passive attitude to auditions and rehearsals, contributing nothing to the vision or detail of the new production other than his own performance, which remained the same as it had been in San Francisco. As a performer, McKayle conceded, Jon took choreographic direction reasonably well but spent the rest of the time during rehearsals working on the *Los Angeles Times* crossword. Despite these complaints, the LA run was successful, continuing for a year at the Westwood Playhouse. But when McKayle dropped in on one of the performances, he was astonished to hear Jon, in his role as a minister, incorporating a commercial for his albums as part of his onstage sermon. In the intermission Judith sat in the lobby in her costume, selling the records and promising purchasers that Jon would be happy to autograph them at the end of the show. Sure enough, after the entire cast had paraded to the exit Jon—still in costume—took up his position at the sales booth. McKayle was outraged: "I walked over and looked squarely in Jon's face as he reached out his hand expecting another record and gushing compliment. 'Jon, I had such respect for you … I'm sorry I ever met you,'" he huffed. And this was far from the end of the affair.

After *Evolution of the Blues* had been running for two years in Los Angeles, Jon and Judith decided to take a vacation. It was then that the trouble started. "While we were gone," said Jon, in an interview with Mike Joyce for *Cadence* magazine, "they wiped us out of the play, put new people in it. I had to go through lawyers, and lawyers are slow, the courts are so slow, by that time they were in Chicago." In early 1981 he sued the producers for effectively stealing his show while he was away. The legal case was over breach of contract and to wrest back the rights to his own work. The defendants were Mark Green, Burton Lane, and Hal Grossman. Donald McKayle—whom Jon described as "the villain of all time"—was guilty, he alleged, of stealing not only *Evolution* but also an idea Jon had outlined for a Duke Ellington show:

Mark Green is a lawyer and he knows that if you take something that's a literary work, anyone who wants to claim it has got to go to court and he's gotta hire a lawyer, and he knows how much lawyers cost. I mean, it's ten thousand dollars when you walk in the office, and who's got ten thousand dollars? So they just took it. That's the way the law is in this country. Somebody can steal your work, like if you're writing a book, somebody could take your idea for the manuscript, publish it—now in order to get it back *you've* got to go to a lawyer, and the lawyer's gonna want ten thousand bucks from you. The reason you were writing the book was to make ten thousand bucks, so where you gonna get the ten thousand? So the guy gets away with the book.

Jon surely had right on his side. While they were locked out of the show, Judith said, they were forced to scratch around doing club dates to keep enough cash coming in to fight the case. But another issue not mentioned by Jon at the time was his insistence on Judith remaining in the production. This was a sticking point for the investors, who seemed to share his belief that *Evolution* had a good chance of making it to Broadway in New York—but not if it featured the singing of Mrs. Hendricks. In another twist to the story, it was said that Green and his colleagues were lawyers for TV talk show star Johnny Carson and that it was he who wanted to take over the production so that they could rework the structure and put it on in New York. The struggle then became more personal—and more painful. Jon discovered that the lawyers also acted for Bill Cosby. Conscious that he himself had been instrumental in helping Cosby to get his start in showbiz at the start of the sixties, Jon called him in the hope of enlisting his help to get the lawyers off his back. But not only did Cosby refuse, he went to them with the privileged information that Jon had given him. It was something the Hendrickses were always reluctant to talk about, but they never forgave Cosby.

8 No Chord is Better Than the Wrong Chord

Throughout the seventies Jon toured Europe regularly, including return visits to the UK. Late one night—after a week of shows at the Opposite Lock club in Birmingham, England—the manager presented him with a check in payment. But despite having played at the club on several previous occasions, Jon refused to accept it and demanded to be paid in cash. The manager could not authorize this, as it had to be agreed by the club's owner, Martin Hone. The latter was at home in bed, laid low with a severe case of influenza. Although he knew about this, Jon nonetheless drove to Hone's house and hammered on the door, demanding he get up and give him the money. Hone, who never kept cash in the house, was forced to crawl from his pit and send him on his way. But this was the only unpleasantness during many years of an otherwise harmonious relationship. More typical was a later encounter when Hone was in Los Angeles on unrelated business, and spotted in the *Los Angeles Times* an advertisement for *Evolution of the Blues*. With some difficulty, he managed to get the last available tickets for the show. On arriving at the theater, he sent an anonymous note backstage. It read, "Your greatest fan from England is sitting in the audience tonight. See you after the show." Two-thirds of the way through the evening, there was a scene set in a jazz club. Jon began reminiscing about jazz clubs he knew, mentioning one that he particularly liked in the middle of England. He then jumped off the stage and—as the house lights came up—ran along the aisle, pushed his way past a row of seats and hugged Martin Hone in full view of the audience.

While touring in the USA, Jon or Judith would often drive a station wagon, while the baggage and instruments would be towed behind in a U-Haul trailer. At other times Jon would fly to the destination the day before to do radio promotions for the gig, and someone in the band would drive. When the Hendrickses were out on the road, the old race problem remained. In the South, it was as if they had stepped into a time machine and been transported back to the early fifties. As a mixed race couple, Jon and Judith had to hide their relationship: it was always Judith who went in and booked the hotel room, because if the locals saw any of the others coming, all of a sudden the hotel would be full. Even to buy gasoline, they would have to lie on the floor of the car as Judith operated the pump. Nothing much had changed since the Louis Jordan band's experiences of a quarter of a century before, when the *Green Book* was an essential guide to avoiding trouble in the South. The Jordan band would pull down the shades so no-one could see in, while the bus driver and the trombonist, both white, went into the diner and bought fifty or sixty hamburgers and a case of Coca Colas. If anyone asked, they would explain that the bus contained a team of athletes, and that they were all sleeping.

Jon liked to tell the story of how, while playing at the Village Vanguard in New York, probably in 1972, he and his brother Jimmy (his manager at the time) found themselves being driven in a yellow cab by a young man called Tim Hauser. Hauser, who was living with his girlfriend Janis Siegel, told them he was planning to form a Lambert, Hendricks & Ross-type band with Janis and another singer called Laurel Massé. Jon gave Tim his card and told him to call as and when the project came together. A year later, Jon said, he received a call to say that Tim and his group were signing with Atlantic Records and wanted Jon to sing on a track with them. The album's title (and the group's name) was *The Manhattan Transfer*, and it made a minor dent on both the album and singles pop charts. However, Jon's collaborations with The Manhattan Transfer didn't actually begin until *Extensions*, their fifth studio outing, on which he contributed lyrics to their version of Joe Zawinul's "Birdland." They had originally commissioned Eddie Jefferson to do it, but on May 9 Eddie was murdered by his former dancing partner. The following year Jon himself gave a different account. He told Bill Moody that the lyrics were originally written for the Swingle Singers but, when they didn't use them, he made them available to The Manhattan Transfer. "They told me they had a couple of tracks open, so I said, I got a song for you," he explained. However it came about, it marked the beginning of a close working relationship between Jon and the group—one characterized as mentor and students. "He had pretty strong ideas about what was right and wrong," said Janis Siegel. "Strong philosophical ideas, strong political ideas." She found him to be a strange mixture of hipster and preacher. It was a fruitful partnership: the vocalized "Birdland" went on to become the group's anthem, earning them their first two Grammys for Best Jazz Fusion Performance, Vocal or Instrumental, as well as Best Arrangement For Voices for Janis Siegel's work on the song. The group had been strongly influenced by Lambert, Hendricks & Ross from the beginning: the first lyric Janis and Tim wrote—"You Can Depend On Me"—was inspired by them. And even before they knew Jon they would perform "I Want You To Be My Baby" and "Four Brothers," as well as Annie Ross's "Doodlin'." That said, they sensibly avoided being pigeonholed as a mere retread of Lambert, Hendricks & Ross, preferring to list as their influences the "jazz, R&B, pop, rock 'n' roll, salsa and swing" heard all over Manhattan when they formed in the early seventies. In fact, The Manhattan Transfer modeled themselves more on the smooth close harmony of wartime singing combos like the Pied Pipers and the Merry Macs; Lambert, Hendricks & Ross, on the other hand, had been first and foremost a group of three soloists who, thanks to Dave Lambert's arranging prowess, were able to approximate the feel and sound of the Basie or Ellington Orchestra. As Janis Siegel put it:

> From the very beginning of Manhattan Transfer we were interested in the art of vocalese ... because it's more challenging. In the same way that bebop grew out of the big band era, because musicians were weary and bored with just playing standards with the old chord changes, and they wanted a bit of a change and a challenge. And along came Charlie Parker, writing these new melodies to "How High the Moon" and "I Got Rhythm," and opening up a whole new world to every instrumentalist.

As she began to spend a lot of time hanging out with Jon, Janis became familiar with his lyric-writing routine. Jon would sit wearing his bathrobe, with a yellow legal pad on his knee, listening to the instrumental music on a cassette over and over again, until suddenly he would start to write. It would be very quick, she noticed, more like translation than pure invention—translation from music to words, from one language to another, as if someone was whispering in his ear.

Meanwhile, trouble was looming in the touring group now known as Jon Hendricks & Company. The current line-up consisted of Jon, Judith, Michele, and Eric. Then one Thursday, after a major bust-up, Eric quit. They had a show scheduled at Fat Tuesday's in New York, starting early the following week, so Jon asked Michele to call Bobby McFerrin. She had first heard McFerrin at an afternoon jam session at a club in San Francisco, when he got up and sang a swing version of "Misty." Wowed by his performance, Michele went up and introduced herself. Until very recently, McFerrin told her, he had not been a singer at all but a keyboard player in funk and fusion bands, dance workshops, and cheesy piano bars. It turned out that he had moved to the city only a month earlier, and he and his wife were living just a block away from Michele. "And so we became friends," she said, "and I kept saying to Dad, come and hear this guy, and he finally did come one night, and he was pretty impressed with him." Now, in their hour of need, McFerrin agreed to join the Hendricks group. With the New York dates only days away, Michele and Bobby locked themselves in a room for the next seventy-two hours. By the end of it, Bobby had learned the whole repertoire—not just the tunes and the words but all the intricate lyrics Jon had set to improvised instrumental solos.

McFerrin stayed with Jon Hendricks & Company for only a few months. "Jon and I worked very well together all in all," he recalled:

Hendricks family on stage: Eric, Colleen, Jon and Judith (courtesy Aria Hendricks)

We argued a lot, though never in a malicious sort of way, and I usually wound up giving in out of admiration for him and a desire to please him and keep my job. I remember once we were planning a tribute to Eddie Jefferson at Carnegie Hall, and we argued *for days* about the solo I was supposed to take on my featured number with Jon's daughter Michele. Jon wanted me to sing the solo note for note the way Eddie had recorded it, and I could see his point in a way because that is what Jon Hendricks is all about, not adding anything to a solo and not taking anything away from it either, but respecting it for what it is and trying to be absolutely faithful as you add words or sounds to it. Maybe because I'm from a later generation of singers, my position was that you take the material you're working with and use it as the springboard for the creation of something completely new.

During the run of shows, the perfidious Bill Cosby came in and was so taken with McFerrin that he hired him to be his opening act. And when Miles Davis heard him, he did the same. It was clear that Bobby McFerrin's singing career had assumed a momentum of its own and, after less than a year, he quit.

So once again the group were without a second male singer. They briefly tried Los Angeles-based Bruce Scott but, when that didn't work out, it was Bob Gurland who got the call. As a child Bob had loved Lambert, Hendricks & Ross. While still at Columbia University in the early sixties he had been a member of the Even Dozen Jug Band, whose members included such future stars as John Sebastian, Stefan Grossman, and Maria Muldaur. He had first met Jon Hendricks in 1974 at the Greenwich Village music club The Bitter End. Having just been introduced to Bob Dylan by their mutual friend David Bromberg, and while jamming along with Dylan in the dressing room, Gurland became aware that someone was accompanying them on double bass—vocal double bass. He looked up and saw that it was Jon Hendricks. Much as he revered Dylan, as far as Gurland was concerned Hendricks was nothing less than a god, and off he went with the jazz singer, leaving Dylan blowing in the wind. It "sounded so groovy," according to Jon, that he asked Bob to join the family group then and there. "We're doing a festival at Monterey soon," said Jon, "Why don't you come out with me?" But Bob had only just started his career as a lawyer with Atlantic Records so, with great regret, he turned the offer down. A few years later, Jon Hendricks & Company were playing at The Bitter End. Bob went to see them, reintroduced himself to Jon and, before he knew it, Jon had invited him up on stage. From that point on, this became a routine whenever Jon was in town. What appealed to him about Bob Gurland was the latter's extraordinary skill on the vocal trumpet. So convincingly trumpet-like did he sound that he was credited on the Even Dozen Jug Band album not as a singer but simply as "Bob Gurland—trumpet".

In 1981 Jon offered him the job again. "Can you be in LA tomorrow?" he asked. Bob hesitated. His career as a music business lawyer in New York was now well established. Did he really want to give it all up to sing with Jon Hendricks? "Listen," said Jon, "We're working our way across the country and we'll be in New York in about two weeks. That should be long enough to figure things out." This time Bob decided to go for it. Having taken the plunge he, like Bobby McFerrin, then had to learn the Hendricks repertoire. He already knew many of the tunes from albums he owned. But once again it was Michele—the only member of the group who could read music—who taught him the finer points. Unlike her, Bob didn't read music (at least, not well) so Michele would sit down with him and go over the parts. In every case, her father insisted they go back to the original recordings—often by Basie or Ellington—and listen to what the trombone (in Bob's case) was play-ing, although the individual members of the Hendricks group didn't stick rigidly to one instrument.

In Bob's first year with Jon Hendricks & Company they received a Grammy nomination and played gigs opposite Ella Fitzgerald, Sarah Vaughan, Carmen McRae, and Dizzy Gillespie. A highpoint for Bob came at one San Francisco Jazz Festival. Jon—who had just come offstage from playing a slot with Dexter Gordon, Connie Kay, Percy Heath, and Les McCann—urged Bob to get up and join them. "Bob," he said, seeing the terror on his face, "This may be the only chance you get in your whole life to play with these guys." So up he went and, for a few brief minutes, had some of the greatest names in jazz history as his backing band. This spontaneity was typical of Jon Hendricks's *carpe diem* approach to life, as fundamental to his philosophy as "just listen." Touring was rather less glamorous. Seven of them—singers and band—traveled in a Dodge van with all their equipment and luggage: two in the front, three in the second row of seats, and the remaining two sliding around on a mattress in the back with all the gear, plus pots and pans for cooking the food the Hendrickses considered essential for good health.

At the time, The Manhattan Transfer were preparing their *Mecca for Moderns* album. For this project, they asked Jon to write lyrics to Freddie Green's "Corner Pocket," a tune recorded by the Basie orchestra in 1957. As usual, the job included lyricizing all the solos. Later, having recorded it—and feeling very happy with the outcome—they heard from a man named Don Wolf. "Excuse me," he said, "I am the lyricist, and you have to pay me and give me credit, because people like Sarah Vaughan have recorded my lyrics." So they struck a compromise with him, going back into the studio and re-recording the head with Wolf's lyrics, which they considered horrible. But at least it meant they were able to keep Jon's solos, and in performance they always used Jon's lyrics. It was worth all the effort. Their version of the song, renamed "Until I Met You," won them a Grammy for Best Jazz Vocal Performance by a Duo or Group. And on the same album Jon got to sing Eddie Jefferson's lyrics to Charlie Parker's "Confirmation," here renamed "(The Word of) Confirmation."

On May 5, twenty-five-year-old Colleen Hendricks, the youngest of the four children from Jon's first marriage, was found dead from a suspected drug overdose. "Pops was too broken up to go and identify her body," Jon Jr. said:

> I had to go into the coroner's office at the morgue and identify her. I looked over her body and I noticed she had needle marks on her right arm—and she was right-handed. So right away I told the guy, "Did you guys inject something? What is this?" And he said, "We don't know ..." And I said, "She's right-handed—why would the injections be in her right arm?" She passed away in the Buckeye Hotel in [San Anselmo, a few miles north of] Mill Valley, abandoned by three other women she was with. As soon as she passed, or got sick, they ran out of the room.

Life went on. In August the Hendricks group, bolstered by the singer Leslie Dorsey, started recording an album called *Love* for Joe Fields's Muse label, credited to "Jon Hendricks & Company featuring Michele Hendricks." The basic tracks were laid in Hollywood and San Francisco, then completed in New York the following February. Michele vividly remembered the process of preparing the arrangements for her father. It was arduous work, but valuable ear training at the same time: Jon would choose a number from the Count Basie or Duke Ellington repertoire and tell her to pull four vocal parts out of it. There was no point in writing the parts out, since they would mean nothing to anybody. Instead she had to sing each person's part for them, along with the original recording, so they could listen to it and memorize it. After the main recording sessions Bob Gurland found himself dipping into his own pocket to pay for extra studio time, since there were mistakes that needed fixing—indeed, some that were never quite fixed. Despite this, *Love* is a thoroughly enjoyable album (characterized by *Jazz Journal* as "witty, civilized and swinging") although slightly uneven, with three different pianists (Jimmy Smith, Eric Doney, and David Hazeltine) playing on the various sessions.

It must have sounded somewhat dated when it came out in 1982: after all, at that time Michael Brecker and Don Grolnik were continuing their fusion experiments in Steps Ahead, Stanley Jordan was inventing new ways to play the guitar, and Michael Franks was introducing a smoother, more romantic singing style to contemporary jazz. The high point of *Love* is not the ensemble singing but Michele Hendricks performing "Angel Eyes," straightforwardly but gorgeously, with only Ray Scott's acoustic guitar as accompaniment. In the liner notes Jon reveals that his favorite composer is Randy Weston, and he includes two of Weston's songs here: the highly syncopated "Willie's Tune," with a whistled Jon Hendricks solo, and the title track "Love" (a.k.a. "Berkshire Blues"). There is also the usual complement of previously recorded numbers: no "Cloudburst" this time, but "Good Ol' Lady" had come out before, on *Fast Livin' Blues* two decades ago; "Li'l Darlin'," here with a lovely, fully harmonized melody, had previously appeared on both *Sing a Song of Basie* and *Times of Love*; the new album also marked the third recorded outing for "I'll Die Happy," which dated back to 1959's *A Good Git Together*, and Jon had recorded it again on *Fast Livin' Blues*; "Tell Me the Truth," his dyspeptic update on "Anything Goes," was the title track of his 1975 album. With his vast knowledge of songs, one might ask why he continually repeated himself. Whatever the reason, *Love* was both his first and last recording of the 1980s and, as with Arista, it was his only album for the Muse label. In fact, from this point on—aged just sixty—he released only two more albums. There is a clue in the liner notes: "Jon Hendricks & Company are the successors to Lambert, Hendricks & Ross," writes Jon. "We will continue the tradition where LH&R left off … We humbly invoke the spiritual good wishes of Dave Lambert and Annie Ross upon us." Further notes by Joel Vance also invoke the vocal trio's fading memory. For Jon, however, making records always ranked well below *the gig*. At the height of their touring days, Hendricks and Company were on the road three hundred nights of the year. In April 1982 the *New York Times* reported that they would be making "a rare weeklong appearance … at the Blue Note in Greenwich Village." The accompanying trio was certainly in the Rolls Royce class—Hank Jones on piano, Red Mitchell on bass, and Philly Joe Jones on drums.

During Bob Gurland's sojourn in Jon Hendricks & Company, the band went through five or six different piano players. Then, one afternoon in late summer of 1982, twenty-five-year-old David Leonhardt attended a cattle call audition held at a club called Lush Life on Bleeker Street, New York. Jon Hendricks had an apartment in the same building at the time; the club became the Hendricks home base until it eventually closed for good. Leonhardt had been in town about a year and a half, having grown up in Louisville, Kentucky. The Hendricks gig was coveted by many piano players—not only because it was Jon Hendricks, but because it was a full-time job. Around thirty hopefuls arrived for the audition; each got to play just one song. All were fine musicians, but the canny Leonhardt was the only one who turned up wearing a three-piece suit: he had heard about Jon's old-school attitude to clothes and image, and was afterwards convinced that that was the reason he got the nod ahead of some equally good players.

After playing a semi-private gig with the band in Vermont he flew with them to play a jazz festival in Israel, in the midst of its invasion of Lebanon. At this point the other two band members were drummer Marvin "Smitty" Smith and Australian bassist Murray Wall. But soon afterwards Smitty left the band for a while, to be replaced by Al Dreares. As soon as they returned from Israel, everyone piled into the Dodge van and spent the next three days traveling from New York to San Diego. (Judith particularly loved driving at night.) But, after one gig, Dreares became ill and had to be flown back to New York and taken to hospital. Drummer Doug Sides took his place but had a mental breakdown after a few months (apparently due to his Vietnam experiences), and was replaced by Clifford Barbaro. In San Diego, they played a concert opposite Dizzy Gillespie and his band. It was sweltering on stage and, in the suit and tie that Hendricks insisted everyone wore, Leonhardt was suffering mightily. When he could stand the heat no longer, he took off his jacket and laid it on the piano bench. Backstage, Hendricks was incandescent. "I'm the star," he raged, "I can take my jacket off. You're the accompanist, you can't take your jacket off!" But, somehow, Leonhardt survived the indiscretion. A big incentive to staying in the band was that, within two months of his arrival, he and Michele had begun a long-term relationship; eventually Leonhardt came to be treated as a member of the family, spending the next four years with them touring Europe, South America, the US, and Canada playing jazz clubs and festivals.

The *Love* album won a Grammy nomination in the category Best Vocal Performance, Duo or Group, and there were also awards for a television documentary that Jon Hendricks wrote and voiced for the KCBS Los Angeles. *Somewhere to Lay My Weary Head* told the story of the Dunbar Hotel on Central Avenue. Built in 1928 and black-owned, the Dunbar provided 115 rooms of first-class accommodation where black jazz musicians and others who were denied hotel rooms in the racially segregated Los Angeles of the 1930s could stay for a dollar a day. Conveniently, it was also next door to the Club Alabam—an entertainment hotspot that hosted the likes of Dexter Gordon, Charles Mingus, and Art Pepper.

Despite all the recent attention, Jon's live gigs now took a bit of a downturn. He was in dispute with his agent and, at the same time, the climate for bebop singers in New York had gone cold: even Shirley Horn and Mel Tormé were playing to half-empty houses. The situation was made worse by one of Jon's personal weaknesses: he could not bring himself to play straight with his business partners, whether they were managers or promoters. "He was a flawed guy," said David Leonhardt:

> He loved to win, in any situation. He didn't trust people. He had a falling out with everyone he was in any kind of business relationship with, even people that were doing great things for him. Eventually he would do some crazy, stupid, petty, dishonest thing. He would cheat them out of a thousand dollars, even though [it meant] he would lose fifty thousand dollars later. He was an idiot about stuff like that.

There were also long-standing, unresolved tensions between Jon and Michele. When she left the group in 1983, Jon called the young jazz singer Holli Ross and told her to learn five or six tunes. For the audition there was no sheet music, just a recording with the lyrics written on a piece of paper. Holli disliked this method; as a trained singer who could read music easily, she preferred the certainty of a properly written chart. So she wrote her own part out, mentioning the fact to David Leonhardt. The pianist warned her not to tell Jon about this ability of hers, or she would end up being the group's dogsbody. So, when she went to the audition, she kept her music hidden and sang instead from Michele's hand-written lyric sheet. In the event, the gig went to Stephanie Nakasian. Judith—noticing how attentive Jon had been towards the young, blonde Holli Ross—was the one who nixed her.

Stephanie had not started out as a jazz singer, but became one after she met her future husband, the bebop pianist Hod O'Brien. Up until then she had worked as a successful Wall Street trader in currency futures, with no background whatever in jazz. David Leonhardt heard her sing at an open-mic session and called to ask if she'd like to audition for Jon Hendricks. She knew almost nothing about the great man and had no idea of audition protocol. As she took her turn at the microphone, Judith asked for her name, phone number and birthdate. When she said August 29, 1954, Judith was delighted: Stephanie was a Virgo, which meant there would be two Virgos and two Cancers in the group. All the other *habituées* of the New York vocal jazz scene who auditioned were aghast that she was chosen, because they'd never heard of her. "If I had known more," she confessed, "I would have been more freaked out." But the decision had been made. They handed her dozens of tapes to listen to and told her they were going to Buffalo a few days later to do a gig at the Tralfamadore, so she plugged herself into a tape player for the duration of the journey by van. There was only one solo to learn but, although she instantly felt very at home on the road with the Hendrickses (more so than trading currency futures), the music was difficult. Judith constantly pushed them to perform new, complicated material. Later the routine of learning everything by ear at Jon's apartment—with nothing written down except the lyrics—proved challenging, to say the least.

But it was the same for everyone. On one occasion, Jon gave Duke Ellington's "April in Paris" to Frank Foster and asked him to separate it out into four vocal parts. Stephanie was tasked to go and pick up the transcriptions from Frank. "He was so upset because it was so hard to hear those parts—they were all on top of each other and mangled," she said. And for her, learning the solos was especially difficult. As others had found before her, there was no alternative: you just had to listen. And listen to the originals—not to the Joni Mitchell or Annie Ross version. You were expected to go back to Wardell Gray and make sure you reproduced his phrasing.

In the fall of 1983, at the Vine Street Bar and Grill in Los Angeles, Jon was playing with a different backing band than usual, featuring a different pianist who had set up a series of dates for them in California. During the break after the first set on the first night, Jon called David Leonhardt at home in his New York apartment and said, "I just booked a ticket for you. You're taking a flight out from JFK tomorrow morning, and you're gonna finish the tour." David did as instructed, arriving hotfoot from LAX—his plane having been delayed—and went straight to the dressing room with his suit bag for the first set of the second night. To his surprise, the other pianist was still there: Jon had not told him he was about to be replaced. As the band prepared to go back on stage, Jon said to the pianist, "Hey, come here, I need to tell you something: I brought my pianist from New York. He's gonna finish the tour with us. You go ahead and play the trio songs. He's coming up with us." One can only imagine how the pianist felt. He was an excellent player, it was his first job for a long time, and he had been Jon's accompanist years before.

As much as he was sometimes capable of such brutality, Jon was also quite capable of shooting himself in the foot. The Modern Jazz Quartet hired him and the band to be the warm-up act for their sold-out reunion concert at Lincoln Center. It was a high-profile booking, and anyone who was anyone in jazz was at the concert. Jon was nervous: he was always looking to get himself "back on top" in his career, and he was desperate for the gig to go well. At the soundcheck, he didn't like what he was hearing—it was a symptom of his nerves—and there was an altercation with the sound engineer. Hours later, during the concert, he was right in the middle of a big number when all the sound went dead. All the audience in the huge hall could hear was the piano, bass and drums with no amplification. The engineer simply turned it off for five minutes, destroying the vibe and completely ruining Jon's big number. Afterwards he shrugged and said, "Oh, I don't know what happened."

Despite the scrapes, the arguments, and the occasional unpleasantness, almost all the musicians and singers who went through the Jon Hendricks band found the experience an unmixed joy. The music performances were at a high level and the audience response was exhilarating. "I loved every minute of it, until the end," said David Leonhardt:

> I was young ... and I got an internationally touring gig, and we went overseas and all through the States, and all these big venues. It was my dream come true. We did radio shows, we did concerts, we did TV shows. It was what I'd wanted to do all my life. We went to South America, went to Brazil for three weeks, and then we went to Europe. The first time we went to Europe, we went for three months. We had a month of gigs, and then a month off, and then another month of gigs.

For their month off, he and Michele rented a car and drove around the south of France and Italy. Once—in the Les Baux de Provence region of the south of France, while playing at a club called Hot Brass—they stayed in an old, collapsing villa with no running water, sleeping on mattresses. One day Jon announced that he was going to treat everyone to lunch at the Michelin-starred L'Oustau de Baumanière restaurant. Even back then, the bill came to five hundred dollars. Afterwards they went to the pool and had champagne cocktails. "Jon had a big heart," recalled David. "He wanted people to experience all the wonderful things he himself had experienced."

After Bob Gurland left in 1984, he was briefly replaced by Avery Brooks. But the rhythm section remained stable as Leonhardt, Wall, and Barbaro built a solid partnership behind the singers. On Friday August 30, 1985, Jon brought Annie Ross back for another reunion—this time at the Chicago Jazz Festival—which was captured in a live coast-to-coast TV broadcast. The preparation for this consisted of Annie joining the Hendricks gang in the south of France for two weeks, while they were playing a club in Aix-en-Provence from ten o'clock each night to two in the morning. Annie would hang out and sing a song or two; the idea was for her to rehearse during the day. In fact, all she did was play poker with the band and they never rehearsed once for the Chicago gig. As Daryl Runswick had noticed in London, Jon and Annie were friendly and polite towards each other; her coolness toward him was explained, at least in part, when Annie told one member of the party that Jon had cheated her out of her royalties for "Twisted." In the late fifties, the dark days of her heroin addiction, she'd had no idea what was going on and had carelessly signed over the rights to Jon and Dave. The resentment was not mutual, however. When Jon appeared in the 2012 documentary film about her, *No One But Me*, he discussed his former bandmate and friend with great affection.

The last concert David Leonhardt played with Jon Hendricks was on New Year's Eve, in Connecticut. The band were paid their performance fee but then, when they arrived, it turned out that the show was being recorded for broadcast. The musicians had previously negotiated long and hard with Jon and Judith about fees—which would vary depending on whether it was a club date, a concert, or a recording—and they expected to be paid extra for a recording. Their cut would only have amounted to a couple of hundred dollars each, even if Jon had honored the contract. But Jon insisted that no-one was getting paid extra for it, not even him. What he had failed to realize was that the recording had been booked through the musicians' union. Because David's name was included on the contract that Jon had signed for the recording, David had received a copy of it through the mail a few days later. It revealed that Jon was getting eight thousand for the recording—a lot of money in 1986. Just before they went on stage, David told him he had to get his share of the money or he would not play the concert. He was by now the longest-standing member of the band and, as the others looked away, he stuck to his guns—knowing that by doing so, he was quitting. "OK, I'll pay you," said Jon, through gritted teeth.

This unfortunate end to their professional partnership may give the impression that Jon consistently exploited his musicians. But David Leonhardt stayed in the group for four years because Jon was actually excellent company and a very fair employer, most of the time, often urging David to go and earn some serious money by getting himself a job with a pop act. He could always play bebop at home, Jon told him. Amongst other things, David credits him with showing him how to be the fine accompanist he became. Once, at a gig in Minnesota, Jon called a song that David had never played before—"Every Time We Say Goodbye." David recalled:

> I thought I knew it, and I didn't. It's not one of those songs like a blues, where you can figure it out. So we started playing it, and this was a concert, and I started playing all the wrong chords—I was trying to figure it out on the spot, as we were playing. And it was just awful. Halfway through, Jon walked over and said to me, very quietly, "No chord is better than the wrong chord." And it hit me—don't get in the way: if you don't know what to do, don't play. Don't make it worse.

Another important lesson he learned, as an accompanist, was to understand that the singer was the most important member of the ensemble and that the accompanist has to follow the singer. "You have to listen to everything they do, and you have to watch 'em physically. You have to watch 'em take a breath. And I could see it in his shoulders, I could play something to fill that space," he said. The most important rule he learned was this: the only reason the accompanist is there is to make the singer sound better:

> Take the word "comping." It's short for *accompanying*, but it's also short for *complementing*. You're complementing what they do. So

I adopted an attitude that I would not play anything, whether it was a chord or a fill, or an introduction or an ending, if it didn't make the singer sound better. It wasn't about me sounding good, like look at what I'm doing, or how fast I can play, or how interesting I am. And because Jon had four singers, there was a group of about twenty arrangements that we did that were reproductions of Basie or Ellington songs. So I had to learn what I called the optimal comp, which is the very best way to comp behind a group. It took me about six months behind the band to really refine it.

In other words, by then it was not a matter of being creative; it was a matter of playing the same thing every night because it fitted perfectly with what the singers were doing. By contrast, during Jon's solo set, when he sang standards, David found he could be creative and play quite long solos.

The Manhattan Transfer *Vocalese* album (1985) was their ninth and the one in which Jon Hendricks was most heavily involved, writing the lyrics to every tune and singing on two of them. On the front of the liner were the words "featuring the lyrics of Jon Hendricks" and on the back he was pictured in a white dinner jacket, laughing along with the rest of them. But Ahmet Ertegun, the president of Atlantic Records, didn't think it was a good idea to devote an entire project to out-and-out vocal jazz. Although the group had recorded ten hit albums by then, Ertegun was convinced this one would be a flop, telling them, "You're going to break the chain, and you're gonna hurt yourselves." But the band argued that they'd earned the right to do it, having already made a lot of money for the company, and threatened to take the project elsewhere. So Ertegun reluctantly agreed. Jon did a low-key West Coast tour with them—"just little saloon-type places where nobody knew us." In the end, the critical acclaim for *Vocalese* was overwhelming and the group received twelve Grammy nominations, winning in three categories. It was a feat surpassed only by Michael Jackson's *Thriller*. Jon shared Best Jazz Vocal performance (Male) with Bobby McFerrin for "Another Night in Tunisia." But in other ways Ahmet Ertegun was right: despite the awards and the acclaim, the highest chart placing for *Vocalese* according to *Billboard* was seventy-four, making it their second-lowest ranked album since their debut *Jukin'*—although on the jazz charts it reached number two. Later Tim Hauser got married, inviting Jon and Judith to the wedding. As Jon crossed the dance floor at the reception he bumped into Nesuhi Ertegun, Ahmet's brother, who asked him. "What did you think [*Vocalese*] was gonna do for The Manhattan Transfer?"

Jon replied, "Well, I think this album is gonna do for The Manhattan Transfer what *Sing a Song of Basie* did for Lambert, Hendricks & Ross."

"Oh you do, do yer?' sneered Nesuhi.

Returned Jon, "Yes I do, do I?" Many years later, he recalled:

> I was ready to punch him out! Little bastard! So I split—walked
> away from him. So I get back to New York, and immediately I get
> a call from Tim, and Tim says, "Guess what?" I says "What?" He
> says, "Guess who's taking me to dinner tonight?" I said, "Who?" He
> says, "Nesuhi." I said, "Halleluyah." He said, "He's so excited about
> the album sales. It's number one in Japan." And so forth. And he
> said, "You know what he said? He said, 'This album is gonna do for
> The Manhattan Transfer what *Sing a Song of Basie* did for Lambert,
> Hendricks and Ross.'" ... I said, "Look, these guys are not creative
> artists, they're record people. They make a good record, they repeat
> it for the rest of their lives. And that's creativity for them." I said, "If
> you want their opinion, you have to give it to them."

Subsequently, The Manhattan Transfer used Jon's "Blues for Pablo" lyrics on
their Grammy-winning *The Offbeat of Avenues* album.

After Bob Gurland left Jon Hendricks & Company, he was replaced for
a short time by Mark Ledford. But the most long-standing member of the
family group was Kevin Burke, a friend of Aria's from California. Burke had
grown up in Larkspur, a couple of miles up the road from Mill Valley. His
sister Kelly was friends with Aria through their mutual interest in the theater.
When Kevin moved to New York in August 1985 he had nowhere to stay, so
Kelly suggested he ask Aria. He went out to dinner with her and her friend
Linda Goldstein (now Bobby McFerrin's long-time manager) and they all
became friends. Kevin enrolled at Hunter College on the Upper East Side to
study music. Meanwhile, in the first week of July, Jon and Judith appeared at
the Lugano Jazz Festival in Switzerland with Kim Lindsay and Mark Ledford,
with a band consisting of Cyrus Chestnut, Larry Gales, and Al Levitt. Soon
after, on a visit to Jon and Judith, Aria and Kevin found her father engaged in
a heated phone conversation with Mark Ledford. Jon knew that Kevin was
a singer, albeit one fresh out of high school. Cupping the phone Jon asked
Kevin, "Can you handle my material?" And Kevin, to his eternal credit, said,
"Yes sir!" Jon uncapped the phone, barked "You're fired!" and slammed it
down.

Kevin owned a Fostex four-track recorder for writing songs and overdubbing his own vocal harmonies. Jon said he had heard some of the songs and
needed a couple more singers (including Aria) for a revival of "Reminiscing in
Tempo," Duke Ellington's lament for his dead mother, at Umbria Jazz Festival.
In preparation for the performance they rehearsed at the Henry Street
Settlement arts center, on the Lower East Side, with director and choreogra-
pher Louis Johnson. Before that, Kevin was asked to sing at a Nat King Cole
tribute with the group, opening for George Benson and Natalie Cole at the
Lincoln Center on June 26—which meant he had a week to learn it all. It was

a familiar story, typical of Jon's "last-minute" policy. There seemed to be no process—just an instantaneous decision, followed by an assurance that "It's gonna be great!" In Aria Hendricks's view the constant, all-enveloping chaos that resulted from her father's approach to his career was what made it less successful than it could have been; the concept would be ambitious, but the preparation would always be done in a rush at the last minute and rehearsals often went on until three in the morning. It meant there were sometimes train wrecks on stage, as Judith had a tendency to learn her own part by rote rather than be aware of what was going on around her. Consequently, if she got lost, it was very difficult to find her way back and, because of this, some venues would not book the group. Jon's inability to read or write music was another frustration, as the only way to make others understand what he wanted was to sing everything. He had to hire people to write charts, which was not only expensive but caused further delays. He would usually try to get someone to do it for free—someone not necessarily qualified to do a complete and accurate job.

Like nearly all the singers and players who had preceded him in the group, Kevin Burke was grateful for the musical education he received at the hands of Jon Hendricks and forgave the occasional hassles. At Hunter College he learned about vocal improvisation almost entirely from a harmonic perspective—what note could fit with what chord. But his experience with Jon taught him that a better approach to the vocal solo was to treat it more like a drum solo. In other words, it was the rhythmic underpinning that was crucial to the overall effect. Jon's genius was his ability to hear tunes at multiple levels, so that if someone suddenly decided to cut the rhythm section and pointed to him, he would immediately start to sing the bass part.

In the spring of 1987, when Buddy Rich was dying in hospital with a brain tumor, Jon paid him a visit, taking Annie Ross along with him. After a few minutes Buddy said to Jon, "You see that cupboard over there? I gotta bottle of brandy. Let's have a few drinks." To the patient's disgust, his visitors declined the offer. "Listen," said Buddy, "Tell you what, if you go into my pocket there's a white line in there we could snort together. Let's just have a last little session." Jon shook his head, sadly. "Buddy, I got to tell you, I gave all that up forty years ago. There's no drugs inside me now, I'm clean as a whistle." The great drummer was not finished yet. "Hey, I'm making it big with that red-headed nurse down the way. Why don't you bring her in? We'll have a gangbang."

One day Jon Hendricks went to do a master class at the New School in Manhattan, whose jazz program had just started. He was one of many New York-based musicians who came to talk to the students, one of whom was a nineteen-year-old pianist called Larry Goldings. The tutor had asked Larry to accompany the guest as part of the student rhythm section. Four months later his phone rang—it was Jon, asking him if he would be able to come over to their Gateway Plaza apartment. Once there, he learned that the pianist Danilo Perez had just quit the Hendricks band. After an hour or so of chat and anecdotes, Jon asked Larry if he knew the brief Red Garland piano intro to Miles's "Bye Bye Blackbird." At the time Larry was only dimly aware of Lambert, Hendricks & Ross, and even then, only as their influence had filtered into The Manhattan Transfer. But he did know his bebop chops and, as it happened, he did know the intro. Jon was testing him, a white teenager from Boston, to make sure he had absorbed enough of the tradition that Jon himself worked in. This meant knowing not only the music of Louis Armstrong from the thirties and before, but also of Jobim in the sixties—along with everything in between. "We're going to Paris in two weeks, for two weeks," he told Larry, "but we don't have a book for the rhythm section, because the last piano player took it with him." Like so many before him, the young pianist was given a box of tapes so he could transcribe the whole repertoire. By the time he arrived at the Méridien Hotel, where they would be living as well as performing for the next fortnight, he was still furiously writing charts. And soon afterwards he learned that he was also expected to be the leader of this rhythm section, consisting of bassist Andy McCloud and drummer Clifford Barbaro. Jon liked to have a young band—he felt comfortable in the teacher/boss position and liked to show them all the ropes. At one point during their Paris residency, they were playing a fast rhythm changes tune when Jon called to Larry Goldings, "Stroll!" Larry had no idea what he meant and so, taking a wild guess, he started to play in the stride style. "Lay out!" yelled Jon; "stroll," it turned out, was an old bebop term for "stop playing."

Larry Goldings stayed with the Hendricks group for about a year and a half. Even during that brief time, musicians were constantly coming and going from the band. Jimmy Cobb and Larry Gales joined them for some gigs, and later Tyler Mitchell and Duffy Jackson. They played all over the world—with jazz festival bookings at Montreux and Nice—and back in the USA there was some television, including *The Arsenio Hall Show* where they were joined by Bobby McFerrin and Al Jarreau. Larry was full of admiration for how hard the Hendrickses worked, as well as noticing the baggage—both literal and figurative—that they carried with them. It seemed to him that the whole family dynamic was one of great neurosis. Traveling as they did, like an old-fashioned entertainment troupe, didn't come without a cost: Jon was hard to handle, and Judith was the one holding it all together. Singing in a style that was years past its peak of popularity, Jon could still make a living and feed his family. Despite the stresses and strains of living and working together, the Hendrickses welcomed Larry Goldings into their midst, taking him under their wing. Jon dubbed him "the reincarnation of Sticky Mack"—an early twentieth-century jazz piano pioneer.

By the end of the decade there was another departure. Michele had had enough of the endless touring, and left the family group. In 1991 she moved permanently to Paris, where she married a French sound engineer and launched a solo career as a singer and teacher. But first she became part of an album project that turned out to be one of the greatest of her father's career.

9 We Need You to Control Him

Jon Hendricks's final studio album was 1990's *Freddie Freeloader.* In common with most jazz musicians, he was used to recording albums in a day or two, but his involvement with *Vocalese* had shown him what could be achieved with a bigger budget. The Manhattan Transfer album had been a lavish exercise involving dozens of musicians and production staff. The genesis of the project that became *Freddie Freeloader* was a spontaneous gig: George Benson, Al Jarreau, Bobby McFerrin, and Jon discovered they were all playing in New York at the same time, and thought it would be fun to perform as a unit—a bebop boy band, if you will—during McFerrin's Blue Note gig. It wouldn't be advertized; it would just be a one-off. Jon, now approaching seventy, was still looking for ways to get "back on top" in his career. Now he had the brainwave of bringing these singers with him into a recording studio; he just needed someone to pay for it. The first part wasn't so difficult: Jon had been around a long time, knew everybody, and was liked and admired by nearly all of them. In addition to Benson, Jarreau, McFerrin, and the singing Hendrickses, he recruited Tommy Flanagan, Stanley Turrentine, Jimmy Cobb, Al Grey, Wynton Marsalis, The Manhattan Transfer, and the Count Basie Orchestra—plus a rhythm section. Larry Goldings, who had just turned twenty-one when recording started, also became a part of *Freddie Freeloader*, sharing piano duties with Tommy Flanagan.

At first, Jon's optimism looked misplaced: no American record company would offer more than twenty-five thousand dollars for the album. But, in the end, the Japanese Denon label showed interest and he succeeded in persuading them to part with the kind of budget—a hundred thousand dollars—required for such an ambitious undertaking. Aria Hendricks did her utmost to convince her father to hire a producer. Tim Hauser would have been the obvious choice: he had produced most of the Manhattan Transfer albums, including *Vocalese*, and would probably have been prepared to take on Jon's project for a fee of around $2,500. For Aria, getting a producer wasn't about the artistic side but the business, efficiency, common-sense side. What was needed was someone with the practical expertise not to book the Count Basie band on a Sunday, for which they had to be paid time-and-a-half. But Jon had already made up his mind to supervise the recording and mixing himself and was serenely uninterested in any practical considerations—despite Aria's dogged arguments. The project was wildly ambitious not only in logistical terms, but artistically: on the face of it, the idea of writing lyrics to Trane's famous *Freddie Freeloader* solo was insane. It simply could not be done. "The fact that he was able to write those lyrics was a miracle in itself," said Aria. "I don't understand how it was done, even though I watched it with my own eyes. It was like watching a magician." Jon's approach to lyric writing for vocalese had not changed since the earliest days. He would sit and listen for about four days to whatever he was working on. There would be no test runs or drafts of any kind. He just listened with an intense, unshakeable focus. You could have had a marching band right next to him, complete with crashing cymbals, and it would not distract him from his attention to listening. After four days the lyrics would come out in about twenty minutes, fully formed, Aria recalled. "Maybe he would end up scratching out two or three words here or there, sometimes a whole line, but that was it," she added. "The way that he described it was, 'I'm just listening to what the instrument is saying.'"

However much her father disdained administration or even basic economics, Aria was impressed by the line-up he assembled for the album. "He always thought big. It was a testament to how well his work was thought of," she said. The famous singers—George Benson, Al Jarreau, and Bobby McFerrin, all of them supremely accomplished musicians—were daunted by the task and Jon found himself constantly encouraging and reassuring them. In truth, he couldn't really see what their problem was, since he himself found this kind of thing quite straightforward.

But as usual, he was disorganized; not only did he waste much of Denon's hundred thousand dollars, but he was forced to spend a further twenty-five thousand of his own money just to finish the project. What happened was that, after a few hours of mixing, the sixty-nine-year-old producer fell asleep on the studio couch, leaving Judith to make the decisions. As a result, she and Jon were mixed too loud, making it difficult to hear either the backing singers or the band. Inevitably, when Denon heard the mix, they rejected it. The problem was only resolved after a thirty-six-hour marathon remix session, and this was the version that was released. Aria's insistence on an experienced producer had been proved one hundred percent correct but, for her, witnessing all the wastage of time and money was a deeply upsetting experience. "And trust me," she said later, "I rubbed their noses in it for a long time!"

A mess it may have been, but in the end it was a musical triumph. Jon had thrown everything he knew into it. Yes, there was the usual complement of old recycled material: "Jumpin' at the Woodside"—now on its third outing in Hendricks's recorded *oeuvre*—likewise "Fas' Livin' Blues" (it had lost a *t* in the intervening years). But the album succeeds magnificently because of the palpable sense of energy and excitement it generates, as well as the sheer scale of the arrangements. The title track's lyric concerns Miles Davis's friend Fred Tolbert, a bartender at a 1950s Philadelphia jazz spot called The Nightlife. The recording is a *tour de force*. The chorus of voices singing "Fre—ddie" at the start is thrilling, the outpouring of lyrics for the solos is astonishing, and all the solo vocalesers are brilliant. "In Summer" (a.k.a. "Estate") features a lovely modernist string arrangement by David Berger. Jon's lyrics are stunningly beautiful: more than a match for the two English language lyrics previously written, on top of Bruno Brighetti's Italian original. Jon sounds old and vulnerable, the sensitivity of his vocal rendition adding to the poignancy of the song itself. Stanley Turrentine's "Sugar" features another Hendricks lyric to a tune that already had two different sets (by Turrentine himself and by Rare Silk producer Ted Daryl). Wynton Marsalis uses the half-valve trumpet technique pioneered by Louis Armstrong, in which the valve is pushed down a little to allow a more fluid, glissando style of playing. In his extensive liner notes, Hendricks brackets the tune "The Finer Things in Life" with "Gimme That Wine" as an "Anthem for the Agonized." Certainly he had not lost his gift for devil-may-care lyrics, and the Basie band backing, complete with shout chorus, is terrific fun. "Listen to Monk"—originally Monk's "Rhythm-a-ning"—was recorded on a whim during a break, and features wonderful scatting—first by George Benson, then by Al Jarreau, and finally by Hendricks himself.

There are a few issues with the vocal performances: Cheryl Bentyne's bat-squeaks on "High as a Mountain" are not pleasant to listen to, sounding like a stunt designed to impress. On Monk's "Trinkle Tinkle" Jon scats as if swilling mouthwash, while Judith sings noticeably flat on the incredibly high notes towards the end of "Swing That Music." But *Freddie Freeloader* was a critical success—seeming to vindicate Jon's initial idea, despite the cost overruns and family strife—and it was nominated for a Grammy. *Jazz Journal's* reviewer echoed the opinion of most critics: "As effervescent as it is thoroughly arranged, the music succeeds admirably in reviving glorious moments in jazz, while avoiding any hint of the museum," he said, describing it as "the best record I have heard from Hendricks in a long time." In later years, Jon said he thought it was the best of all his albums and that George Benson was the world's best jazz singer, never mind his prowess on the guitar. Unfortunately there was to be no second album with Denon, because soon afterwards the Japanese economy went into recession and the days of big recording budgets were over.

That said, for Jon Hendricks it was another in a long line of one-off projects. There seems to be no single straightforward answer to the question of why he never enjoyed a long and fruitful relationship with a single record company except that, perhaps as a man with some legal training and an eye for detail, he never saw a contract he liked the look of—i.e. one which didn't have at its core an attempt to rip him off. Another likely reason is that Hendricks would not brook any interference with his artistic vision. In the nineties, marketing came to dominate every aspect of life—including creative production—and he never recorded anything substantial in a studio again, despite a career that was to last another twenty-five years. A further reason for his less-than-prolific studio output may have been that his own questionable business ethics had finally caught up with him. A couple of years earlier, when Carmen McRae was preparing to record *Carmen Sings Monk*, she wanted to use some of the lyrics that Hendricks had written to Thelonious Monk's tunes. However, Hendricks was by now known by some music business insiders for his predatory behavior when it came to lyricizing tunes written by other people: he would sometimes claim them for his own company, Hendricks Music Inc. Before Carmen McRae could record the Hendricks lyrics to Monk's tunes, Hendricks was told to sign an agreement with Thelonious Music Corp. guaranteeing that all the titles would be changed. This would ensure that there would be no confusion about royalty payments. "Pannonica," for example, had to be renamed "Little Butterfly" (a title based on the Hendricks lyric), before Carmen's recording of it could go ahead. To make doubly sure that Hendricks did not try to claim the tunes for himself, a separate company was formed called Boobar (named after Monk's daughter Barbara, a.k.a. "Boo-boo") and Monk's songs were housed there.

But Jon was reluctant to sign the agreement. Carmen called him and said: "Listen you motherfucker, either you sign this agreement, or tomorrow when I go to the [studio] I'm gonna record someone else's lyrics." At this point, Jon decided to make himself scarce—but his lawyer Bill Krasilovsky had power of attorney to act for him, so in the end it was Krasilovsky who signed the agreement. Carmen then went ahead and recorded the songs. Once these were safely in the can, Jon resurfaced and all of a sudden it seemed that Krasilovsky did not have the right to sign the agreement after all. Jon then went ahead and claimed the songs for his own company. Today, ASCAP's entries for the Monk catalogue do not name Jon Hendricks as one of the writers, but advise "Contact ASCAP for more information." And on *Carmen Sings Monk*, every track is listed with a separate title for the lyricized version.

Undaunted, when it came to recording *Freddie Freeloader*, Jon was determined to include his lyricized version of Monk's "Trinkle Tinkle," which he put on the album with its original title—although he renamed "Rhythm-a-ning" as "Listen To Monk." As was his habit, he went ahead and claimed "Trinkle Tinkle" for Hendricks Music Inc., despite being told by Monk's son T. S. ("Toot") that he had no right to do so and that, moreover, Toot was vehemently opposed to him doing it.

Not everyone stood so firm; many were too dazzled by Jon's charm, affability and sheer genius to object. One of them was Benny Golson. Hendricks had registered Golson's famous "I Remember Clifford" with PRS in the UK, listing himself as sole author, which had allowed him to collect all the money for the song—whether instrumental or vocal. But Benny Golson was reluctant to pursue the matter, preferring to believe Jon when he said he would get around to changing the title—a promise he had no intention of honoring. Sometimes, faced with no alternative, Jon would preface a tune's original title with the word "Sing," hence Gigi Gryce's "Social Call" is listed in ASCAP both under its original title and as "Sing Social Call." Hence also "Sing Joy Spring," "Sing Blues for Pablo," and "Sing Shiny Stockings." Now and then, he missed a trick. For years he had been getting paid for both the vocal and the instrumental versions of the Bobby Timmons tune "Moanin'." But when the lyric copyright came up for renewal, Jon forgot to do the paperwork and so the whole song—music and lyrics—reverted to Timmons.

Soon after recording *Freddie Freeloader*, Larry Goldings accepted an offer from Maceo Parker to tour with him (and later on with Jim Hall and many others). For his replacement in the Hendricks rhythm section he recommended Slovenian-born Renato Chicco, who had just been with Lionel Hampton's big band. "Dress good," was Larry's only advice. When Renato went to the Battery Park apartment at two in the afternoon he found Jon still in his pajamas, drinking tea, and singing along with a Charlie Parker solo. Judith showed Renato into a room with a piano, put a cassette into the recorder, pressed record, and left him to play by himself for half an hour. Afterwards Jon regaled him with anecdotes for two more hours and that was the extent of the audition. It was followed by some rehearsals. If Renato played a chord that was different to what was on the original recording, Jon heard it and Renato would have to change it to the right one. Later, during the transition period, when Larry Goldings couldn't do all five nights of the group's engagement at the Catalina Jazz Club in Los Angeles, they flew Renato out to play on the fifth night. Arriving a day or two early, he was able to listen to Larry and to form a reasonably clear picture of how the band worked. As usual there were no charts—it all had to be learned from scratch. Larry Gales, Monk's last bass player, was also on that gig and a couple of subsequent nights in San Francisco. The endless churn of musicians continued and, like Larry Goldings and many others before him, Renato soon found he was expected to be the recruiting sergeant and boss for the rhythm section. Over the following years Reggie Nicholson, Joe Farnsworth, and for a long time Andy Watson all played drums; the bass slot was taken by Ugonna Ukegwo and Paul Gill. The next seven years became a blur, with gigs at places like Fat Tuesdays in New York, major festivals in Europe, and tours to Japan and Hong Kong, until economic conditions got worse and the gigs became fewer.

Touring was the circus it had always been. The Hendrickses did not believe in traveling light and checked in around twenty-five suitcases at every airport or train station; just getting from place to place was a logistical feat. And being late was the norm; planes would just be caught in time, or just missed. On one occasion, they had finished a show in Paris and we were heading for the south of France. Michele and her husband, Aria, Judith, Jon, Renato Chicco, and Kevin Burke assembled at the Gare de Lyon. Michele had a show of her own to do, with her Parisian rhythm section. For once they had succeeded in getting there early to avoid the usual stress, so everybody could relax a little. In fact, they had arrived at the station two hours ahead of time. This, in Jon's view, gave him ample opportunity to buy his newspaper and wander around the train station. Daughters and wife wagged their fingers in his face, warning him, "Don't get lost! Don't be late!" When the time came to board the train, pushing two big baggage carts with all the suitcases, there was of course no sign of Jon. It was a long train, divided into two sections with a locomotive in the middle, so that passengers could not walk between the two sections. Whoever made the train reservations had booked Aria and Renato into one section with all the suitcases and Judith, Jon, and Michele into the other. In those pre-cellphone days they could only hope that everyone else was on board—and that Jon would join them in time.

The minutes ticked by. Just before the train was due to depart, Judith leapt to her feet and said, "I have to go look for him." The train pulled out with both of them now missing. To make matters worse, Judith had everyone's tickets with her—which would have been a problem even if the party had not become separated into what was now three sub-groups. When the ticket inspector came along, Aria and Renato told him, "We don't have our tickets, they're in the other section of the train." "Well," said the ticket inspector, "There's a phone, so you can call the other side." Meanwhile, Michele and her husband were hoping that Jon and Judith were in the other section of the train. Just then an announcement came over the tannoy: "We ask Jon and Jimi Hendrix to please come to the phone." This set the entire train laughing. Michele went to the phone and asked, "What's going on?" At this point the truth became clear: neither Judith nor Jon, nor anyone's tickets, were on board.

Back at the Gare de Lyon, Judith finally gave up looking for her husband and went back to the train. Not to the same train, however, but a different one that was simply parked on a track and going nowhere. When the original train containing the rest of the group arrived at Avignon, Aria and Renato busied themselves unloading the twenty-five suitcases on to the platform. Michele and her husband ran along to help, since the train would only be stopping for two or three minutes. As they did so, they spotted a figure running toward them. It was Jon.

"Hey, I'm here!" he called.

"So where's Judith?" they asked.

"Well," explained Jon, proudly, "I took a taxi to the airport, a plane to Marseilles, and then a taxi to here." The taxi had traveled a hundred kilometers (around sixty-two miles).

"So where's Judith?" asked the daughters again.

"She's not here?" said Jon in surprise. Judith ended up taking another train to Avignon, arriving hours later. In truth, it was she who usually made the travel arrangements in their New York apartment, with the aid of a secretary. Said Renato:

> We would travel incredible distances and then not make much money at the end, so you had to take it in a spirit of adventure and learning. [Jon] would call me every gig because he needed me, and I would never ask about the pay. But for other members of the rhythm section [the money situation] was hard to deal with sometimes. There were … arguments about where we were staying, and do we have to share rooms?

SONGS FROM ALBUM

GROUP — SINGLES

JUMPIN' AT THE WOODSIDE — IN SUMMER — Eb
FREDDIE FREELOADER — STARDUST — Bb
SUGAR — EAS' LIVIN'
TAKE THE A TRAIN — C — TRINKLE TINKLE — Eb
HIGH AS A MOUNTAIN — THE FINER THINGS IN LIFE
(DON'T NEED THIS ONE) — LISTEN TO MONK/RHYTHMING
SWING THAT MUSIC — Ab
SING SING SING. — E---A-

JON'S SINGLE TUNES DONE FREQUENTLY

TELL ME THE TRUTH
EVERYTHING HAPPENS TO ME — G
FINER THINGS IN LIFE *
I STILL LOVE YOU (JOBIM) — G → RETRATO EM BRANCO E PRETO
GET ME TO THE CHURCH — G
SEPTEMBER OF MY YEARS — Gb
STARDUST — Bb
BACK IN YOUR ARMS (JOBIM) — A → CAMINHOS CRUZADOS
RHYTHMING — Bb
I'LL DIE HAPPY
LAMENT — A-
EVERYTHING STARTED IN THE HOUSE OF THE LORD *
C. C. RIDER
SAVEN MO
ROLL 'EM PETE
REFLECTIONS — Ab
DAYBREAK / ON THE TRAIL
BLUES FOR STRAYHORN — D
I REMEMBER CLIFFORD — C

A typical set list from the Nineties (courtesy Andy Watson)

As a rule, the shows would begin with the vocal big band and then, in the middle of the concert, there would be just the quartet. In this part of the show, Jon would sometimes construct a set around the work of a particular composer, with the tunes linked by anecdotes. He still loved ballads, such as "September of My Years," and the repertoire he took from Frank Sinatra— particularly the recordings Sinatra made with Basie. The set would include plenty of Monk—"Evidence," "Rhythm-a-ning," "In Walked Bud," "Reflections," "Round Midnight." He also often played Lee Morgan's "The Sidewinder." And there would always be a section of *Evolution of the Blues*, lasting anything up to forty-five minutes, complete with his versified links.

In 1992 Jon made a singing-only cameo appearance in the film *White Men Can't Jump*, as a member of the fictional Venice Beach Boys—three old black men who hang out and sing on the sidewalk in the opening credits. Hendricks, fellow jazz singer Bill Henderson, and soul artist Sonny Craver perform the traditional gospel tune "Just a Closer Walk with Thee." The same year, Jon was awarded a National Endowment for the Arts (NEA) American Jazz Masters Fellowship—along with Joe Williams and bass player Milt Hinton. The award, worth twenty thousand dollars, was designed for people who have made a significant impact on jazz. Afterwards Jon sent a note to James Zimmerman (who had proposed him via a friend, Cheryl Goodman), saying, "I'll enjoy spending our money." That year he recruited drummer Andy Watson, who stayed with him on and off until 1997 and thereafter full-time, until Jon finally stopped doing live gigs. Andy had been working with Renato Chicco at Augie's, a no-frills Upper West Side club in New York (since upscaled and renamed Smoke). Renato had recently secured the Jon Hendricks gig and, when the drum chair became available, Jon asked Andy to come over to his place and rehearse. Their first gig was in Reykjavik, Iceland. Another new member of the regular combo was guitarist Paul Meyers, who joined a tour with Jon, Judith, Aria, and Kevin Burke on which there were five horns as well as a rhythm section. On these gigs the set would always include a bossa nova or samba, often a slow one in a minor key called "Every Time They Play This Song," which Jon never recorded. He was also still relying heavily on the old Lambert, Hendricks & Ross material, because people always wanted to hear it—and he was happy to play it. In fact, he would probably have lost some of his audience if he hadn't played it. And, in any case, Jon had never really liked any music recorded since the early sixties.

Years after he had first thought of the idea, he continued to work spo- radically on lyricizing Miles Davis's *Miles Ahead*. Saxophonist and arranger Frank Griffith became involved in this long-standing project when a col- league, Mark Lopeman, asked him for help with the orchestrations. Frank's task was to transcribe the original Gil Evans arrangements by ear (no pub- lished scores existed then) and then transpose them into Jon's key, since his voice was considerably lower than Miles's trumpet. The next step was to reorchestrate the parts from a score originally written for around twenty players—mostly horns, with no piano or guitar—to a nonet with five horns and a rhythm section. But having the chord instruments, which do not appear on the original *Miles Ahead*, allowed him to shift several of the horn parts to piano and guitar. And from Frank's point of view, the presence of bass player Paul Chambers on the *Miles Ahead* recordings was very helpful: Chambers was an excellent reader, and it became evident to Frank that the bassist was playing specific written notes rather than simply responding to the roots of the chords. All the work of transcribing and adapting was difficult, but for him it was mitigated by the sheer enjoyment of getting to know great music so intimately. Jon's enthusiasm for the project was infectious and inspiring; Frank was more than happy to be a part of it. Later, Jon asked him to adapt Gershwin's "Oh Bess, Oh Where's My Bess?" from *Porgy and Bess*. After he had copied the chart by hand, they discovered at rehearsal that its key of D♭ was not suitable because one high note at the end was beyond Jon's reach. This meant it had to be rewritten in its entirety into the key of C—and this in the era before music software allowed charts to be transposed with the click of a mouse. The rewrite took Frank a week. When he rang Jon to discuss his key for "The Maids of Cadiz," he suggested E♭ might be a better key than E, to which Jon enquired, "Which one's higher?" Frank was not sure if he was serious or not, but it seems likely that he was. He also asked Frank to adapt some Basie arrangements, including a bluesy Basie/Joe Williams tune called "The Comeback." Typically, Jon would think of a song and want the arrangement to be ready the next day.

In the middle of the decade, Jon and Judith moved into a thirty-third floor apartment at Gateway Plaza in the Battery Park district, and remained there on and off for the next twenty-five years. The apartment overlooked the Hudson River going north. From the living room window you could see the Battery Park City promenade directly below and the New Jersey shoreline across the river. It was a compact little place and its walls were soon lined with framed posters of Duke Ellington, Louis Armstrong, and Billie Holiday—and of Jon himself, performing with Aria and Michele. At first, Aria hated it. "It had a fantastic view of the Statue of Liberty but I called the area 'the concrete desert,'" she said. "There was nothing else there." When Frank Griffith visited, he usually found Jon and Judith's apartment to be a hive of activity. The second bedroom was used as an office and was often full of young people, tending to such matters as publishing royalties and gig bookings. In fact, the Hendrickses owned two apartments which faced each other across a corridor. The second one was used for guests and also contained a lot of Jon's music. The couple's lifestyle and work were inseparable, with no demarcation between them: they lived for the work. This, combined with the good nature and optimism that shone through whenever Jon picked up a microphone, may have played a role (along with good genes) in his exceptional longevity.

After *Freddie Freeloader*, Jon guested on albums by several other artists—among them Al Grey, Georgie Fame, Joyce Moreno, Patti Dunham, Italian jazz singer Gegé Telesforo, and the Japanese DJs United Future Organization. The latter put out a hip new version, featuring Jon, of "I'll Bet You Thought I'd Never Find You," from the *Tell Me the Truth* album. Then, in 1993, Telarc agreed to release a live album with a combo called Jon Hendricks and the All-Stars. The name was not an exaggeration: *Boppin' at the Blue Note* features Aria, Judith, Michele, and Kevin Burke, with the current Hendricks rhythm section, plus Wynton Marsalis, Benny Golson, Red Holloway, and Al Grey. The *Boppin' at the Blue Note* album was to be recorded live over six nights at the New York club over the Christmas period. There were a lot of people involved but, even after decades in the business, Jon still had no idea how to run a rehearsal. His lack of interest in the conventions of jazz meant that he didn't even know how to refer to sections in a tune (section A, section B, etc.). If anyone asked he would reply, "Follow me!" In fact, this was his standard response to any musician who asked for some idea of what they were supposed to be playing. He used to tell a story about going to a job with a band who were already in the club. He had the songs he wanted to sing and, fortunately, the band knew them all. The club's owner came in to listen to a rehearsal and afterwards asked Jon, "How do they stay with you, when you're doing all this stuff?"

"Osmosis," Jon replied.

"Well how does it work by osmosis?"

"Ah's Moses, dey follows me."

Rehearsals for the Blue Note opening night, which was a Tuesday, started at two in the afternoon and continued until showtime at eight. By then, everyone was exhausted. Clark Terry's vision had deteriorated so badly due to his diabetes that he could barely read, so they had to give him a chart in three times the normal print size. After the second night Clark gave up and Jon was at a loss, because on the third night they were supposed to be recording. But his luck was in, on this occasion: he called Wynton Marsalis and asked whether he could recommend a suitable replacement. "Yes," said Wynton, "Me!" Meanwhile the afternoon-long rehearsals continued, in an effort to get the band tighter. Sometimes the rehearsals would stop for forty-five minutes while Jon told stories. For him a rehearsal was just a social event, but for the others, conducted in this way, they were a source of annoyance. There was also trouble in store on the technical front. The common way to record a live gig—a quartet, say—would be to mix it live to two tracks. But in this case there were five singers, four horns, and a four-piece rhythm section. The job of mixing so many sources live, unless the engineer had been working with them at gigs for at least a year, would have been well-nigh impossible. The best approach, in 1993, would have been to use several Alesis Digital Audio Tape (ADAT) machines, which would have allowed some degree of control over the mix, but Telarc refused to pay for them. As a result, the album was mixed badly and, not for the first time, Jon had to pay for studio overdubs. Listening today, it's hard to understand the point of *Boppin' at the Blue Note*.

It was yet another live album in a patchy recording career that had featured very many of them. Not only that, but Jon had released no fewer than seven of the eleven tunes before, meaning that the only "new" songs were the show tunes "I'm Getting Married in the Morning" and "Almost Like Being in Love" (a showcase for Michele), plus the old Big Joe Turner blues "Roll 'Em Pete" and Aria's impressive solo spot "Since I Fell for You." There was no sign of the new Miles Davis material. That said, Jon is in good voice and, as usual, succeeds in getting the audience chuckling. "Everybody's Boppin'" itself, which first appeared on *The Hottest New Group in Jazz*, gives everyone in the band a scat solo. It's a lot more fun than it sounds, with bits of "Popity Pop" thrown in for good measure. But overall, the album confirms what we already knew: that Jon was treading water, as he had been for decades. We could have been back in 1961.

Meanwhile, there were the usual college and private party gigs for the Hendricks group. At one private gig, in a swanky hotel, the musicians had been promised a hundred dollars each—a paltry amount, even then—but no cash appeared on the night. When some of the band members complained, Jon blandly assured them that they would get paid at some point. Eventually they received checks, but the hoo-hah was typical of the little hassles that would always accompany other people's professional dealings with Jon.

Kevin Burke took a break from the group to study between 1995 and 1997, and was replaced by Miles Griffith. By now, Jon had begun performing with a large ensemble called The Jon Hendricks Explosion. In April 1995—when they played the Banlieues Bleues festival in Paris—it featured Jon, Judith, and Aria, with the five horns (Andy Farber on tenor sax, Jay Brandford on alto, Gideon Feldstein on baritone, Kenny Rampton on trumpet, Wayne Goodman on trombone), plus Paul Meyers on guitar, Renato Chicco on piano, Paul Gill on double bass, and Marcello Pellitieri on drums. But as the nineties wore on, work became less plentiful in New York and in 1997 Renato decided to go back to Europe, recommending Peter Mihelič (another Slovenian) to take his place.

Even if the repertoire had become predictable, Jon (now aged seventy-six) found himself enjoying an increasingly exalted status in the jazz world, as one of its revered elder statesmen. Who else had been around at the birth of bebop, and was still alive? There were a few: George Shearing was and he remained active well into the twenty-first century, along with Barry Harris and Hod O'Brien. But Bird was long dead, Miles had passed in 1991, Dizzy in 1993, and Mulligan in 1996. Of the great singers, Ella also died that year and Sarah Vaughan was gone in 1990. Sinatra and Mel Tormé were still alive, but they had not sung with Charlie "Bird" Parker or hung out with Monk. Every successive Jon Hendricks birthday therefore became a celebration. Jon's seventy-fifth, on September 16, kicked off the Lincoln Center's 1996–97 season with a star-studded bash at Avery Fisher Hall. As well as Wynton Marsalis conducting the Lincoln Center Jazz Orchestra there was Judith, Aria and

Michele, Bobby McFerrin, Al Jarreau and The Manhattan Transfer, Dianne Reeves and Tony Bennett, plus Frank Foster and James Moody. Even after all these years, Jon was still hoping to get *Evolution of the Blues* to Broadway and he revived it again that year at the Monterey Jazz Festival, with Joe Williams and Dianne Reeves in the cast. He had recently toured Europe in a show called *Forty Years of Benny Golson* with a cast that included Golson himself, trumpeter Art Farmer, and trombonist Curtis Fuller. And when Wynton Marsalis wrote his oratorio *Blood on the Fields*, who else was he going to choose as his librettist but Jon Hendricks, whom he always insisted on addressing as "*Mister* Hendricks." In January 1999, Jon and Annie Ross had one of their reunions performing the old Lambert, Hendricks & Ross repertoire—"Down For Double," "Come On Home," "Centerpiece," "Cloudburst"—as a duo. Guitarist Paul Meyers played the third part when the singers couldn't cover it themselves. Leaving it until the last minute, as usual, Jon didn't call Paul until the first gig (at Shanghai Jazz in New Jersey) was only a week away. That week was spent listening to records in Jon's apartment; Jon would try to sing Dave's part but, since he didn't actually know it, Paul had to figure it out from listening. It was a huge amount of work, since nothing was in the original keys: the natural ageing process of their voices had seen to that. But, with repetition, it gradually became easier and Paul eventually figured out what he was supposed to do—namely, configure his part to fit in with Jon and Annie. "The first gig went great because no-one was paying any attention to my part anyway," he said. "Everyone was checking out just the fact that there's Jon Hendricks and Annie Ross on stage again for the first time in years."

For the guitarist, every gig with Jon Hendricks was a joy. Jon knew his stagecraft. He liked the band to go out and play an instrumental before he came on. This created extra anticipation and lifted the audience when he did appear. But, as a musician, no-one was going to get rich working with Jon. True, you were never going to get rich playing jazz anyway. Certain gigs would pay well and others would not, paying only enough for the players to continue working with him, which they all wanted to do. Paul and Jon bonded over their shared love of bossa nova, but Paul was also adept at comping in the Freddie Green style on the Basie material. And because he also took the trouble to learn the vocal parts and the rhythmic hits, he was able to add to the vocal ensemble. Even after Annie Ross was no longer there, he could add support to all the vocal parts. This meant that he would sometimes let the piano player do all the comping, while he doubled the background parts that Kevin Burke and Aria were singing together behind him (as on the Basie material) or add another voice, so it would approximate the sound of three horns. At a gig in Switzerland, Clark Terry sat in and they did "Mumbles" together—a tune of Clark's that Jon had adapted into "Jon's Mumbles." And at Minton's Playhouse in New York, Andy Bey and Jon sang "Bye Bye Blackbird" together, and both scatted on it. An appearance at the Blue Note was followed by one at Symphony Hall in Chicago, then the Jazz Bakery in Los Angeles. At one point during the Blue Note engagement, Jon spoke to Gene Lees on the telephone. Performing at his age was no longer a breeze.

"Are you going to be home over the weekend?" asked Lees.

"You bet," said Jon, "Flat on my back."

"Are you sick?"

"No!" said Jon, "Exhausted! This takes concentration!"

There was more to Judith's role than singing and handing out the band checks at the end of the night. She also had to keep Jon on the straight and narrow, getting him to cut down on the drinking and staying up late. For the Hendrickses, the wrong diet was the root of all sickness. They ate the best quality health foods, traveling everywhere with an industrial-sized juicer, which they would use to process the organic fruit and vegetables they bought. Their own health regime was a necessity: gigs could be long and punishing. At Ronnie Scott's, for example, there would be an opening band, followed by a long set from Jon and the band, then a break, and then the same sequence repeated. Then there would be the late jam session, which went on until three in the morning. Perhaps thanks to all the raw carrot juice, Jon still possessed extraordinary reserves of energy: once, after the main houses had finished and the jam had started, Paul Meyers was relaxing at the bar with his wife when he realized that Jon was back on stage, singing with the young musicians in the jam. Meanwhile, Judith was fretting and wondering how she would ever get him to come off. Even when he was backstage, Jon loved to talk to all the people who wanted to meet him—and there would be the inevitable stories. If Judith had not put him to bed, he would never have gone to sleep. It is to her eternal credit that she kept her husband healthy and enabled him to do what he did for so long.

In May 1999, through the combined efforts of Aria Hendricks and Roger Ray in the humanities department, Jon was awarded an honorary doctorate by his alma mater, the University of Toledo and, soon afterwards, a teaching position. In some ways, this was an amazing achievement, since Jon had never actually graduated. On the other hand, as Aria pointed out at the time, "All these jazz legends have one, two, three, four honorary degrees, why not him?" As well as recognition for all his years of achievement in jazz, the teaching post would provide Jon and Judith with an annual income for the first time in their lives, with a salary of around a hundred thousand dollars.

But, as with all things Hendricks, the path to academia was not smooth. To begin with, Judith had spent most of her life in New York, Marin County, or London and did not want Jon to take the job, telling him, "I did not marry you to be dragged off to your stupid little hometown!" Aria was furious with them both. "Are you out of your minds?" she asked, "You are no longer young!" The advancing years were something the Hendrickses never acknowledged. A commercial breakthrough was always just around the corner; they were always going to be "back on top." Aria pointed out their touring situation (not much happening) and the fact that they had no new recordings out, which made it increasingly difficult to get gigs. "How are you going to continue spending all this money if none is coming in? You need input in order to have output." This was the argument that finally gained some traction. "Negotiate with [the university]," she urged, "Talk to them about being able to leave to do your gigs and your projects, as needed."

The university agreed. Accommodation was the next issue. Aria assumed they would get along fine in Toledo with a modest, two-bedroom, furnished apartment; this would allow them to retain their two apartments in New York. It wasn't until two and a half years later that she learned they had bought a house. And not just any house, but a gracious mansion a few blocks from the campus at 3478 Brookside Road, in the exclusive Ottawa Hills. It was only about five miles west of where Jon was brought up, but a world away socially. Yet again, Aria hit the roof. It was partly that they had not told her, knowing how enraged she would be. They seemed to have no idea how to manage money. After a tour, whatever they had made would immediately be spent on a vacation. "How," she asked, "can you spend every dime you're earning ... in *Toledo*—the 'stupid little hometown?' Why are you spending all your money on a five-bedroom house, and you are two elderly people?" The answer eventually emerged: the house was a statement. Jon told the film-maker Audrey Lasbleiz that having a white wife and moving into a wealthy white area was a form of revenge. He was not blind to the fact that some of the middle-class whites who now courted him regarded him as "safe," a sort of "house nigger"—perhaps the educated, well-mannered kind of black man portrayed by Sidney Poitier in *Guess Who's Coming to Dinner* all those years ago. As he explained to his University of Toledo colleague Gunnar Mossblad:

> See that park over there? When I was a boy, they used to have swings and stuff, and we'd come over from the ghetto, and come into the park, and try and use the swings, 'cos we didn't have any-thing where I lived. And the police would run us off, every time. They wouldn't let us be in that park playing. So I decided to get the house across the street.

Perhaps it was not revenge, as such, but poetic justice. For good measure, he enjoyed parking his fat, shiny, white Lincoln Continental in the driveway for all to see.

As far as the job went, Jon also began to see it as an opportunity to give something back to the community he grew up in. He told Monk Rowe that his vocalese studies program would result in vocalese proliferating all over the world—Hank Jones, Ray Brown, and Max Roach had already agreed to be the band! Jon's idea of vocalese was not merely singing, but storytelling. "The setting of lyrics to established American jazz instrumentals, in a form so that it tells a story, with a beginning, middle and an end—a plot," was how he described it. The story always emerged from the song's title. The horns were

The house In Ottawa Hills (author photo)

the cast of characters. "All this has to work like an opera, or a well-constructed theatre piece, like a drama," he said. "Each person has to be a character within a previously defined plot structure." For Jon, true vocalese combined elements of theatre, literature, and above all poetry—even philosophy. "So it's a completely new form, but it's based on the depths of old established forms," he added (see lyrics chapter).

It was a grand vision but, before it could be realized, there were some practicalities to consider. At first, the university had no idea how to marshal the force of nature that was Jon Hendricks. He wanted to teach jazz history as well as vocalese—it was, after all, something he had done in California in the seventies and it would give him the chance to tell the thousands of stories he had at his disposal, as well as imparting his trenchant views on American social history. As one might expect, Jon's teaching style was not exactly founded on modern pedagogical theory. There were no lesson plans or learning outcomes—he would simply stand up and riff for forty-eight minutes—but if you were interested in the history of jazz, it was all gold. Even if you weren't, there would usually be some point that you could take away from the class. Yet again, he used what he had learned from his father's preaching: the parable, the sermon, the ability to draw something true and universal from an apparently rambling anecdote.

Jon founded a vocal group, The Jon Hendricks Vocalstra, made up of a combination of students and people from the local community who wanted to work with him. The aim was to do what he and Dave Lambert had originally intended to do on *Sing A Song of Basie*—having sixteen voices sing Basie. The rehearsals were very old-school: timetabled from four in the afternoon until six, Tuesday to Thursday, they might actually start at any point between those times and carry on into the night. Judith would bring food along and people would eat while they listened to the music Jon wanted to work on.

The timing of his appointment was lucky: on September 11, 2001 he and Judith were already up in Toledo for the beginning of the new academic year, when the Battery Park area where they lived was devastated by the destruction of the Twin Towers. Their daughter was less fortunate: Aria experienced the full horror, since her apartment was just down the hall from theirs. Earlier that year, the World Trade Center had featured in the shooting of the sleazy thriller *People I Know*, starring Al Pacino and Ryan O'Neal, in which Jon Hendricks was cast as himself. The film—with a score by Terence Blanchard— was ultimately delayed, as the World Trade Center scenes had to be re-edited to reflect the new reality.

Meanwhile, the university managers were becoming increasingly alarmed by Jon's demands for money and his habit of going his own way. He seemed to have no idea of the limits to what he could spend on projects which, he took for granted, would include first-class overseas travel. There was also some understandable resentment in the faculty about how much he was getting paid. Since neither organization nor fiscal discipline were his strongest suits, the university hired Gunnar Mossblad as Director of Jazz Studies the following year. The idea was to help Jon and his students by putting the whole jazz program on a firmer footing—or, as the faculty boss told Gunnar, "We need you to control him." For one thing, the Vocalstra would have to be less of a social gathering for Jon and more of a music rehearsal. Soon afterwards, there was an opportunity to take the whole Vocalstra group to England, and one of Gunnar's first jobs was to explain to Jon that the university couldn't afford it. In the teeth of his deep suspicion, Gunnar next began organizing the Vocalstra group and changed the history teaching schedule. Every year from now on, there would be one Vocalstra concert and one concert with the faculty group—as well as a gala fundraising event for the Jazz Studies program—all arranged around Jon's external commitments. He also persuaded the university to employ a full-time (instead of part-time) rehearsal pianist for the Vocalstra.

But there was more to the job than merely creating order out of chaos, and reining in the excesses of Dr. Hendricks; Mossblad saw it as his responsibility to educate the faculty and wider community about the importance of Jon Hendricks to the profile of the university and to jazz as a whole. Once they realized this, the Hendrickses started to warm to him and ended up treating him as one of the family. The Vocalstra students revered Jon; knowing his significance in the history of jazz, undergraduate and graduate students alike would enrol in the course purely because of his presence, and local people would join the Vocalstra for the same reason. For the non-music students taking the history class, who were unaware of him, an introduction would be given at the beginning of the semester. Jon certainly didn't hold back when it came to correcting attitudes about jazz:

> Teaching jazz, I have realized how de-culturalized America really is. This is America, with a culture of its own, that comes from its African people. I am intently concerned with acquainting the American people to the fact that not only do they have a culture, but if they are not up on that culture, how *stupid* they are, because there's not a country on this planet that does not love our culture.

In Paris, Anne Legrand, who was then studying for a music MA at the Sorbonne, as well as writing for a student newsletter about jazz, took a call from a man who introduced himself as Jon Hendricks. She started to laugh, assuming it was a friend playing a prank. But it turned out that it was indeed Jon Hendricks, and he wanted her help to bring his student Vocalstra to Paris. The concert duly took place on May 7, 2002 with the students of several Paris-based jazz singing teachers (including Michele Hendricks) as well as Jon's own Vocalstra. A few days earlier, on the fourth, he had delivered a talk at the Bibliothèque Nationale de France on the history of jazz singing and scat, with the same participants. And afterwards on the eleventh—again with Anne Legrand's help—he played a gig at Paris's Duc des Lombards club. In an article for *Jazzman* magazine, she reported that Jon had been listening intensively to classical music at home. Why should the classics not be lyricized? If vocalese was the serious art form Hendricks believed it to be, the work of classical composers could certainly be deepened and improved by the addition of lyrics. Rimsky Korsakov's *Shéherazade* and *Porgy and Bess* were on the same level, artistically. He was also setting words to Rachmaninoff's Second Piano Concerto and working on lyrics to Gershwin's Piano Prelude no. 1 ("Music of the Spheres") for *Across the Blue Meridian*, a 2004 album by the New York a cappella ensemble Pieces of 8. As far as he was concerned, part of his mission as an educator was to link the worlds of jazz and classical music. And perhaps, he thought, it was time to assemble a larger Vocalstra.

On October 3 of the previous year, Jon had recorded some tunes in Berkeley, California, with his old sixties bandmates Larry Vuckovich and Noel Jewkes. These ended up on an album under Larry's name called *Reunion*. (Twenty years earlier, he had also contributed to the latter's album *Cast Your Fate*.) After the recording, Noel drove Jon over to see his sister-in-law Bernice in Larkspur, near Mill Valley—and that was the last time he ever saw him. "I don't think Jon was really at his best on that session," remembered Noel, "His voice started to crack a bit ... He made up for it with his humor and spontaneity. We did a couple of small festival dates at that time, one in Fairfax and one in San Rafael."

Perhaps Jon was aware of his declining vocal powers. At any rate, for the first time in his life, he decided to take some singing lessons with university vocal tutor Eric G. Johnson. Judith learned that, as a faculty spouse, she too was entitled to lessons, so Eric agreed to work with both of them. But, having personally witnessed Jon performing with Annie Ross and Aria, trading fours and eights at a concert at the university, he found it difficult to imagine what he could possibly teach the eighty-one-year-old jazz legend. His default aim as a singing coach was to promote a sense of ease and a good sound with the least amount of breath. As a disciple of Berton Coffin, author of the book *Overtones of Bel Canto*, Eric believed that vowel sounds should be the main focus. In particular, how could singers succeed in reaching high notes? The technique was to tune the vowel using the International Phonetic Alphabet (IPA), the most basic vowel sound of which is *uhhh*—the sound you make if you simply open your mouth and make a sound without shaping it. Eric had also reached the conclusion that many singers' vocal problems would go away if they simply practiced singing in French, since a nasal intonation eased the transitions between sounds. In the end he did around eight lessons with Jon but, as he had suspected, there wasn't much he could do to improve Jon's singing. "I really couldn't do anything with Judith either," he admitted. "She had learned to sing those notes that Annie Ross could sing in the arrangements, and they were pretty awful."

As agreed, the outside projects continued alongside the teaching. In June 2002 Jon began rehearsing for a show at Chicago's Park West, with the other three members of a vocal ensemble called Four Brothers. This was the brainchild of Kurt Elling—to put together a group of male jazz singing legends, consisting of himself, Jon Hendricks, Kevin Mahogany, and Mark Murphy. On the fifteenth they opened for Nancy Wilson and Ramsey Lewis at the Ravinia Festival. In the summer of the following year they went on tour in Europe and the US, with a final performance back in Chicago in the Summer of 2005—this time at the Millennium Park. Kurt had first met Jon Hendricks when the latter was conducting a master class during a previous Ravinia Festival, and he himself was one of the participants:

> I did "Doodlin'," and Jon sat on stage and laughed as if I had made up every joke. Almost tears in his eyes, laughing. And he just got up from his chair and embraced me. There wasn't any advice, just, "This is what it sounds like."

Thereafter came lunches and dinners and sitting-in at gigs, as they became friends.

The Four Brothers planning took years. Everyone's individual tour dates had to be worked around, then there was the scheduling of rehearsals and preparation of charts, but it was all only logistical—there was the will to make it work on all sides. They rehearsed at Kurt's house in Hyde Park near

Poughkeepsie, New York. An interesting contrast of characters and styles soon emerged: Kevin Mahogany was never one for a lot of homework, which caused a certain amount of friction. Mark Murphy was anxious about singing defined parts, and had worked hard and come well prepared—especially with the Miles vocalese—but still needed some guidance. ("Never the same note once," as Kurt put it.) Jon Hendricks could only sing the melody or harmony parts that he already knew and there could be no jumping to some new part, such as the alto rather then the tenor—it was too deeply ingrained.

Mark Murphy and Jon Hendricks at Kurt Elling's house (credit: Marc PoKempner)

10 Keep Smiling

Jon's phenomenal work rate continued unabated. In 2002 he told the world that he had written his autobiography, with the title *Mind On Fire*. On February 3, 2003 it was announced on his website that he had acquired a new assistant, who was helping him answer questions on his message board and—more importantly—work on his lyric books (he was hoping to have the first volume out later that year). He also had in mind to write a book of jazz history. Meanwhile, he continued to perform occasionally with Jon Hendricks & Company, and periodically reunited with Annie Ross. In January 2004 the Vocalstra performed for the International Association of Jazz Educators Conference, in the Mercury Ballroom at the New York Hilton. That summer, the Toledo Jazz Festival invited Mark Murphy to come and sing. Jon Richardson, one of the organizers, had urged Mark to sing some ballads—of which he was an acknowledged master—but as soon as Mark realized Jon was in the audience, he scatted the entire set. "He didn't give a damn who else was there," said Jon Richardson, "It was for no-one's benefit but Jon's."

On June 6, during the sixtieth anniversary of the D-Day landings, France honored Jon Hendricks with its highest decoration—the Legion d'honneur— for his army service during the conflict, as well as for his extensive contribution to vocal jazz. He featured in the event's TV coverage and in an article in *Le Monde*: "La Guerre en Noir et Blanc," by Benoit Hopquin, which told the story of his wartime experiences. He was presented with the award in Herouville-Saint-Clair by the governor of Normandy and it reinforced the love and respect he had always proclaimed for France and the French people, because it also honored his international performing career. Jon had always said that his ideal was to live in France: as well as loving the culture, he was proud of his long-term popularity there. Whilst in Paris he sang at the Duc des Lombards club and at a private concert for Gérard Bremond (the club's owner at the time). In August he and Michele appeared at Festival de Jazz de Ramatuelle, a small village in the south of France, and were filmed by Audrey

Lasbleiz. It was the beginning of her five-year documentary project, called *Tell Me the Truth*.

Back home, Judith had not only come to terms with living in Toledo but, contrary to her expectations, it had turned out to be the best time of her life. She loved the town, and she loved the house. No matter that the nearby creek overflowed every year, causing water to flood the basement three times during their tenure, damaging Jon's archive of charts and other paperwork shipped over from Mill Valley (as did a fire, on one occasion). The house also contained a music room that was stuffed full of tapes, LPs, and manuscripts. It was not so much an office—more a listening space. When friends came over to listen to music, there would be none of the usual anecdotes and self-aggrandizement; he would simply sit listening, staring at the floor. (The power of the music always seemed to render him a humble listener.) Local musicians would be invited to come over and play in the Hendricksces' living room and there was a jazz club in Toledo that Gunnar Mossblad would take his students to, and which Jon and Judith would sometimes attend. Other local jazz musicians would turn up too and, on these occasions, Jon would exercise his uncanny knack of creating instant *esprit de corps*.

In 2005 Jon created a new vocal group called Lambert, Hendricks & Ross Redux, in which he and Judith toured with Toledo singer and musician Joel Hazard. They performed at the Blue Note in Milan, the Blue Note in New York, the Jazz Bakery in Los Angeles, and on New Year's Eve at the Kennedy Center with the Lionel Hampton Orchestra. At the New York Blue Note the three of them were accompanied by a trio consisting of Peter Mihelič on piano, Neal Miner on bass, and Andy Watkins on drums. Hendricks's solo set consisted of "Feed Me," "Home Cookin'," "Tell Me the Truth," "Estate," "Blues March" (a Benny Golson tune that he never recorded) and "Swingin' Till the Girls Come Home," before the other two came on and sang "Take the A Train," "Everything Happens to Me," and "Avenue C" with him. He revived the trio in 2008, replacing Hazard with Kevin Burke, who had now completed his academic studies, and they premiered their show at the Jazz Standard on July 5. Jon told Sanford Josephson:

> We had standing ovations every show. Then we went up to Boston and did the Regattabar in the Charles Hotel. It was unbelievable. We did two full houses each night to standing ovations. Then we did the Providence Jazz Festival. The mayor gave us the key to the city.

The Redux repertoire was old Lambert, Hendricks & Ross material like "Centerpiece" and "Jumpin' at the Woodside," because theirs was an older, nostalgia-seeking audience, "but I did add some new things that were mostly duets between my daughter [Aria] and me," he said, "like 'Four.' She loves that. She did Miles and I did Horace Silver's piano solo." They played four nights at the Jazz Standard in New York with Ray Gallon on piano, Paul Gill on bass, Andy Watson on drums, and guitarist Paul Meyers. However, the *New York Times* reviewed the gig and came away with the distinct impression that the old magic was fading. "Of L, H & R Redux, it can be said that at least the spirit is intact," conceded Stephen Holden:

> As long as Mr. Hendricks, one of the most joyous performers I've ever seen, is at the helm, it could hardly be otherwise. He is an intrepid musical missionary for a difficult style that has its own set of complicated but flexible rules: solos must not only follow the same notes as improvised instrumental solos, they should also take into account the timbre, note-bending and dynamics of those solos, as well as the sounds of the particular instruments on which they were played. Some attempt must be made to articulate words that often flow in semi-nonsensical torrents. When the three voices sing together, a semblance of a coherent harmonic blend is essential.
>
> On Thursday Ms. Hendricks's bright, shiny voice, leaping into twirly peaks, was the trio's sonic linchpin. Mr. Burke offered witty muted trumpet imitations. But Mr. Hendricks's voice was husky and wavering. He sounded strongest outside the trio, singing "September of My Years." But another solo, the chromatic João Gilberto classic "Estate," mostly eluded him. As the Lambert, Hendricks and Ross standards "Cloudburst," "Centerpiece," "Jumpin' at the Woodside" and "Moanin'" were dutifully trotted out, the enthusiasm was there, but the blend wasn't.

Whatever Hendricks's waning powers, it struck his UT colleague Gunnar Mossblad—as a tenor saxophone player himself—how much Jon was essentially a tenor saxophonist too, but without the saxophone. Jon had been personally close to John Coltrane, but lost touch after Trane started playing in his "sheets of sound" style. To Hendricks, there could be nothing better than playing bebop melody; Coltrane's strange, hypnotic deluge of notes made no sense to him. One of the first things Gunnar wanted to work on with Jon, therefore, was Trane's 1965 masterpiece *A Love Supreme*, but Jon pulled the shutters down on that idea—at first:

> I wanted to bring him back to Coltrane, because I love Coltrane. So I asked him, knowing that his dad was a preacher, and that he was very spiritual, I asked him, "Would you consider just coming back and doing your thing with Trane's prayer?" And he said, "Fine, we'll do it."

Coltrane had written the words in early December 1964 and—on the ninth of that month, in a kind of reverse vocalese—played them note-for-note in the out-of-time tune "Psalm," the fourth movement of the *Love Supreme* suite. He had put the handwritten poem on the music stand in front of him, and "played" it, as if reading notes on a stave. "Trane played the words," said Gunnar, "so I had Jon read the words, and then I echoed them [on tenor], and it came out beautiful. And from then on, he was back with Trane, and reconnected with him spiritually." They recorded it in November 2007.

An elderly man with diminishing energy, Jon now found it hard to manage more than one teaching session per day, whether it was a lecture or the Vocalstra. In the same year a new interim dean, who had no idea who Jon Hendricks was, looked at his light schedule and tried to replace it with a full teaching load. Jon put his foot down and filed an age discrimination grievance against the university, asking Gunnar to attend some of the meetings, at which the latter articulated Jon's importance and defended his position to the university. Admitting defeat, the dean and other administrators took the famous jazz singer out to a very fancy dinner and gave him a year off, at full pay. In 2008 Jon came back to take on the more realistic teaching schedule that Gunnar had persuaded both him and the university to live with.

Audrey Lasbleiz's documentary *Jon Hendricks, Tell Me The Truth* was finally completed in 2009 and debuted at Le Balzac cinema on the Champs Elysée in Paris on October 4, in the presence of Jon himself. (It was later shown on French TV.) In 2010 Holli Ross, who had known Jon for years, asked him if he would contribute the liner notes for her forthcoming album, *You'll See*. It was a reasonable request: for many years she had been constantly guest-listed into his gigs, invited on stage to sing, and generally treated as a good friend. Jon enthusiastically agreed. But as time went by, there was no sign of the notes. Holli was driven to calling Judith and asking her to prompt him. When he finally wrote something, it was his well-worn story about Rodgers and Hammerstein and their wives, and he went on to talk about himself as a lyricist, but entirely failed to mention either Holli Ross or her music. "Well," he explained, when Holli queried this, "I didn't want to be critical." She decided to delve deeper. "What do you hear when you listen to my tunes? Who are the influences? What about those vocaleses? What do you think I'm trying to do?" It was a struggle but, in the end, she was able to piece together from his replies all the things that she had been hoping for from his liner notes. ("As a lyricist, Holli speaks from the heart and she does it well with relevance and quick wit.")

While Jon's capabilities in other areas were obviously in decline, he continued to shine as brightly as ever on the live stage, where he frequently appeared with his daughters and Kevin Burke. In November 2010 he went to London to play Ronnie's during the London Jazz Festival. The gig sold out, with the master on top form and up to his old tricks, including playing the flute on a drumstick. ("This is my flout. It's different from a flute. I flout convention.") The two sets were composed of classic cuts from the Hendricks catalogue: a breathy and poignant "Desafinado," a magnificent "Listen to Monk" from the

Freddie Freeloader album, "Everybody's Boppin," and other familiar Lambert, Hendricks & Ross numbers like "Centerpiece" and "Moanin'"—as well as his perennial choice of ballad, "September of my Years." The following September, back in New York, he played at the Lincoln Center's Rose Theater with Jimmy Heath. Dianne Reeves and Bobby McFerrin were also on the bill. These days standing ovations were the norm, as was the ancient material: "It's Sand, Man," "Come On Home," "Jumpin' at the Woodside," and "In Walked Bud." Along with his usual group of back-up singers there was the eight-piece band directed by tenor saxophonist Andy Farber. "Never missing a note, he mentioned his recent ninetieth birthday on Sept. 16," reported the *Amsterdam News*. "Dianne Reeves asked, 'Did you find the Fountain of Youth?' Hendricks responded laughingly, 'I had a séance with Ponce de León.'"

A witty rejoinder. But one of the penalties of a long life is to experience the deaths of those younger than yourself; far worse when your own offspring pre-decease you. Jon had already lost his daughter Colleen. In April 2012 his younger son Eric, whose type two diabetes had been affecting him severely for the last twelve years, died aged only fifty-seven. Judith had been diagnosed with with melanoma in January 2006, but had since been declared clear of cancer. The Hendrickses' healthy eating regime was a bulwark against its return.

How much longer could Jon carry on? A group dedicated to the close harmonies of Lambert, Hendricks & Ross and The Manhattan Transfer booked him for a studio recording at Water Music in Hoboken in July 2012. The Royal Bopsters Project was a well-timed swansong for Mark Murphy, Jon Hendricks, Bob Dorough, and Annie Ross (all of whom have since died), plus Sheila Jordan. Jon's contribution was the opening track, "Music in the Air" (a.k.a. Art Farmer's "Wildwood").

The Hendrickses' erratic form in business matters came to light once again after the group played four nights at the Duc des Lombards in Paris later that year. On the first night Van Morrison came to listen, sitting in the balcony wearing shades, with his hat pulled down over his eyes. He'd flown in from Belfast especially, with no entourage. The next evening he visited Jon in the dressing room. ("I've come to get some healin'," he explained.) Invited to sit in he sang "Centerpiece," which expanded into some other old blues. Six months later, in spring 2013, Jon was at Ronnie Scott's and still showing extraordinary vitality, playing two sets a night for three or four nights in a row. At the final gig they couldn't get him off the stage, as he sat in for over an hour with the band. Again Van Morrison showed up backstage. Discussions began about some possible recording project the two could do together—perhaps four Hendricks tunes, four Morrison tunes, and a couple of classics? (They had worked together before on a 1991 Georgie Fame album called *Cool Cat Blues*.) The project began to take shape. Eventually they agreed on four days of recording in Bath, England. Van would pay for everything. Jon would receive twenty-five percent and not have to put in a penny himself. All the travel and accommodation would be taken care of. Judith reminded Van's people that Jon was ninety-two and would need to come over three days early to give him time to recover from the transatlantic journey. That was fine, and everything was booked. At this point Judith insisted that they be paid *in cash*. This they could not agree to, and the project fell apart.

It was a major lost opportunity. Such was Van Morrison's fan base that anything he released would automatically sell a quarter million copies. The idea had been to record the album then tour, with Jon opening for Van. It would have exposed Jon to a potentially new audience, and there could have been TV shows too. Even if not quite "back on top," Jon's career would have gained a big boost if, behind the scenes, he'd had someone like Tony Bennett's son Danny, who refreshed Tony's career by getting him on MTV and pairing him with modern singers like Amy Winehouse. Despite the album debacle, there were no hard feelings and the Hendricks group sang with Van in New York at Madison Square Gardens' Hulu Theatre and at the Beacon Theatre on successive nights.

By now Jon and Judith were spending more time in New York than Toledo, and eventually they sold the house in Ottawa Hills. Although Judith enjoyed their quiet life in Ohio, Jon found it too slow, missed his New York jazz friends, and wanted to go back. He continued teaching his history of jazz classes at the university, and all went well for a number of years. (During his final years at the university, when Jon and Judith came to town, they lived in a residential hotel.) His teaching assistant Atla DeChamplain told the *Toledo Free Press*:

> Most of [the students] aren't music majors and we show a lot of black-and-white footage. They wonder why it's relevant. They'll be like, why do we care? Then [Jon] comes in and totally hooks them. He charms them, he gets them engaged, and makes it real.

Then, in 2013, a new head of department was installed; the following year, he made another effort to get rid of Jon. Gunnar Mossblad—well aware of what the authorities were up to—told them, "Look, you don't tell Picasso he can't paint any more. Why should you do that to Jon?" But his arguments fell on deaf ears, and once again the ninety-two-year-old was saddled with a full faculty teaching load—a schedule that lasted all day, Monday to Friday. Jon refused even to consider it, and the harassment began all over again. This time, he did not bother with middle management, instead going direct to the president of the university (as was his inclination in most business affairs) and negotiated a buy-out. He wanted three years' pay and benefits. The university offered him one year, so in 2015 he simply failed to show up. They continued to pay him, however, and in 2016 he finally retired (with a one-year buyout), so it was a victory of sorts.

Before Jon left the University of Toledo for good, and mindful of his still uncompleted Monk project, Gunnar recorded him singing seven or eight of his previously unrecorded lyrics to Monk tunes. Over the years he had lyricized "Trinkle Tinkle," "Evidence," "Rhythm-a-ning," "In Walked Bud," "Reflections," and many others, but had not recorded them all. Gunnar arranged the song structures and endings in the way that that Jon wanted and he then overdubbed the singing, just a couple of tunes at a time. "I wanted to document him doing it, a little at a time," said Gunnar. "Obviously he was not in his prime voice, but it is moving." In 2019 Gunnar was still hoping to put out this multitracked recording with Monk's son T. S., who owned the rights to his father's music, playing drums.

On November 18, 2015, and in the midst of Jon's final battle with the university, Judith Hendricks suddenly and unexpectedly died from an aneurysm. Aria had had a long telephone conversation with her at around 12:30 a.m. At 7:15 a.m., she received the call that her mother had passed away half an hour earlier. Judith, sixteen years her husband's junior, had for years borne the strain of looking after her elderly husband, who was now suffering from dementia. Ironically, Aria had finally convinced her to hire some professional help, a woman who was only on her second day in the job when Judith died. Jon and Judith were "more entwined and closer than any couple you've ever encountered," said Aria:

> They were married fifty-six-and-a-half years, and with almost no exceptions, they were together twenty-four seven that entire time. I can remember three days that they were apart in the late seventies and again between 2007 and 2008 when she was ill.

Aria began traveling with Jon in Judith's place and became very close to her father over that period. She moved in with him, fearing that the shock would cause him to follow Judith very quickly. His own decline had begun some time before. On the road, the dementia was becoming noticeable, although it didn't seem to render him angry, depressed, or sad. In recent years Judith had always made sure he had his lyrics in front of him, which seemed ridiculous for a man whose memory had once been like a steel trap. Now, his inability to recall the lyrics and linking dialogue from *Evolution of the Blues*, which he'd performed on and off since 1961, was difficult to watch. On one occasion, he started repeating a section they had sung ten minutes earlier. The overseas touring ceased soon afterwards and they stuck to gigs like Minton's, but nowadays the fog would descend. Towards the end, Jon not only needed the lyrics on stage in front of him but Aria would have to be there too, ready to point to the right line.

But musicians still wanted to work with the great Jon Hendricks. He appeared on three tracks of a 2016 release by the J. C. Hopkins Biggish Band titled *Meet Me At Minton's*: performing vocalese on "In Walked Bud," singing as part of the ensemble on the album's title track, and crooning a duet on the Monk tune "Ask Me Now" with the singer Jazzmeia Horn (seventy years his junior). But that year marked the end of his live performances. Aria believed her father's dementia had begun as early as 1996. Prior to its onset, he had a vast amount of material in his pad and was willing to sing almost anything, but gradually he would attempt fewer and fewer new songs, until his repertoire was distilled down to two sets. His onstage shtick would sometimes stray beyond the bounds of the good-natured banter that had characterized his career. After making some observations about his children, he would say:

> My kids are doin' it themselves. I'm not leavin' them *nothin'*. Because when I die, in my will it says, "I Jon Hendricks, bein' of sound mind, leave my kids *nothin'*, 'cos I *spent it!*"

It got the cheap laugh, but to some observers it looked as if he meant it. Towards the end of Jon's life there was an evident closing down of his interests until, just before his death, the only thing he seemed to care about was food. He had become the opposite of his old self. Aria said:

> He [had been] extremely verbose and very plugged in and thoroughly aware of everything that was happening, and always had something to say about everything, and always had an interesting turn of phrase, or a pun or a comment. And he went from that to its inversion—of being silent. It was so strange. He retreated.

There was one final triumph in the musical career of Jon Hendricks, for which we need to rewind a few years. Back in February of 2011, he had conducted a master class at the Royal Academy of Music (RAM) in London. A jazz choir—The London Vocal Project, directed by the RAM's Professor of Jazz Composition Pete Churchill—performed some Lambert, Hendricks & Ross material in his honor, welcoming Hendricks with "Li'l Darlin'" and "Swingin' Till the Girls Come Home." The Australian jazz singer Anita Wardell joined him on "Moanin'." Then followed the master class and Churchill interviewed Hendricks, mentioning how groundbreaking the overdubbing of *Sing a Song of Basie* had been. Churchill and Hendricks discovered that they shared a background of growing up in a church environment, Churchill's father having been the organist and choir director at London's St. Martin-in-the-Fields. They also bonded over the language of the church, particularly Jon's deep familiarity with the King James Bible. "I got his references," said Churchill. The conversation came around to Jon's cherished *Miles Ahead* project, which he had now been working on for half a century. The *Tell Me the Truth* album had included his "Blues for Pablo" lyric, and *Billboard* reported at the time that he plans recording all of the tunes in that Davis evergreen, creating his own unique lyrics for Davis' solos. Several of these Davis tunes are already in the can and will appear on his second Arista LP.

As we know, this LP was never recorded. Interviewed more than twenty years later, Jon claimed that he had now finished all the words and said he was just looking for a record company to record it. In fact, the lyrics were far from complete, even then. Another fifteen years passed and, as soon as Jon mentioned *Miles Ahead*, it was immediately obvious to Pete Churchill that such a piece would be perfect for the London Vocal Project—if it were ever completed. He suggested the idea to Hendricks, who liked it. Churchill emailed Judith and asked when they were coming back to Europe. It turned out they were going to be in Paris in July, so on the appointed day he caught a Eurostar train at six in the morning and met them there.

Jon was leaving the next day, so they got down to work immediately. As Pete had requested, Jon had brought all his lyric sheets plus some transcriptions of Gil Evans's scores from the Smithsonian. At this point it became clear not only how much work Jon had done, but also how much there was still to do. As they spent the next eleven hours going through each score, Pete realized there were no lyrics at all for the track "Miles Ahead," and that Jon was blocked on "Springsville." The three tunes nearest to being finished were "My Ship," "The Maids of Cadiz," and "The Duke," and for the next couple of years these were the target for completion. In the meantime, Junko Arita at the New School in New York did some work on the project with Jon, but progress was slow. Pete thought they could finish "My Ship," but they still needed the intro—which was the link from the previous tune—and they also needed the intro to "The Duke." He kept pressing Jon, who finally grabbed a pencil and started writing on his yellow legal pad, and the entire lyric came out in one piece. It all flowed beautifully, complete with rhyme wherever the music suggested words ought to rhyme. It seemed to Pete (as it had to many of his previous colleagues) that Jon was not imposing his ideas on the music, but rather, through some strange alchemy, pulling out lyrics that were already there. "My Ship" was a tune that already had lyrics (by Ira Gershwin), but many more were needed for the full lyricization of Gil Evans's orchestrations and Miles Davis's solos—and Miles's phrasing of the melody did not match the original lyrics. (It was the same story with "Summertime," hence Jon's abbreviated "Summertime, and the livin' ain't bad" lyric.) Overall, Pete found that Jon had written lyrics for most of Miles's solos and his playing of the melodies, but not the orchestrations—especially the backing figures and shout choruses. But "My Ship" was completed and the London Vocal Project tried it out, live at London's The Forge, with Anita Wardell singing Miles's trumpet parts.

Finishing the whole thing, however, was a protracted business and the next meeting between Churchill and Hendricks wasn't until 2014. The choir was due to perform a gig one Sunday afternoon at Ronnie Scott's, where more of the material would be heard in public for the first time. But the tunes they wanted to do had still not been completed, so the choristers clubbed together and paid for Churchill to go to New York, where he stayed in the Hendrickses' guest apartment. Full lyrics to "The Duke" emerged on the first day. Churchill immediately sent it to Anita Wardell in London; she learned it, recorded it and sent the recording back three days later. By now Churchill had figured out how to work with Jon Hendricks. Unwittingly, he had slipped into the same role that Dave Lambert had occupied all those years ago. Each morning he would knock on Hendricks's door and say, "Time to get to work." The two of them would sit together on the piano stool and whole lyrical phrases would now start to emerge. There were some inner parts that Hendricks knew but had not yet articulated. Sometimes they would spend two hours on eight bars and nothing would happen. Bearing in mind the underlying concept of the suite as a musical dialogue between Miles Davis's trumpet and the other instruments, the trick was to turn it into a verbal dialogue, a conversation. "I'd try—'Well, Miles is saying this, so what's Gil saying?' And you'd get that Greek chorus thing—the truth is in the backing vocals," said Churchill. It helped that Hendricks had already written his "Blues for Pablo" lyrics. This one completed tune served as a template for the rest: the conversation between soloist and choir.

With Pete Churchill in Jon's apartment (courtesy Pete Churchill)

At one point, Hendricks began to speak and Churchill failed to realize at first that he was coming out with the lyric for the tune "Miles Ahead." In keeping with the solo/backing vocal dialogue idea, it turned out that Miles's trumpet was saying, "This is the promised land," while the orchestra was warning, "But the journey never ends." Over the decades, Hendricks had devised his own creative strategies for lyric writing. When he was blocked, he would sometimes write the entire lyric out again up to the point where the block was, in the hope that the momentum of the creative flow would make the next line obvious. But it didn't always work. On the tune "Miles Ahead," a method Churchill tried was to suggest lyrics that he knew were appalling, knowing that Hendricks would be so incensed that he just *had* to come up with something better.

As Churchill passed Judith in the kitchen, she murmured, "I can hear what you're doing, it's great!" And when Hendricks complained he couldn't do any more, Judith would say, "Jon, he's come three thousand miles—you're gonna do this shit." As she passed around the mud-colored fruit and vegetable juices, which sometimes tasted as bad as they looked, she'd say to her husband, "You're gonna live to 140—you've got a lot more work to do." Jon described himself as her first child. Frequent diversions into anecdote were met with, "Oh, is it story time now, or are you going to do some work?" She was a slave driver, albeit not in the league of Willard Alexander. On one occasion, Jon was on his way to Chinatown for acupuncture because of a trapped nerve in his hand due to a fall. Afterwards they went to eat in a Chinese restaurant and he ordered lobster and tore it to pieces with gusto. It was a twenty-five-minute walk back to the apartment and Judith pressed on ahead, calling behind her, "Come on, Jon! This is the only way I'm gonna keep you fit." Jon, hobbling behind her, called, "Wait up, Judith," and then he fell into the gutter. "Oh you're all right," declared his wife, striding on.

The original Gil Evans scores were all written for the individual instruments, in concert, E♭ or B♭. One necessary task, Churchill realized, was to reduce them to the point where they could be played on the piano. It was an essential interim stage before the parts could be distributed among the singers. In performance there would be no piano—merely bass, drums, and voices.

In December he returned to New York and this time they were able to finish the whole project. Aria came over to the apartment, they opened the champagne, and only then did it hit Pete that his choir would have to learn the whole thing. The initial idea was to perform it in London, but complications immediately ensued: key people were never available when needed and finding the right venue proved a major headache. "I was losing the will to live," said Pete. Then, in July 2016, the RAM presented Quincy Jones with an honorary doctorate and asked Pete to look after him for the day. Chatting with Quincy in the principal's office, Pete reminded him that Jon had lyricized

Oscar Pettiford's "Swingin' Till the Girls Come Home," and they spontaneously sang it together.

By this time, Pete was growing increasingly anxious that Jon might not live to hear the choir sing his cherished Miles Davis opus. He gave up trying to stage *Miles Ahead* in London and decided to relocate it to New York. He emailed Quincy, who had given him his business card, and asked if there was any way he could help. It turned out he could, donating twenty thousand dollars for travel and accommodation for the choir. Then there was the question of venue. He first considered the Apple Room at the Lincoln Center, whose acoustic is ideal for voices. But even with what they called "a deal," they quoted him thirty-two thousand dollars to rent the room. Wendy Oxenhorn at the Jazz Foundation of America then suggested St. Peter's Church on Lexington Avenue, known as the Jazz Church and frequently used for the funerals of jazz musicians. The fee here was a far more modest two thousand dollars—less than the cost of hiring the sound system. The concert was booked for Friday, February 17, 2017, at 7 p.m.

Pete organized London–New York flights and Airbnbs for twenty-six people. The soloist Anita Wardell went, with bass player Dave Whitford and drummer Steve Brown, as did Michele Hendricks from Paris. One member of the choir, Mishka Adams, was interrogated for an hour by the immigration authorities before she was allowed to enter the USA (a recently imposed Trump policy, because she had once visited Iran). When they reached New York, they learned that Jon had been taken into hospital. "He was the only reason we'd gone," said Pete. "I didn't care about everybody else." When Friday rolled around, the night of the gig, Jon, Aria, and a nurse arrived at the church with seconds to spare. It was very much a characteristic of Jon's life that everything came together in the final moments, so his joy at the *Miles Ahead* event, and his participation, was a significant return to form. Afterwards they went out to a restaurant and drank champagne, and Pete Churchill pushed the great jazz singer back home through the streets of Manhattan in his wheelchair. Since Judith's death the original apartment had been sold, and Jon and Aria were living in what had been the guest apartment.

Jon's favorite place to dine was the French restaurant Bouley in Tribeca, which was about to close down. On the last day of July, Jon went along for its final night in the company of Aria and Kevin Burke, who had offered to host the meal. The original plan had been for lunch, but something intervened and it became dinner. Bouley was expensive, even more so in the evening than at lunchtime, but Burke figured that since it was Jon's favorite restaurant, and since he himself had been treated hundreds of times by the Hendrickses, he was hardly going to quibble—even if the bill did come to five hundred dollars or more. Jon was in good spirits, having recovered sufficiently from his last illness to flirt with the foxy young waitress. Then David Bouley, the owner, came to their table and declared he was going to cook personally for Jon. In the event the bill came to an eye-watering $1,200, which included the cost of two glasses of champagne between the three of them.

It was hard to begrudge Jon even this wallet-slimming encounter. For him—brought up in poverty, suffering through World War II, starving in professional obscurity until his mid-thirties—the consumption of food was an all-important ritual. It was a topic that had dominated his lyrics: "Feed Me," "Home Cookin'," "Contemporary Blues," "Cookin' at the Continental," and even "Doodlin'," with its events set in a restaurant. Wherever they went for dinner, he was known. He always ordered more than anyone thought he could eat, sometimes demolishing two entrées.

In the hospital, about six weeks before he died, Jon fell over again and broke his hip and in the same incident ruptured his intestines, which meant he could no longer be fed. After that he declined rapidly.

Jon Hendricks died at 3:12, p. m. on November 22, 2017, aged ninety-six. "When a man like this dies," said his friend the broadcaster Claude Carrière, "it's like a museum burned down."

In the view of his daughter Aria, Jon remained a besotted fan of jazz and a worshipper of the jazz composers and musicians he came to know and work with. At heart, perhaps, he never really believed that he belonged in the company of people like Armstrong, Ellington, Gillespie, and Basie. The super-confidence he projected was overcompensation, because he was intimidated by them. Being unable to read music bothered him more than he let on—he regretted that he had never learned. Yet, being stubborn, he was too proud to provide any formal musical tuition for his children, preferring just to throw them into it as he himself had been. Flamboyant and relaxed on stage, and never less than voluble in interviews, Hendricks was in domestic life a quiet man who spent a lot of time doing crossword puzzles. As extraordinary as his early life was, he was reluctant to share his experiences with his children. "You had to pull everything out of him," said his daughter Michele. "He would hold court, but that's different to holding a conversation." He was less secure in himself than he appeared, often referring to the jazz singers who came after him, such as Al Jarreau and Bobby McFerrin, as his "children." The word sounds kindly and paternal; after all, he did bring them, and many other singers and players, to public attention and train them in the niceties of jazz singing and presentation. But the suggestion that he was their (spiritual) "father" also has proprietorial implications, as if he himself deserved the credit for their contributions to jazz.

Yet in many ways he did, which is why Jon Hendricks's musical legacy lives on. The songs and lyrics he wrote continue to be performed and recorded. Today, the obscure art of vocalese is still very much alive among jazz singers, many of whom also relish (and fear) the challenge of the scat solo. Singers continue to add their own lyrics to existing jazz instrumentals, because Jon Hendricks showed them how. As Jon's publicist Don Lucoff pointed out:

Since Jon wrote about topics as diverse as numerology, history, substance abuse, the blues, politics, Picasso, and cuisine, his work as a lyricist means that any singer who also wants to write new vocalese lyrics has almost unlimited vistas of possibility when it comes to content. Imagination alone is the limit!

There is striking unanimity amongst almost everyone interviewed for this book that Jon Hendricks was great company—a fountain of good humor, warmth, bonhomie, and terrific stories. Ben Sidran expressed the recollections of many:

> Through it all, he was such a generous spirit, and he radiated love and affection for the music and the people who made it. The idea of a greater humanity, that we were all part of this family—he believed that firmly ... The feeling that I take away from Jon was positive, was love, was swing, was humor, fun, pleasure ... that's what it felt like.

His personality was so magnetic that when he was in the room, it was *his* room. "He was a natural leader, said bass player Daryl Runswick. "[He] always had an idea about which song to do next on a gig. No-one else would dream of putting forward ideas. Jon had a formula which always worked." The charisma he radiated had nothing to do with physical stature or movie star looks; he was of below-average height and wore thick glasses much of the time. But he always dressed like a star, from his admiral's hat to his handmade English shoes, with tailored suits in expensive fabrics and a silk handkerchief bursting from his breast pocket, perfectly complementing a bold necktie. He retained his flamboyance almost to the end, resplendent in a purple or silver suit whenever he left his apartment.

In his liner notes for Jon's 1965 album *Live at the Trident*, the critic Leonard Feather described him as

> an incurably happy man. This warning about his condition is posted here partly as a warning to those who like their music heavy and cerebral ... Happiness and a buoyant beat are the predominant characteristics in most Hendricks performances ... But the essence of Jon Hendricks'[s] individuality, I think, lies in his congenial, non-neurotic approach to music. He has a good time; he wants the audience to share in his pleasure. This attitude is regarded with condescension and suspicion in some modern musical circles.

Those who worked with Hendricks loved simply being with him. "Jon was always a scream to be around," recalled drummer Andy Watson:

I can't remember one time being around him when he wasn't laughing or trying to make you laugh. He'd be holding court, cracking everyone up, and we would be trying to make a plane, and meanwhile we didn't get to the gate on time.

He also had a very simple approach to dealing with people who could potentially frustrate him: don't get involved in direct confrontation and, wherever possible, keep smiling.

Appendix A: The Voice, the Scat, the Vocalese

Strange to say, Jon Hendricks never regarded himself as a singer, but as someone who used his voice to express the sound of a horn in the hands of a jazz musician; in other words, he was someone who played the horn without the horn. The "real" singers, he thought, were Tony Bennett, Vic Damone, Mel Tormé, Joe Williams, and Billy Eckstine. Bennett in turn had a very high regard for Hendricks, envying his ability to do things with his voice that Bennett himself could not do. Hendricks said that even when he sang a ballad, he was always thinking that he was playing an instrument such as a saxophone or a trombone; conversely, he valued the singers he liked according to the natural qualities of their voices—in other words, those with a good "instrument" of their own. Some of his choices are surprising. Today some might regard Perry Como as bland and lacking in energy but Hendricks said he would pick him or Andy Williams as a lead alto [sic] voice. He liked Williams's clear tone, his lack of vibrato, and ability to stick to the melody. When it came to female singers, he liked Rosemary Clooney and Doris Day for similar reasons.

Was Hendricks right about not being a "real" singer like those just mentioned? The answer depends on what you want or expect from a singer. Technically, Hendricks was limited: his pitching often left a lot to be desired and he didn't have much range. He made no attempt to widen it or even train his voice in any way. He didn't bother to practice; he didn't even do warm-ups before gigs. In the opinion of Holli Ross, "He was a better singer than Eddie Jefferson, but King Pleasure … was a better singer [than Jon]." The natural timbre of his voice was dry and raspy, but with an abundance of character, style, and jazz feel. When he sang he exuded energy, warmth, passion, and humor; on record he is as instantly identifiable as Frank Sinatra or Eddie Jefferson. Within that overall sound, his singing style varied according to the material: a repertoire that extended from the jump-blues and early R&B of the mid-forties to the bebop of the late forties and early fifties, the Miles Davis/Gil Evans collaborations of the late fifties, and the Brazilian jazz of the early sixties—but nothing that came after that. His singing style developed in tandem with his lyric writing. When he wasn't singing lyrics, he was scatting and, when it came to jazz feel, who else could scat with such incredible velocity whilst hitting the changes with pinpoint accuracy—and all the time swinging like crazy?

Of course, the rhythm always comes first. Drummer Andy Watson enjoyed playing in Hendricks's late combo precisely because of the rhythmic sense that the singer possessed. This was particularly evident when he was scatting. "It had an explosive quality to it," he said. "Until I started working with him I did not like scat singing. But with Jon it was like playing with a great tenor player or trumpet player—the way he sang through the chord changes. It was a gift from God." Jon himself considered that it was his background as a drummer that had trained him to swing:

> Everything you do has to swing. The drummer, as Duke Ellington said, is the bandleader. If he's swinging, the whole band will swing. If he's not swinging, the band is going to sound very ponderous ... So the drum—the sound that you hear in your ear for the rhythm— is very important, because that's going to underline everything that you do. So it's best to have your own drum in your ear and to play from that, [rather] than to depend on the drummer who's actually working behind you, because they very seldom have the idea that you have.

Stephanie Nakasian described Jon's rhythmic singing style as a process linking something very grounded and physical with something that feels intensely spiritual:

> Swing provides a grounding for you to take off. You know the way the whirling dervishes do their dance? They have one hand that goes on the ground and one hand that goes to the stars. And you have to be grounded, and for me the rhythm is the grounding part of it, and then what happens out of that whirls you up into the stratosphere.

Scat singing is spontaneous, improvised vocal soloing, with nonsense syllables pitched to form the notes that would otherwise be played on an instrument; the term **vocalese** refers to lyrics written to fit a specific recorded instrumental solo whose melody was spontaneously improvised at the time it was committed to disc or tape, but which the singer must learn and perform note by note. Alongside his lyric writing (see next chapter), Jon Hendricks is perhaps most celebrated as a master of both scat and vocalese.

Scat singing is surely as old as music itself though, if we really want a historical marker, it has often been said that Louis Armstrong accidentally invented it when he dropped his lyric sheet while recording "Heebie Jeebies" in February 1926. In fact, the Fletcher Henderson band had included scat almost two years earlier when Don Redman sang a scat chorus on "My Papa Doesn't Two Time, No Time" on April 24, 1924; when he joined the band, Louis himself added a scatted coda to "Everybody Loves My Baby" that November. What is significant, in the context of Jon Hendricks's approach to scatting, is the way Armstrong was able to emulate vocally his own trumpet techniques—with all its subtle inflections, note-bending and vibrato—and retain the same relaxed style. Cab Calloway and Leo Watson went on to popularize the technique, although each had a different approach: Calloway was a showman and an entertainer whose songs often featured characters such as drug-taking Minnie the Moocher, in which his scatting would reflect the voice of the character; Watson—through his jazz comedy work that reached its peak with Slim Gaillard—was more a precursor of the bebop singers of the decade that followed, his voice taking on the instrumental qualities of a trombone (though he was also a drummer). He was an inspiration to Mel Tormé, who eventually eclipsed him and almost everyone else. Early on, Watson learned his technique from horn players, but without simply imitating them. The zaniness of Jon Hendricks and Lambert, Hendricks & Ross owes much to Watson. The almost-forgotten George "Bon Bon" Tunnell was another early influence. A black singer employed by white bandleader Jan Savitt, Tunnell was equally adept with ballads as he was with swing and was another of those who influenced both Tormé and Hendricks. The scatting on his Decca and Victor recordings in the early 1940s sounds more structured and deliberate than Watson's.

After rhythm, the next most fundamental skill required of a scat singer is to "hit the changes" during a solo—in other words, to sing notes that fit with the changing harmony as the tune progresses. Blues songs are the easiest to scat over because the harmony barely shifts: the soloist only has three chords to worry about, and the singer need only sing one scale over them. The very best scat singers—Ella Fitzgerald, Jon Hendricks, Jazzmeia Horn—have the ability to improvise with their voices on a level that matches the greatest instrumentalists. They are able to string together long, musically coherent passages with a sense of narrative purpose. For example, they may start with a few notes and build up to a torrent of them. Or they might trade fours or eights with an instrumentalist, perhaps beginning with the last note or phrase played by the other. "Listen to the great horn players," Jon urged. "Ella was listening to everybody. She learned to scat by listening to the cats and copying their solos, and she was very much aware of Bird, of Diz, of Ben."

But many great singers never scatted at all, including Billie Holiday and Frank Sinatra. So what prompted some of them to start? Without scat, a singer simply performs the head and then has to keep quiet until all the instrumentalists have finished their solos, whereupon he or she sings the head again. But in the meantime, the soloists have had all the fun. So perhaps envy was one motivation. The freedom, even wildness, of bebop—but also the virtuoso technique needed to play it—seems to have emboldened certain singers to scat. But scat has not always been popular with audiences, critics, and singers. Wielded by the underprepared or uncertain, it is a dangerous and unstable technique. Even when done well, scat is often more fun to sing than it is to listen to; a little goes a long way. Mel Tormé was of this opinion. Leonard Feather went so far as to write that "scat singing—with only a couple of exceptions—should be banned." Jon Hendricks, of course, felt it had its place in jazz, although even he had his reservations: "One can never say that in order to be a jazz singer you have to scat ... What one *can* say is that it helps."

There is an argument that says singers should express the emotion of a song not through a scat solo but by working harder on the delivery of the lyric. Betty Carter drew an important distinction between the skills needed for singing the lyrics of a song and those needed for scatting, which she called "another art form altogether." The effort—and the mistakes—can be too obvious: spontaneity and fun are sometimes lost when singers launch into a scat solo, as they strain every sinew to master this difficult technique. As Mel Tormé put it:

> [The] truth of the matter is that scat singing is the toughest kind of singing ... I'm talking about how your mouth is stretched out of shape. I'm talking about taking a specific chord pattern and ... never knowing what you're gonna sing at that moment.

Familiarity with, and then mastery of, a song's harmonic structure is essential if scatting is to be done well. Helen Merrill had the wisest counsel for would-be scat singers: "If you're going to scat, you'd better be able to play as good as any of the jazz musicians, that's all." And the best scat singers can. "When you know a tune well enough to scat on it, you don't think about it any more," Jon Hendricks said. "What I think about is, how can I make it pretty?" And that, of course, is what makes it worth hearing. But a scat solo can inspire terror in even the greatest jazz singers. Jon told a story about scatting once alongside Ella Fitzgerald, and how she put her arm around his waist. He reciprocated. Afterwards she said she did it because she was scared. "The secret of great art is desperation," said Jon, "because you never really know how you're doing." He went on to say that at Ronnie Scott's sometimes he would sit backstage hating himself for being so bad, and yet the audience still loved it.

Hendricks's early training at the knee of Art Tatum embedded scat so deeply in his brain that it became second nature to him when he was in his early teens. Working with Tatum taught him that

> music is made up of melody, harmony and rhythm, and it's played over chord structures—that each song has a chord structure, that it's not just "Lady Be Good" the melody ... but there are the chords

that go underneath that make that song. It made it fuller. It made a song not just a melody that I sang, but a chord structure that I hadn't even thought about, let alone thought about singing ... Scatting ... is merely singing the chord structure to the song while you subconsciously have the melody in your mind.

This also has the advantage of freeing the singer from having to hit certain notes that may be beyond his or her range, since a different note would fit equally well—providing it is contained in the underlying chord, or at least within a scale that works with the chord sequence.

Hendricks went far beyond merely improvising over the changes; his body became a musical instrument. The biggest influences in the development of his own scatting were all trumpet players—Louis Armstrong, Harry "Sweets" Edison, and Dizzy Gillespie—not, you will notice, other singers. While scatting, however, he would always hold his hands as if he was playing a saxophone. "If you move your hands like an alto or tenor player, that's how you're gonna sound," he told Roseanna Vitro. "There are other cats who do that, too, like Al Jarreau. You'd be surprised how many notes come out." But he was able to use different styles depending on the specific instrument he had in mind for his solo. As he pointed out, there is a great difference between soloing like Ben Webster and soloing like Louis Armstrong. The vowel and syllabic sounds he made depended on what instrument he had decided to be:

Are you going to be standing up in the saxophone section and blowing? Or are you going to be standing up in the trumpet section? Are you going to be the trombone? Are you going to be the piano? Or are you going to be the guitar? What instrument are you going to be? That determines the sound that you're going to make.

If you were going to be a saxophone, for example, you should make more use of the tongue than you would if you were a piano. Similarly, your sound will be more *legato* when it's a saxophone than when it's a guitar—whereas the trumpet is more percussive. When The Manhattan Transfer went on the road with Hendricks before recording their *Vocalese* album, he would coach them to emulate the timbre of an instrument. In his own scatting he went further still: he possessed the ability to emulate the playing styles of particular musicians. The most jaw-dropping example is on "Swingin' Till the Girls Come Home" (*The Swingers*, 1959), where he calls out the names of four different bass players and performs consecutive improvised solos in the style of each. He could do it because he listened with great concentration, over and over again, to what they were doing and how they were doing it.

The same close attention to each minute detail of performance was needed for vocalese, the other technique that Hendricks mastered. He didn't invent it, any more than he invented scat, but he came close to perfecting it. Vocalese dates at least as far back as 1934, when the singer Marion Harris recorded "Singing the Blues" with her own lyrics to Bix Beiderbecke's 1927 cornet solo, fluting in a sweet and innocent voice about shooting her lover in the head with a Gatling gun. "Every person who ever sang vocalese was influenced by King Pleasure," said Hendricks. As a singer, he found merely singing the first chorus and the head out too limiting; there was always more he wanted to say. Other lyricists would get round this by writing alternative lyrics to the same song. But vocalese gave Pleasure the means to extend his lyrics beyond the first chorus. "That opened up a whole world for me," said Hendricks. The saxophonist Noel Jewkes, who played with him in the sixties, added, "He was gifted with the ability, in his vocalese, to transform a jazz solo into something which actually enhanced the original solo and made it more understandable to a wider audience." This explains why Hendricks thought it was so important to give the utmost attention and respect to the original soloist.

It was of course Eddie Jefferson who had originally given Pleasure the idea for vocalese, but Hendricks expanded the technique by applying it to big band arrangements—with words not just for the central melody but for the lines played by individual sections. This was how he arrived at his own definition of vocalese: it wasn't what Pleasure did, singing just a single horn line, but singing a complete orchestration. "Vocalese is collective," he insisted. "King Pleasure, Eddie Jefferson, Kurt Elling are soloists. So they can't be vocalese. Vocalese is at least four [voices]." One might question Hendricks's definition, which conveniently allows him to *own* vocalese, since he was the first one to adapt it for multiple voices. But he had the authority of Leonard Feather behind him, since it was Feather who coined the word in an article he wrote in response to the multi-voiced *Sing a Song of Basie*.

There are, however, some problems with vocalese that lay open to question Hendricks's assertion that it should be considered as "a new cultural artform on the planet." One is that of authorship. In a traditional songwriting team, one person may write the tune and another may write the lyrics. But when that tune comes to be recorded, at least one other person plays a spontaneous instrumental solo that then forms the basis of the vocalese lyrics. These, in turn, have been written by a fourth person. And what if there are two, three, or more solos by different players on the original recording? In the case of *Sing a Song of Basie*, there were many soloists to take into consideration. Authorship, and hence intellectual property, is therefore something of a quagmire. When Prestige released as a single King Pleasure's "Moody's Mood For Love" (originally "Moody Mood for Love") the label read "Dedicated to James Moody," but the writer's credit which would normally appear in brackets under the song title was conspicuously absent; that is to say, there was no mention of Jimmy McHugh who wrote the tune, or Dorothy Fields who wrote the original lyric—nor indeed is Eddie Jefferson credited with the vocalese lyric.

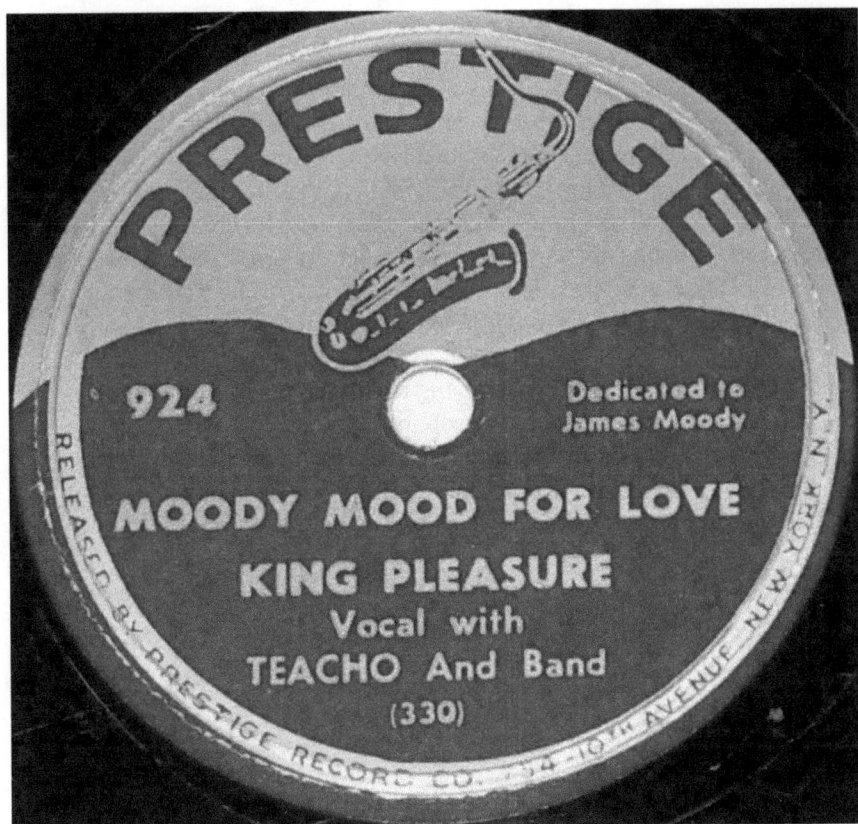

On "Don't Get Scared," Hendricks's recording with Pleasure (also for Prestige) the label reads "Dedicated to Stan Getz." This time the tune is credited to Pleasure-Getz-Hendriks [*sic*], thus robbing Lars Gullin of any authorship—despite the fact that Hendricks's vocal solo would not exist without Gullin's original baritone solo. In short, how can vocalese claim to be a new art form when it is entirely dependent on—and indeed secondary or tertiary to—another artist's work? In drama, for example, Shakespeare may have appropriated existing stories for his plays but his dramaturgy was not tied hand and foot to them, as he could equally well have invented the stories himself. He reworked and expanded the source material in ways that rendered his plays infinitely more detailed and complex than the sources. The same cannot be said of vocalese, which must duplicate the exact notes played by an earlier artist.

This restriction causes another problem: lack of choice, and lack of choice can result in lack of inspiration. Too many vocalese lyrics are nothing more than tributes to the musicians who originally recorded the tune in question. For instance, in his lyrics to Coleman Hawkins's famous "Body and Soul" solo, Eddie Jefferson sings Hawk's praises—"Don't you know, he was the king of saxophones." Likewise, Hendricks's "I Remember Clifford"—"The ever-present sound that abounds in his praise echoes throughout the universe." And his lyric to "In Walked Bud" is more of the same. One may also cite Christopher Acemandese Hall's lumpen lyrics, recorded by Jefferson, for "So What," and Eddie's own for "Now's the Time." If, as a lyricist, one has nothing more creative to add to a tune other than salaams to its creator and his associates, it was probably not worth the effort. Such encomia tend to cheapen the value of vocalese, rendering it as something less than the new art form that Hendricks claimed it was. As Will Friedwald put it:

> Jefferson and Pleasure were trying to expand the length of time a vocalist stood in front of a microphone, and wound up with a repertoire full of numbers about five times as long as any Cole Porter song without a tenth of Porter's wit. They want us to listen to them longer but don't give us any good reason why we should.

All this may be ungenerous. For Hendricks, what really mattered was live performance. That was where the magic happened.

Appendix B: The Lyrics

As a young man, whenever he heard the spiritual "Joshua Fit the Battle of Jericho," Jon Hendricks always felt irritated by the word "fit." The English major in him couldn't help but feel that "fit" was wrong, because the past tense of "fight" is "fought." Eventually he realized that the words were composed by African slaves: English was not their first language. Now, "Joshua Fit the Battle of Jericho" sounded absolutely right. As he studied the great song lyricists—W. S. Gilbert, Oscar Hammerstein II, Lorenz Hart, Cole Porter, and Johnny Mercer (his favorite)—it seemed to Hendricks that "none of them had the true poetry of those nameless, faceless slaves who wrote the lyrics to the spirituals." He could find nothing more poetic and beautiful than "Heaven, heaven, everybody talkin' about heaven ain't goin' there." He admired the Ohio-born black writer Paul Laurence Dunbar whose gift, he believed, was Shakespearean and who could write with equal fluency in the mode of Shelley or Byron. But Hendricks was equally impressed by Dunbar's work in African American dialect, saying, "I like that line where he says, 'They set down to some unskun coon.' Unskun. Of course 'skun' is the past tense of 'skin.'" Black people had made English language hipper, he maintained. For example, where a white person would say, "What's the matter with you?" a black person would say, "Smatterchoo?"

Hendricks could have turned his hand to any form of writing. One major reason for coming to New York in 1952, he said, was that he always wanted to write short stories and plays. Instead he applied what he had learned from his study of literature—particularly drama—to his lyrics. One important reason why his lyrics work so well, and have been sung so often, is that they are colloquial and therefore trip naturally off the tongue. He had the gift of writing in a conversational way—a way that never sounds forced or literary. He understood that, unlike a piece of literature designed to be read on the page, a lyric should appeal to the ear by employing the vocabulary and the syntax that real people use when they speak. This allows the words to be sung with authentic-sounding cadences. In fact, Hendricks did not see himself as a mere lyricist but as a poet, because he thought all the best lyricists *were* poets. "The difference between lyrics and poetry is philosophy," he said. "Lyrics often lack philosophy, but poetry never lacks philosophy."

His approach to writing lyrics did not vary according to the composer. He felt there was little difference between writing them for Duke Ellington and writing them for Monk because philosophy was at the heart of what they both did, and Monk's approach derived from Ellington's, both being steeped in religious philosophy. With Miles, he thought, there was

> a more secular, hip, light, airy, whimsical, quixotic, affected way that you can take. It's not as deep as either Monk or Duke Ellington is, but it's cute, and sometimes it's very pretty, like in the *Miles Ahead* things and "My Ship." The way he sings "Bess, where is my Bess?" is heartbreaking, just gorgeously beautiful. He has great beauty about him, but the depth belongs to Monk and Duke. They're the deep ones.

He thought Randy Weston, influenced mostly by Monk, was part of that same cultural and philosophical lineage. The "philosophical" component applied to most of the lyrics that Hendricks wrote; even something as apparently frivolous as "Jive Samba," whose words do no more than explain why the tune isn't really a samba. It was all about his worldview, and his fascination with every conceivable aspect of life. For example, it became fashionable during the fifties to go to an analyst. "Doodlin'" could be seen as no more than a ridiculous anecdote inspired by Annie Ross's "Twisted." Like "Twisted," "Doodlin'" makes fun of the whole idea of psychiatry as a way of healing people. Jon explained:

> You see I don't believe that psychiatry has ever healed anybody. So I constructed this little story—"Using the phone booth, making a few calls." The guy doodles on a restaurant tablecloth and the waiter calls the police and they take him to the psychiatrist. The psychiatrist, while he's doodlin', begins to flirt with his girlfriend. It's really an exposé of psychiatry from a comical standpoint.

In other words it was satire, which always expresses a philosophical attitude. In Hendricks's mind, just as there was a lineage from Duke to Monk to Weston, there was also a seamless connection between lyric writing, poetry, philosophy, and religion:

> It's a part of the culture of jazz. You get the chance to delineate the life that went on. Jazz came out of a culture. So these lyrics are actually folk poetry that delineates cultural aspects of the society

that produced jazz music. I always had a story to tell and a sermon to preach actually. My lyrics are actually sermonettes.

In keeping with this quasi-religious terminology, writing lyrics was a mystical process for him, as we have seen throughout this book. Many of his associates saw him doing it, and all described it in exactly the same way. David Leonhardt remembered watching him write lyrics in the van on their way to and from gigs. At the time he was writing a whole album for The Manhattan Transfer, he would wear a Walkman and have a yellow legal pad on his knees, listening and writing the lyrics. He wrote very fast, with very little editing. He was able to do this with confidence throughout his life because of his extraordinary belief that the words were not coming *from* him, but *through* him:

> When I'm writing these lyrics, I am watching the end of the pencil to see what is coming out of the pencil. And then after they're written, I don't know them. If I'm going to sing them, I'm going to have to learn them all over again. So it doesn't come from me, it comes through me.

As The Manhattan Transfer's Tim Hauser said:

> He listens to these solos, these instrumental solos, and then he gets a story. And a lot of times he says, "I dunno, it comes from somebody else." Sometimes I feel it's automatic writing. He doesn't even believe it's [him] who's doing the writing. He feels like he's got some higher power, a spirit who's working through him.

So when Hendricks wrote something, he did not regard it as an act of creation:

> I'm like a secretary, and I take the pen and the Entity dictates to me and I start writing. It's not mine, because I read every line and I say, "Whoo-hoo!" I laugh at the funny stuff. Well, if I was doing it and thinking it, I wouldn't laugh at the funny stuff. So I know what creative work is. It's out-of-body. So I think if you hem it in too much, you know, you kill it. I like the way it happens with me. I get an idea that I want to do the lyrics to a song. I put it on, and I play it, and then I play it again, and then I put it on again, and I start writing. And the words come so fast that it can't be me thinking and putting it down. I'm taking dictation, and sometimes—well no, not sometimes, most of the time—my original lyrics are one-time.

So although his production of lyrics *appeared* to be supernaturally fast, he had already spent a lot of time thinking about the construction of the piece as a whole. The composition formed in his head before it appeared on the page.

The "mystical" nature of the writing process would therefore seem to apply only to this final phase. As well as describing it as taking dictation from some "entity" outside himself, he also said it was "like translating a novel. You listen to the notes again and again and find the words that make the closest sounds in English." He thought the words were already there; getting them on paper was simply a matter of digging them out:

> Well, I listen. The main thing—I figure—this is true of anybody, if you listen long enough, you'll hear it finally. And when you hear it and you can get it to the point where you can hum it on the subway or walking down the street, then after a time, words begin to come to you, whatever the horn is saying, they just form themselves, some of the phrases, like that on "Let Me See," that just screams, "How d'you do there?" It shouts, just like what he was saying.

Asked if he was a religious man, Hendricks said he thought all artists were, by definition, religious:

> If we're in the arts, we live, work and do our thing in the spirit …
> The most charming, the most well-informed, the funniest people in the world are jazz musicians, because their minds are constantly creating, and so they can create in any area. If they have a conversation with you, it's a creative thing.

His lyrics for "Let Me See" were based on a 1941 solo that Lester Young recorded with Count Basie. Hendricks described a spiritual experience he'd had in the Alvin Hotel after writing the lyrics, whose last eight bars were:

> I'm wise,
> Your ever-watching eyes are busy looking constantly,
> But you gotta listen if you wanna hear what's missin',
> then you really can see.

Excited at having captured what he felt was the perfect lyrical expression of the tune, he went up to Prez's room and said he had something he wanted to sing to him. Before he had sung a word, Young said, "You know, man, I never use my eyes, I always use my ears, and you gotta nice sound." Understandably, Hendricks thought there was something deeper going on here than mere coincidence.

When preparing to write a lyric for an existing tune, the first thing he would do was learn the song's melody and familiarize himself with the solos. At this stage he would not learn these in detail, but simply be aware that the first solo was played by a trumpet or tenor, or whatever the instrument was, and know where it came in. Then, he said, he would think about the title of the song. Wherever possible he would ask the composer of a tune what he'd had in mind when giving it its title. This then became the subject of the story that he would construct. "Jumpin' at the Woodside" was the example he gave most frequently. He learned, by asking Basie and older members of his band, that the Woodside was a Harlem hotel where they stayed when they were in town during the thirties and forties. It was run by a man and a woman who worked in vaudeville, and they didn't mind musicians practicing at eleven or midnight, or jam sessions going on at two in the morning. All the other guests were in the entertainment business too. No-one would knock on the walls or complain about the noise; they were up all night anyway, and would either come and listen, or join in.

Having done his research, Hendricks would then begin to dramatize the story by bringing to life the personalities who would inhabit it, with a beginning, middle and an end—a plot. The horns were the cast of characters, and their solos were a commentary on the subject matter, which was determined by the title. It had to work like an opera or a drama:

> So I had this line and I would begin to talk and their feelings about living at the Woodside and why they lived there and the philosophy that I imagined each of the musicians blowing would express about it. That's why it helps to know each artist playing a solo, because when I wrote the first solo, Buck Clayton's, I tried to speak in a way that Buck Clayton would speak. Like when you write a solo by Lawrence Brown, you have to use precisely correct English because Lawrence spoke very well. He never engaged in vulgar expressions, there were never any slang expressions used around Lawrence. Many members of the Ellington band were like that.

When lyricizing "Shorty George" from the *Sing Along with Basie* album, Hendricks didn't know who Shorty George was. All Basie told him was, "That's the cat that comes in the back door." The hint was enough for Hendricks to create the whole story. With the character of Freddie Freeloader:

> I had to tell who he was in the melody …. With the way the song is constructed on one riff repeated over and over. You don't have much room to go into too much delineation, so you had to tell who Freddie was with those melodic designs. So "Freddie, Freddie, Freddie, Freddie, free booze, free blues, free dues." That basically is what Freddie was. He was a guy that gave liquor away to jazz musicians … first he gives you the booze, that gives you the blues, and you definitely will pay dues.

Unlike Lawrence Brown, most people use slang, and a lyric will always sound more authentic when slang is a part of it. "Slang is beautiful," said Hendricks:

> Somebody once said that slang is rolling up its sleeves and going to work, because it is the best way that ordinary not-well-educated people have of expressing themselves, and it has a beauty about it ... I like to write in the vernacular. You can express yourself much better in the vernacular than I think you can in so-called literary terms.

For Holli Ross, Hendricks's lyrics to Clifford Brown's "Joy Spring" were a game-changer:

> He quotes Shakespeare in his vocalese, and I can't get over how brilliant it is. How he managed to get just the right quote in a rhythmical figure that it fit ... A good lyrical writer will choose words that are easy to sing. For example, if you had a phrase like "Next train out," you would have to place it in a slow, emphatic context. You couldn't sing it fast because you couldn't get it past your tongue and teeth. It's like forcing a jigsaw piece into a space that it just doesn't fit. A good lyric just floats off the tongue. Jon was perfection at this.

There were technical issues to resolve too: Hendricks said "Jumpin' at the Woodside" was the hardest tune to lyricize because of all the repetitions of the main phrase. With Monk's song "Evidence," he was faced with a series of single notes:

> For that I did "Black, white, day, night, sunshine, bright, evidence, right, you dig it?" That's very hard to do—to write in those contexts ... If you have to choose one word that says a whole lot it's very difficult, because the word has to be well known enough and important enough to bring up a myriad of ideas ...

It was never enough merely to fill out the line and make it rhyme. You had to express a thought.

> Words are the best methods that humans have for expressing a thought, but when you consider the thought seeking to be expressed, words are a very poor instrument. That's why, for what people want to say, they often say, "I just can't find the words," because thoughts are so much bigger and wider and deeper than words can express.

Lyrics were important to Hendricks in part because of their importance to players as well as to singers; an instrumentalist needs to know the words to a song before he or she can play it effectively. "A lotta cats just run the chords and when you hear what they play, you can tell that," he said. "But if you are going to express the thoughts that the song has to offer, you have to know what the words are."

Hendricks was prone to go too far in his assertions about all manner of things. Perhaps because most of the tunesmiths he had approached about writing lyrics had apparently been happy to accept them, he believed that all instrumental music was meant to have words:

> I believe that if you could talk to any composer—Bach, Brahms, Beethoven—they would tell you, "Oh yes, if I could find words, I would love to have them." Every composer that writes a piece of music would love, I'm sure, to have words to his music. They're just not lyricists: they're musicians. Monk told me this, you know: he says every song he writes he's thinking in terms of words for it eventually. I think with every musician, words and music go together.

He thought of Jobim as the Tchaikovsky of his age:

> I want to have English lyrics to all his songs ... He is the composer whose sense of melody is just so beautiful. Henry Mancini was another composer of that type. Richard Rodgers, of course. Their melodies are so beautiful that they cry out for words. Of course Richard Rodgers had some of the greatest poets ... Johnny Mercer is a great folk poet. His lyrics—I think he is the American lyricist with the most range in expression. He can write folksy, shoes-off, barefoot type stuff like "Lazybones" ... [he went on to quote lyrics from "On the Atchison, Topeka, and the Santa Fe," "Ac-Cent-Tchu-Ate the Positive," "Dream," "Moon River," and "Laura."] That's gorgeous. It's so poignant and so beautiful.

Jon Hendricks thought big, and he knew no boundaries. This could have its drawbacks. Not all his lyric writing really suited the material it was meant for. Holli Ross remembered having to learn "Gone" from the Gil Evans/Miles Davis *Porgy and Bess* recording.

> It was so hard, and actually in my opinion, it was not a great vocal choice. I learned it, and I could do it with the ensemble ... But even when it was all rehearsed and ready for performance, I still think it missed the mark. But my point is, Jon thought outside the box. I don't think he cared that it missed the mark—it was Miles, it was

Gil, and it was an important orchestral piece. And that's what he tried to do, with four singers, and before, three singers. With four singers he wanted to create this orchestration. Sometimes you have to admit, nah, it's not working. But he went to those uncomfortable places, and made music as he saw fit.

Very many of the vocalese lyrics he wrote have never seen the light of day, including Charlie Parker solos from *Charlie Parker with Strings*, such as his entire "Just Friends" solo and the "Night and Day" solo from the same record. It is to be hoped that at least some of these will eventually find a book publisher, or better still musicians and singers willing to record them.

Appendix C: The Wisdom and Philosophy

Not only was Jon Hendricks interested in everything that went on in the world, but he was well-informed, although some of his beliefs were bizarre. What follows is a selection of his thoughts on a variety of topics. In keeping with his gifts as a raconteur, we begin with talk.

On speaking

> People nowadays, with the lessening of education, just don't know how to speak well. So more and more writing is being done in a more and more vulgate idiomatic English language. I don't think that's necessarily such a good thing. I think Duke Ellington was right. "To speak well is to live well." I think you should know how to speak well. You should be taught how to speak well. I think not to speak well is dangerous, because it lowers the level of the mind, and when your mind level is lowered, you're subject to the dark forces creeping in on you. You very seldom hear a junkie talking in high literary terms. He's usually talking in extreme profanity and the most basic and base language possible, because his tone level has been lowered so much that this expression is the best he can manage.

On medicine and diet

Interviewed at the age of seventy-eight, Hendricks put his health and youthfulness down to being interested in everything. This included medicine—but not the modern kind, which was not healing but socially acceptable drug pushing, in his view. Surgery was mere licensed butchery, because all the doctors did was cut out the affected part. He was an admirer of Hippocrates, the Ancient Greek father of Western medicine who, he said, never operated, and treated nervous disorders using numbers. The wrong diet was the root of all sickness.

He and Judith took their ideas about health and diet to extremes. Each morning they would brew up some coffee, let it cool, and then administer an enema in order to cleanse their intestines, and encouraged others to do the same. The coffee enemas seemed to most of the people around them like an addiction. One morning while they were touring with Tommy Flanagan, they were staying together in a house in Virginia. The Hendrickses were brewing the coffee in their room as usual. Flanagan got up and said, "Oh that coffee smells good." "Oh," said the others, "You don't want any of *that* coffee." The practice continued, although Jon also suffered badly from hemorrhoids, which the coffee enemas were not exactly helping.

On race

The uniquely toxic nature of race relations in the US is due to slavery, Hendricks believed, with many whites still viewing blacks as ex-slaves and hence an inferior species. It was not the same in Europe, because there had never been slavery there. In the US, the antagonism came from the top echelon of society because it had to do with the control of money rather than genuine, out-and-out hatred. How could whites hate the blacks who cooked their meals and looked after their children? It was in the interests of the powers that be to maintain black people in a state of subjugation, and to maintain the social divisions that reinforced their position.

But somehow, in the midst of their oppression, black people had succeeded in creating a beautiful art form. And the struggle for jazz to find its place in popular culture was also due to race. "You can't respect a person's art form if you can't respect the person himself," he pointed out. Before the French sold Louisiana to the USA, you could hear the music out in the streets. It was the USA that put it in the whorehouses:

> That was the only place you could go to hear the blues ... we comprise ten percent of the population. Well it's a bit unrealistic to expect the other ninety percent of that population that controls all the money to—with that disrespect of the people—to give them what they deserve artistically ... What they did was they took it and put it in the mouths of their own children, and *then* they bought it. Which brings us to the phenomenon of the four little boys from Liverpool. The United States put itself in the position of paying four English boys twenty million dollars for playing a third-hand version of their own art form. Because they didn't have the [black]

faces, they had white faces, so they could accept the music from those faces.

He spoke bitterly about the enormous commercial success enjoyed by James Taylor and Carole King who, he thought, had appropriated black music:

You can go into a church at random in almost any city in the United States and you can hear somebody playing that kind of piano and singing much better [than Carole King]. And you see them making all this money, it's got to be a conspiracy. There's no way possible that these people can make all that money out of their version of something unless there is a conspiracy.

Hendricks did not blame the white performers. "You don't have to attack the people, you have to attack the social force that makes this thing possible," he said. "I don't get mad at anybody making money off jazz, I get mad at the fact that it's such a sick society that pay a third party to bring the music to the people, rather than pay the people themselves."

Conversely, Benny Goodman was "an American social hero" who could not understand why he couldn't have black musicians like Lionel Hampton, Charlie Christian, or Teddy Wilson in his band.

It hurt Hendricks that most African Americans had turned their backs on jazz, that they did not come to his gigs; it was a problem that dated back as far as the end of World War II. He attributed it to the slave mentality; this was the only reason he could think of to explain why black people had rejected their own greatest contribution to the world. It was the same story with the blues. "Through the social struggle to become equal they've lost their roots and in a very big way they've become ashamed of their roots, so that they don't want to sing the blues any more," he said in 1971. "Take a guy like Joe Williams, the greatest blues singer in the world, doesn't want to sing the blues, he wants to sing ballads like Frank Sinatra or Tony Bennett. That's ridiculous."

As for his own experience of racism, he had learned how to deal with it from his father:

If someone has made any racial remark to me, I've always felt more like—I don't know what word to use, but I've always felt a kind of pity for that person, rather than any pain to myself. I always felt, oh man, what a terrible way to go around looking at the world. I've always felt what a sadness in your life you must have.

The best way to combat hatred was with love:

You can't fight love. See hate, they can fight that. They can lynch you, and they can kill you. But if you love them, they can't fight you. You disarm them. It's a very strong force, and it's what Christ preached. Christ in the New Testament brought man from the Mosaic law into the ... psychological law. If a man hits you, and you say, "I love you," you drive him nuts. He gets so mad, he hits you again, and you say, "Why are you hitting me when I love you?" Then he just drops his weapon and starts to weep, because you call upon the essential humanity that is in him. He is, after all, a man and a human being, and you call upon this humanity. You call forth past the beast that's manifesting and beating you. You call ... into being the essential him.

He had been dealing with the problem since serving in World War II:

I ran into this USO place ... I went and I found this one table. It had two chairs. I sat in one to eat my donuts and drink my coffee. This one white boy—he was maybe about nineteen years old. He was a kid. He came in. He walks through the place, looking for a place where there were no black soldiers. The only chair he saw was mine. He passed my table three times. Finally, finding no other place, he sat there, but he thought he had to let me know, so he sat down, he looked at me and he said, "I don't like niggers." I said, "Me neither." Of course, this was using the words of Jesus. If a man strikes you on one cheek, turn the other cheek. Agree with thine adversary quickly lest he deliver you to the sheriff ... it was using the words of Christ. That guy got so upset, that kid. He looked like he was going to cry. He didn't know what to do, he was so taken aback. So he started to talk, and he started talking to me. We had a long conversation. We ate our donuts, drank our coffee. At the end, before he left, he said, "If you ever get to Mobile, this is my address." He gave me his address in Mobile, Alabama and asked me to come by. That's the power of the message of Jesus Christ, which is love. It's powerful and it works. I've used it all the time.

Racism was not something that should rouse one to anger:

Because if someone calls you a name, and you get angry about it, then isn't that anger an acceptance of the fact that you are whatever name it is they called you? ... That's not me. What are you getting mad at? Because if you're mad, then you're a nigger. I said no, that ain't me.

Some people, of course, were beyond reform. When a red-faced individual came up to him in Indianapolis and said, "I don't like your group!" Hendricks simply smiled, thanked him, and walked away. "He was very nonplussed: he had nothing to vent his anger on," said Jon. "You can turn anger around with love, and wipe it out. But if you go against it, then it feeds itself." He did not feel that anyone could mistreat him, because he could simply never accept the image they had of him. "I'm immune to such things," he said. "They can do whatever they want, but I'm always sitting there feeling sorry for them. I only get incensed at the mistreatment of somebody else."

But Hendricks was conflicted about his attitude towards white people. Both of his marriages were to white women. Although he had long-term relationships with black women, which produced children, there never seemed to have been any question of him marrying them. His daughter Aria believed her father found safety in white people—sanctuary from a very difficult, challenging life. It was a matter of acceptance, more than money, which was not important to him. And although he was outspoken on issues of race and social justice, Hendricks did not take part in marches and demonstrations. Unlike so many with his background, he didn't hate whites, perhaps because he had been helped by them as often as he had been threatened or abused by them. Harry Belafonte had counseled him early in life how to avoid conflict with whites, and to master the art of negotiation with them. Belafonte also taught him the importance of maintaining one's dignity in the presence of whites, however great the provocation. "I hate what this country does," Hendricks said, "not just to us [blacks] but to anyone they don't like. I am very dissatisfied with the wrongs that take place in this country. My country right or wrong? OK, *right the wrongs*, then I'll go with you."

On conspiracies

He subscribed to the discredited mid-nineteenth century theory that it was Francis Bacon who had actually written the work attributed to his contemporary William Shakespeare. The idea was comprehensively debunked in the 1950s by means of detailed textual analysis. But Hendricks liked to quote Mark Twain on the subject: "Anyone who thinks Shakespeare wrote those plays is a damned fool." In fact no such quote has been recorded, but Twain did write an essay titled *Is Shakespeare Dead?* in which he revived the controversy, perhaps out of sheer mischief. Soon after arriving on the faculty at the University of Toledo, Hendricks became involved in a long discussion with the head of the theatre department about it. His interest dated back to his visit to England with Basie and Lambert, Hendricks & Ross in March, 1962. Even more absurdly, while the accepted view has always been that the King James Bible was written by several anonymous hands in the sixteenth century, Hendricks claimed it was again all Francis Bacon's work. Not only that: Bacon had apparently "codified and made up the entire English language out of German, French, Spanish and Italian." All this work, he said, was an early seventeenth-century philanthropic project of the occult Society of the Rosy Cross, or Rosicrucian Order, of which Bacon was a member.

It should also come as no surprise that Hendricks also scoffed (as many do) at the official explanations for events like the Kennedy assassination and the 9/11 attacks ("an inside job").

On art

> Music is endlessly occult and secret. It's a spiritual art form. All art is spiritual. Painting is spiritual. Painting and music and poetry and dance. Plato put them all together. He called architecture "frozen music." Painting is visual poetry. They're all tied together. The arts are all tied together. So-called civilized man in the West unties them and separates them. That's actually primitive, because primitive so-called uncivilized people keep them together. Look what they've done to poetry. Poetry was sung. They've taken the music away. Now they have a composer and a lyricist. The true poet sang both the music and the words at the same time. So we haven't progressed. We've actually retrogressed in many ways.

On musical knowledge

Like Jon Hendricks, Erroll Garner was a non-reading jazz musician. Towards the end of his life Garner came up to Hendricks, put his arms around him and said, "Hey Jon—you learned to read yet?" And Jon said, "No ..." And Garner said, "Well hold out, brother, hold out." It was entirely typical of Hendricks's positive outlook and self-justification that he turned this shortcoming into a virtue. It was not necessary to read music, he said:

> The secret of my art is ignorance, because I [didn't know] that you can't do this and you can't do that. So I just did it. When I told Johnny Mercer that I wrote a song a week, he said "You can't do that." I said, "Yeh yeh I did that for six years." He said, "How the heck did you do that?" I says, "They told me that that's what they wanted."

Jon would remind interviewers that Buddy Rich and Elvin Jones were also non-readers. "I think there's a great spirit to art that transcends intellectual knowledge," he said. Many have marveled at his achievement in becoming such an extraordinary singer without being able to read music. Part of it was his endlessly repeated mantra—"just listen." He liked to quote Dizzy Gillespie: "If you can hear it, you can sing it, and if you can sing it, you can play it." In his long interview with James Zimmerman, Hendricks gave the finest argument ever made for *not* writing music down on a stave. For him, music needed to be *rescued* from its written representation. "The music of the world is not made by people who can read music," he began:

> Reading music is the intellectual approach to music ... The people who make the music cannot read. The great operatic arias of Guiseppe Verdi are taken from the folk songs of the Neapolitan fishermen. They can't read. They wouldn't know a note if you put it on a boat ... It's the hearing of the music that's the important thing, I think. If you can hear it, you can sing it or play it. Then, if you learn how to do it intellectually, you of course can write it. But the writing of it is not the execution of it. I know great symphonic musicians who, if you say, "Play 'Stardust' for me," they can't play it until you go get a lead sheet and put it in front of them. Then they can play it. To me that's ... not a musician. That's a person who practices the art of playing music, but a musician to me is someone who can play any tune you name without looking at anything .... Because the one who can't play it without the music is totally dependent on the intellect, and the intellect has never created any art form in the history of this planet ... In the Bible, the intellect is symbolized by King Herod, who is looking for the Christ-child that he's been told is coming, and so slaughters all the children. This is what the intellect does in the heart of the human being that engages the intellect over the spirit. The intellect is a great servant to the spirit, but it is a tyrant if it is used instead of the spirit. It will murder the Christ-child.

Count Basie was a quiet man, but "nothing happened until he moved." When he and his band appeared in London, Basie was due to give an interview with *The Times*. He was nervous and asked Hendricks to sit in with him in case anything needed "translating." The reporter said, "You have a style of playing the piano. You don't seem to play too many notes. You're *economical* in your style of playing. How did you arrive at such a style?" Basie replied, "I just can't play no more piano." In the article, the writer commented on Basie's modesty. Hendricks claimed that when Basie started out, he could only play in the key of E♭, and that on "One O'Clock Jump" you can hear the band modulating to D after his E♭ intro. In fact this is incorrect: on the original recording, Basie plays in F, and when the band comes in it is in D♭. But by the early thirties he had improved markedly; he could hear when a soloist was running out of ideas, and would feed him some in the form of one or two notes on the piano.

On accompanists

Asked what advice he would give to pianists about playing with singers, he said, "It's called 'accompaniment.'" If a pianist found it in some way insulting to be called an accompanist, then they had the wrong attitude, because playing with a singer is not about what the pianist wants:

> You're not here to get what you want and just be here for that only. You get what you want when you give something back ... I would explain to them what the word accompanist means. When you are accompanying a singer, you are playing the chords of the song in such a way that you never get in the way of the melody the singer is singing. You always lay it down, and then, three bars later, the next phrase, and then it becomes a marriage. It's a work in which everybody takes part as an accompanist somehow, and it's healthy. If it's done right, it's artistic as hell.

Even late in Hendricks's life, Art Tatum was still his favorite accompanist. "It was like I had the whole Philadelphia Symphony back there when I was singing with him." Asked what he wanted from a bassist, he said, "In a bassist you look for thumpin'! *Boom*! Ding! Ba-doom, dup, dup ... You're looking for that!" As for drummers, he would tell people:

> You've got a vocalist here. No instrument is weaker than the human voice. So to accompany something as weak as the human voice, you've got to stay under it. And you have to have the willingness to do that. Everybody knows you want to be heard, so you should have a solo to show the audience that you are an artist, and be heard. But all of that "being heard" should not be going on over the singer. If you feature the band and let them blow on something so they can shine, it's good for them and for the audience.

On solos

He would sometimes quote something Basie used to tell his own band members: "You played a great solo last night—play it again tonight!"

On jazz and rock

Despite his innovations in vocal jazz, Hendricks was musically conservative. For him, jazz reached its apogee with bebop, and it never reached such heights again. As a performer and recording artist, therefore, he felt it was his duty to preserve it. He agreed with the sign on the wall in the bathroom at Keystone Korner in San Francisco: "Bebop is the music of the past, present and future." Music is the world's oldest art form, he explained. Jazz is the youngest form of music, and bebop is the highest form of jazz, because the bebop pioneers were intellectuals. On one occasion, he admitted, "I don't think I've ever really evolved. I think I just kept going."

By around 1970, he had lost patience with the direction jazz was taking, under the influence of rock and funk. There was a link between jazz and rock, he believed, albeit a hierarchical one:

> You won't find any rock musician worth his salt who is not a jazz fan, because they know where they come from. They all started out to be jazz musicians. When I lived in London, the Monday night relief player at Ronnie Scott's was Elton John. He was trying to sound like Horace Silver. All those guys love jazz, because they started out to be jazz musicians. What became rock was the would-be jazz musicians playing the blues. That's what rock is.

His contempt for rock was thinly-veiled; he echoed Mark Murphy in saying that an appreciation of jazz requires a greater intellect:

> That's why there's so many more pop and rock fans than there are jazz fans, because there are so many more mundane people than there are really intelligent people ... I don't mean to disparage all rock music now, there's some good music that came out of rock, and continues to, but I do say that if you are of the age sixteen-to-twenty and are a rock fan, it's perfectly normal. But if you are thirty-five and a rock fan, I believe you to be in a state of arrested cultural development.

He thought that the arguments jazz artists made for going into fusion music were simply a cover story for wanting to make money:

> Look what happens to them. Cats like Chick Corea are now trying to swing again. I had a nineteen-year-old pianist from Japan playing like Oscar Peterson. He ain't been messin' with no fusion. European musicians, even Japanese, are keeping our culture alive by playing jazz.

At other times, however, he could see that rock had opened up a conduit to to jazz. "I remember when 'ofays' couldn't clap their hands on two and four," he said. "But thanks to rock, sociologically at least, the way has been paved for mass acceptance of jazz for the first time in the history of America. And that's an important step."

On the avant-garde

He had no truck at all with the experimental and free-form music that went under the name of jazz from the sixties onwards. For him it was a movement away from jazz, it was a mistake for musicians to get involved with it, and people who thought otherwise were probably involved in it in some way:

> You can hear a thousand definitions of what jazz is, but one definition that you'll always hear is that it swings. As Mr. Ellington says: "It don't mean a thing if it ain't got that swing." Well, one thing I notice about the avant-garde: it doesn't swing. Therefore to call it jazz is, in some cases, misguided; in others, it's pure charlatanism, chicanery—just phoney posing. I think it will pass, but in the meantime it will have caught in its snare many otherwise promising musicians, some of whom may be ruined forever by it.

On the music industry

The music industry changed profoundly after the fifties, in Hendricks's view. In those days, the heads of all the record companies were musicians and artists. They had their business departments with their lawyers and book keepers and accountants, but the decisions that affected the work were made by artists:

> The head of RCA Victor played with the Philadelphia Symphony Orchestra—he played the clarinet and the bassoon. The head of Columbia Records was Goddard Lieberson, who worked in the English music hall—he could play the piano and do a dance for you—he was an artist. Decca was headed by Milt Gabler … But now they've taken the lawyers and accountants and bean counters and put them in charge of the music. Put a fox in charge of the chicken coop and see how many chickens you have left at the end of the summer. You have a lot of people recording, but where's the great art?

In later life, Hendricks did not have managers and agents taking care of his career:

> I'm my own manager, and on this next tour to Europe [1995] we're taking, I'm also my own agent. I've done it all, because I get tired of these agents telling me "that's all I could get for you," and then I call the venue and I find out that they're willing to pay more, and they probably *are* paying more, but between the agent who collects it and me when I get it, a lot of it disappears. A lot of agents

use what's called a double contract—they'll have an agreement between themselves which they sign and they'll make another one between themselves and you, the artist. They'll sell you for $3,500 per concert, and then they'll sell you to the promoter for $5,000. But you see that's $1,500 difference—he keeps that. Then they take ten percent of your $3,500 too! So he's made $1,850 on your gig."

The job of a good manager, thought Hendricks, was to be aware of double contracts and to tell the agent to go to hell.

On Miles Davis

Miles and I remained friends until his death. He allowed me the freedom to detest what he was doing when he died. He knew I hated it, but he never took umbrage at me, or even questioned me about it. I think the legacy he left jazz singers is wonderful. If you want to know how to sing, especially jazz music, Miles Davis is the greatest singing teacher I ever had. This man could sing. Ben Webster was another one. You want to know how to sing a ballad? Just listen to Ben Webster play a ballad. He teaches you how to sing.

Miles only came across as a tough guy because he was protecting the tender side of himself. "He was a Gemini—two-sided people," said Jon. "But he was also a gentle soul. 'Cos you cannot play that beautifully without being a gentle soul, not just pretending to be." The interviewer remarked that Miles was a singer on his instrument. "Yes," agreed Hendricks, "He's my favorite vocalist."

On studio recording

He did not approve of modern recording techniques, with voices and instruments recorded on separate mics:

You can't hear what the other person's singing, so you lose the blend. Whatever blend you attain comes from the engineer. I think it should come from the singers. I don't agree with a lot of modern recording technique. I think it's good for the record companies, but it's not good for the art form that they're recording. I think it's destructive to the art.

The problem lay in the isolation of the instruments, which made life easier for engineers, but adversely affected the music:

We're there to recreate a spontaneous cultural art form that's done openly and honestly and right out. So to go into all this stuff is just making the art a slave to the—what can I say?—the techniques and the business. What are we doing? Are we doing art? Or are we doing technique? Why don't we just record the engineers?

Consequently, he said, he got into a fight every time he went into the studio, and gave as an example a recent recording he had made with Dave Brubeck:

They had a drummer over there, isolated. The bass player was over here, isolated. The tenor player—one of the Brecker Brothers, Michael I think it was—in isolation over there. And me in the middle, between them, in isolation. So Dave and I just said, "Hey why don't we at least get together?" So Dave told everybody, he says, "Let Jon stand right by the piano, so we can feel each other and be together." The engineers complained, but afterwards they were the first to come out and tell the musicians how great it sounded. The life of the music is the proximity of the musicians to each other.

Asked how the multitracked voices of *Sing a Song of Basie* translated into live performance, he responded:

You don't have to sound a note for the audience to hear that note … If you have [two instruments] sound their two notes correctly, the audience will automatically, subliminally, subconsciously hear the third note … They'll put it in there with their ear.

He gave the example of Ahmad Jamal using silences. Once piano, bass and drums have played a phrase, if piano and bass lay out and the drummer just plays his part, the audience will "hear" what the other two would have played. "That's the way the human ear works," he said. "It hears what's not there if it's heard it there before … So you can … take three notes and you can voice them so that the notes in between each of them will be subliminally heard." This, of course, is the obverse of Miles's famous dictum "Don't play what's there. Play what's not there." Miles also said, "I always listen to what I can leave out." It was all about listening, and "listen" was Hendricks's most consistent word of advice for musicians.

On critics

"Anybody with a big mouth and access to a newspaper can be a jazz critic," declared Hendricks, the former jazz critic:

If a critic played, he would know that when you're up on the stage you're trying to engender warmth, beauty and contentment in the audience. And if you succeed in doing this, then there can be nothing wrong with what you've done. It's just damn foolishness to suggest that there is. One thing I do is please audiences. If people are liking it and applauding, you're succeeding in your objective, which is to bring them happiness.

I read a review of me the other day, and I didn't recognize me there. My picture was there; that's all I recognized. None of it had to do with what my work really is.

On stage outfits

In his dressing room, he once showed Kurt Elling how to hang and fold his sweaty performance clothes inside out so that they could dry and be wearable the next day. "This is the way Duke (Ellington) taught me when we were on the road," he said, "'cause you'll have to be clean again tomorrow, when you sing again."

On jazz clubs

"I like the Blue Note," he said. "Arturo's is fun here in NYC. But my favorite is Ronnie Scott's club in London."

On the audience

He was opposed to dumbing down, believing it was better to elevate the taste of your audience rather than pander to it, since this simply kept them in their existing condition of poor understanding. That did not help them, or improve the work itself:

> It's really the job of the artist, to raise the consciousness of the audience ... and they start thinking on a much higher plane than they do ordinarily every day. I think what the arts do now, especially in the movies, is to pander and play down to the audience so much that they keep the audience in a state of abject stupidity and ignorance and animalism ... I think that's the degradation of art and not the purpose of art at all.

Playing jazz to a mass audience was always going to involve compromise, he conceded: "If you have a French restaurant that serves thirty people and then expands to serve three hundred, the food has got to drop in quality, unless you stick to your guns. That's what jazz artists have got to do."

It was also one of Jon's theories that jazz is always more popular with audiences during hard times, such as the Great Depression of the 1930s, although he did not offer any explanation for why this might be.

On leaving everything until the last minute

Hendricks was well-known for leaving everything to the last minute, at times literally still writing as he walked on stage. Needless to say, there was method in this apparent madness. "Duke was the same. The minute you put it on paper it starts to die … As long as it's in your mind, it's alive," he said. Hendricks told the story of how in 1941 Orson Welles hired Ellington and Strayhorn to provide the music for an RKO film he was making for Howard Hughes, and put them up in the Chateau Marmont, a luxury hotel in Los Angeles. Welles told them what he wanted, but they wrote nothing and spent the next four weeks eating, drinking, and entertaining. Then,

> on the last weekend, on the Friday morning of the last weekend, Orson called up and said, "Duke, we need the music on the set Monday." Duke says, "Strays, we have to go to work." That Friday, they started working. Monday morning, they had all that music at RKO.

On ego

Duke was also aware of the perils of an unleashed ego. To avoid this, one should acknowledge one's predecessors. "Duke just wanted an orchestra that would approach that of Fletcher Henderson," said Jon. Music is spiritual work, not the product of ego. "If you let your ego rise too high, it kills your creativity." Humility was the way to learn and the way to improve, and there was always someone out there who knew something you didn't. Therefore you should try to get close to that person, and find out how they go about it. And in turn, you should offer to serve them in some way, even if it's just running errands for them:

> And nobody will turn you down, because you are offering to be a personal assistant. People are flattered by that. If you do that, you can get all the knowledge you want. Many band singers that I worked with helped me. I later asked them why they had taken the time to share with me. They told me that it was because they knew

I was sincere, that I wanted to better myself, and I wasn't trying to "out-star" them. So they gave me all the knowledge they could.

He recommended this as a good way to hold your ego down. "Some people have an attitude, 'I don't serve nobody!' I say, that's okay. You don't have to serve me. Then I'm gone. I wouldn't say that's a good friend to have."

On his place in history

On being told he had a special place in jazz history, Hendricks replied:

I don't want a place in history. I want a place in the House of Lords. They made me an honorary member of the House of Lords, and an honorary member of the House of Congress, and in France, they made me a member of the Legion d'honneur, comprised of musketeers—the regiment who protects the king. Athos, Porthos, and Aramis, the famous Three Musketeers, belonged to the Legion d'honneur. That means I can go to the Mayor's mansion in Paris and show them my pin, and go right into the Mayor's office. They've given me much more than my own country.

On religion and the supernatural

Most of Jon's ideas on religion were derived from Christianity, and Judith's from Judaism, but both were in flight from any kind of orthodoxy in their respective creeds. Where they met was somewhere in the middle, where the two religions were esoteric, metaphysical. Jon often talked about spiritual matters and his belief in God, but he was not actively religious and never went to church. His interest in Christianity and the Bible was more from a scholarly or philosophical viewpoint. In fact, the established churches were finished, he believed, including the Catholic Church. This distrust of organized religion dated back to his belief that his father was worked to death by the African Methodist Episcopal Church. Hendricks also believed it was wrong for any church to think they could intercede with God on man's behalf; that was something you had to do for yourself. "We have a direct line to the creator of the heavens and the earth, and I don't think we need anybody in between," he said.Spiritual awareness and growth was one's own responsibility, with practical outcomes. This was because we all have within us a propensity to attract whatever befalls us:

Once we know that, we can begin to prepare ourselves so that we can attract less of what is bad and more of what is good. When you realize that everything of a terrible nature that has happened to you has happened only because there is inside you a force that is attracting this thing and saying "come here, happen to me, I'm ready for this"—if you realize that, then you can begin to battle, because life is one battle after another. The Bhagavad Gita tells the story about Arjuna, who's constantly enjoined to fight, fight, fight. He says, "But I don't want to fight. I am a man of peace." "You must fight." This is the battle of life, so that you fight the forces that are arrayed against you and that come towards you, because of what is inside you attracting them.

He thought that most people, not knowing this, tend to externalize their own interior weaknesses (or as Freud called it, projection): those who are intolerant of laziness in others subconsciously dislike it in themselves. But failing to recognize where this dislike of laziness actually comes from, these people allow their own laziness to persist and get stronger until it dominates their lives.

That's the way life works. We are magnets. We are electrical magnetized beings, and we attract to us that which is going to do us harm, because we have hidden and made subliminal by our subconscious mind, these thoughts inside ourselves. The whole syndrome of our life in the South can be shown through that. In the South, the people who enslaved us called us lazy, shiftless and ignorant. But at the same time, who did the work while they sat on the porch and rocked and drank mint juleps? We did the work.

Hendricks did not pretend to be a saint. He openly acknowledged his own failures—his lying, his adultery, and drug abuse. "These are crimes against your spirit ... The body's made to last forever," he said. "We kill it with what we do." But he also acknowledged that he loved ice cream. "All this talk of knowledge, but when it comes to what you really want, you're an ignoramus!"

When one of his sons died (he did not specify which one), he told King Pleasure about it, and Pleasure said, "Nobody dies! They just leave here." This idea appealed to Hendricks. "When I say, Nobody dies, I mean it literally." His belief in the supernatural extended to his first encounter with Judith. While studying at Toledo University, he had taken a fine art course. "I used to draw pictures all the time, and I would draw faces. I drew the face of this girl ... When I got through drawing, I'd end up drawing this face. I'd always feel a stirring in my heart when I looked at that face that I had just drawn. Now I know that I was in love with that face. This happened for about five or six years .... Then I met Judith and there that face was. I almost fainted ... My throat dried up. My eyes watered. I became deaf. My knees weakened. I started to itch. It was the most amazing thing. I met her in Birdland ... I

thought God, that's the most beautiful thing I've ever seen in my life. That's my face."

As a couple, Jon and Judith were firm believers in astrology. Important acts, such as the signing of contracts, could only take place when the stars were auspiciously aligned.

The astrologer Gavin Arthur drew up the Hendrickses' charts:

> He said, "I've got to show you something." He took my chart and laid it out, and then he did a transparency of Judith's chart. He laid the transparency of Judith's chart over my chart, and all the planets in our two charts went like this in every house. It was amazing. He said, "This marriage was made in heaven."

He believed that maintaining a positive mindset—especially if one was an artist—opened one's mind to being helped by the spirits that are all around us. "The human family is surrounded by spirits at all times," he said. "And they actually are taking care of us. If we were paying attention to what they tell us, we wouldn't have these tragedies that we go through."

Discography

The main source for this discography is Tom Lord's *The Jazz Discography* (West Vancouver: Lord Music Reference, 1992–). Some additional recordings were found at https://de.wikipedia.org/wiki/Jon_Hendricks/Diskografie.

Unless stated otherwise, the credited artist is Jon Hendricks (vocals), and the country of origin is the USA.

Instruments: arr = arranger, as = alto sax, b = bass, bgo = bongo, bsx = bass sax, bs = baritone sax, btb = bass trombone, cl = clarinet, cng = congas, cnt = cornet, d = drums, dir = director, eb = electric bass, fog = flugelhorn, fl = flute, g = guitar, hrp = harp, kyb = keyboards, narr = narrator, org = organ, p = piano, perc = percussion, ss = soprano sax, synth = synthesiser, tamb = tambourine, tb = trombone, tp = trumpet, ts = tenor sax, tu = tuba, v = vocal, vbs = vibraphone, vla = viola, vln = violin

King Pleasure
King Pleasure (v), Quincy Jones (tp), J. J. Johnson, Kai Winding (tb), Lucky Thompson (ts), Danny Bank (bs), Jimmy Jones (p), Paul Chambers (b), Joe Harris (d)
New York, 1953

    Don't Get Scared

Prestige 913

Jon Hendricks/Dave Lambert
Teacho Wilshire (p), unknown bass and drums, Dave Lambert, Butch Birdsall, Harry Clark (v)
New York, late 1953

    Four Brothers (side 1 and side 2)

Avalon 63695

Jon Hendricks and the Dave Lambert Singers (single session)
The Dave Lambert Singers (v), with unknown rhythm section
New York, May 1955

Cloudburst
Four Brothers

Decca 9-29572

Single session
Unknown band.
Probably New York, some time before October 27, 1956

Crazy, Crazy, Crazy 'Boutcha Baby
You Baby

Pleasure Records 1001

Lambert, Hendricks & Ross: Sing a Song of Basie
Dave Lambert, Annie Ross (v), Nat Pierce (p), Freddie Green (g), Eddie Jones (b), Sonny Payne (d)
Beltone Studios, New York

August 25, 1957

It's Sand, Man
Little Pony
Blues Backstage
Down for the Count

September 16

Avenue C

October 11

Down for Double
Fiesta in Blue

November 26

Two for the Blues
Every Day I Have the Blues
One O'Clock Jump

ABC223/ABCS223—*Sing a Song of Basie*

Count Basie and his Orchestra, with Lambert, Hendricks & Ross: Sing Along with Basie
Dave Lambert, Annie Ross, Joe Williams (v) Count Basie (p), Freddie Green (g), Eddie Jones (b), Sonny Payne (d), Snooky Young, Thad Jones, Wendel Cully, Joe Newman (tp), Al Grey, Henry Coker, Benny Powell (tb), Marshal Royal (as, cl), Frank Wess (as, ts,fl), Frank Foster, Billy Mitchell (ts), Charlie Fawlkes (bs)
Capitol Studio, NYC

May 26, 27, 1958

Let Me See
Swingin' the Blues
Li'l Darlin' [b]

September 2, 3, 1958

Goin' to Chicago

Tickle Toe [ab]
Every Tub

October 15, 1958

Jumpin' at the Woodside [ab]
Shorty George [a]
Rusty Dusty Blues [a]
The King [ab]

M-Squad Theme (unissued)

Roulette R-52018—*Sing Along with Basie*
[a] Roulette CD 795332
[b] Roulette REP-1024

Lambert, Hendricks & Ross (single session)
Dave Lambert, Annie Ross (v), Nat Pierce (p), Kenny Burrell (g—although more likely to be Freddie Green), Addison Farmer (b), Osie Johnson (d)
New York, August 1, 1958

Doodlin'
Spirit Feel

United Artists 45-156, Yorkshir 711

George Russell and his Orchestra: New York, N.Y.
Art Farmer, Doc Severinsen, Ernie Royal (tp), Bob Brookmeyere, Frank Rehak, Tom Mitchell (tb), Hal McKusick (as), John Coltrane (ts), Sol Schlinger (bs), Bill Evans (p), Barry Galbraith (g), Milt Hilton (b), Charlie Persip (d), Jon Hendricks (narr), George Russell (arr, dir)
September 12, 1958, New York

Manhattan

Art Farmer, Ernie Royal, Joe Wilder (tp), Bob Brookmeyer, Jimmy Cleveland, Tom Mitchell (tb), Phil Woods, Al McKusick (as), Al Cohn (ts), Gene Allen (bs), Bill Evans (p), Barry Galbraith (g), George Duvivier (b), Max Roach or Don Lamond (d), Jon Hendricks (narr), Al Epstein (bgo), George Russell (arr, dir)
November 24, 1958, New York

A Helluva Town
Manhattan-Rico

Art Farmer, Joe Wilder, Joe Ferrante (tp), Bob Brookmeyere, Frank Rehak, Tom Mitchell (tb), Phil Woods, Al McKusick (as, fl, cl), Benny Golson (ts), Sol Schlinger (bsx), Bill Evans (p), Barry Galbraith (g), Milt Hilton (b), Charlie Persip (d), Jon Hendricks (narr), George Russell (arr, dir)
March 25 1959, New York

Big City Blues
East Side Medley: Autumn in New York/How About You

Decca 9216—New York, N.Y.

Lambert, Hendricks & Ross: The Swingers!
Dave Lambert, Annie Ross (v), Zoot Sims (ts), Russ Freeman (p), Freddie Green, Jim Hall (g), Eddie Jones (b), Sonny Payne (d)
The Crescendo, Hollywood, CA

March 21, 1959

> Jackie
> Where
> Little Niles
> Four
> Swinging Till the Girls Come Home
> Babe's Blues
> Airegin
> Airegin (alt take)

March 24, 1959
Jim Hall replaces Freddie Green

> Love Makes the World Go Round
> Dark Cloud
> Now's the Time

World Pacific 1264—*The Swingers!*

Duke Ellington, Harry James, Herb Pomeroy, Jon Hendricks: Europa Jazz

Ernie Andrews (v), Harry James, Nick Buono, Art Depew, Don Paladino, Bob Rolfe (tp), Bob Edmonson, Bob Robinson, Ray Sims (tb), Herb Lorden, Willie Smith (as), Corky Corcoran, Frank Polifroni (ts), Ernie Small (bs), Larry Kinnamon (p), Allen Reuss (g), Russ Philips (b), Buddy Rich (d)
Live recording, 1959

> Flying Home

Europa Jazz EJ 1022—*Europa Jazz* (Italy)

A Good Git Together

Pony Poindexter (as), Gildo Mahones (p), Wes Montgomery (g), Monk Montgomery (eb), Walter Bolden (d)
Recorded live at Fugazi Hall, San Francisco, CA, 1959

> A Good Git Together [a]
> Feed Me

Ike Isaacs (b), Jim Wormsworth (d), replace Monk Montgomery (b), Walter Bolden (d), Buddy Montgomery (vbs), Bill Perkins (tamb) added, probably Gildo Mahones (p) added

> Everything Started in the House of the Lord [a]
> I'll Die Happy [b]
> Minor Catastrophe

Nat Adderley (cnt), Julian "Cannonball" Adderley (as), Gildo Mahones (p), Wes Montgomery (g), Monk Montgomery (eb), Walter Bolden (d)

> Music in the Air
> Pretty Strange
> The Shouter
> Social Call [b]
> Out of the Past

World Pacific 819 WP (ST) 1283—*A Good Git Together* (1959)
[a] World Pacific X-819 (single)
[b] World Pacific S-204 (single)

Lambert, Hendricks & Ross: The Hottest New Group in Jazz
Dave Lambert, Annie Ross (v) Harry "Sweets" Edison (tp), Gildo Mahones (p), Ike Isaacs (b),
Walter Bolden (d)
New York, August 6, 1959

Centerpiece [b]
Moanin' [a]
Charleston Alley
Twisted
Cloudburst [a]

November 4, 1959

Harry Edison (tp, v); Jimmy Wormsworth (d) replaces Walter Bolden

Gimme That Wine [b]
Bijou
Sermonette
Summertime (HE vcl)
Everybody's Boppin' (HE vcl)

Columbia CL1403—*The Hottest New Group in Jazz*
[a] Columbia 4-41468 (single)
[b] Columbia 4-41588 (single)

Annie Ross with Lambert and Hendricks
Possibly Tommy Flanagan (p), Joe Benjamin (b), Elvin Jones (d)
RCA Studios, New York, October 1, 1958

Jackie (Annie Ross with Lambert and Hendricks)
Where (Jon Hendricks)

World Pacific S-202

Lambert, Hendricks & Ross: Sing Ellington
Dave Lambert, Annie Ross (v), Gildo Mahones (p), Ike Isaacs (b), Jimmy Wormsworth (d)
New York, May 9, 1960

Midnight Indigo
What Am I Here For (unissued)
In a Mellow Tone
All Too Soon

May 12

Happy Anatomy
I Don't Know What Kind of Blues I've Got
Cottontail (unissued)
Rocks in My Bed (unissued)

June 2

In a Mellow Tone
Cottontail
Main Stem
Things Ain't What They Used to Be

August 18

    What Am I Here For
    All Too Soon
    Rocks in My Bed
    Caravan

Columbia CL1510—*Sing Ellington*

Evolution of the Blues Song

Jon Hendricks (v, narr), Big Miller, Jimmy Witherspoon, Hannah Dean (v); Eric Gale, Gildo Mahones (p), Bobby Gibbons (g), Ike Isaacs (b), Jimmy Wormsworth (d), Ben Webster, Pony Poindexter (ts)
Los Angeles, September 21 1960

    Amo
    Some Stopped on de Way
    Swing Low, Sweet Chariot
    New Orleans
    I Had My Share
    Please Send Me Someone to Love
    Sufferin' Blues

September 1960

    That's Enough
    Aw, Gal
    See See Rider
    Jumpin' with Symphony Sid
    The Sun Gonna Shine in My Backdoor
    WPA Blues
    Sometimes I Feel Like a Motherless Child

Columbia CL1583—*Evolution of the Blues Song*

Lambert, Hendricks & Ross: High Flying

Same personnel as *Sings Ellington*
Chicago, March 13–14, 1961

    Halloween Spooks
    Mr PC [a]
    Hi-Fly
    Come On Home
    Farmer's Market
    Popity Pop
    The New ABC
    Cookin' at the Continental
    With Malice Towards None

Chicago, March 14, 1961

    Home Cookin'
    Blue

Columbia CL1675—*High Flying*
[a] Columbia Stereo Seven JS7-72—*Various Artists: Who's Who in the Sixties*

Lambert, Hendricks & Ross
May 4, 1961

Deck Us All with Boston Charlie (no cat. no.)

Count Basie and his Orchestra: Basie at Birdland
Sonny Cohn, Lonnie Johnson, Thad Jones, Snooky Young (tp), Henry Coker, Quentin Jackson, Benny Powell (tb), Marshall Royal (cl,as), Frank Wess (as, ts, fl), Frank Foster (ts), Charlie Fowlkes (bs), Count Basie (p), Freddie Green (g), Eddie Jones (b), Sonny Payne (d)
Birdland, New York, July 28, 1961

Whirly Bird

Roulette R52111—*Basie at Birdland*

Salud! Joao Gilberto
Gildo Mahones (p), George Tucker (b), Jimmie Smith (d), plus on some tracks six-piece string section, Buddy Collette (fl), Frank Messina (acc), Pete Candoli or Conte Candoli (tp), Milt Bernhart (tb), Ray Sherman (org), uncredited (g), Antonio Carlos Jobim, Johnny Mandel, Walter Wanderley, John Carisi (arr)
Los Angeles, 1961

The Duck (O Pato)
Quiet Nights (Corcovado)
You and I (Voce e Eu)
Love and Peace (O Amor Em Paz)
Little Paper Ball (Bolinha de Papel)
Longing for Bahia (Saudade da Bahia)
Little Train of Iron (Trem de Ferro)
No More Blues (Chega de Saudade)
Rosa Morena
The Most Beautiful Thing (Coisa Mais Linda)
Samba of My Land (Samba de Minha Terra)
Once Again (Otra Vez)
Jive Samba

Reprise 6089—*Salud! Joao Gilberto*

Fast Livin' Blues
Joe Newman (tp), Al Grey (tb), Billy Mitchell (ts), Pony Poindexter (ts, ss), Freddie Green (g), Gildo Mahones (p), Ike Isaacs (b), Stu Martin (d)
September 6, 1961, New York

What Would You Do
Fast Livin' Blues
Saturday Night Fish Fry

September 18

Stop and Go Blues
I Never Get Enough of You
Good Old Lady
Contemporary Blues

September 27

Do You Call That a Buddy?
I'll Die Happy
Another Git-Together
Don't Mess Around with My Love

Columbia CL1805—*Fast Livin' Blues*

Various Artists: The Real Ambassadors
Louis Armstrong (tp, v), Dave Lambert, Annie Ross (v), Trummy Young (tb, v), Joe Darensbourg (cl), Dave Brubeck (p), Billy Kyle (p), Irving Manning (b), Danny Barcelona, Joe Morello (d)
New York

September 12, 1961

Everybody's Comin' (LA vcl, JM d)
Blow Satchmo (JM d)

September 19, 1961

Cultural Exchange (LA, tp/vcl, BK p, IM, b, JD cl, DB, d)

Columbia Masterworks 5850—*The Real Ambassadors*

Lambert, Hendricks & Ross
Dave Lambert, Annie Ross (v) acc by Pony Poindexter (as), Gildo Mahones (p), Ron Carter (b) Stu Martin (d)
New York, February 19, 1962

Walkin' [c]
This Here (Dis Hyunh) [ac]
Swingin' Till the Girls Come Home [bc] (PP out)

March 9

Twist City [c]
Just a Little Bit of Twist [c]
A Night in Tunisia [b]
A Night in Tunisia (alt take) [c]

[a] Columbia CL1970; Various artists: Columbia 8770—*The Giants of Jazz*
[b] Columbia FC38508
[c] Columbia C2K 64933 (CD)

Lambert, Hendricks & Bavan: Live at Basin Street East
Dave Lambert, Yolande Bavan (v), Pony Poindexter (ss, as), Gildo Mahones (p), George Tucker (b), Jimmy Smith (d)
Recorded live at Basin Street East, New York
September 6, 1962

This Could Be the Start of Something
Melba's Blues
Doodlin'
unknown title (unissued)

September 7, 1962, same venue

> Feed Me
> Swingin' Till the Girls Come Home
> Dis Heah
> One Note Samba

September 8, 1962, same venue

> Cousin Mary
> April in Paris
> Shiny Stockings
> Desafinado/Slightly Out of Tune
> One O'Clock Jump

RCA Victor LSP2635—*Live at Basin Street East*

Ralph Gleason's Jazz Casual: Count Basie, Lambert, Hendricks & Bavan
Dave Lambert, Yolande Bavan (v), Pony Poindexter (as, ss), Gildo Mahones (p), George Tucker (b), Jimmie Smith (d), Ralph Gleason (interviewer)
February 22, 1963

> Sugar Hill Blues (instrumental, PP sop)
> Another Get Together (ditto)
> This Could Be the Start of Something Big (LHB + band from now on)
> Melba's Blues
> Shiny Stockings
> Cousin Mary
> Cloudburst

[These LHB tracks were paired with a Basie TV broadcast from the same series in May 1968. The Spanish released DVD of it is also available: Idem Home Video—IDVD 1003]

Koch Jazz KOC CD-8568—*Ralph Gleason's Jazz Casual*

Lambert, Hendricks & Bavan: At Newport '63
Dave Lambert, Yolande Bavan (v), Coleman Hawkins (ts), Clark Terry (tp, fgl), Gildo Mahones (p), George Tucker (b), Jimmy Smith (d)
Recorded live at Newport Jazz Festival, Freebody Park, Newport, RI, July 5, 1963

> One O'Clock Jump
> Watermelon Man
> Sack o' Woe
> Deedle-Lee, Deedle Lum
> Gimme That Wine
> Yeh Yeh
> Walkin'
> Cloudburst

RCA Victor LPM2747—*At Newport '63*

Dizzy Gillespie: Dizzy for President
Dizzy Gillespie (tp), Hidehiko "Sleepy" Matsumoto, James Moody (ts), Kenny Barron (p), Chris White (b), Rudy Collins (d)
Recorded live at the 1963 Monterey Jazz Festival

> Vote Dizzy (Salt Peanuts)

Douglas AD-04—*Dizzy for President* (France)

Single session
Unknown band, prod by Sonny Burke, probably 1963

> Watermelon Man
> Jive Samba

Reprise R-20 167

Lambert, Hendricks & Bavan: Havin' a Ball at the Village Gate
Dave Lambert, Yolande Bavan (v), Thad Jones (cnt, fgl), Booker Ervin (ts), Gildo Mahones (p), George Tucker (b), Jimmy Smith (d)
Recorded live at the Village Gate, New York, December 20–21, 1963

> Jumpin' at the Woodside
> Meetin' Time
> Days of Wine and Roses
> Rusty Dusty Blues (TJ and BE out)
> Three Blind Mice
> Nothin' for Nothin'
> With' er 'ead Tucked Underneath 'er Arm (TJ and BE out)
> It's Sand, Man
> I Wonder What Became of Sally (JH vcl only)
> Stops and Goes Blues

RCA Victor LSP 2891—*Havin' a Ball at the Village Gate*

Jon Hendricks
Unknown band
September 10, 1964

> Sister Sadie (unissued)
> River's Invitation (unissued)
> The Comeback (unissued)

No catalogue no.

Recorded in Person at the Trident
Noel Jewkes (ts), Flip Nunes (p), Fred Marshall (b), Jerry Granelli (d)
Recorded live at the Trident Club, Sausalito, CA, 1965

> This Could Be the Start of Something Big
> Watermelon Man
> Old Folks
> Gimme That Wine
> One Rose
> Cloudburst
> Shiny Stockings
> Yeh! Yeh!
> I Wonder What Became of Sally
> Stockholm Sweetnin'
> Jon's Mumbles

Smash MG27069—*Recorded in Person at the Trident*

Duke Ellington: A Concert of Sacred Music from Grace Cathedral

Cat Anderson, Cootie Williams, Herbie Jones, Mercer Ellington (tp), Chuck Connors (btb), Lawrence Brown (tb), Jimmy Hamilton (ts, cl), Paul Gonsalves (ts), Harry Carney (bs, cl), Russell Propcope (as, cl), Johnny Hodges (as), Duke Ellington (p), John Lamb (b), Louis Bellson (d), The Herman McCoy Choir
Grace Cathedral, San Francisco, September 16, 1965

In The Beginning God

Status DSTS1015—*A Concert of Sacred Music from Grace Cathedral*

Red Allen, Clark Terry, Dizzy Gillespie Trumpet Giants: Jazz Collection

Red Allen, Clark Terry (fgl), Rex Stewart (cornet), Chris White (b), Kenny Barron (p), Rudy Collins (d).
Recorded live at the Monterey Jazz Festival, September 19, 1965

Sometimes I'm Happy

I Giganti del Jazz—*Jazz Collection* (ten-album set, Italy)

Moe Koffman

1966. No recording information.

Mighty Peculiar
Archie Buckle-up

Columbia C42721 (Canada, single)

Various Artists: Jazz Monterey 1958–1980

Larry Vuckovich (p), Bob Maize (b), Clarence Becton (d)
Recorded live at the Monterey Jazz Festival, September 17, 1966

All of You

Palo Alto PA8080-2—Jazz Monterey 1958–1980

Single session

Bill Kreutzmann (d), Bob Weir (g, v), Jerry Garcia (g, v), Phil Lesh (b, v), Ron "Pigpen" McKernan (kyb, v) a.k.a. The Grateful Dead
Columbus Recorders, San Francisco, March 1967

Fire in the City
Sons and Daughters

Verve VK10512
Rhino 8122-74391—*Birth of the Dead*

Thelonious Monk: Underground

Thelonious Monk (p), Larry Gales (b), Ben Riley (d)
New York, February 14, 1968

In Walked Bud

Columbia CS 6392—*Underground*

Single session
Prod Ray Horricks, arr John Cameron, with unknown band

No More
Rainbow's End

Verve 45VS572 (UK)

Various Artists: Jazz Am Rhein—1967 to 1968
Johnny Griffin (ts), Sahib Shihab (as, bs, fl), Dusko Goykovich (tp), Ake Persson (tb), Francy Boland (p), Jimmy Woode (b), Kenny Clare, Kenny Clarke (d), Larry Vuckovich (v)
Recorded live at Jazz am Rhein (Koln), August 30-September 1, 1968

A Handful of Soul
He's Got the Whole World
The Jamfs Are Coming

Be! Jazz 6262-67—Jazz Am Rhein: 1967 to 1968 (6 CD set, Germany)

Cloudburst
Larry Vuckovich (p), Isla Eckinger (b), Kurt Bong (perc)
Recorded live at the Domicile Club, Munich, Germany, 1969 or 1970

No More
It Was A Dream
Shiny Stockings
Jon's Mumbles
Here's That Rainy Day
Cloudburst
Watermelon Man
Every Day I Have the Blues
Gimme That Wine
Arastão

Enja (G)4032 (Germany, 1982), Enja 25MJ3322 (Japan, 1982)—*Cloudburst*

Jon Hendricks Live
Pete King, Ronnie Scott (ts), Harold McNair (fl, ?as), Barry Roberts, Hank Shaw (tp), Reg Powell (p), Daryl Runswick [not Runsworth as printed] (b), Bill Moody (d), Kofi Ayivor, Reebop Kwakubaah (perc)
Recorded "as live" at Philips Studios, London, 1970

Home
Come Sunday
Ain't No Excuse
Low Down Dirty Blues
Fast Living Blues
Reza
Times of Love
Rainbow's End
No More
Lament

Fontana 6438 019—*Jon Hendricks Live* (UK)

Single session
Wally Stott (MD) with unknown band, probably London, 1971

> I Got Soul (Cass, Hendricks)
> Slow Train (Williams)

Philips 6006-088 (UK)

Times of Love (UK)/September Songs (US)
Wally Stott (MD) with unknown orchestra, Ronnie Scott, Bob Efford (ts)
London, 1972

> Times of Love
> Once Upon a Summertime
> It Could Happen to You
> One Rose
> Nature Boy
> I Concentrate on You
> September Song
> Li'l Darlin'
> Where
> We'll Be Together Again

Philips 6414302—*Times of Love* (UK, 1972); Stanyan SR 10132—*September Songs* (USA, 1975)

Art Blakey and the Jazz Messengers: Buhaina
Woody Shaw (tp), Carter Jefferson (ss, ts), Cedar Walton (p), Mickey Bass (b), Art Blakey (d), Tony Waters (cng)
Fantasy Studios, Berkeley, CA, March 1973

> Moanin'
> Along Came Betty

Prestige PRST-10067—*Buhaina*

Tell Me the Truth
Hadley Caliman (ts, fl), Larry Lofton (tb), Eddie Duran (g), Boz Scaggs (g), Clint Mosely (g), Melvin Seals (org), Ben Sidran, Larry Vuckovich (p), Thomas Rutley (b), Eddie Marshall, Lennie McBrowne (d); Benny Velarde (perc), choir: Bianca Thornton, Joyce Beasley, Judith Hendricks, Reggie Hanbury, Verlin Sandles
Wally Heider Studio, San Francisco, mid-1975

> Flat Foot Floogie (Judith Hendricks, Pointer Sisters, vcl; LM, d)
> Naima (CM, lead g)
> No More (Boz Scaggs, rhythm g)
> On the Trail
> Tell Me the Truth
> Old Folks (BS piano)
> I Bet You Thought I'd Never Find You
> Blues for Pablo (choir)

Arista AL4043—*Tell Me The Truth*

Stan Getz presents Jimmie Rowles: The Peacocks

Elvin Jones (d), Buster Williams (b), Judith Hendricks, Michele Hendricks, Beverly Getz (v)
Unknown studio, New York, October 1975 (instrumental session—vocals added at a later date)

The Chess Players

Columbia JC34873—*Stan Getz presents Jimmie Rowles: The Peacocks*

Various Artists: Giants of Jazz Volume 1

Gary Pribek, Paul Moen, Steve Marcus (ts), Barry Kiener (p), Lionel Hampton (vbs), Tom Warrington (b), Buddy Rich (d), Candido Romero (cng)
New York, October 19, 1977

Hamp, Rich, Dido Blues

Who's Who in Jazz WWLP 21012—*Giants of Jazz Vol.1*

Manhattan Transfer: Mecca for Moderns

Prod. Jay Graydon. Alan Paul, Janis Siegel, Laurel Massé, Tim Hauser (v), Richie Cole (as), Milcho Leviev (kyb), Abraham Laboriel (b), Steve Gadd (d)
Dawnbreaker Studio, San Fernando, CA/Garden Rake Studios, Studio City, CA, 1981

(The Word of) Confirmation

Atlantic SD 16036—*Mecca for Moderns*

Jon Hendricks & Company feat. Michele Hendricks: Love

Michele Hendricks, Judith Hendricks, Leslie Dorsey, Bob Gurland (v), Marvin "Smitty" Smith (d all tracks)
Harry "Sweets" Edison (tp), Jerome Richardson (ts), Jimmy Smith (p), John Williams (b)
P-D Recorders, Hollywood, CA, August 1981

Good Ol' Lady
The Swinging Groove Merchant

Eric Doney (p), Ray Scott (g), James Leary (b)
Russian Hill Recording, San Francisco, CA, September & November 1981

Li'l Darlin'
Tell Me the Truth
In a Harlem Airshaft
Angel Eyes

David Hazeltine (p), John Burr (b)
Sundragon Studio, New York, January & February 1982

Royal Garden Blues
Bright Moments
Willie's Tune
I'll Die Happy
Love (Berkshire Blues)

Muse MCD 5258—*Love*

Janis Siegel: Experiment in White
Janis Siegel (v), Frank Foster (ts), Jimmy Owens, Lew Soloff (tp), Lou Marini (as, fl), Gerald Chamberlain, Gregory Williams, Robin Eubanks (tb), Howard Johnson (tu), Ted Dunbar (g), Kenny Barron (p), Ron Carter (b), Grady Tate (d)
Atlantic Studios, New York, 1982

   Don't Get Scared

Atlantic 80007-4—*Experiment in White*

Charles Schwartz: Solo Brothers
John Faddis, Jimmy Maxwell (tp), Sonny Fortune (as, ss), Kenny Burrell (g), Jon Hendricks (narr), Joan Heller (v) with the Philharmonia Virtuosi of New York cond by Richard Kapp.
New York, 1983

   Snake Hips
   Shimmy
   Romp
   Stomp

Inner City IC 1164—*Solo Brothers*

Larry Vuckovich with Jon Hendricks: Cast Your Fate
Prod. Herb Wong. Larry Vuckovich (p), Hein van de Geyn (b), Gaylord Birch (d), Kenneth Nash (perc)
Mobius Studio, San Francisco, CA, October 1982

   Cast Your Fate to the Wind
   Sweet Lorraine
   I Want to be Happy
   Concerto de Aranjuez
   Walkin'
   I'll Walk Alone
   Reza
   Ah, Se Eu Pudesse

Palo Alto PA 8042-N—*Cast Your Fate*

The Manhattan Transfer: Vocalese
Alan Paul, Cheryl Bentyne, Janis Siegel, Tim Hauser (v), Bobby McFerrin (v, b, perc), John Barnes (synth)
Recorded at various studios, Autumn 1985

   Another Night in Tunisia (BM) [1]
   Ray's Rockhouse (JB)

Atlantic 781 266-1—*Vocalese*
[1] Blue Note BT 851 Bobby McFerrin—*Spontaneous Invention*

Michele Hendricks: Keepin' Me Satisfied
David "Fathead" Newman (r), David Leonhardt (p), Ray Drummond (b), Marvin "Smitty" Smith (d)
Home Base Studio, New York, 7 & 9 May, 1988

   Everybody's Boppin'

Keepin' Me Satisfied (Muse 5363)

Wynton Marsalis: Crescent City Christmas Carol
Wynton Marsalis (tp), Wycliffe Gordon (tb), Todd Williams (ts, ss), Wes Anderson (as), Marcus Roberts (p), Reginald Veal (b), Ben Riley (d)
RCA Studio, January and April 1989

Sleigh Ride

CBS 465879-1—*Crescent City Christmas Card*

Al Grey: Fab
Clark Terry (tp, fgl), Al Grey, Mike Gray, Delfeayo Marsalis (tb), Virginia Mayhew (as), Norman Simmons (p), Joe Cohn (g), J. J. Wiggins , Bobby Durham (d)
A&R Studios, New York, February 2 and 7, 1990

Save the Grease

Capri Records 74038—*Fab*

Jon Hendricks and Friends: Freddie Freeloader
A&R Studios, Sound Track Studios, TMF Studios
Count Basie Orchestra, Frank Foster (ts)
January 15 and March 17, 1990

Jumpin' at the Woodside

Larry Goldings (p), Barry Finclair (vla), Al Rogers, Andy Stein (vln), Romero Lubambo (g), Andy McCloud (b), Clifford Barbaro (d), Ron McBee (perc)
March 15 and 17, 1990

In Summer

George Benson, Al Jarreau, Bobby McFerrin (v), Tommy Flanagan (p), George Mraz (b), Jimmy Cobb (d)
June 17, July 9, 1989

Freddie Freeloader

Aria Hendricks, Judith Hendricks, Kevin Fitzgerald Burke (v), Randy Sandke (tp), Britt Woodman (tb), Jerome Richardson (as), Joe Temperley (bari), Larry Goldings (p), Tyler Mitchell (b), Jimmy Cobb (d)
March 2 and 11, 1990

Stardust
Swing that Music

Aria Hendricks, Judith Hendricks, Kevin Fitzgerald Burke (v), Wynton Marsalis (tp), Stanley Turrentine (ts), Larry Goldings (p), Tyler Mitchell (b), Jimmy Cobb (d)
January 14, 18 and 20, 1990

Sugar

Aria Hendricks, Judith Hendricks, Kevin Fitzgerald Burke (v), Joe Temperley (bs), Britt Woodman (tb), Lew Soloff (tp), Larry Goldings (p), Tyler Mitchell (b), Jimmy Cobb (d)
March 14 and 17, 1990

Take the A Train

Count Basie Orchestra, inc Rufus Reid (b), Al Grey (tb), Frank Foster (ts)
January 15, February 13, 1990

Fas' Livin' Blues
The Finer Things in Life

Alan Paul, Cheryl Bentyne, Janis Seigel, Tim Hauser (The Manhattan Transfe—v), Rufus Reid (b), Margaret Ross)(hrp), Ron McBee (b)
August 16, 17, 1989

High as a Mountain (Song no.2)

Wynton Marsalis (tp), Tommy Flanagan (p), George Mraz (b), Jimmy Cobb (d)
December 12, 1989

Trinkle Tinkle

George Benson, Al Jarreau (v), Tommy Flanagan (p), George Mraz (b), Jimmy Cobb (d)
June 7, 1989

Listen to Monk (Rhythm-a-ning)

Aria Hendricks, Judith Hendricks, Kevin Fitzgerald Burke (v), Larry Goldings (p), Tyler Mitchell (b), Duffy Jackson (d)
March 11, 19, 20, 1990

Sing Sing Sing

Denon COCY-630—*Freddie Freeloader* (Japan)

Al Grey and Friends: Christmas Stockin' Stuffer
Al Grey, Mike Grey (tb), Joe Cohn (g), Steve Novosel (b)
M&I Recording Studios, August/September 1990

Christmas Stockin' Stuffer
How Santa Got Thin

Capri Records 74039—*Christmas Stockin' Stuffer*

Georgie Fame: Cool Cat Blues
Georgie Fame (org, v), Van Morrison (v)[a], Richard Tee (p)[a], Michael Weiss (p)[b], Robben Ford (g)[a], Will Lee (b)[a], Dennis Irwin (b)[b], Steve Gadd (d)
Skyline Studios, New York, Spring 1991

Moondance (JH vcl solo) [a]
Little Pony (JH vcl) [b]

Go Jazz vBr 2043—*Cool Cat Blues*

Joyce: Linguas & Amores
Joyce Moreno, Lizzie Bravo, Tony Battaglia (v), Joyce Moreno (ac g), Kenny Werner (p), Rodrigo Campello (cavaquinho), Paul Socolow (b), Gil Goldstein (keys), Tutty Moreno (d, perc), Duduka da Fonseca, Joaozinho (perc)
Studio 900, New York, 1991

Taxi Driver

Verve 849 346—Linguas & Amores (Brazil)

Patti Dunham: Repertoire
Gary Haberman (arr, p, synth), Phil Woods (as), Tom Rotella (g), Norman Geller (p), Vincent Fay (b), Rick Petrone (b), Harvie Swartz (b), Shem (b, d, v), Bruce Rogers (v), Danny Gottlieb (d), Tommy Igoe (d), Grady Tate (d), James Saporito (perc)
A&R Studios, NY; Hallmark Productions, Westlake, CA; Manhattan Recording Studios, NY; NewFound Sound, Fairlawn, NJ; Nola Recording, NY; Red Rock Recording, Saylorsburg, PA; Tullen Sound Recording, Morristown, NJ, 1992

Why Don't You Walk Away

LaJacher L5-88-9—*Repertoire*

Gegé Telesforo: Gegé and the Boparazzi
Gegé Telesforo, Georgia Todrane (v), Clark Terry (tp, v), Marco Tamburini (tp), Bob Berg (ts), Stefano di battista (as), Marco Rinalduzzi (g, v), Ben Sidran (kyb), Danelo Ria (kyb, Rita Marcotulu (kyb), Max Bottini (eb), Enzo Pietropaou (b), Roberto Gattio, Salvatore Carrazzo, (d), Candido (perc)
Polucino's Studio, Rome, and Skyline Studios, New York, 1993

The Sidewinder
Mumbles

Go Jazz GoJ/vBr 2118—*Gegé and the Boparazzi* (Germany)

Antonio Carlos Jobim: Antonio Carlos Jobim and Friends
Gal Costa (v), Joe Henderson (ts), Oscar Castro-Neves, Paulo Jobim (g), Antonio Carlos Jobim, Herbie Hancock, Gonzalo Rubalcaba (p), Ron Carter (b), Harvey Mason (d), Alex Acuña (perc)
Recorded live at Free Jazz Festival, Sao Paulo, September 27, 1993

Chega de Saudade (OCN, HH, RC, HM, AA)
The Girl from Ipanema

Verve Records POCJ-123—*Antonio Carlos Jobim and Friends* (Japan)

United Future Organization
Sanshiro (fl), Hiroyuki Komagata (g), Alex Gray (vln), arr by Raphael Sebbag and Tadashi Yabe
1993

I'll Bet You Thought I'd Never Find You

Talkin' Loud—TLKDJ55 (EP)

Wynton Marsalis and the Lincoln Center Jazz Orchestra: Blood on the Fields
Wynton Marsalis, Russell Gunn, Roger Ingram, Marcus Printup (tp), Wayne Goodman, Ron Westray (tb), Wycliffe Gordon (tb, tu), Wess Anderson (as), James Carter (bari, bass sax, clarinet), Victor Giones (ts, ss, clarinet, bcl), Robert Stewart (ts), Michael Ward (vln), Eric Reed (p), Reginald Veal (b), Herlin Riley (d, tamb)
Grand Hall of the Masonic Grand Lodge, New York, January 22–25, 1995

Juba and a O'Brown Squaw

Columbia CXK 5769—*Blood on the Fields*

Jon Hendricks and the All-Stars: Boppin' at the Blue Note

Aria Hendricks, Judith Hendricks, Michele Hendricks, Kevin Fitzgerald Burke (v), Wynton Marsalis (tp, v), Benny Golson (ts), Red Holloway (as), Al Grey (tb), Mark Elf (g), Renato Chicco (p), Ugonna Ukegwo (b), Andy Watson (d)
Recorded live at the Blue Note, NY, December 23–26, 1993

> Get Me to the Church on Time
> Do You Call That a Buddy?
> Good Ol' Lady
> Contemporary Blues
> Everybody's Boppin'
> Almost Like Being in Love
> Roll 'Em Pete
> It's Sand, Man
> Since I Fell for You
> Shiny Stockings
> One O'Clock Jump

Telarc CD 8332—*Boppin' at the Blue Note*

Dave Brubeck: Young Lions & Old Tigers

Dave Brubeck (p)
Clinton Recording Studios, NYC, June 6, 1995

> How High the Moon

Telarc 8334—*Young Lions & Old Tigers*

Benny Carter: Songbook

Benny Carter (as), Warren Vac (cornet), Chris Neville (p) , Steve Laspina (b), Sherman Ferguson (d)
Probably Master Sound, Astoria, NY, July 26–28, 1995

> Cow Cow Boogie

Music Masters Jazz 01612-65134—*Songbook*

Benny Carter: Songbook II

Benny Carter (as), Warren Vaé (cornet), Chris Neville (p) , Steve Laspina (b), Sherman Ferguson (d)
Master Sound, Astoria, NY, July 26–28, 1995

> Doozy

Music Masters Jazz 01612-65152—*Songbook II*

Michele Hendricks: A Little Bit of Ella (Now and Then)

Michele Hendricks (v), Brian Linch (tp), Robin Eubanks (tb), Dd'Nd "Fathead" Newman (ts), Tommy Flanagan (p), Peter Washington (b), Lewis Nash (drums)
New York, January 7–8, 1998

> How High the Moon

Cristal CR37—*A Little Bit of Ella (Now and Then)* (France)

Kurt Elling: Live in Chicago

Von Freeman, Eddie Johnson or Ed Petersen (ts), Laurence Hobgood (p), Rob Amster (b), Michael Raynor (d), Kahil El-Zabar (perc)
Green Mill, Chicago, July 14–15, 1999

Don't Get Scared
Goin' to Chicago

Blue Note 522 22—*Live in Chicago*

George Duke/Various Artists: Going Home: a Tribute to Duke Ellington

Alvin Chea, George Duke, Al Jarreau, Joey Kibble, Mark Kibble, Claude McNight, David Thomas (v)
Probably 2000

Going Home

Platinum 37—*Going Home: a Tribute to Duke Ellington*

Larry Vuckovich: Reunion with Jon Hendricks

Larry Vuckovich (p), Noel Jewkes (ts, ss, cl, fl), Jules Brossard (ts, as), Allen Smith (tp, fgl), Josh Workman (g), Nat Johnson (b, v), Harold Jones, Omar Clay (d), John Santos, Orestes Vilarto, Enrique Pedraza (perc)
Bay Records, Berkeley, CA, October 5, 2001

Lester Leaps In
Last Train from Overbrook
Shorty Indigo
Tickle Toe
Do You Call That a Buddy?
Bye Bye Blackbird

Tetrachord 682

Various Artists: The Legacy Lives On

Kenny Burrell, Larry Koonse (g), Teddy Edwards, James Moody (ts), Louis Taylor (bs), Oscar Brashear (tp), Cedar Walton (p), Ray Brown, Luther Hughes, Al McGibbon (b), Roy McCurdy, Steve Williams, Paul Kreibich, Wille Jones, Stix Hooper (d)
February-May 2000, unknown location

Cloudburst
When Lights Are Low
Last Night When We Were Young
New Rhumba

Mack Avenue Recos—The Legacy Lives On

Karrin Allyson: Footprints

Karrin Allyson, Nancy King (v), Bruce Barth (p), Peter Washington (b), Todd Strait (d)
Fantasy Studios, Berkley, CA; Sear Sound Studios, New York, NY, September 4—October 18, 2005

Strollin'
Everybody's Boppin'
Airegin

Concord Jazz CCD-2291-2—*Footprints*

Take 6: The Standard
Al Jarreau, Mark Kibble (v), Till Bronner (fgl)
Recorded at The MeeDee Room, Woodland Hills, CA; Till's Studio, Berlin, Germany, 2008

Seven Steps to Heaven

Heads Up International HUCD 32—*The Standard*

Count Basie Orchestra: Swinging, Singing, Playing
Arr/cond/tb Dennis Wilson. Jamie Cullum (p, v), Curtis Fuller (tb), Bill Hughes (btb), Grant Langford, Marshall McDonald (as), Doug Lawrence, Doug Miller (ts), John Williams (bs), William "Scotty" Barnhart, Michael Williams, Kris Johnson, James Zollar (tp), Dave Keim, Clarence Bank, Alvin Walker (tb), Barry Cooper (btb), Will Matthews (g), James Leary (b), Marion Felder (d)
Probably 2009

Blues on Mack Avenue

Mack Avenue 10P—*Swinging, Singing, Playing*

Andy Farber and his Orchestra: This Could Be the Start of Something Big
Andy Farber (as, ts bs, fl), Chuck Wilson, Jay Brandford (as), Dan Block (ts, cl), Marc Phaneuf (ts), Kurt Bacher (bs), Brian Pareschi, Kenny Rampton, Irv Grossman, Alex Norris (tp), Art Baron, Wayne Goodman, Harvey Tibbs (tb), Max Seigel (btb), Bob Grillo (g), Kenny Ascher (p), Jennifer Vincent (b), Alvester Garnett (d), Aria Hendricks, Kevin Fitzgerald Burke (v)
Sear Sound, NYC, June 29, 2009

This Could Be the Start of Something Big
Roll 'em Pete

Black Warrior BWR15—*This Could Be the Start of Something Big*

3 Cohens: Family
Avishai Cohen (tp), Anat Cohen (ts, cl), Yuval Cohen (ss), Aaron Goldberg (p), Matt Penman (b), Gregory Hutchinson (d) Systems Two, Brooklyn, NY, April 17 and 18, 2011

On the Sunny Side of the Street
The Mooch

Anzic ANZ72—*Family*

Sachal Vasandani: Hi-Fly
Ambrose Akinmusire (tp), John Ellis (ts), Jeb Patton (p), David Wong (b), Kendrick Scott (d) Water Music, Hoboken, NJ, probably 2011

One Mint Julep
Hi-Fly

Mack Avenue MAC10—*Hi-Fly*

The Royal Bopsters Project
Prod Amy London (v); Darmon Meader, Dylan Pramuk, Holli Ross (v); Steve Schmidt (p); Sean Smith, Cameron Brown (b); Steve Williams (d); Steven Kroon (perc)
Water Music, Hoboken, NJ, June 12, July 6–7, 2012

Music in the Air (Wildwood)

Motéma 2348—*The Royal Bopsters Project*

Connie Evingson & The John Jorgenson Quintet: All the Cats Join In

Connie Evingson (v), John Jorgenson (g, cl, v), Doug Martin (g), Jason Anick (vln), Simon Planting (b), Rick Reed (d)
Probably 2014

Medley: All the Cats Join In / Tickle Toe

Minnehaha MM20—*All the Cats Join In*

J.J.C Hopkins Biggish Band: Meet Me at Minton's

Prod J.C.C Hopkins (p); Christopher McBride (as), Troy Roberts (ts), Philip Dizack (tp), Corey Wallace (tb), Claire Daly (bs), Solomon Hicks (g), Brandee Youngrp)(hrp), Joseph Doubleday (vbs), Noah Jackson (b), Charles Goold (d), Andy Bey (celeste), Ismel Wignall (cng), Jazzmeia Horn, Aria Hendricks, Kevin Burke (v)
'Dedicated to Judith Hendricks'
The Bunker, Brooklyn, probably 2016

Suddenly (In Walked Bud) w. Jazzmeia Horn
How I Wish (Ask Me Now) w. Aria Hendricks, Kevin Burke

Harlem Jazz Records (no cat no.)—*Meet Me at Minton's*

Notes

Introduction—The Verge of Impossibility

performing Miles Ahead at Jon's bedside ... Pete Churchill interviewed by the author, August 3, 2018.

I was knocked out ... Aria Hendricks interviewed by the author, January 10, 2018.

the greatest stories ever told ... Ben Sidran interviewed by the author, June 20, 2019.

that is the history of jazz ... Jon Richardson interviewed by the author, July 1, 2019.

really important to him ... Ben Sidran interviewed by the author, June 20, 2019.

any saxophonist who ever lived ... https://www.youtube.com/watch?v=Ul54NWmwLxs

great gymnasts at work ... Gene Lees "Jon Hendricks and Annie Ross Together Alone," *Jazz Times*, April 25, 2019.

Drives them crazy ... Interview August 17–18, 1995, by James Zimmerman, Smithsonian National Museum of American History. https://amhistory.si.edu/jazz/Hendricks-Jon/Hendricks_Jon_Transcript.pdf, p. 75

Joni Mitchell ... Don Heckman, *Los Angeles Times*, November 27, 2017.

sick as a dog ... Kurt Elling interviewed by the author, March 11, 2019.

like a work of art ... David Leonhardt interviewed by the author, January 18, 2019.

Chapter 1—You've Got Something Money Can't Buy

west to Columbus ... https://www.raremaps.com/gallery/detail/38892/railroad-map-of-ohio-published-by-the-state-1914-columbus-lithograph-co

he was a runaway. ... Zimmerman, pp. 12–13

Jon's great-grandmother ... In later interviews, Hendricks sometimes seemed confused about which parent had Cherokee blood. Both his daughter Michele and his niece Bonnie Hopkins confirmed it was the mother's side.

Jon's mother ... Zimmerman, p. 14

devote his life to God ... Aria Hendricks interviewed by the author, September 29, 2019.

African Methodist Episcopal Church (AME) ... In a *Pace Report* interview, October 4, 2011, Hendricks referred to his father's friend as Rev. Thomas Waller, but Thomas was the given name of Edward's son, better known as Fats. https://vimeo.com/30011118

reinvigorating it ... Hendricks told an interviewer that the Bishop was called C. J. Ransom, but it seems more likely he meant Reverdy [*sic*] Cassius Ransom, "the Sage of

Tawawa," a Christian socialist who spent his career in Ohio heading up the Church's 3rd Episcopal District. https://wilberforcepayne.libguides.com/library/ransom

three to a bed ... Marc Myers interview, JazzWax. https://www.jazzwax.com/2017/11/jon-hendricks-1921-2017.html

Robert and Lola Mae ... Zimmerman, pp. 1–2

food on the table ... Myers

as the kids grew up ... Michael Mwenso interview for Jazz at Lincoln Center, 2015. https://www.youtube.com/watch?v=FRc-wZHDoqY

children around the house ... Lee Ellen Martin. *Jon Hendricks, Father of Vocalese: A Toledo Story* (University of Toledo thesis, May 2010), p. 18 http://citeseerx.ist.psu.edu/viewdoc/download?doi=10.1.1.884.6959&rep=rep1&type=pdf

kind and affectionate father ... John Jeremy, background interview for *Jazz Is Our Religion*, November 23, 1971 (British Library).

I've never felt poor ... W. Patrick Hinely interview, *Jazz Forum* no.94, March 1985, p. 36

who would wash last ... Zimmerman, p. 2

clean and tidy ... Martin (2010), p. 18

my brothers and sisters ... Myers. Charles Hendricks eventually became the maître d' at a fancy restaurant where they would cook table-side. Once, in the seventies, he took a gun away from a man who had just shot his wife dead in front of a whole room of people, singing, "I did it my way," and making no attempt to escape (interview with John Richardson, July 1, 2019).

you respect all life ... Martin (2010), p. 19

What time does it start? ... ibid.

All right, Reverend, said the lawman ... Monk Rowe interview (2000), Fillius Jazz Archive, Hamilton College. https://www.youtube.com/watch?v=aM89KH1mYao

the seventh son ... ibid. Interviewed by Monk Rowe in 1995, Hendricks had gone further. A believer in numerology, he pointed out that he was not only the seventh son but the ninth child. "Nine and seven are sixteen. I'm born the ninth month on the sixteenth day, and one and six are seven." Fillius Jazz Archive, Hamilton College. https://www.youtube.com/watch?v=eX7sGSgjNXo

came into the ministry ... Private recording courtesy of Pete Churchill.

Rev. Hendricks's next sermon ... Mwenso

spiritual thing to do ... Roseanna Vitro interview, *Jazz Times*. https://jazztimes.com/columns/voices/jon-hendricks-poet-laureate-godfather-of-jazz-vocalese/

a powerful voice ... The microphone, Hendricks believed, had caused a lot of people to lose that vocal power. Ian Carr interview January 14, 1992, in New York (British Library).

the source of the blues ... *Pace Report* October 4, 2011. https://www.youtube.com/watch?v=4QK27ByLWSw

allowed to stay in Toledo ... Leonard Feather/Ira Gitler. *The Biographical Encyclopedia of Jazz* (OUP 1999, p. 313)

west to Chicago ... Map of the north-central and Great Lakes region, published 1881. https://www.loc.gov/resource/g4071p.rr001330/?r=0.074,0.267,1.167,0.439,0

desperate for entertainment ... Francis Davis. *Village Voice*, October 3, 2006. https://www.villagevoice.com/2006/10/03/territorial-imperatives/

both black and white families ... James Lester. *Too Marvelous for Words: the Life and Genius of Art Tatum* (OUP, 1994), p. 19. Todelo neighborhoods were far less segregated by color than they appear to be now. The house where the Hendricks family lived is no longer standing.

Zuttie and Vivian ... Hendricks said his mother was once fired from a good job as a cook at Ohio State Penitentiary for putting too many eggs in a pound cake. (Molly Murphy interview for the National Endowment for the Arts, January 10, 2008. https://www.arts.gov/honors/jazz/jon-hendricks.)

no money for a ticket ... Zimmerman, p. 4

the request was turned down ... Martin (2010), p. 35

song he had learned at school ... The lyrics to *Torna a Surriento*. ibid., p. 27

he would get the nickel ... Rowe (1995). The owner, Stanley Cowell Sr., was the father of Stanley Cowell the pianist (Zimmerman, p. 72).

his vocalese compositions ... Terry Perkins interview, *Jazz Standards*. http://www.jazzstandards.com/What%27s%20NewJon%20Hendricks.htm

Russ Columbo ... Zimmerman, pp. 7–8

a church full of people ... Martin (2010), p. 28

Memphis Slim ... Ashley Stephens interview, February 9, 2009. https://www.youtube.com/watch?v=ElN_BVI6Xgg

through a skylight ... Hinely, pp. 35–6

banquets and other functions ... ibid.

better than one's audience ... Undated video interview by John Cleveland. https://www.youtube.com/watch?v=2fSHQsToqec

vetoed the idea ... ibid.

Art is practicing ... Ralph Gleason, *Conversations in Jazz: the Ralph J. Gleason Interviews* (2016, Yale Uni Press), p. 265. Interview conducted March 9, 1959. The house still stands, although now boarded up. An Ohio Historical Marker identifying it as Art Tatum's house was erected outside in 2003.

Hendricks also participated ... Carr

I'll never forget that ... Vitro

avoided the melody ... Rowe (1995)

rigorous ear training ... Martin (2010), pp. 28–9

hear around corners ... Cleveland

entertained at parties ... Martin (2010), p. 29. Blind Tom was indeed born a slave in 1849. His genius was such that an Albany, NY, newspaper reported on one performance as follows: "With his right hand he plays '*Yankee Doodle*' in B♭. With his left hand he performs '*Fisher's Hornpipe*' in C. At the same time he sings '*Tramp Tramp*' in another key, maintaining three distinct processes in that discord, and apparently without any effort whatever." Quoted in Lester, p. 39

sounds like a brass band ... Lester, pp. 75–6

miracles of performance ... Schuller. *Swing Era*, quoted by Lester, p. 9

sounded two-handed ... Balliett. *Ecstasy*, quoted by Lester, p. 9

far more about harmony ... Vitro

accurately in every key ... Zimmerman, p. 15

substitute chord structures ... ibid., p. 19. In his biography of Parker (*Chasin' the Bird*, OUP 2005, p. 115) Brian Priestley quotes Don Byas: "Bird got a lot of things from me ... I played all that stuff from Tatum. That F-sharp, B-natural, E, A, D, G, C, F, like in '[I Got] Rhythm,' instead of playing [the first four bars of] 'Rhythm' chords."

two or three choruses ... David Lee interview, Jazz FM, June 3, 1990 (British Library).

illegal whiskey ... Sanford Josephson *Jazz Notes: Interviews Across the Generations* (Praeger, 2009), p. 131

most of whom were Jewish ... Zimmerman, p. 14

Chateau le France ... "I wish I had a better sense of time. My wife knows all these things. I usually ask her. When someone asks me so-and-so, I say, 'Hey Judith, when was this?' She knows when my mother died. I don't know the dates. I remember the day, but I don't believe in time. I think time is a man-made thing. In the spirit there is no time, and I'm always in the spirit of things." Ibid., p. 12

I loved to sing. ... Martin (2010), p. 32, quoting Steven Cornelius, *Toledo Blade*, October 3, 2004; December 3, 2009.

save me the last corner ... Hinely, p. 37

headlining artists ... Martin (2010), p. 30

full of grays ... ibid., p. 31

anything from tablecloths to liquor ... Cleveland. Hendricks used his own strange logic to explain why jazz thrived during Prohibition: the Sicilians who ran the clubs loved jazz because they were not really Italians, but Libyans, from Africa, only a few miles south across the Mediterranean.

followed by a tap dancer ... Mike Joyce interview, *Cadence*, January 1983, p. 5

get me in trouble ... Vitro

actually a strip club ... Aria Hendricks interviewed by the author, January 10, 2018.

Scott's-a-Poppin' ... Zimmerman, p. 11

financial stability ... Martin (2010), pp. 35–6

the way we should swing ... ibid., p. 26

whenever he was in town ... Aria Hendricks interviewed by the author, 29 September, 2019, and Jon Hendricks Jr. interviewed by the author on August 10, 2018. Jon Jr. became friends with Dwight and Thelma.

Jesse Jones Band ... Feather/Gitler, p. 313

Juice Jones ... Zimmerman, p. 9; Martin (2010), pp. 35–6

lived with his sister Vivian ... Bonnie Hopkins interviewed by the author, September 26, 2019.

Hendricks met Dizzy Gillespie ... Curiously, the Detroit Federation of Musicians, which has represented local players since 1881 and keeps historical records for the period in question, has no record of Jon Hendricks. Email to author from AFM Local 5, November 10, 2019.

Indiana Avenue ... Toledo's Jazz Tradition, on Toledo.com. https://www.toledo.com/news/2008/06/05/intoledo/toledos-jazz-tradition/

drafted into the army ... Josephson, p. 132

Chapter 2—Mitigating Circumstances

America entered the war ... According to Ulysses Lee's *The Employment of Negro Troops* (Library of Congress 66-60003, 1966), the bulk of US black soldiers were employed in supply and construction units (p.vii). https://history.army.mil/books/wwii/11-4/index.htm#contents

soldiers like slaves ... There are many documented incidents of American military police harassment of and violence toward black GIs stationed in the UK. See, for example, Linda Hervieux's *Forgotten: The Untold Story of D-Day's Black Heroes, at Home and at War* (Harper Collins, 2015). https://www.telegraph.co.uk/history/world-war-two/12035018/Revealed-How-Britons-welcomed-black-soldiers-during-WWII-and-fought-alongside-them-against-racist-GIs.html

constant racial strife ... Martin (2010), p. 40. The information about Jon's wartime experiences is culled from the Martin paper, the *Blues March* website and various interviews. The author has tried to reconcile Jon's sometimes contradictory accounts.

demoralizing for us ... *Tell Me the Truth* (dir. Audrey Lableiz, Mosaïque Films, France, 2008).

singers and dancing girls ... Zimmerman, p. 10. The USO (United Service Organizations) provides support for the military by providing entertainment, social activities and welfare.

without a weapon ... Audrey Lasbleiz interviewed by the author, January 22, 2019.

treated him as an equal ... *Tell Me the Truth*

Quartermaster's Headquarters ... Hinely, p. 38

made up the battalion ... Hendricks talked about reporting to both a captain and a major. It is not clear whether this was one and same person.

quote one of the Articles ... Hinely, p. 38

I hereby resign ... Joyce, p. 6

penalty for desertion ... Martin (2010), p. 44

Eric Douglas Hendricks ... Jon Hendricks Jr. interviewed by the author, October 8, 2018.
south to Besançon ... In another version of the story, the town was Dijon (Moody, p. 118). Roger appears in the account given in *Blues March*.
a truckload of gas ... Martin (2010), p. 45
a Frenchman's house ... The word used in Martin's interview (p.46) is not "cans" but "patens."
passed along to the next man ... ibid.
You're talking to an officer ... According to the court martial document, he was not an officer but a private.
send us another counsel ... This narrative is a composite of two accounts: Martin, pp. 46–7; Joyce, p. 6
a hanging offense ... Martin (2010), p. 47
all his back pay ... Joyce, p. 6
live in the ghetto ... Martin (2010), p. 49
the title was "Salt Peanuts" ... Hendricks told an interviewer that the label was Musicraft, but the red Guild label was the one he meant: Guild 1003 was recorded on May 11, 1945, and credited to Dizzy Gillespie, Charlie Parker, Sydney Catlett, Al Haig and Curly Russell, collectively billed as the All Star Quintette. (Uncredited, Sarah Vaughan is the one chirping "Salt peanuts, salt peanuts." She recorded her solo debut "Lover Man" the same day with the same line-up.) "Salt Peanuts" was written by Dizzy and drummer Kenny Clarke. The B side features Tad Dameron's "Hot House."
like being in Heaven ... Ken Burns. *Jazz* (2000), quoted in Martin (2010), p. 50

Chapter 3—We Don't Want No Singers, Man

The Pythodd ... The Pythodd became a popular jazz venue in the 1950s. In his autobiography *Satchmo: My Life in New Orleans* (Prentice Hall, 1954, p. 163), Louis Armstrong stated that the Knights of Pythias was "my lodge."
the recently-passed GI Bill ... The Servicemen's Readjustment Act (1944) was commonly known as the GI Bill.
what the drums should do ... *UT Times*, June 12, 2000:, pp. 3–6, quoted in Martin (2010), p. 54
the Second Great Migration ... "Between 1940 and 1950 ... one and a half million blacks left the South, as many in one decade as in the previous three." Thomas C. Holt and Molly Hudgens, *The Second Great Migration, 1940–70* (University of Chicago). http://www.inmotionaame.org/migrations/topic.cfm?migration=9&topic=1
nobody was beaten ... *Tell Me The Truth*
majoring in English ... Feather/Gitler, p. 313
racially-based legal actions ... Myers
United World Federalists ... Founded in 1947, the World Federalist Movement was a loose association of activist organizations from different countries whose main aim was the prevention of future wars following World War II. http://www.wfm-igp.org
United States of the World ... Martin (2010), p. 55
pianist Buster Hawkins ... Jeremy
she became pregnant ... Martin (2010), pp. 53–57
she was divorcing him ... ibid., p. 59
the sheriffs would intercept it ... Beverly Willett. *Washington Post*, June 19, 2017.
GI benefits ran out ... Lee Mergner. *Jazz Times*, November 22, 2017.
first student A grades ... Myers
get in touch with you ... Martin (2010), p. 58
near Columbia University ... Hendricks said the hotel was on 110th Street, so it can't have been the famous Claremont Inn, a once-swanky live music venue on 124th Street

and Riverside Drive that was in a state of dilapidation by 1951, when it finally burned down.

exactly as Bird had said ... *Sojourner's Truth*, vol. 5 no. 16; Marc Myers. Interview: Jon Hendricks (Part 1), JazzWax, July 13, 2009. https://www.jazzwax.com/2009/07/interview-jon-hendricks-part-1.html

he reached the Apollo ... Toledo's Jazz Tradition, on Toledo.com. https://www.toledo.com/news/2008/06/05/intoledo/toledos-jazz-tradition/

quite a nice place to live ... Zimmerman, p. 27

sold the song to Hoagy ... Gregg Akkerman. All About Jazz, March 27, 2012. https://www.allaboutjazz.com/jon-hendricks-still-creative-still-outspoken-jon-hendricks-by-gregg-akkerman.php?pg=1

alleged to have sold it ... Hendricks's allegation is unfounded, there being no conclusive proof of Fats Waller's authorship. Jazz Standards. http://www.jazzstandards.com/compositions-1/icantgiveyouanythingbutlove.htm

two evils of Loesser. ... Akkerman

get home to Pittsburgh ... Zimmerman, p. 31

dispute was finally settled ... *Billboard*, March 7, 1953, p. 16

briefly shared an apartment ... This was verified in a conversation between Pete Churchill and Quincy Jones (Pete Churchill interviewed by the author, September 4, 2018). Quincy and his wife were living at Oscar Pettiford's apartment, during which time it is likely that Quincy arranged Pettiford's "Swingin' Till the Girls Come Home," to which Jon wrote lyrics.

selling the same song ... Gunnar Mossblad interviewed by the author, March 7, 2019.

an unfamiliar horn ... *There I Go, There I Go*. BBC Radio 3, presented by Brian Morton, March 1, 1998 (British Library).

with perfect accuracy ... Martin (2010), p. 10. In *Jazz Singing: America's Great Voices from Bessie Smith to Bebop and Beyond* (Da Capo Press, 1996), Will Friedwald states that Pleasure also claimed authorship of the lyrics.

became a hit record ... See Scat and Vocalese chapter for authorship issues relating to vocalese. For reasons that remain a mystery, Pleasure abruptly quit showbiz in 1956, only re-emerging in 1961 with his *Golden Days* album. According to Jon Hendricks's interview with Joyce (p.7), Pleasure's disappearance was because he had got heavily into the occult. But in the interim, Lambert, Hendricks & Ross stole his thunder and become rich and famous. (Distilled from Daniel Halperin's liner notes to *Golden Days*.)

the norm in jazz tunes ... Josephson, p. 133. By this Hendricks meant that, with vocalese, a singer would have more to sing than the traditional allocation of thirty-two bars at the beginning and end of the tune.

track down Louis Jordan ... John Chilton, *Let the Good Times Roll* (University of Michigan Press, 1992), p. 266

Billboard Hot 100 ... https://www.allmusic.com/artist/lillian-briggs-mn0000289901

thirty-three recorded versions ... In 1995 Hendricks told James Zimmerman that he was still chasing his publisher for unpaid royalties on "I Want You To Be My Baby" (Zimmerman, p. 31). https://secondhandsongs.com/performance/460866/ versions#nav-entity

Ray didn't even know about it ... Martin (2010), pp. 65–68

"Don't Be Afraid" ... Friedwald, p. 237

"Four Brothers" ... "Four Brothers" is a contrafact on "Jeepers Creepers," a contrafact being a tune written using the chord sequence of an existing tune, but with a new melody.

pianists and composers ... In another account, Hendricks said Teacho Wiltshire went with him to meet Dave. It was apparently Brooks who had first showed the musically untrained Dave Lambert how to write out the vocal parts he heard in his head.

looking at me very funny … John S. Wilson. *New York Times*, April 2, 1982. https://www.nytimes.com/1982/04/02/arts/pop-jazz-jon-hendricks-brings-back-style-of-big-band-era.html

working on the same idea … Friedwald, p. 239–40

serving in World War II … Feather/Gitler, p. 399

Buddy was killed … Mark Chilla. https://indianapublicmedia.org/afterglow/dave-lambert-centennial/ (June 23, 2017)

pulled the plug … Priestley, p. 189. Hal McKusick told Marc Myers the whole story: https://www.jazzwax.com/2008/01/charlie-parker-and-voices-part-one.html. All the vocal takes were released in 1999 as bonus tracks on the CD re-issue of the Bird album *Big Band*.

his royal highness replied … Bill Crow. *Jazz Anecdotes* (OUP, 2005), p. 64–5

lacked the confidence … Zimmerman, pp. 51–52

crazy madrigal club … *DownBeat*, January 13, 1954, p. 20

get a beat … *Metronome* February 1954, p. 24

a gas as soloists … *DownBeat*, October 5, 1955, p. 24

number sixteen on the singles chart … Not number one, as Hendricks claimed.

she hit the bottle … Martin (2010), p. 64

always blowing his horn … Jon Hendricks Jr. interviewed by the author, October 8, 2018.

look after the children … Michele Hendricks interviewed by the author, October 10, 2018. After leaving Jon, Connie remarried at least twice and went on to have six more children.

Chapter 4—The Most Beautiful Thing

Quincy Jones writing and directing … *DownBeat*, February 8, 1956, p. 6

he had a spare room … Today, visitors to the Blue Note Jazz Club need only walk a few yards around the corner to see Cornelia Street.

let the good times roll … Bill Crow. *From Birdland to Broadway* (OUP, 1992), p. 44–48

bodies in tunnels … Martin (2010), p. 70

split his fee with Jon … ibid., p. 73

weekly lecture-demonstrations … *DownBeat*, May 16, 1956, p. 6

elected to ASCAP … *DownBeat*, September 5, 1956, p. 35

cut them off … Zimmerman, p. 34

he started work … Martin (2010), pp. 75–6

less happily with Charlie Parker … Friedwald, p. 230

Blues Backstage … *DownBeat*, September 17, 1959, p. 17. Drug use referred to by Jon in a conversation with Amy London.

walked forty-six blocks … Hinely, p. 33

red-haired girl … Hendricks's description.

Annie was intrigued … Anthony Brown interview with Annie Ross for Smithsonian Oral History Program, January 13–14, 2011. https://jazzday.com/media/AC0808_Ross_Annie_Transcript.pdf, p. 24

fresh out of university … Jon Hendricks interviewed by John Cleveland, January 13–14, 2011. https://www.jazzwax.com/2008/05/interview-creed.html

close Basie associate … Hinely, p. 34

have a ball and get high … Ben Sidran interview for *Talking Jazz* project November 12, 1985. bensidran.com

took them around six months … Cleveland

Your Hit Parade … *DownBeat*, September 17, 1959, p. 17

the young Mark Murphy … Peter Jones *This is Hip: the Life of Mark Murphy* (Equinox, 2018), pp. 19–20 *another was Georgia Brown* ... Joyce, p. 8

laying back and slowing down ... Marc Myers interview with Creed Taylor, JazzWax. https://www.jazzwax.com/2008/07/interview-cre-1.html

seventh one or the ninth one ... Sidran op. cit.

be born with it ... Annie Ross "Interview NPR on Fresh Air." NPR Music, August 25, 2005. Quoted by Martin, p. 77

Walter Schumann sings Count Basie ... Crow. *From Birdland to Broadway*, p. 163. Walter Schumann recorded a number of easy-listening albums with choirs in the early fifties.

couldn't swing if you hung 'em ... Friedwald, p. 241

seems a little hot in here ... Lee

innocent as a baby lamb ... Zimmerman, p. 38

the various Mafiosi ... *The Pace Report* op. cit.

Our Gang Follies of 1938 ... Annie Ross in "Loch Lomond," from The Our Gang Follies of 1938. https://www.youtube.com/watch?v=_enNo0qFxm8&index=12&list=RDaN-PHp0RBWYY

Let's Fly ... Revived by the Royal Bopsters on their eponymous 2015 album, with added vocalese written by Amy London.

James Moody and Jack Dieval ... Documentary film *No-One But Me* (dir. Brian Ross, BBC Scotland, 2012). In a 2001 interview with Monk Rowe, Annie also mentioned other Paris exiles Willie "The Lion" Smith, Sidney Bechet, "Big Chief" Russell Moore, as well as Mary Lou Williams, with whom she shared an apartment. https://www.youtube.com/watch?v=LccR9TidLmc&t=1710s

closing after three weeks ... Friedwald, pp. 241–3

build radio sets ... *The Pace Report*

turn three into twelve ... Friedwald, p. 243

worked for Columbia Records ... Martin (2010), pp. 78–9. In her PhD dissertation, *Validating the Voice in the Music of Lambert, Hendricks and Ross* (University of Pittsburgh, 2016, p. 170) Martin adds that it was Greenbaum's suggestion to overdub the voices of Lambert, Hendricks & Ross, quoting his autobiography *In One Ear, and In the Other: Memories of 48 Years in Recording* (Abraham I. Greenbaum Inc., 2000), pp. 84–5

made some pioneering records ... History of the Ampex Corporation as recalled by John Leslie and Ross Snyder in 2010. http://www.aes.org/aeshc/docs/ company.histories/ ampex/leslie_snyder_early-days-of-ampex.pdf. You can see a tongue-in-cheek TV demonstration from 1953 here: https://www.youtube.com/watch?v=VCEmAgak9V8

wow and flutter ... Wow and flutter is caused by slight irregularities in tape drive speed during recording, which create fluctuations in pitch.

the newsprint factory ... According to Tom Lord's *Jazz Discography*, the tracks were recorded in four sessions: on August 25—"It's Sand, Man," "Little Pony," "Blues Backstage," "Down for the Count"; on September 16—"Avenue C"; on October 11—"Down for Double" and "Fiesta in Blue"; and on November 26—"Two for the Blues," "Every Day I Have the Blues," and "One O'Clock Jump." But this orderly, albeit protracted, sequence simply does not square with the story told by those who were there. Since the tracks were being recorded covertly, it is possible that Taylor simply created fake studio bookings to make it look to ABC-Paramount as if everything was proceeding as planned. He apparently told Stanley Dance, who wrote the liner notes for the 1965 Impulse re-release of *Sing a Song of Basie*, that the whole process took sixty hours.

never heard anything that beautiful ... Martin (2010), p. 80

worked day and night ... Lee

both of them loved it ... Brown, p. 25

top of the list ... *DownBeat*, vol.3 no.1 1958, p. 7

outstanding listening experiences ... *DownBeat*, April 17, 1958, p. 33

great interpreters ... *Metronome*, July 1958, p. 27

entertainment value ... *Jazz Journal*, November 1958, p. 13

back of the liner ... Murphy

Greyhound bus to Pittsburgh ... Les Tomkins interview 1968 (National Jazz Archive, UK).

the chair fell over ... Lee

do-re-mi. ... Martin (2016), p. 170

four or five singers ... Crow. *From Birdland To Broadway*, p. 163

reproducing it on stage ... Brown, p. 26

syrupy baritone ... Rowe (1995). Not long after the album's release, Leonard Feather wrote a very detailed analysis of it, showing how and where it diverged from the original Basie recordings. Some of the voicings were apparently modernized by Frank Foster after transcription. "An Explanation of Vocalese" in *Jazz: a Quarterly of American Music*, Summer 1959, pp. 261–7 (this periodical, edited by Ralph Gleason, lasted only for five issues).

dispute with Neal Hefti ... *DownBeat*, January 22, 1959, p. 40

command of the combo ... *Metronome*, July 1959, p. 37

already their trademark ... Count Basie. *Good Morning Blues* (Heinemann, 1986), p. 329

E for effort ... *DownBeat*, April 2, 1959, p. 29

vaudeville turn ... *DownBeat*, September 18, 1958, p. 19 [Williams]

another rave from DownBeat ... *DownBeat*, October 2, 1958, p. 22. In his autobiography, Basie said they first got together with the trio in May 1959. *Good Morning Blues*, p. 328

Billboard reviews ... Martin (2016), p. 184

genre of rap ... According to Aria Hendricks, an academic who was writing a paper on the history of rap music considered this to be the world's first rap recording. (Interviewed by the author, May 10, 2018.)

all the introducing musically ... *DownBeat*, November 27, 1958, p. 9

Boston's Storyville ... *DownBeat*, December 25, 1958, p. 44

Steve Allen's NBC show ... *DownBeat*, vol.4 no.1, 1959, p. 25

trumpet, clarinet or trombone ... *Ebony*, February 1959, pp. 33–35

the Hi-Lo's ... *DownBeat*, December 25, 1958, p. 24

a country mile ... ibid., p. 19

may tour England ... *DownBeat*, February 19, 1959, p. 10

only a matter of time ... *Jazz: A Quarterly of American Music* (Summer 1959), pp. 261–7

apartment sixteen ... Leonard Feather, *New Encyclopedia Yearbook of Jazz* (1958, p. 132)

Red Hill Inn ... Gleason. *Conversations in Jazz*, p. 268

Sunset Boulevard ... ibid., p. 269

man, you ate my steak ... Joyce, p. 8. Hendricks often told this story, but in the version he related to Zimmerman (p.82), the tune in question was "Four."

Royal Festival Hall ... Zimmerman, p. 58

under arrest in South Africa ... Gleason. *Conversations in Jazz*, p. 271

hungry i residency ... Josephson, p. 134

stage presence ... UK tour program, 1962.

the Four Freshmen ... http://www.awardsandshows.com/features/grammy-awards-1959-may-238.html

a fast segue ... *Good Morning Blues*, p. 332

a bashing conclusion ... *DownBeat*, August 6, 1959, p. 12

beating Ray Charles ... ibid., p. 19

marked time in the background ... Don Loving. *Jazz Notes*, August 1959, p. 1

the crowd loved it ... David Leonhardt interviewed by the author, January 18, 2019.

Favorite Jazz Vocal Group ... *DownBeat*, August 20, 1959, p. 82

where she later died ... http://www.toledoblade.com/Deaths/2015/11/19/Judith-Hendricks-1937-2015-Wife-was-driving-force-behind-world-jazz-icon.html

white and colored people ... https://news.gallup.com/poll/163697/approve-marriage-blacks-whites.aspx

borscht with boiled potato ... Willett. The journalist added that a young couple—a black woman and a white man—had been arrested in 1958 in their bedroom in Central Point, VA, and thrown in jail. The couple, Mildred and Richard Loving, had married in Washington, which had no anti-miscegenation law, then returned to their native Virginia. They were convicted, but released on the condition they leave and not return together for twenty-five years. They brought their case before the Supreme Court. On June 12, 1967, the court struck down all interracial marriage bans as unconstitutional.

careers were blooming ... Albert Goldman. *Ladies and Gentlemen—Lenny Bruce!!* (Pan, 1976), p. 225

his wife was white ... "Trouble For Jon in Chicago," *DownBeat*, December 8, 1960, p. 11. Quoted in Martin (2016), p. 192

Lorton Reformatory ... ibid., pp. 198–200

desegregation of buses ... ibid., p. 208

data's too demanding ... His biographer can attest to this.

they sing jazz! ... *DownBeat*, September 17, 1959, p. 18

Charleston Alley ... Or was it, as the New York Voices' Darmon Meader claims, Edgar M. Sampson (who also wrote "Stompin' at the Savoy")? Then again, saxophonist and bandleader Charlie Barnet recorded it first in 1941, and it's also often credited to him.

have his head examined ... Nat Hentoff. *Listen to the Stories* (Harper Collins 1995), p. 63

still understand the words ... Monk Rowe interview, January 13, 2001. https://www.youtube.com/watch?v=LccR9TidLmc&t=1710s

there would be no Jon Hendricks ... This information was provided by a music business insider who requested anonymity. It was confirmed by a second source.

Keester Parade ... Doug Ramsey, "Finding Mandel," in Rifftides at artsjournal.com. https://www.artsjournal.com/rifftides/2005/10/finding_mandel.html. Secondhandsongs.com credits the song to Edison, Mandel and Hendricks, while C. Michael Bailey claimed in 1999 that the song was originally based on an earlier tune called (appropriately enough) "Nobody Knows." https://www.allaboutjazz.com/the-bill-perkins-octet-on-stage-cy-touff-his-octet-and-quintet-bill-perkins-review-by-c-michael-bailey.php

alcohol had been prevalent ... Brown, p. 26

blazing log fire ... "This was filmed at the original Playboy Club on Michigan Ave. in downtown Chicago" (comment on YouTube, since deleted). It was aired on February 13, 1960.

Every Day and The King ... https://www.youtube.com/watch?v=aNPHp0RBWYY

"Doodlin'" ... https://www.youtube.com/watch?v=9Lu1nVQDThI&list=RDaNPHp0RB-WYY&index=3

because he was white ... Zimmerman, p. 38

multitrack Duke Ellington ... ibid., p. 67

heroin addiction ... James Gavin, *New York Times*, October 3, 1993. See also Goldman. In Hendricks's case, his past heroin addiction had caused chronic constipation and hemorrhoids.

deep-toned bluesy style ... The review is uncredited but the name "Milkowski"—presumably present-day jazz critic Bill Milkowski—appears at the end. https://www.pastemagazine.com/articles/2010/02/lamberthendricks-and-ross-doodlin-horace-silver.html *darted from the stage* ... John Johnson, "Untouchables," *Ebony*, December 1959, p. 90. Quoted in Martin (2016), p. 187

Avenue C ... https://www.youtube.com/watch?v=E99TIXB_swg

best known number ... *Jazz Me Blues: the Autobiography of Chris Barber* (Equinox, 2014), p. 72

something about the blues ... James L. "Jimmy" Lyons was the Festival's manager from 1958 until his retirement in 1992.

every Negro person in America ... Joyce, p. 8

circuit rider ... He had described his father as a "runaway" before. Slavery was officially abolished at the end of the American Civil War in 1865. For his father to run away from whatever Virginia plantation he had been born on, he must have been at least eight years old, which would have made him around sixty-four by the time Jon was born in 1921. By this reckoning he would have been over eighty by the time he died in Greenup, KY, some time in the 1950s.

political/educational credo ... Aria Hendricks interviewed by the author, May 10, 2018.

on stage with him ... 1975 show program on Larry Vuckovich's website.

justified its existence ... Quotes taken from the liner notes of the album release. Kofsky was a jazz aficionado and Professor of History at Cal State University.

that's what they had to do ... Josephson, p. 134

she had to quit ... Myers https://www.jazzwax.com/2009/03/interview-carol-sloane-part-2.html

comedic talent ... Aria Hendricks interviewed by the author, May 10, 2018.

arranged by Jobim ... This was almost certainly *O Amor, O Sorriso E A Flor*, released by Capitol in the US with the clumsy title *Brazil's Brilliant João Gilberto Pops in Portuguese with Antonio Carlos Jobim's Orchestra*.

integration crisis ... Faubus brought in the Arkansas National Guard to prevent young African Americans attending Little Rock Central High School, even though it was part of federally ordered racial desegregation. Charles Mingus made his own comment on the affair with his celebrated tune "Fables of Faubus" on *Mingus Ah Um* (1959).

mouthful of hot rice ... Ottney, *Toledo Free Press* Star, September 19, 2012, p. 6

the subject of race ... Karl Ackermann, All About Jazz, April 27, 2018 https://www.allaboutjazz.com/state-and-mainstream-the-jazz-ambassadors-and-the-us-state-department-by-karl-ackermann.php?page=1

flashed to the forefront ... Program for UK tour, 1962.

mix all kinds of stuff. ... Brown, p. 27

merry-go-round ... Paul Roland consultant ed. *Jazz Singers: the Great Song Stylists in their Own Words* (Hamlyn 1999), pp. 101–2

oh I don't know ... A sound recording from one of the last Lambert, Hendricks & Ross concerts, in Bremen, Germany, April 23, 1962, was available online at the time of writing: https://crooksandliars.com/gordonskene/newstalgia-downbeat-lambert-hendricks-

Chapter 6—Everybody Got Tired

strict quota system ... Hendricks saw this discrimination as political, a way to pack the country with a right-wing constituency of Irish Catholics.

the way was cleared ... Zimmerman, pp. 44–5

a never-ending melody ... Pat Thomas, Julie London and Ella Fitzgerald all released their own versions with the Hendricks lyrics in October 1962.

extraordinarily successful ... *Jazz Journal*, June 1963, p. 32

there wasn't the fire ... John S. Wilson op. cit.

interviewed by the host ... *Ralph Gleason's Jazz Casual* was produced for KQED San Francisco and ran for eight years and thirty-one episodes on National Educational Television (NET). These are available on video and CD.

make the trip himself ... "The Year Dizzy Gillespie Ran for President—Spoiler Alert, He Didn't Win," DangerousMinds.net. https://dangerousminds.net/comments/the_year_dizzy_gillespie_ran_for_president_1964_spoiler_alert_he_didnt_win

went to the hospital ... Aria Hendricks interviewed by the author, September 25, 2019.

Dave quit the group ... Feather/Gitler, p. 399

it didn't work out ... Lees op. cit.

being shocked ... Aria Hendricks interviewed by the author, May 10, 2018. A photograph of Pat Harris "of Jon Hendricks's trio" appeared in *Ebony*, December 1964 (p.62), but Harris was dark-haired. The magazine reported that she and Chastain had sung with Hendricks at that year's Monterey Jazz Festival (p.57).

beat it out of them ... Michele Hendricks interviewed by the author, October 10, 2018.

locked them in the closet ... Aria Hendricks interviewed by the author, September 29, 2019.

Kingston Trio ... Whilst at the Vanguard, Ganapoler was said to be the only club manager who succeeded in getting his money's worth out of Miles Davis. At the time Miles would often disappear to score drugs after playing only one set. Other club owners complained about the amount of money they had to pay him for one show per night. When Lou booked Miles, he told him he was going to pay him per show, not per night. After that Miles always played two sets.

if the mood took him ... Noel Jewkes interviewed by the author, November 7, 2018.

took some persuading ... Zimmerman, pp. 60–1

the music of Edu Lobo ... Larry Vuckovich interviewed by the author, September 3, 2018.

writing lyrics to his tunes ... Jon told it slightly differently to Gunnar Mossblad. In this version, he and Monk were talking about writing lyrics, and Jon was bragging he could write lyrics to anything, whereupon Monk challenged him to lyricize his tunes.

It took me six months ... Paul Meyers interviewed by the author, June 12, 2018.

Crepuscule with Nellie ... Interviewed after a gig at North Sea Jazz Festival July 17, 1982, in The Hague (World of Jazz Videos). https://www.youtube.com/watch?v=QyA9Qc17SBk. Also see chapter 10 about some unreleased recordings made in Toledo around 2014.

no fewer than eight ... Renato Chicco interviewed by the author, December 18, 2018.

no aspirin, no headaches ... https://www.youtube.com/watch?v=r8T5-AxBUwI

the dancing of Bunny Briggs ... Duke Ellington. *Music Is My Mistress* (W. H. Allen, 1974), p. 263

The Warlocks ... https://archive.org/details/gd1966-12-05.sbd.kimbro.23064.sbeok.shnf. According to the band's Bob Weir, Hendricks performed with them in 1967 (https://www.jazzwax.com/2017/09/ad-hed.html)

for them it was perfect ... In Leonard Feather's *Encyclopedia of Jazz in the Sixties* (Da Capo, 1966, p. 156), the Hendrickses' address is given as 68 Cloudview Road, Sausalito.

Irene Kral and June Christy ... Larry Vuckovich interviewed by the author, September 3, 2018.

Detroit and elsewhere ... The earliest recording featuring both was "All Of You," performed live at Monterey Jazz Festival, September 17, 1966. *Jazz Monterey 1958–1980* (Palo Alto PA8080-2)—see Discography.

from swing to bebop ... Noel Jewkes interviewed by the author, November 7, 2018.

other freelance work ... Feather/Gitler, p. 399

producer George Avakian ... They were Mary Vonnie, David Lucas, Sarah Boatner and Leslie Dorsey, with George Duvivier on bass.

Avakian declined ... https://vimeo.com/2681835 A later recording of Dave Lambert performing may exist—see below.

when they were struck ... The Norwalk Hour, November 5, 1966. This contemporary news report does not mention Dave's girlfriend but see Marc Myers's interview with Yolande Bavan. https://www.jazzwax.com/2007/11/a-chat-with-yol.html

Pennies from Heaven ... Crow. *From Birdland to Broadway*, p. 163

packed memorial concert ... Dave's last recording was apparently made at the 1965 Charlie Parker Memorial Concert, where he sang "Donna Lee." Unfortunately, the video is no longer available on YouTube. Richard Vacca: https://www.troystreet.com/tspots/2013/06/19/june-19-1917-dave-lambert-born/

he'd show you. ... Zimmerman, p. 68

Happy Days ... Dee Lambert on her father, Dave Lambert, July 24, 2014. https://jazz.fm/dee-lambert-my-dad-dave-lambert/

a bottle of champagne ... Marc Myers. Jazzwax interview with Yolande Bavan

every day of my life ... Lees

wardrobe from Holsten ... Carr

babysitters ... Michele Hendricks interviewed by the author, September 12, 2018.

some total stranger ... Aria Hendricks interviewed by the author, September 25. 2019.

his son Eric ... Jon told his interviewer, Dave Lee, that Eric was ten.

his birth mother, Connie ... Aria Hendricks interviewed by the author, January 10, 2018.

understood what he was saying ... Hendricks did not share these insights. https://www.toledo.com/news/2008/06/05/intoledo/ toledos-jazz-tradition/

Mongo Santamaria ... There is no sign of Hendricks on anything Mongo released.

producer Teo Macero ... Jon said it was Monk himself who asked. According to Monk's biographer Robin D. G. Kelley, Columbia had commissioned Hendricks to write lyrics three years earlier for "all of Monk's tunes, as the company contemplated featuring Hendricks on an all-Monk LP. Like so many Columbia projects, it never came to fruition, but not because Monk objected ... In the end Monk was pleased with the lyrics." *Thelonious Monk: the Life and Times of an American Original* (Free Press, 2010), p. 394

not realizing ... Zimmerman, p. 66

Chapter 7—The Mistakes Are the Only Part That's Jazz

fur coats and jewelry ... Aria Hendricks interviewed by the author, January 10, 2018.

nowhere on either list ... Melody Maker, February 24, 1968, pp. 18–19

Jon's live album ... Larry Vuckovich interviewed by the author the author, September 3, 2018. The liner notes state that the album was recorded in 1972, but according to Larry it was 1969 or 1970.

house near Marble Arch ... Conversation with Val Wilmer (2018, undated).

make a living ... Melody Maker, April 13, 1968, p. 8

his own scat solo ... Tomkins (1968)

they could go home ... Michele Hendricks interviewed by the author, October 10, 2018.

passenger on that ride ... Aria Hendricks interviewed by the author, May 10, 2018.

opportunities to make friends ... Michele Hendricks interviewed by the author, September 12, 2018.

TV and radio appearances ... Three tunes—"A Handful of Soul," "He's Got the Whole World" and the oddly-titled "The Jamfs Are Coming," with members of the all-star international Clark-Boland band, were recorded for posterity and released on the compilation album *Jazz Am Rhein: 1967 to 1968* (see Discography).

the house they lived in ... Lee

Maynard Ferguson ... Moody, p. 180

very acceptable ... Zimmerman, p. 65

five nights at the club ... ibid.

Marquee Club ... The gig was on December 26, 1969. http://www.45worlds.com/live/artist/jon-hendricks

He's lost his mind! ... Michele Hendricks interviewed by the author, September 12, 2018.

living in the UK ... http://www.michaelvalentinestudio.com/jazz_gallery/king_lockett/index.php

Reebop Kwakubaah ... Ghanaian-born Anthony "Rebop" Kwaku Baah also worked with Randy Weston, the rock group Traffic, Steve Winwood and Eric Clapton, among others.

Bassist Dave Green ... Green received £9.10s for the date (roughly equivalent to £150 in 2019).

American musician friends ... Daryl Runswick interviewed by the author, June 25, 2019.

the group became a quartet ... Wilson

push her on stage ... Aria Hendricks interviewed by the author, January 10, 2018.

never come back ... ibid.

a separate person ... Aria Hendricks interviewed by the author, September 25, 2019.

the next forty-eight years ... Norma Winstone interviewed by the author, December 15, 2018. She finally got to sing it in London in December 2018.

the Monk project ... *Miles Ahead* was completed just before Jon died. See chapter 10.

The Young Generation ... BBC genome

Hommage à Cole Porter ... Wilson

Hampstead Theatre Club ... *Evolution* played at The Blackie on March 16–17, 1972 with Lee Scones (p), Alan Cooper (b), Les Cirkel (d), Lord Eric (bgo) with George Margo staging/directing.

pay attention ... Les Tomkins interview, *Crescendo*, February 1973, pp. 15–17

West Indian-born musicians ... See also John Fordham *Let's Join Hands and Contact the Living* (Elm Tree, 1986), p. 143

five pounds for a gig ... Dave Green interviewed by the author, February 1, 2019.

don't have to pay them ... Email from Frank Griffith.

huffing about "sacrilege" ... Aria Hendricks interviewed by the author, September 25, 2019.

his favorite ... Hinely, p. 33

a good enough booking ... Zimmerman, p. 45

Rolling Stone ... Ben Sidran interviewed by the author, June 20, 2019.

teaching jazz history ... *Evolution* program 1974

Country Joe MacDonald ... http://www.45worlds.com/live/artist/jon-hendricks-and-family

Along Came Betty ... Message on Jon's website dated January 3, 2003. As with "Watermelon Man," Jon claimed he never got paid.

phony expenses claims ... *New York Times*, June 22, 1973; April 24, 1977

ended up on the record ... Ben Sidran, *A Life in the Music* (Taylor Trade Publishing, 2003), pp. 123–4

fixed performance ... Aria Hendricks interviewed by the author, September 25, 2019.

relevant to the Trump era ... The singer Roseanna Vitro pointedly recorded her own version in 2018.

communications vehicle ... Eliot Tiegel, *Billboard*, July 12, 1975

WTTW Chicago ... https://www.youtube.com/watch?v=PgYAS6mhn7A

okay the lyric. ... Dan Morgenstern. *Living with Jazz* (Pantheon, 2004), p. 377–8

excellent voice ... Jon Hendricks Jr. interviewed by the author, August 10, 2018.

later renamed Edward ... Michele Hendricks interviewed by the author, September 12, 2018.

sorry I ever met you ... Donald McKayle. *Transcending Boundaries: My Dancing Life* (Routledge, 2002), pp. 233–4

The defendants ... At this point in the interview, which was conducted in Washington, DC on March 7, 1981, Green is rendered as "Mark Queen," and Burton Lane has become "Bert Marks" (Joyce, p. 8).

ten thousand bucks ... ibid., p. 9

the singing of Mrs. Hendricks ... Eric G. Johnson interviewed by the author, September 26, 2019.
they never forgave Cosby ... Gunnar Mossblad interviewed by the author, March 21, 2019.

Chapter 8—No Chord is Better Than the Wrong Chord

full view of the audience ... Martin Hone interviewed by the author, January 9, 2019.
radio promotions ... Eghosa Osarabo interviewed by the author, August 11, 2018.
operated the pump ... Michele Hendricks interviewed by the author, October 10, 2018.
they were all sleeping ... Bob Burgess's account of a 1951 tour, quoted in Chilton, p. 164
project came together ... Rowe (2000) and Ashley Stephens interviews. In fact there had been an earlier version of The Manhattan Transfer founded in 1969 that recorded an album (*Jukin'*, 1971) for Capitol, before breaking up. It may be that the encounter took place in the late sixties, and that Jon conflated these two eras in the group's history.
former dancing partner ... Jones, p. 74
I got a song for you ... Moody, p. 117
hipster and preacher ... Janis Siegel interviewed by the author, October 16, 2018.
Best Arrangement ... https://manhattantransfer.net/about/
whispering in his ear ... Janis Siegel interviewed by the author, October 16, 2018.
something completely new ... *In the Moment: Jazz in the 1980s* by Francis Davis (OUP, 1986), pp. 54–55
join the family group ... Wilson
essential for good health ... Bob Gurland interviewed by the author, March 12, 2019.
Charlie Parker's "Confirmation" ... Janis Siegel interviewed by the author, October 16, 2018.
ran out of the room ... Jon Hendricks Jr. interviewed by the author, October 8, 2018. "Their names are known," he added.
Joe Fields's Muse label ... On September 19, 1988 the *New York Times* reported that Leslie Dorsey was moonlighting as a taxi driver on Labor Day when he was killed during a robbery, shot point-blank in the back of the head and robbed by one of three men in his cab. At the time he was scheduled to sing in the chorus of seven operas at the New York City Opera.
the original recording ... Michele Hendricks interviewed by the author, October 10, 2018.
the various sessions ... *Jazz Journal*, October 1982, p. 41
Rolls Royce class ... Wilson
different piano players ... Bob Gurland interviewed by the author, March 12, 2019.
Clifford Barbaro ... David Leonhardt interviewed by the author, January 18, 2019.
entertainment hotspot ... Ted Gioia *West Coast Jazz* (OUP 1992), p. 5. See also https://www.laconservancy.org/locations/dunbar-hotel The hotel fell into disrepair in the 1960s but was renovated and reopened in 2013 as Dunbar Village to provide permanent accommodation for families and senior citizens. Frustratingly, despite contacting KCBS and the Emmy, Peabody, and Iris awarding bodies, the author has been unable to find any trace of *Somewhere to Lay My Weary Head*.
half-empty houses ... Stephanie Nakasian interviewed by the author, February 3, 2019.
a series of dates ... The pianist in question accompanied Jon Hendricks on numerous occasions, both before and after.
wonderful things ... Bob Gurland interviewed by the author, March 12, 2019.
Avery Brooks ... Brooks, who was also an actor, ended up playing Captain Benjamin Sisko in *Star Trek: Deep Space Nine*, which ran from 1993 to 1999.
signed over the rights ... David Leonhardt interviewed by the author, January 18, 2019.
quite long solos ... ibid.
made it less successful ... Aria Hendricks interviewed by the author, May 10, 2018.
not necessarily qualified ... Note from Gunnar Mossblad, February 17, 2020.

we'll have a gangbang ... Martin Hone interviewed by the author, January 9, 2019.
Sticky Mack ... Larry Goldings interviewed by the author, December 23, 2019. Larry later commemorated this in the tune "Sticky Mack" on his *Awareness* album (1997).

Chapter 9—We Need You to Control Him

it wouldn't be advertized ... Stephanie Nakasian interviewed by the author, February 3, 2019.
thirty-six hour marathon ... Kevin Burke interviewed by the author, March 14, 2019.
Philadelphia jazz spot ... https://indianapublicmedia.org/nightlights/hipsters-flipsters-onthescenesters.php
in a long time ... *Jazz Journal*, March 1991, pp. 34–5
prowess on the guitar ... Anne Legrand interviewed by the author, February 5, 2019. As previously mentioned, on other occasions he said *Times of Love/September Songs* was his best.
the Japanese economy ... Kevin Burke interviewed by the author, March 14, 2019.
Contact ASCAP ... https://www.ascap.com/repertory#ace/writer/63612886/HENDRICKS%20JON
reverted to Timmons ... This information was provided by a music business insider who requested anonymity. It was confirmed by a second source.
versified links ... Renato Chicco interviewed by the author, December 18, 2018.
bass player Milt Hinton ... https://www.arts.gov/honors/jazz/year-all
enjoy spending our money ... James Zimmerman interviewed by the author, February 15, 2019.
Reykjavik, Iceland ... Andy Watson interviewed by the author, December 10, 2018.
performing with Aria and Michele ... Greg Thomas interview, All About Jazz, April 18, 2008.
nothing else there ... Aria Hendricks interviewed by the author, January 10, 2018. By 2019 the area had become highly desirable—and expensive.
a lot of Jon's music ... Pete Churchill interviewed by the author, September 4, 2018.
exceptional longevity ... Frank Griffith: https://lance-bebopspokenhere.blogspot.com/2017/12/the-real-j-hendricks.html
osmosis ... Eric G. Johnson interviewed by the author, September 27, 2019.
a source of annoyance ... Renato Chicco interviewed by the author, December 18, 2018.
studio overdubs ... Kevin Burke interviewed by the author, March 14, 2019.
professional dealings ... Frank Griffith interviewed by the author, August 24, 2018.
Lincoln Center ... *DownBeat*, January 1997, p. 13; *Amsterdam News*, October 19, 1996.
Joe Williams and Dianne Reeves ... Bruce Crowther and Mike Pinfold. *Singing Jazz: the Singers and their Styles* (Blandford, 1997), p. 96
as a duo ... http://downbeat.com/archives/detail/down-for-double
both scatted on it ... Paul Meyers interviewed by the author, December 6, 2018.
this takes concentration! ... Lees
kept her husband healthy ... Paul Meyers interviewed by the author, December 6, 2018.
annual income ... Gunnar Mossblad interviewed by the author, September 26, 2019.
difficult to get gigs ... Aria Hendricks interviewed by the author, September 25, 2019.
a form of revenge ... Audrey Lasbleiz interviewed by the author, January 22, 2019.
poetic justice ... Gunnar Mossblad interviewed by the author, March 7, 2019.
old established forms ... Rowe (2000)
rambling anecdote ... Jon Richardson interviewed by the author, July 1, 2019.
sixteen voices to sing Basie ... Post on Jon's website February 3, 2003. http://www.harmonyware.com/JonHendricks/index.html
just down the hall ... Aria Hendricks interviewed by the author, January 10, 2018.
unaware of him ... Gunnar Mossblad interviewed by the author, March 7, 2019.
they have a culture ... Thomas op. cit.

on the same level ... The Vocalstra performed his lyrics to Nikolai Rimsky-Korsakov's *Schéherazade Op. 35* with the Toledo Symphony Orchestra at the Cathedral of St. John the Divine in Toledo.

a larger Vocalstra ... Anne Legrand interviewed by the author, February 5, 2019.

small festival dates ... Noel Jewkes interviewed by the author, November 7, 2018.

they were pretty awful ... Eric G. Johnson, interviewed by the author, September 27, 2019.

too deeply ingrained ... Kurt Elling interviewed by the author, March 11, 2019.

Chapter 10—Keep Smiling

Mind On Fire ... It was never published. https://www.pbs.org/weta/onstage/twain2002/bios/hendricks.html

no-one's benefit but Jon's ... Jon Richardson interviewed by the author, July 1, 2019.

international performing career ... Martin (2010), p. 51

long-term popularity ... Michele Hendricks interviewed by the author, December 9, 2018.

Gérard Bremond ... Anne Legrand interviewed by the author, February 5, 2019.

five-year documentary project ... Personal communication from Audrey Lasbleiz.

she loved the house ... Aria Hendricks interviewed by the author, September 25, 2019.

shipped over from Mill Valley ... Conversation with Aria Hendricks, March 19, 2019. Whatever exists of Jon's autobiography *Mind On Fire* probably lies buried somewhere amid mountains of household stuff in a Toledo storage facility. However it is not known how much he had written, only that he began writing it after he and Judith moved to Toledo. According to one account, he got no further than World War II

a humble listener ... Jon Richardson interviewed by the author, July 1, 2019.

esprit de corps ... Eric G. Johnson, interviewed by the author, September 27, 2019.

Blues March ... http://www.jazzitalia.net/iocero/JonHendricks_NewYork_eng.asp#.Xf_GdC2cai4

key to the city ... Josephson, p. 136

the enthusiasm was there ... Stephen Holden, *New York Times*, July 5, 2008.

notes on a stave ... http://www.openculture.com/2014/07/john-coltrane-turn-handwritten-poem-into-musical-passage-on-a-love-supreme.html

"September of my Years" ... https://theartsdesk.com/new-music/jon-hendricks-london-jazz-festival-ronnie-scotts

Ponce de León ... Ron Scott "Jon Hendricks Smokes, Dizzy's Jam," *Amsterdam News*, September 28, 2011. According to popular legend, the Spanish conquistador Ponce de León discovered Florida while searching for the Fountain of Youth.

healthy eating regime ... Thomas

sat in for over an hour ... Kevin Burke interviewed by the author, March 19, 2019.

the Hendricks group sang with Van ... Kevin Burke interviewed by the author, March 14, 2019.

missed his New York jazz friends ... Priscilla Florence interviewed by the author, September 26, 2019.

he gets them engaged ... *Toledo Free Press*, September 19, 2012, p. 5

don't tell Picasso he can't paint ... Eric G. Johnson, interviewed by the author, September 27, 2019.

a victory of sorts ... Email from Gunnar Mossblad, October 21, 2019.

Monk's son T. S. ... The full track listing was "Blue Monk," "Pannonica," "Evidence," "Crepuscule with Nellie," "Rhythm-a-ning," "Monk's Mood," "Trinkle Tinkle," "Hackensack," "Round Midnight," "In Walked Bud," "Ask Me Now," and "Well You Needn't."

became very close ... Aria Hendricks interviewed by the author, January 10, 2018.

dementia was becoming noticeable … His stories became wilder, including one about Duke Ellington who, he claimed, had once conducted an affair with a certain European head of state.

cheap laugh … Holli Ross interviewed by the author, January 3, 2019.

looking for a record company … https://wyntonmarsalis.org/videos/view/jon-hendricks-and-wynton-marsalis-share-stories-from-the-history-of-jazz-ch

are you going to do some work? … Private recording, courtesy of Pete Churchill.

he fell into the gutter … Pete Churchill interviewed by the author, April 9, 2018.

the guest apartment … Pete Churchill interviewed March 8, 2018.

two glasses of champagne … Kevin Burke interviewed by the author, March 14, 2019.

ruptured his intestines … Bonnie Hopkins interviewed by the author, September 26, 2019.

like a museum burned down … Claude Carrière interviewed by the author, February 15, 2019.

over-compensation … "The important thing, whether you use words or not, is to try to think like a horn, which I've always done. As you know, there's an age-old antipathy between musicians and singers. Musicians don't want to hang around with singers! So I tried to sound as much like an instrument as I could, in order to get the cats to accept me." Leonard Feather, "Feather's Nest," *DownBeat*, January 28, 1953, p. 17, quoted in Martin (2016), p. 8

imagination alone is the limit! … 2018 PDX Jazz Festival Program. http://kurtelling.com/news/press_article_1133.php

humor, fun, pleasure … Ben Sidran interviewed by the author, June 20, 2019.

a bold necktie … Kurt Elling. https://jazztimes.com/features/tributes-and-obituaries/kurt-elling-jon-hendricks-farewell/

retained his flamboyance … Holli Ross interviewed by the author, January 3, 2019.

he'd be holding court … Andy Watson interviewed by the author, December 10, 2018.

keep smiling … Gunnar Mossblad interviewed by the author, March 7, 2019.

Appendix A—The Voice, the Scat, the Vocalese

without the horn … Zimmerman, p. 92

female singers … ibid., pp. 92–3

warm-ups before gigs. … ibid., p. 6

better singer … Holli Ross interviewed by the author, January 3, 2019.

a gift from God … Andy Watson interviewed by the author, December 10, 2018.

your own drum … Zimmerman, p. 81

into the stratosphere … Stephanie Nakasian interviewed by the author, February 3, 2019.

"Everybody Loves My Baby" … Alyn Shipton. *A New History of Jazz* (London, Continuum, 2001), pp. 576–7

more structured and deliberate … Crowther and Pinfold, p. 129. You can hear him with Savitt's orchestra on Slim Gaillard's "Vol Vistu Gaily Star." https://www.youtube.com/watch?v=ms2TXoW1u9w

of Bird, of Diz, of Ben … Murphy

envy was one motivation … Crowther and Pinfold, p. 130

another art form altogether … ibid., p. 131

make it pretty … Jeremy

for being so bad … Carr

the melody in your mind … Zimmerman, p. 16

within a scale that works … ibid., p. 20

soloing like Louis Armstrong … Mwenso

that determines the sound … Zimmerman, pp. 80–1

Gatling gun … https://www.youtube.com/watch?v=NCtPfP1MCuc

enhanced the original solo ... Noel Jewkes interviewed by the author, November 7, 2018.
the original soloist ... Janis Siegel interviewed by the author, October 16, 2018.
individual sections ... Carr
vocalese is at least four ... Stephens
article he wrote in response ... "Hendricks is one of several singers who have been involved with a form that has come to be known in recent years as vocalese." Feather. *Jazz: a Quarterly of American Music*, p. 261
art-form on the planet ... Morton
the vocalese lyric ... The lack of a writing credit for McHugh and Fields resulted in them suing both James Moody and King Pleasure. They were eventually rewarded with a share of the recording profits. Alyn Shipton. *The Life of Jimmy McHugh* (University of Illinois Press, 2009), p. 205
without a tenth of Porter's wit ... Friedwald, p. 238

Appendix B—The Lyrics

unskun coon ... Zimmerman, p. 6
Smatterchoo? ... *The Pace Report*
study of literature ... Gleason. *Conversations in Jazz*, p. 268
cultural and philosophical lineage ... Zimmerman, p. 80
a ridiculous anecdote ... "Annie's a genius. I have one regret that's always haunted me ... I completely intimidated Annie ... accidentally. By writing those lyrics, some of which were wonderful, it made Annie feel like she didn't want to write any more lyrics, especially when she was working with me. And she is one of the greatest lyricists ... The woman is marvelous." (Carr)
sermonettes ... Morton
very little editing ... David Leonhardt interviewed by the author, January 18, 2019.
some higher power ... Morton
my original lyrics ... Murphy
the closest sounds in English ... Mark Fisher, *Washington Post*, January 14, 2000
it shouts ... Gleason. *Conversations in Jazz*, p. 267. The "he" in this case presumably being Lester Young.
you gotta nice sound ... ibid.
an opera or a drama ... Rowe (2000)
the Ellington band ... Hinely, pp. 31–2
create the whole story ... Gleason. *Conversations in Jazz*, p. 268
what Freddie was ... Zimmerman, p. 76
so-called literary terms ... ibid., pp. 76–8
floats off the tongue ... Holli Ross interviewed by the author, January 3, 2019.
all the repetitions ... Gleason. *Conversations in Jazz*, p. 269
a myriad of ideas ... Zimmerman, p. 76
express the thoughts ... Lee
words and music go together ... Tomkins (1968)
uncomfortable places ... Holli Ross interviewed by the author, January 3, 2019.
Charlie Parker solos ... Paul Meyers interviewed by the author, December 6, 2018.

Appendix C—The Wisdom and Philosophy

the best he can manage ... Zimmerman, pp. 76–8
the root of all sickness ... Rowe (2000)
reinforced their position ... Moody, p. 118

a beautiful art form … *Jazz Is Our Religion*
pay the people themselves … Jeremy
couldn't have black musicians … Rowe (1995)
contribution to the world … Mwenso
that's ridiculous … Jeremy
a sadness in your life … Zimmerman, p. 35
the essential him … ibid., p. 42
the message of Jesus Christ … ibid., p. 43
that ain't me … ibid., p. 14
mistreatment of somebody else … Tomkins (1968)
acceptance, more than money … Aria Hendricks interviewed by the author, October 5, 2018.
maintaining one's dignity … Anne Legrand interviewed by the author, February 5, 2019.
right the wrongs … Cleveland
sheer mischief … Interested parties may consult the online facsmile of *Is Shakespeare Dead?* https://en.wikisource.org/wiki/Index:1909._Is_Shakespeare_Dead%3F_From_My_ Autobiography.djvu
head of the theatre department … Eric G. Johnson, interviewed by the author, September 27, 2019.
Rosicrucian Order … Cleveland
frozen music … This quote is usually attributed to Goethe.
we've actually retrogressed … Zimmerman, pp. 40–41
hold out, brother … Pete Churchill interviewed by the author, September 4, 2018. One of Hendricks's many unrealized projects was to lyricize the whole of Garner's *Concert By The Sea.*
great spirit to art … Zimmerman, p. 59
murder the Christ-child … ibid., p. 17
so they can shine … Vitro
a great solo … Larry Vuckovich interviewed by the author the author, September 3, 2018.
past, present and future … ibid.
the bebop pioneers … Ben Sidran interviewed by the author, June 20, 2019.
I just kept going … Zimmerman, p. 55
that's what rock is … ibid., p. 29
greater intellect … Jones, p. xi
arrested cultural development … Carr
keeping our culture alive … Moody, p. 122
'ofays' … ibid., p. 118. A disparaging term for white people, the origins of which are unknown.
ruined for ever … Tomkins (1971)
where's the great art? … Rowe (1995)
go to hell … Hinely, p. 42
he teaches you … Murphy
my favorite vocalist … Carr
Dave Brubeck … The album *Young Lions & Old Tigers*—see Discography.
the proximity of the musicians … Zimmerman, pp. 39–40
word of advice … Extract from *Miles Beyond: the Electric Explorations of Miles Davis 1967–1991* (Watson Guptill, 2001). http://www.miles-beyond.com/ch1.htm
that's all I recognized … Tomkins (1968)
clean again tomorrow … Lucoff
Ronnie Scott's club in London … Vitro
the purpose of art … Zimmerman, p. 53. This was apropos of slowing down the first vocal recording of "Four Brothers."
why this might be … Moody, p. 119
Monday morning … The film in question may have been *It's All True*, three stories about Latin America. It was supposed to be Welles's third project for RKO after *Citizen Kane*

and *The Magnificent Ambersons*. But Welles and RKO failed to see eye to eye, the film was never completed, and some of the original negative ended up being dumped in the Pacific Ocean. Meanwhile, Duke Ellington allegedly received $12,500 for writing twenty-eight bars of music, which he subsequently mislaid. See *Reminiscing in Tempo: a Portrait of Duke Ellington* by Stuart Nicholson (Pan, 2000, pp. 235–6). Another school of thought, namely Harvey Cohen in *Duke Ellington's America* (Chicago, University of Chicago Press, 2010, p. 329) suggests that Welles hired Duke for twelve weeks to work on a film outlining the history of jazz. "Then there never was a movie, but I never forgot the theme," he told Bill Ladd. Cohen says the theme resurfaced in Duke's 1956 jazz opera *A Drum is a Woman*.

Fletcher Henderson ... Rowe (2000)

kills your creativity ... Stephens

a good friend ... Vitro

my own country ... ibid. In fact there is no such thing as an honorary member of the UK's House of Lords nor, in the USA, of either House of Congress. These assertions may have been sheer playfulness on Hendricks's part, but given that the interview took place in 2014, they may have been an unfortunate indication of his dementia.

the two religions ... Aria Hendricks interviewed by the author, October 5, 2018.

interest in Christianity ... Michele Hendricks interviewed by the author, October 10, 2018.

a direct line ... Cleveland

drank mint juleps ... Zimmerman, pp. 83–4

you're an ignoramus! ... Rowe (2000)

nobody dies ... Mwenso. Even in his nineties Hendricks believed he was able to communicate with his dead parents, especially in times of trouble. (Private recording courtesy of Pete Churchill.)

made in heaven ... Zimmerman, p. 46. Hendricks goes on to say that astrological references, as well as references to reincarnation, are "hidden" in the King James Bible. Judith "makes charts and reads palms and does numerology." (p.47)

these tragedies ... Vitro

Bibliography

NB: *Where the name of the writer, author or editor is unknown, the title of the publication or website takes precedence. All weblinks were functional as of June 2020.*

45worlds "Jon Hendricks – Live Music" gig diary. http://www.45worlds.com/live/artist/jon-hendricks

Ackermann, K. "State And Mainstream: The Jazz Ambassadors And The U.S. State Department." All About Jazz. Last modified April 27, 2018. https://www.allaboutjazz.com/state-and-mainstream-the-jazz-ambassadors-and-the-us-state-department-by-karl-ackermann.php?page=1

Akkerman, G. "Jon Hendricks: Still Creative, Still Outspoken." All About Jazz. Last modified March 27, 2012. https://www.allaboutjazz.com/jon-hendricks-still-creative-still-outspoken-jon-hendricks-by-gregg-akkerman.php?pg=1

Ankeny, J. "Artist Biography by Jason Ankeny" of Lillian Briggs. AllMusic. https://www.allmusic.com/artist/lillian-briggs-mn0000289901

Armstrong, L. *Satchmo: My Life in New Orleans*. Prentice Hall, 1954.

ASCAP "Welcome to ASCAP" society homepage. https://www.ascap.com

Awards & Shows, "Grammy Awards 1959 (May)" retrospective. http://www.awardsandshows.com/features/grammy-awards-1959-may-238.html

Bailey, C. M. "Bill Perkins/Cy Touff (Pacific Jazz/West Coast Classics: The Bill Perkins Octet: On Stage/Cy Touff: His Octet And Quintet," All About Jazz. Last modified March 1, 1999. https://www.allaboutjazz.com/the-bill-perkins-octet-on-stage-cy-touff-his-octet-and-quintet-bill-perkins-review-by-c-michael-bailey.php

Barber, C. *Jazz Me Blues: the Autobiography of Chris Barber*. Equinox, 2014.

Basie, C. *Good Morning Blues*. Heinemann, 1986.

BBC "Welcome to the BBC Genome Project" homepage. https://genome.ch.bbc.co.uk

Billboard untitled article on the Churchill Kohlman legal case. March 7, 1953

Bourne, M. "Jon Hendricks and Annie Ross: Down for Double." *DownBeat*. September 1999. https://downbeat.com/archives/detail/down-for-double

Brown, A. "Annie Ross: NEA Jazz Master (2010)" interview transcript. Smithsonian National Museum of American History, Jazz Oral History Program. January 13–14, 2011. https://jazzday.com/media/AC0808_Ross_Annie_Transcript.pdf

Carr, I. Untitled transcript of an interview with Jon Hendricks, New York. British Library, January 14, 1992.

Cerulli, D. *DownBeat* untitled review of Sing a Song of Basie. April 17, 1958.

Chilla, M. "Dave Lambert centennial." Afterglow: Jazz and American Popular Song. Last modified June 23, 2017. https://indianapublicmedia.org/afterglow/dave-lambert-centennial.php

Chilton, J. *Let the Good Times Roll.* University of Michigan Press, 1992.

Cleveland, J. "Sight & Sound – Jon Hendricks (Part 1)" interview recording. https://www.youtube.com/watch?v=2fSHQsToqec&t=761s

Cohen, H. *Duke Ellington's America.* University of Chicago Press, 2010.

Crow, B. *From Birdland to Broadway.* OUP, 1992.

Crow, B. *Jazz Anecdotes.* OUP, 2005.

Crowther, B. and Pinfold, M. *Singing Jazz: the Singers and their Styles.* Blandford, 1997.

Dangerous Minds. "The Year Dizzy Gillespie Ran for President." Last modified October 21, 2014. https://dangerousminds.net/comments/the_year_dizzy_gillespie_ran_for_president_1964_spoiler_alert_he_didnt_win

Davis, F. *In the Moment: Jazz in the 1980s.* OUP, 1986.

Davis, F. "Territorial Imperatives." *The Village Voice.* October 3, 2006. https://www.villagevoice.com/2006/10/03/territorial-imperatives/

DownBeat untitled review of the original "Four Brothers." January 13, 1954.

DownBeat untitled review of "Four Brothers"/"Clouburst." October 5, 1955.

DownBeat untitled article on Jon Hendricks/Quincy Jones collaboration. February 8, 1956.

DownBeat untitled article on Hendricks lecture-demonstrations. May 16, 1956.

DownBeat untitled article on Hendricks being elected to ASCAP. September 5, 1956.

DownBeat publication of ABC-Paramount advertisement. Vol. 3, no. 1. 1958.

DownBeat untitled review of Great South Bay Festival. September 18, 1958.

DownBeat untitled review of Randall's Island Jazz Festival; announcement of *Sing Along with Basie.* October 2, 1958.

DownBeat untitled article on Hendricks lyric for "Little Niles." October 30, 1958.

DownBeat untitled article on Carnegie Hall poll winners. November 27, 1958.

DownBeat poll results. December 25, 1958.

DownBeat untitled article on the *Steve Allen Show.* Vol 4, no. 1. 1959.

DownBeat untitled article on dispute with Neal Hefti; review of Sing Along with Basie. January 22, 1959.

DownBeat untitled article on possible England tour. February 19, 1959.

DownBeat untitled article on Johnny Mandel Blindfold Test. April 2, 1959.

DownBeat untitled article on writing *Sing a Song of Basie.* September 17, 1959.

DownBeat untitled article on Newport Jazz Festival. June 8, 1959.

DownBeat publication of Billboard poll advertisement. August 20, 1959.

DownBeat untitled article on Jon Hendricks. September 17, 1959.

Ebony untitled article on John Hendricks's Trio. December 1964.

Elling, K. "Kurt Elling Remembers Jon Hendricks." *Jazz Times,* Last modified April 25, 2019. https://jazztimes.com/features/tributes-and-obituaries/kurt-elling-jon-hendricks-farewell/

Ellington, D. *Music Is My Mistress.* WH Allen, 1974.

Feather, L. *New Encyclopaedia Yearbook of Jazz.* Arthur Baker, 1958.

Feather, L. "An Explanation of Vocalese." *Jazz: a Quarterly of American Music.* Summer 1959.

Feather, L. *Encyclopedia of Jazz in the Sixties.* Da Capo, 1966.

Feather, L. and I. Gitler. *The Biographical Encyclopedia of Jazz.* OUP, 1999.

Fisher, M. "Back in the Swing of Things." *Washington Post.* January 14, 2000.

Fordham, J. *Let's Join Hands and Contact the Living.* Elm Tree, 1986.

Friedwald, W. *Jazz Singing: America's Great Voices from Bessie Smith to Bebop and Beyond.* Da Capo Press, 1996.

Gallup. "In U.S., 87% Approve of Black-White Marriage, vs. 4% in 1958." Last modified July 25, 2013. https://news.gallup.com/poll/163697/approve-marriage-blacks-whites.aspx

Gavin, J. "Annie Ross: A Free-Spirited Survivor Lands on her Feet." *New York Times*. October 3, 1993. http://jamesgavin.com/page6/page67/page67.html

Gioia, T. *West Coast Jazz*. OUP, 1992.

Gleason, R. *Conversations in Jazz: the Ralph J. Gleason Interviews*. Yale University Press, 2016.

Goldman, A. *Ladies and Gentlemen – Lenny Bruce!!* Pan, 1976.

Gordonskene. "Newstalgia Downbeat – Lambert, Hendricks and Ross – Live in Germany – 1962." Crooks & Liars. https://crooksandliars.com/gordonskene/newstalgia-downbeat-lambert-hendricks-

Green, B. "Lambert, Hendricks and Ross" article in Count Basie UK tour program. 1962.

Griffith, F. "The 'Real' J Hendricks." Be-Bop Spoken Here. Last modified December 30, 2017. https://lance-bebopspokenhere.blogspot.com/2017/12/the-real-j-hendricks.html

Harmonyware. "Jon Hendricks" personal homepage. http://www.harmonyware.com/JonHendricks/index.html

Heckman, D. "Jon Hendricks, the 'James Joyce of Jazz', Dies at 96." *Los Angeles Times*. October 27, 2017. https://www.latimes.com/local/obituaries/la-me-jon-hendricks-snap-story.html

Henry, T. "Judith Hendricks: 1937–2015; Wife was driving force behind world jazz icon." *Toledo Blade*. November 19, 2015.

Hentoff, N. *Listen to the Stories*. Harper Collins 1995.

Hervieux, L. *Forgotten: The Untold Story of D-Day's Black Heroes, at Home and at War*. Harper Collins, 2015.

Hinely, W. P. "Jon Hendricks: Poet Laureate of Jazz." *Jazz Forum*. No. 94. March 1985.

Holden, S. "A Musical Missionary Returns, Joyful Spirit Intact." *New York Times*. July 5, 2008 https://www.nytimes.com/2008/07/05/arts/music/05hend.html

Holt, T. C. and Hudgens, M. "The Second Great Migration, 1940–70." In Motion AAME. University of Chicago. http://www.inmotionaame.org/texts/viewer.cfm?id=9_000T

Internet Archive. "Grateful Dead Live at Studio on December 5, 1966." https://archive.org/details/gd1966-12-05.sbd.kimbro.23064.sbeok.shnf

Jazz Journal review of *Sing a Song of Basie*. November 1958.

Jazz Journal review of *Lambert, Hendricks & Bavan: Live at Basin Street East*. June 1963.

Jazz Journal review of *Love*. October 1982.

Jazz Journal review of *Freddie Freeloader*. March 1991.

Jazzitalia. "Jon Hendricks & Company." http://www.jazzitalia.net/iocero/JonHendricks_NewYork_eng.asp#.XtzX0i2ZNBw

Jeremy, J. Interview with Jon Hendricks for *Jazz Is Our Religion* documentary. November 23, 1971. British Library.

Johnson, D. "Hipsters, Flipsters, And On-The-Scenesters." Night Lights. January 6, 2016. https://indianapublicmedia.org/nightlights/hipsters-flipsters-onthescenesters.php

Jones, M. Untitled Jon Hendricks interview. *Melody Maker*. April 13, 1968.

Jones, P. *This is Hip: the Life of Mark Murphy*. Equinox, 2018.

Josephson, S. *Jazz Notes: Interviews Across the Generations*. Praeger, 2009.

Joyce, M. Untitled Jon Hendricks interview. *Cadence*. January 1983.

Kelley, R. D. G. *Thelonious Monk: the Life and Times of an American Original*. Free Press, 2010.

Lasbleiz, A. (dir.) *Tell Me the Truth*. Mosaïque Films, 2008.

Lee, D. Interview with Jon Hendricks, *Jazz FM*, March 6, 1990. British Library.

Lee, U. *The Employment of Negro Troops*. Library of Congress, 1966.

Lees, G. "Jon Hendricks and Annie Ross Together Alone." *Jazz Times*. April 25, 2019.

Leslie, J. and Snyder, R. "History of the Early Days of Ampex Corporation." AES Historical Committee, December 17, 2010. http://www.aes.org/aeshc/docs/company.histories/ampex/leslie_snyder_early-days-of-ampex.pdf

Lester, J. *Too Marvelous for Words: the Life and Genius of Art Tatum.* OUP, 1994.

LOC.gov. "Railroad map showing the lands of the Standard Coal and Iron Co. situated in the Hocking Valley, Ohio, and their relation to the markets of the north and west." https://www.loc.gov/resource/g4071p.rr001330/?r=0.074,0.075,1.167,0.822,0

Los Angeles Conservancy. "Dunbar Hotel." https://www.laconservancy.org/locations/dunbar-hotel

Loving, D. "French Lick Jazz Festival." *Jazz Notes.* August 1959.

Lyall, S. "Requiem for a Victim: A Singing Cabby." *New York Times.* September 19, 1988. Accessed at https://www.nytimes.com/1988/09/19/nyregion/requiem-for-a-victim-a-singing-cabby.html

McGirt, E. "Watch John Coltrane Turn His Handwritten Poem Into a Sublime Musical Passage on A Love Supreme." Open Culture. Last modified July 4, 2014. http://www.openculture.com/2014/07/john-coltrane-turn-handwritten-poem-into-musical-passage-on-a-love-supreme.html

McKayle, D. *Transcending Boundaries: My Dancing Life.* Routledge, 2002.

Manhattan Transfer, The. "TMT History" page of website. https://manhattantransfer.net/about/

Melody Maker untitled poll winners report. February 24, 1968.

Martin, L. E. *Jon Hendricks, Father of Vocalese: A Toledo Story* master's degree thesis. University of Toledo, May 2010. http://citeseerx.ist.psu.edu/viewdoc/download?doi=10.1.1.884.6959&rep=rep1&type=pdf

Martin, L. E. *Validating the Voice in the Music of Lambert, Hendricks and Ross* PhD thesis. University of Pittsburgh, 2016. http://d-scholarship.pitt.edu/27291/1/Martinle_leetdpitt2016_2.pdf

Mergner, L. "Jon Hendricks, Jazz Vocalese Innovator, Dies." *Jazz Times,* November 22, 2017.

Metronome review of "Four Brothers," February 1954.

Metronome review of *Sing a Song of Basie*, July 1958.

Metronome untitled article on Hendricks in command of Lambert Hendricks and Ross. July 1959.

Milkowski, B. Liner notes to *At Newport '63.* Accessed at https://www.wolfgangs.com/music/lambert-hendricks-and-ross/audio/20020380-51328.html?tid=4869885

Morgenstern, D. *Living with Jazz.* Pantheon, 2004.

Morton, B. "There I Go, There I Go." BBC Radio 3. March 1, 1998. British Library.

Murphy, M. Interview with Jon Hendricks for the NEA. Last modified January 10, 2008. https://www.arts.gov/honors/jazz/jon-hendricks

Mwenso, M. "The Poet Laureate of Jazz, Jon Hendricks (Part 1)" interview with Jon Hendricks. https://www.youtube.com/watch?v=FRc-wZHDoqY

Myers, M. "Interview: Yolande Bavan (Part 1)." JazzWax. https://www.jazzwax.com/2007/11/a-chat-with-yol.html

Myers, M. "Charlie Parker and Voices, part 1." JazzWax. Last modified January 30, 2008. https://www.jazzwax.com/2008/01/charlie-parker-and-voices-part-one.html

Myers, M. "Interview: Creed Taylor (Part 1)." JazzWax. https://www.jazzwax.com/2008/05/interview-creed.html

Myers, M. "Interview: Carol Sloane (Part 2)." JazzWax. https://www.jazzwax.com/2009/03/interview-carol-sloane-part-2.html

Myers, M. "Dee Lambert: My Dad, Dave Lambert." Jazz FM. https://jazz.fm/dee-lambert-my-dad-dave-lambert/

Myers, M. "Grateful Dead and Jon Hendricks." JazzWax. https://www.jazzwax.com/2017/09/ad-hed.html

Myers, M. "Jon Hendricks (1921–2017)." JazzWax. https://www.jazzwax.com/2017/11/jon-hendricks-1921-2017.html

National Endowment for the Arts. "NEA Jazz Masters by Year" database. Arts.gov. https://www.arts.gov/honors/jazz/year-all

Newhart, B. "Behind the Curtain: Jon Hendricks." PBS On Stage. https://www.pbs.org/weta/onstage/twain2002/bios/hendricks.html

Nicholson, S. *Reminiscing in Tempo: a Portrait of Duke Ellington.* Pan, 2000.

Ottney, S. "The legend at 91: Hendricks to celebrate birthday at Jazz on the Maumee." *Toledo Free Press Star.* September 19, 2012.

Pace, B. "The Pace Report: 'The Wit and Wisdom of Gentleman Jon Hendricks' The Jon Hendricks Interview wsg Jimmy Heath." The Pace Report. October 4, 2011. https://vimeo.com/30011118

Pennebaker, D. A. (dir.) *Audition at RCA.* 1964. Viewed at https://vimeo.com/2681835

Perkins, T. "Jon Hendricks" interview transcript. JazzStandards.com. http://www.jazzstandards.com/What%27s%20NewJon%20Hendricks.htm

Priestley, B. *Chasin' the Bird.* OUP, 2005.

Quinn, P. "Jon Hendricks: London Jazz Festival, Ronnie Scott's" The Arts Desk. Last modified November 19, 2010. https://theartsdesk.com/new-music/jon-hendricks-london-jazz-festival-ronnie-scotts

Ramsay, D. "Finding Mandel" *Rifftides.* Last modified October 10, 2005. https://www.artsjournal.com/rifftides/2005/10/finding_mandel.html

RareMaps. "Railroad Map of Ohio. Published By The State." https://www.raremaps.com/gallery/detail/38892/railroad-map-of-ohio-published-by-the-state-1914-columbus-lithograph-co

Rauch, M. (dir.) *Blues March: Soldier Jon Hendricks.* Strandfilm GmbH, 2010.

Roland, P. (ed.) *Jazz Singers: the Great Song Stylists in their Own Words.* Hamlyn, 1999.

Rose, C. "Jon Hendricks and Wynton Marsalis share stories from the history of jazz – Charlie Rose Show." September 13, 1996. Viewed at https://wyntonmarsalis.org/videos/view/jon-hendricks-and-wynton-marsalis-share-stories-from-the-history-of-jazz-ch

Ross, B. (dir.) *No One But Me.* BBC Scotland, 2012.

Rowe, M. "Jon Hendricks part 1 Interview by Monk Rowe – 10/18/1995 – NYC." Fillius Jazz Archive, October 18, 1995. Viewed at https://www.youtube.com/watch?v=eX7sGSgjNXo

Rowe, M. "Jon Hendricks part 2 Interview by Monk Rowe – 1/29/2000 – NYC." Fillius Jazz Archive, January 29, 2000. Viewed at https://www.youtube.com/watch?v=aM89KH1mYao

Savitt, J. and Tunnell, B. B. "Jan Savitt – Vol Vistu Gaily Star." Viewed at https://www.youtube.com/watch?v=ms2TXoW1u9w

Scott, R. "Jon Hendricks Smokes, Dizzy's Jam." *Amsterdam News.* September 28, 2011.

Second Hand Songs. "I Want You To Be My Baby" database entry. https://secondhandsongs.com/work/112905

Shipton, A. *A New History of Jazz.* Continuum, 2001.

Shipton, A. *The Life of Jimmy McHugh.* University of Illinois Press, 2009.

Sidran, B. *Talking Jazz: An Illustrated Oral History.* Pomegranate Artbooks, 1992.

Sidran, B. *A Life in the Music.* Taylor Trade Publishing, 2003.

Stephens, A. "Jon Hendricks Interview 2009." February 9, 2009. Viewed at https://www.youtube.com/watch?v=ElN_BVI6Xgg

Thomas, G. "Jon Hendricks: Vocal Ease." All About Jazz. Last modified November 23, 2017. https://www.allaboutjazz.com/jon-hendricks-vocal-ease-jon-hendricks-by-greg-thomas.php

Tiegel, E. "Jon Hendricks: Singer Swings Again Via LP and N.Y. Club Date." *Billboard,* July 12, 1975

Tingen, P. *Miles Beyond: The Electric Explorations of Miles Davis 1967–1991.* Billboard Books, 2001.

Toledo.com. "Toledos Jazz Tradition." Last modified June 5, 2008. https://www.toledo.com/news/2008/06/05/intoledo/toledos-jazz-tradition/

Tomkins, L. Untitled Jon Hendricks interview conducted in 1968. UK National Jazz Archive.

Tomkins, L. Untitled Jon Hendricks interview *Crescendo*. February 1973.

Twain, M. *Is Shakespeare Dead? From My Autobiography*. Harper & Brothers, 1909. Accessed at https://en.wikisource.org/wiki/Is_Shakespeare_Dead%3F

Tyle, C. "I Can't Give You Anything But Love." JazzStandards.com http://www.jazzstandards.com/compositions-1/icantgiveyouanythingbutlove.htm

Vacca, R. "June 19, 1917: Dave Lambert Born." The Troy Street Observer. https://www.troystreet.com/tspots/2013/06/19/june-19-1917-dave-lambert-born/

Valentine, M. "Peter King biography." Michael Valentine Studio. http://www.michaelvalentinestudio.com/jazz_gallery/king_lockett/index.php

Vitro, R. "Jon Hendricks: Poet Laureate, Godfather of Jazz Vocalese." *Jazz Times*. Last modified April 26, 2019. https://jazztimes.com/features/interviews/jon-hendricks-poet-laureate-godfather-of-jazz-vocalese/

WFM. "World Federalist Movement – Institute for Global Policy" homepage. http://www.wfm-igp.org

Wilberforce-Payne Unified Library. "Who is Bishop Ransom?" Wilberforce University. https://wilberforcepayne.libguides.com/library/ransom

Willett, B. "This Interracial Couple Endured Discrimination and Bullying but Loved Each Other Until the End." *Washington Post*. June 9, 2017.

Wilson, J. S. "Jon Hendricks Brings Back Style of Big Band Era." *New York Times*. February 4, 1982. https://www.nytimes.com/1982/04/02/arts/pop-jazz-jon-hendricks-brings-back-style-of-big-band-era.html

WTTW Chicago. "Sing Me a Jazz Song." Viewed at https://www.youtube.com/watch?v=PgYAS6mhn7A

YouTube "Annie Ross almost 20 Years before Lambert Hendricks, and Ross." https://www.youtube.com/watch?v=_enNo0qFxm8&index=12&list=RDaNPHp0RBWYY

YouTube "Duke Ellington – A Concert Of Sacred Music (1965 premiere performance)." https://www.youtube.com/watch?v=r8T5-AxBUwI

YouTube "Lambert Hendricks and Ross airegin." https://www.youtube.com/watch?v=Ul54NWmwLxs

YouTube "Lambert Hendricks & Ross PLAYBOY 60 02 13 4 'Doodlin'" https://www.youtube.com/watch?v=9Lu1nVQDThI&list=RDaNPHp0RBWYY&index=3

YouTube "Les Paul and Mary Ford on 'Omnibus' (1953)." October 23, 1953. https://www.youtube.com/watch?v=VCEmAgak9V8

YouTube "LIVE: Joe Williams with Lambert, Hendricks and Ross – Every Day I Have the Blues." https://www.youtube.com/watch?v=aNPHp0RBWYY

YouTube "Popular 1934 music by Marion Harris – Singin The Blues @Pax41." https://www.youtube.com/watch?v=NCtPfP1MCuc

YouTube "The Duke from Jon Hendricks' Miles Ahead." https://www.youtube.com/watch?v=XIKWolhO-do

YouTube "Interview with Jon Hendricks & Company at the North Sea Jazz Festival • 1982 • World of Jazz." https://www.youtube.com/watch?v=QyA9Qc17SBk

Zimmerman, J. "Jon Hendricks: NEA Jazz Master (1993)" interview transcript. Smithsonian National Museum of American History, Jazz Oral History Program. August 17–18, 1995. https://amhistory.si.edu/jazz/Hendricks-Jon/Hendricks_Jon_Transcript.pdf

Index

9/11 attacks, 148, 188
ABC (Associated Booking Corp.), 61
ABC-Paramount Ampar, 51, 54, 56, 57
"Ac-Cent-Tchu-Ate the Positive," 181
Across the Blue Meridian, 149
Adams, Mishka, 163
ADAT, 142
Adderley, Cannonball, 69, 70
Adderley, Nat, 70, 77
Adler, Richard, 39
African Methodist Episcopal Church
   (AME), 10, 14, 197
"Air Mail Special," 59
"Airegin," 4, 61, 71
Alabam, Club, 124
Alexander, Perry, 39
Alexander, Willard, 57, 62, 63, 72, 76, 162
Almeida, Laurindo, 77
"All Blues," 90
"All Too Soon," 71
Allen, Steve, 60, 87
Allen, Woody, 76
"Almost Like Being in Love," 143
"Along Came Betty," 108
Alvin Hotel, 48, 178
"Amo," 74
Amsterdam News, 156
Anatomy of a Murder, 71
Andrews Sisters Gospel Singers, 73
"Angel Eyes," 123
Annie's Room, 103
Another Night in Tunisia, 129

Anything Goes, 123
Apollo Theater, 40, 61, 63, 68
Apple Room, 163
"April in Paris," 85, 125
Arista Records, 109, 112, 123, 160
Arita, Junko, 160
"Arrastão," 91
Armstrong, Louis "Satchmo", 3, 21, 61,
   74, 78, 85, 100, 112, 132, 135, 141, 164,
   168, 169, 171
Arsenio Hall Show, 132
Arthur, Gavin, 199
Articles of War, 27, 30
Arturo's, 195
ASCAP, 39, 50, 69, 100, 136, 137
"Ask Me Now," 159
At Newport '63, 87, 88, 91
Atlantic Records, 121, 128
Audition at RCA, 94
Augie's, 140
Austin, Gene, 16
Avakian, George, 94
Avalon Records, 42
"Avenue C," 56, 72, 153
Avery Fisher Hall, 143
"Aw Gal," 74, 75
Azzam, Cyril, 107

Bach, Bob, 50
Backer, Steve, 109
Bacon, Francis, 82, 187, 188
Bailey, Pearl, 72

Bankers Club, The, 57
Banlieues Bleues Jazz Festival, 143
Barbaro, Clifford, 124, 127, 132
Basie, Count, 3, 50, 57, 59, 62, 70, 72, 78,
    89, 100, 119, 121, 122, 133, 134, 135,
    140, 141, 144, 164, 178, 179, 187, 189,
    190
Bavan, Yolande, 82–86, 89, 94–96
BBC Radio, 102, 105
BBC Television, 103
Beacon Theater, 157
Beatles, The, 184
Becton, Clarence – see Eghosa Osarabo
Beeks, Clarence – see King Pleasure
Belafonte, Harry, 74, 187
Beltone Studios, 52, 53
Bennett, Danny, 157
Bennett, Tony, 70, 94, 144, 157, 167, 185
Benson, George, 130, 133, 134, 135
Bentyne, Cheryl, 135
Berger, David, 135
"Berkshire Blues," 123
Berry, Alan, 106
Bey, Andy, 144
Bhagavad Gita, The, 198
"Big City Blues," 60
"Bijou," 68
Bijou, The, 53
Billboard, 59, 64, 111, 129, 159
Birdland (club), 61, 64, 65, 198
"Birdland" (song), 118
Birdsall, Butch, 44
Bitches Brew, 102
Bitter End, The, 121
Blakey, Art, 84, 109
Blanchard, Terence, 148
Blind Tom, 18
Blood on the Fields, 144
"Blue," 75
Blue Note, The, 123, 133, 142, 144, 145,
    153, 195
"Blues Backstage," 50, 56, 79
Blues for Pablo, 111, 130, 137, 159, 161
Blues March (film), 25
"Blues March" (song), 153
BMI, 69
"Body and Soul," 173
Bolden, Buddy, 74

Bolden, Walter, 67
Boleyn, Ann, 89
Boobar Publishing, 136
Boppin' at the Blue Note, 142
Both And Jazz Club, 92
Bottom Line, The, 111
Bouley, David, 163
Brandford, Jay, 143
Brecker, Michael, 123, 194
Bregman, Buddy, 70
Bremerhaven, Germany, 30
Bremond, Gérard, 152
Briggs, Bunny, 48, 92
Briggs, Lillian, 41
Brighetti, Bruno, 135
Brill Building, 39
British Museum, 82
Bromberg, David, 121
Bronx, The, 38
Brookmeyer, Bob, 59, 60, 94
Brooks, Avery, 127
Brooks, John Benson, 43
Broonzy, Big Bill, 75
Brown, Clifford, 180
Brown, Georgia, 52
Brown, Lawrence, 15, 179–180
Brown, Ray, 72, 146
Brubeck, Dave, 78, 83, 194
Brubeck, Iola, 78
Bruce, Lenny, 66, 76
Buhaina, 108
Burke, Kelly, 130
Burke, Kevin, 130–131, 138, 140, 142, 143,
    144, 153–154, 155, 163
Burke, Sonny, 87
Burns, Ralph, 68
Burrell, Kenny, 59
Byas, Don, 98
Byron, Lord, 175
"Bye Bye Blackbird," 90, 132, 144

C&L Club, 24
California State University, Sonoma, 109
Calloway, Cab, 169
Camp Rucker, AL, 26
Camp Shelby, MO, 26
Capitol Records, 50
Carmen Sings Monk, 92, 136

"Caravan," 71
Carmichael, Hoagy, 39
Carnegie Hall, 60, 114, 120
Carrière, Claude, 164
Carrington, John, 8
Carrington, Wille Mae – see Wille Mae Hendricks
Carroll, Joe, 34, 37
Carson, Johnny, 116
Carter, Benny, 89
Carter, Betty, 170
Carter, Ron, 78
Cast Your Fate, 149
Catalina Jazz Club, 137
Cavanaugh, Jesse – see Howie Richmond
Caymmi, Dorimel, 77
CBS Records, 109
Cecil Hotel, 48
"Centerpiece," 69, 112, 144, 153, 154, 156
Cerulli, Dom, 55, 58
Chaloff, Serge, 44
Chambers, Paul, 72, 141
Charles, Ray, 41, 60, 63
"Charleston Alley," 68
Charlie Parker with Strings, 182
Chastain, Don, 89
Chateau le France, 20
"Chega de Saudade" – see No More Blues
"Chess Players, The," 112
Chestnut, Cyrus, 130
Chicago Stadium, 72
Chicago Urban League, 66
Chicco, Renato, 137–140, 143
Christian, Charlie, 185
Christy, June, 93
Christian Action, 62
Churchill, Pete, 159–163
CID, 28
Cirkel, Les, 105, 106
Civic Opera House, 87
Clancy Brothers and Tommy Makem, The, 89
Clark, Harry, 44
Clayton, Buck, 71, 179
Clayton, Jay, 1
Clooney, Rosemary, 167
"Cloudburst" (song), 45, 46, 68, 69, 72, 87, 88, 91, 111, 112, 144, 154

Cloudburst (album), 100
Cobb, Jimmy, 103, 132, 133
Coffin, Berton, 150
Cohn, Al, 44, 59, 94
Cole, Nat "King", 19, 107, 130
Cole, Natalie, 130
Coltrane, Jon, 5, 59, 134, 154
Columbia Records, 43, 68, 73, 78, 192
Columbo, Ross, 16
"Come On Home," 79, 84, 144, 156
"Comeback, The," 89, 141
Como, Perry, 167
Concert of Sacred Music, A, 92
Confirmation, 122
Congress of Racial Equality (CORE), 67
"Contemporary Blues," 78, 164
"Cookin' at the Continental," 75, 164
"Cool Cat Blues," 156
Copacabana, The, 50
Corea, Chick, 191
"Corner Pocket," 122
Cosby, Bill, 76, 116, 120
"Cottontail," 71, 72
"Cousin Mary," 87
Cranks, 53
Craver, Sonny, 140
"Crazy, Crazy, Crazy Boutcha Baby," 48
"Crepuscule with Nellie," 91
Crescendo, The, 61, 62
Crockett, Johnny, 22
Crombie, Tony, and his Orchestra, 41
Crosby, Bing, 16
"Cry," 39

Damone, Vic, 167
"Dark Cloud," 61
Daryl, Ted, 135
Dave Lambert Singers, 43
Dave Lambert Sings and Swings Alone, 70
Davis, Clive, 109, 112
Davis, Miles, 1, 55, 62, 69, 88, 90, 94, 95–6, 102, 112, 120, 132, 135, 140, 143, 151, 153, 160, 161, 163, 167, 176, 181, 193, 194
Day, Doris, 167
"Days of Wine and Roses," 89
"DB Blues," 40
D-Day landings, 26, 152

de Moraes, Vinicius, 77
Dean, Hannah, 73, 74
Decca Records, 169, 192
DeChamplain, Atla, 157
Dee, Simon, 102
Dee Time, 102
"Deedle-Lee, Deedle-Lum," 87
Demby, Floyd H., 94
Denon Records, 133–135
"Desafinado," 76, 85, 155
Detroit, MI, 19, 23, 24, 89
Dickstein, Judith – see Judith Hendricks
Dickstein, Maida, 65
Dickstein, Max, 65
Dieval, Jack, 53
"Dis Hyuhn" – see "This Here"
Dizzy for President, 88
Domicile club, 100
Donovan, 99, 101
"Don't Be Afraid"/"Don't Get Scared," 42, 173
"Doodlin'," 59, 61, 62, 70, 71, 72, 79, 118, 150, 164, 176
Dorham, Kenny, 36, 51
Dorough, Bob, 156
Dorsey, Leslie, 122
DownBeat, 40, 45, 48, 50, 53, 55, 57, 58, 59, 60, 62, 63, 67, 68
"Down for Double," 55, 56, 144
"Down for the Count," 50, 56, 79
"Dream," 181
Dreares, Al, 124
"Drinking Wine Spo-Dee-O-Dee," 41
Duc des Lombards, 149, 152, 156
Duke, The, 160, 161
Dunbar Hotel, 124
Dunbar, Paul Laurence, 175
Dunham, Patti, 141
Dwight (son), 23, 114
Dylan, Bob, 94, 121

Earl Hotel, 48
Ebony, 60, 72
Eckstine, Billy, 92, 167
Edison, "Sweets", 17, 21, 68, 69, 171
Efford, Bob, 107
Eisenhower, Dwight, 78
Eliot, T. S., 61

Elling, Kurt, 5, 150, 172, 195
Ellington, Duke, 3, 17, 21, 59, 61, 71, 88, 92, 100, 115, 119, 121, 122, 125, 130, 141, 164, 168, 176, 179, 183, 192, 195, 196
Elliott, Don, 53
Épernay, France, 27
Eros Hotel, 48
Ertegun, Ahmet, 129
Ertegun, Nesuhi, 129, 130
Ervin, Booker, 88
"Estate," 135, 153, 154
Evans, Bill, 59, 60
Evans, Gil, 1, 43, 69, 95, 111, 140, 160–162, 167, 181–182
Even Dozen Jug Band, 121
"Every Time They Play This Song," 140
"Every Time We Say Goodbye," 128
"Everybody Loves My Baby," 169
"Everybody's Boppin'," 69, 112, 143, 156
"Everyday"/"Every Day I have the Blues," 56, 63, 70, 72, 79
"Everything Happens to Me," 153
"Everything Started in the House of the Lord," 70
"Evidence," 140, 180
Evolution of the Blues, 3, 72–75, 93, 105–106, 112, 114–116, 117, 140, 144, 158
"Ev'ry Tub," 58
"Extensions," 118

"Fables of Faubus," 78
Fame, Georgie, 88, 100, 141, 156
Fantasy Records, 109
Farber, Andy, 143, 156
Farmer, Addison, 59
Farmer, Art, 53, 59, 144, 156
"Farmer's Market," 51, 53, 75, 112
Farnsworth, Joe, 137
"Fas' Livin' Blues"/"Fast Livin' Blues," 76–77, 123, 135
Fat Tuesday's, 119, 137
Faubus, Orval, 78
Feather, Leonard, 61, 76, 165, 170, 172
"Feed Me," 85, 103, 153, 164
Feldman, Marty, 103
Feldstein, Gideon, 143

Ferguson, Maynard, 76, 102
Festival de Jazz de Ramatuelle, 152
Fields, Dorothy, 40, 172
Fields, Joe, 122
"Fiesta in Blue," 56, 71
Fillmore, The, 92
"Finer Things in Life," 135
"Fire in the City, 92
Fitzgerald, Ella, 43, 79, 121, 143, 169, 170
Five Guys Named Moe, 41
Flamingo Hotel, 72
Flanagan, Tommy, 19, 23, 133, 184
"Flat Foot Floogie," 111
Fonteyn, Margot, 102
Forge, The, 160
Fort Leavenworth, KS, 30
Forty Years of Benny Golson, 144
Foster, Frank, 82, 125, 144
"Four," 84, 153
"Four Brothers" (song), 40, 42–46, 58, 118
Four Brothers (group), 150
Four Freshmen, The, 60, 62
Foxx, Redd, 72
Franks, Michael, 123
Franz, Johnny, 104, 107
Freddie Freeloader (album), 133–137, 141, 156
"Freddie Freeloader" (song), 135, 179
Freeman, Russ, 61, 70
French Lick Jazz Festival, 63
Friedwald, Will, 174
Freud, Sigmund, 30, 198
Fugazi Hall, 70
Fuller, Curtis, 144

G-Noters, The, 43
Gabler, Milt, 45, 192
Gaillard, Slim, 75, 111, 169
Gales, Larry, 130, 132, 137
Gallon, Ray, 154
Gallup, 65
Ganapoler, Lou, 90
Gare de Lyon, 138
Garland, Red, 132
Garner, Erroll, 22, 188
Garner, Linton, 22
Gasser, A, 70
Gateway Plaza, 131, 141

Gay Nineties, 35
George Wein's Newport All-Stars, 94
German Jazz Festival, 80
Gershwin, George, 141, 149
Gershwin, Ira, 160
Getz, Beverley, 111
Getz, Stan, 42, 44, 112, 173
Giants of Jazz, 88
Gibbons, Bobby, 74
Gibbs, Georgia, 41
Gilbert, W. S., 175
Gilbert and Sullivan, 61
Gilberto, João, 76, 77, 154
Gill, Paul, 137, 143, 154
Gillespie, Dizzy, 24, 32, 33, 47, 61, 78, 82, 88, 94, 98, 111, 121, 124, 143, 164, 169, 171, 188
"Gimme That Wine," 40–41, 69, 72, 78, 79, 87, 91, 135
Gleason, Ralph, 61, 73, 87, 88, 92, 109
"Goin' to Chicago," 56, 79
Goldings, Larry, 131–133, 137
Goldstein, Linda, 130
Golson, Benny, 59, 109, 136, 137, 142, 144, 153
"Gone," 181
Good Git Together, A, 70, 85, 123
"Good Ol' Lady," 123
Goodman, Benny, 185
Goodman, Cheryl, 140
Goodman, Wayne, 143
Gordon, Dexter, 5, 121, 124
Gordon, Max, 107
Grace Cathedral, 92
Grammys, 3, 62, 75, 118, 121, 122, 124, 129, 135
Grand Canyon Suite, 111
Granelli, Jerry, 90, 91
Granz, Norman, 44
Grateful Dead, The, 92
Gray, Wardell, 23, 53, 61, 90, 94, 126
Great Depression, 10, 196
Great South Bay Jazz Festival, 59
Greenbaum, Irv, 54
Green, Benny, 62, 79, 102, 107
Green Book, The, 118
Green, Dave, 104, 105
Green, Freddie, 51, 56, 61, 122, 144

Green, Mark, 115, 116
Greenup, KY, 13, 23
Grey, Al, 133, 141, 142
Griffin, Johnny, 99
Griffith, Frank, 106, 140–141
Griffith, Miles, 143
Grofé, Ferde, 111
Grolnik, Don, 123
Grossman, Albert, 66
Grossman, Hal, 115
Grossman, Stefan, 121
Gryce, Gigi, 59, 70, 137
Guaraldi, Vince, 93
Guess Who's Coming to Dinner, 146
Guiffre, Jimmy, 40, 42
Gullin, Lars, 42, 173
Gurland, Bob, 120, 123, 127
Gypsy, 70

Hall, Christopher Acemandese, 174
Hall, Jim, 61
"Halloween Spooks," 75
Hammersmith Odeon, 102
Hammerstein, Oscar II, 175
Hampstead Theatre Club, 105
Hampton, Lionel, 53, 106, 137, 153, 185
Hancock, Herbie, 87
Handy, Flo, 59
Handy, George, 43
Happening for Lulu, 102
"Happy Anatomy," 71
Harris, Barry, 19, 23, 143
Harris, Marion, 172
Harris, Pat, 89
Harris, Wynonie, 75
Hart, Lorenz, 175
Hauser, Tim, 118, 129–130, 133, 177
"Hava Nagila," 16
Havin' a Ball at the Village Gate, 88–89
Hawes, Hampton, 61
Hawkins, Buster, 34
Hawkins, Coleman, 87, 173–174
Haynes, Roy, 38
Hazard, Joel, 153
Heath, Jimmy, 156
Heath, Percy, 65, 72, 121
"Heebie Jeebies," 169
Hefner, Hugh, 70

Hefti, Neal, 58
"Helluva Town, A," 59
Henderson, Bill, 140
Henderson, Fletcher, 169, 196
Henderson, Horace, 68
Henderson, Joe, 92
Hendricks, Alexander Brooks, 8–14, 73
Hendricks, Aria, 1, 22, 88–90, 94, 96, 99,
    101, 103, 104, 112, 114, 120, 130, 131,
    133, 134, 137, 138, 140, 141, 142, 143,
    144–145, 146, 148, 150, 153–154, 155,
    158–159, 163–164, 187
Hendricks, Charles, 26
Hendricks, Clifford, 26
Hendricks, Colleen (wife), 35–37, 46–47,
    65, 96, 114
Hendricks, Colleen (daughter), 46, 90, 94,
    101, 105, 120, 122, 156
Hendricks, Edward, 26
Hendricks, Eric Douglas, 28, 46, 90, 97,
    101, 103, 104, 105, 119–120, 156
Hendricks, Florence Missouri "Zuttie", 11
Hendricks Getz Rich, 114
Hendricks, Jimmy, 68, 118
Hendricks, Jon
    birth, 8
    siblings, 10
    with Art Tatum, 17–20
    war experiences, 25–32
    first marriage (to Colleen), 35
    moves to New York, 37
    meets Dave Lambert, 42
    splits with Colleen, 47
    meets Annie Ross, 50
    meets Judith, 65
    end of Lambert, Hendricks & Ross, 81
    begins solo career, 90
    lives in London, 99–108
    teaches at University of Toledo, 145–158
    death, 164
Hendricks, Jon Jr., 35, 37, 46–47, 90, 114,
    122
Hendricks, Judith, 45, 72, 76, 78, 88, 90,
    91, 92, 94, 96, 103, 104, 106, 111, 112,
    114, 115, 116, 119, 120, 124, 125, 126,
    129, 131, 134, 135, 137, 138, 140, 145,
    148, 150, 152, 156, 157, 158, 160, 163,
    184, 198, 199

Hendricks, Michele, 1, 2, 42, 90, 94, 96, 99, 101, 103, 104, 105, 106, 111, 112, 114, 119, 121, 122, 123, 124, 125, 127, 137, 138, 141, 142, 143, 144, 152, 155, 164
Hendricks Music Inc., 69, 136
Hendricks, Vivian, 11, 89
Hendricks, Stuart, 33
Hendricks, Willie Mae, 8–10, 14, 73
Herman, Woody, 40, 42, 44, 57, 68
Herod, King, 189
Heyward, DuBose, 69
Hi-Lo's, The, 60
"High as a Mountain," 135
High Flying, 75
Hillman, Richard, 94
Hines, Earl, 59
Hinton, Milt, 140
Hippocrates, 184
Holden, Stephen, 154
Holiday, Billie, 66, 82, 109, 141, 169
Holland, Dave, 99
Holloway, Red, 142
Holloway, Stanley, 89
"Home Cookin'," 75, 79, 153, 164
Hommage à Cole Porter, 105
Hone, Martin, 117
Hopkins, Bonnie, 10, 11
Hopkins, Lightnin', 16
Hopquin, Benoit, 152
Horn, Jazzmeia, 159, 169
Horn, Shirley, 125
Horne, Lena, 72
Hot Brass, 127
Hottest New Group in Jazz, The, 5, 67–69, 87, 143
"How High the Moon," 119
Howard Theater, 68
Hughes, Howard, 196
Hulu Theater, 157
hungry i, the, 62
Hunter College, 130, 131

"I Can't Give You Anything But Love, Baby," 39
"I Concentrate on You," 107
"I Cover the Waterfront," 16
"I Don't Know What Kind of Blues I Got," 71

"I Got Rhythm," 119
"I Got Soul," 107
"I Had My Share," 74
"I Like My Baby's Pudding," 75
"I Remember Clifford," 59, 136, 174
"I Want You to be My Baby," 41, 118
"I'll Bet You Thought I'd Never Find You," 142
"I'll Die Happy," 41, 78, 123
"I'm Getting Married in the Morning," 143
"I'm in the Mood for Love," 40
"In Summer" – see "Estate"
"In the Beginning, God," 92
"In the Still of the Night," 95
"In Walked Bud," 97, 98, 140, 156, 158, 174
International Association of Jazz Educators (IAJE), 152
International Hour: American Jazz, 87
International Phonetic Alphabet (IPA), 150
Is Shakespeare Dead?, 187
Isaacs, Ike, 61, 68, 70, 73
"It Could Happen to You," 107
"It's Sand, Man," 2, 55, 56, 57, 62, 79, 84, 156
"It's the Same Old Dream," 16

"Jackie," 61
Jackson, Duffy, 132
Jackson, Harold, 34
Jackson, Michael, 129
Jackson, Milt "Bags", 59
Jacobs, Dr, 31
Jacques (son), 114
Jamal, Ahmad, 22, 194
James Harry, 57
Jarreau, Al, 91, 132, 133, 134, 135, 144, 164, 171
Jazz Am Rhein Festival, 102
Jazz at Lincoln Center, 125, 130, 143
Jazz at the Maltings, 102
Jazz Bakery, 144, 153
Jazz Casual, 87
Jazz For Moderns, 75
Jazz Foundation of America, 163
Jazz Journal, 55, 85, 123, 135
Jazz Is Our Religion, 105
Jazz Scene, The, 102

Jazz Standard, The, 153, 154
Jazzman, 149
J. C. Hopkins Biggish Band, 158
Jeep Club, 24
Jefferson Airplane, 92
Jefferson, Eddie, 40, 112, 118, 120, 122,
    167, 172, 174
Jennings, Bill, 34
Jennings, Dean, 114
Jesus Christ Superstar, 106
Jewkes, Noel, 91, 93–94, 149, 172
"Jive Samba," 77, 176
Jobim, Antonio Carlos, 3, 76, 85, 181
John, Elton, 191
Johnson, Eric G., 150
Johnson, James P., 19
Johnson, J. J., 73
Johnson, John, 72
Johnson, Louis, 130
Johnson, Osie, 59
Jon Hendricks and his Beboppers, 33
Jon Hendricks & Company, 119, 122, 123,
    130, 152
Jon Hendricks & Family, 109
Jon Hendricks and the All-Stars, 142
Jon Hendricks Explosion, The, 143
Jon Hendricks Vocalstra, The, 147–149,
    152, 155
Jon Hendricks Live, 104, 107
"Jon's Mumbles," 91, 144
Jones, Eddie, 51, 52, 56, 61
Jones, Elvin, 92, 188
Jones, Hank, 19, 23, 123, 146
Jones, Jessie "Juice", 23
Jones, Philly Jo, 102, 123
Jones, Quincy, 39, 42, 48, 51, 162, 163
Jones, Thad, 88, 89
Josephson, Sanford, 75, 153
"Joshua Fit the Battle of Jericho," 14, 175
Jordan, Louis, 2, 40–41, 69, 77, 78, 87, 118
Jordan, Sheila, 1, 156
Jordan, Stanley, 123
"Joy Spring," 137, 180
Joyce, James, 61
Joyce, Mike, 115
Jukin', 129
"Jumpin' at the Woodside," 71, 88, 134,
    153, 156, 179, 180

"Jumpin' with Symphony Sid, 75
"Just a Closer Walk with Thee," 140
"Just a Little Bit of Twist," 78, 79
"Just Because I Kissed the Bride," 34
"Just Friends," 182

Kay, Connie, 121
Kay, Monte, 57
"Keester Parade," 69
Kennedy Center, 153
Kennedy, John F., 88, 188
Kenton, OH, 10
Kettering, UK, 26
Keynote label, 42
Keystone Korner, 191
King, The, 59, 70
King Alfred School, 102
King, Carole, 185
King James Bible, 13, 33, 73, 159, 187, 189
King Gustav VI, 103
King, Martin Luther, 102
King of Thailand, 44
King, Pete, 103
King Pleasure Sings, 43, 55
Kingston Trio, 90
Kirk, Andy, and his Twelve Clouds of Joy,
    15
Kirkland, Leroy, 45, 68
Knights of Pythias, 33
Kohlman, Churchill, 39
KCBS, 124
KQED, 87, 92
Kral, Irene, 93
Krasilovsky, Bill, 136
Kristofferson, Kris, 109
Krupa, Gene, 43
Kwakubaah, Reebop, 103

"La Guerre en Noir et Blanc," 152
"Lady Be Good," 170
Lambert & Co., 94
Lambert, Dave, 42–45, 48–50, 52, 54,
    56–61, 63, 67, 68, 70–72, 80, 82, 83, 88,
    89, 94, 112, 119, 123, 127, 148, 161
Lambert, Dee, 44, 95
Lambert, Hortense, 44
Lambert, Hendricks & Bavan, 84–89, 91,
    94

Lambert, Hendricks & Ross, 4, 5, 44, 56, 60, 61, 63, 65–68, 70, 71, 76, 78, 80, 82, 90, 100, 114, 115, 118, 120, 123, 129, 132, 140, 144, 153, 154, 156, 159, 187
Lambert, Hendricks & Ross Redux, 153–154
Lamond, Don, 60
Lamson's, 16
Lane, Burton, 115
Lang, Don, 46
Lasbleiz, Audrey, 146, 152–153, 155
Lascelles, Gerald, 55
"Laura," 181
Laws, Hubert, 101
"Lazybones," 181
Le Balzac, 155
Le Monde, 152
L'Oustau de Baumanière, 127
"Leaving Town," 59
Ledford, Mark, 130
Lee, Peggy, 72
Lees, Gene, 4, 68, 96, 144
Legion d'honneur, 3, 152
Legrand, Anne, 149
Lieberson, Goddard, 192
Leonard, Jack E., 72
Leonhardt, David, 6, 123–129
"Let Me See," 177
Levitt, Al, 130
Lewis, Jerry, 72
Lewis, Ramsey, 150
Lewis, Ted, 17
Licavoli mob, 20
"Li'l Darlin'," 58, 107, 112, 123, 159
Lindsay, Harold, 24
Lindsay, Kim, 130
Lindy's, 65, 66
"Listen to Monk" – see "Rhythm-a-ning"
"Little Butterfly" – see "Pannonica"
"Little Niles," 59
"Little Pony," 55, 56, 79, 84, 111
Little Rascals, 53
Little Rock integration crisis, 78
Live at Basin Street East, 85, 87, 91
Live at the Trident, 91, 165
Lloyd Webber, Andrew, 106
Lobo, Edu, 91
Logan, Ella, 53

Loesser, Frank, 39
London Jazz Festival, 155
London Vocal Project, 159, 160
Lopeman, Mark, 140
Lorton Reformatory, 66
Los Angeles Times, 115, 117
Love (album), 122, 123, 124
"Love" (song) – see Berkshire Blues
"Love Letters in the Sand," 16
Love Supreme, A, 154–155
Luck, Don and Sandra, 82
Lucoff, Don, 164
Lugano Jazz Festival, 130
Lulu, 102
Lunceford, Jimmie, 17
Lush Life, 124
Lyons, Jimmy, 72–3

Macero, Teo, 78, 98
McCann, Les, 104, 121
McCarran-Walter Immigration Act, 83
McCloud, Andy, 132
MacDonald, Country Joe, 109
McFerrin, Bobby, 119, 120, 121, 129, 130, 132, 133, 134, 144, 156, 164
McGaffick, James Sr., 8
McHugh, Jimmy, 39, 40, 172
McKayle, Donald, 115
McKinney's Cotton Pickers, 15
McKuen, Rod, 107
McRae, Carmen, 78, 85, 92, 121, 136
McVea, Jack, 111
Mahogany, Kevin, 150, 151
Maize, Bob, 93
Makeba, Miriam, 73
Mafia, The, 50
Mahones, Gildo, 61, 70, 73, 75, 78, 87, 91, 101
"Maids of Cadiz, The," 160
Mainstemmers, The, 34, 38
Malcolm X, 88
Man, 102
Mancini, Henry, 181
Mandel, Johnny, 58, 69, 76
Mangual, Jose, 100
"Manhattan-Rico," 60
Manhattan Transfer, The, 118–119, 122, 129, 130, 132, 133, 144, 156, 171, 177

Margo, George, 105
Marsalis, Wynton, 133, 135, 142, 143
Marshall, Fred, 90, 91
Martin, Dean, 72
Martin, Hugh, 76
Martin, Lee Ellen, 23
Martin, Stu, 78
Marquee club, 102
Massé, Laurel, 118
"Me and My Shadow," 17
Mecca for Moderns, 122
Meet Me at Minton's, 158
"Meetin' Time, 89
"Melba's Blues," 87
Melody Maker, 81
Memphis Slim, 16, 56
Mercer, Johnny, 53, 61, 76, 175, 181, 188
Mercury Ballroom, 152
Méridien Hotel, 132
Merrill, Helen, 170
Merry Macs, The, 43, 119
"Messy Bessie," 41
Metronome, 45, 55
Meyers, Paul, 140, 143, 144, 145, 154
MGM, 53
"Mighty Like a Rose," 16
Mihelič, Peter, 143, 153
Miles Ahead (album and project), 1–2,
    111, 140, 141, 159–163
"Miles Ahead" (song), 160, 162
Mill Valley, CA, 93, 109
Millennium Park, 150
Miller, Big, 73, 74, 75
Mills Brothers, 56
Mind on Fire, 152
Miner, Neal, 153
Mingus, Charles, 55, 72, 85, 88, 124
"Minnie the Moocher," 169
Minton's Playhouse, 144, 158
"Misty," 119
Mitchell, Billy, 23
Mitchell, Joni, 5, 69
Mitchell, Red, 103, 123
Mitchell, Tyler, 132
"Moanin'," 68, 109, 137, 154, 156, 159
Modern Jazz Quartet, 57, 60, 126
Modernaires, The, 43
Monk, Barbara "Boo-boo", 136

Monk, Thelonious, 3, 60, 91, 92, 97, 136,
    137, 143, 176
Monk, T. S. "Toot", 136, 158
Monterey Jazz Festival, 72–4, 88, 90, 93,
    114, 144
Montgomery, Buddy, 70
Montgomery, Monk, 70
Montgomery, Wes, 70
Montreux Jazz Festival, 132
Moody, Bill, 103, 105, 118
Moody, James, 40, 53, 144
"Moody"/"Moody's Mood for Love," 39,
    42, 53, 172
"Moon River," 181
Moore, Colleen Jean – see Colleen
    Hendricks
Morello, Joe, 78
Moreno, Joyce, 141
Morgan, Lee, 140
Morrison, Van, 156, 157
Moss, Anne-Marie, 76, 82
Mossblad, Gunnar, 146, 148, 153–158
Muldaur, Maria, 121
Mulligan, Gerry, 38, 70, 143
Mundy, Jimmy, 71
Murphy, Mark, 52, 99, 150–151, 152, 156,
    191
Muse Records, 122
"Music in the Air" – see "Wildwood"
Musicians' Union, 100
My Dancing Life, 115
"My Papa Doesn't Two Time, No Time,"
    169
"My Ship," 160, 176
Myers, Marc, 95

NAACP, 34, 66
"Nagasaki," 23
Nakasian, Stephanie, 1, 125, 168
"Nature Boy," 107
NEA Awards, 140
"Nearer My God to Thee," 14
New Cranks, 82
New Deal, The, 10
New Orleans, 74
New School, 131, 160
New York, NY, 5, 59
New York Times, 87, 123, 154

New Yorker magazine, 73
Newark, OH, 8, 9, 14
Newport Jazz Festival, 62, 71, 87, 114
Nice Jazz Festival, 132
Nicholas, Big Nick, 87
Nicholson, Reggie, 137
"Night and Day," 182
"Night in Tunisia, A," 78
Nightlife, The, 135
"No More," 101
"No More Blues," 77
No One But Me, 127
Nob Hill, 92
"Now's the Time," 62, 174
Nunes, Flip, 90, 93
Nureyev, Rudolph, 102

"O Pato," 77
O'Brien, Hod, 125, 143
Oddfellows, 33
Odetta, 73
Offbeat of Avenues, The, 130
"Oh Bess, Oh Where's My Bess?" 141, 176
"Old Folks," 94, 109, 111
Oliver, Joe "King", 74
On Broadway Theater, 114
"On the Atchison, Topeka, and the Santa
    Fe," 181
"On the Trail," 111
"One Note Samba," 76, 85
"One O'Clock Jump," 55, 63, 84, 87, 189
One Pair of Eyes, 103
"One Rose," 91
O'Neal, Ryan, 148
Opposite Lock club, 117
Osarabo, Eghosa, 93, 100
O'Toole, Peter, 102
Ottawa Hills, 146, 147, 157
Our Gang Follies of 1938, 53
Overtones of Bel Canto, 150
Oxenhorn, Wendy, 163
Oxley, Tony, 99

Pacino, Al, 148
"Pannonica," 91, 136
Paramount Theater, 17
Park West, 150

Parker, Charlie "Bird", 2, 3, 4, 19, 32, 33,
    36–38, 43, 50, 61, 62, 95, 111, 119, 122,
    137, 143, 169, 182
Patrice Munsel Show, 53
Paul Masson Winery, 114
Paxton, Tom, 84
Payne, Sonny, 51, 56, 61
Payne Theological Seminary, 10
Peacocks, The, 112
Pellitieri, Marcello, 143
Pena, Paco, 105
Pennebaker, D. A., 94
People I Know, 148
Pep's Lounge, 76
Pepper, Art, 124
Perez, Danilo, 131
Perry, Mozart, 24
Peterson, Oscar, 191
Pettiford, Oscar, 61, 72, 98, 163
Philips Studios, 104
Pickwick club, 103
Pieces of 8, 149
Pied Pipers, The, 119
Pierce, Nat, 51, 56, 59
Playboy Jazz Festival, 72
Playboy's Penthouse, 70
"Please Send Me Someone to Love," 75
Pleasure, King, 2, 39, 42, 167, 172–174,
    198
Poindexter, Pony, 74, 75, 78, 84
Pointer, June, 111
Pointer Sisters, The, 111
Poitier, Sidney, 146
Ponce de León, Juan, 156
"Popity Pop," 75, 143
Porgy and Bess, 141, 149, 181
Porter, Cole, 107, 174, 175
Powell, Bud, 4, 38, 98
Powell, Reg, 103
"Preacher, The," 2, 79
Presenting Lily Mars, 53
Prestige Records, 43, 53, 55, 68, 172
"Pretty Strange," 70
Prima, Louis, 41, 62
Prohibition, 20
Providence Jazz Festival, 153
PRS, 135

Psalm, 155
Purple gang, 20
Pythodd, The, 33

Rachmaninoff, Sergei, 149
"Rainbow's End," 101
Rainey, Ma, 75
Rampton, Kenny, 143
Randall's Island Jazz Festival, 59
Ransom, Bishop R. C., 10
Rare Silk, 135
Ravinia Festival, 150
Ray, Roger, 145
Razaf, Andy, 39
RCA Records, 94, 192
Real Ambassadors, The, 78
Red Hill Inn, 61
Redman, Don, 169
Reagan, Ronald, 3
Reeves, Dianne, 144, 156
"Reflections," 140, 158
Regal Theater, 68
Regattabar, 153
Reminiscing in Tempo, 130
Reprise Records, 87
Reunion, 149
"Reza," 91
"Rhythm-a-ning," 135, 140, 155, 158
Rich, Buddy, 105, 114, 131, 188
Richardson, Jon, 152
Richmond, VA, 8, 10
Richmond, Howie, 76
Richardson, Jon, 4
Rickles, Don, 72
Rimsky-Korsakov, Nikolai, 149
"River's Invitation," 89
Rivoli Theater, 16
RKO Pictures, 196
Roach, Max, 59, 88, 98, 146
Roberts, Lucky, 39
Robinson Junior High School, 17
Rochester, NY, 33
Rodgers and Hammerstein, 155
Rodgers, Richard, 181
"Roll 'em Pete," 143
Rolling Stone, 108
Rollins, Sonny, 4, 61

Ronnie Scott's club, 99, 100, 102, 103, 104,
    105, 155, 156, 160, 170, 191, 195
Rose Theater, 156
Rosicrucian Order, 188
Ross, Annie, 1, 44, 45, 50, 51–54, 56, 57,
    59–61, 63, 65–70, 75, 76, 79–83, 103,
    105, 112, 123, 127, 131, 144, 150, 152,
    156, 176
Ross, Holli, 125, 155, 167, 181
Ross, Jerry, 39
"Round Midnight," 91, 140
Rouse, Charlie, 98
Rowe, Monk, 146
Rowles, Jimmy, 112
Royal Academy of Music, 159, 162
Royal Bopsters Project, 156
Royal Festival Hall, 62
Royal Roost, 95
Runswick, Daryl, 103, 104, 127, 165
Runswick, Elaine, 103
Russell, Curly, 38
Russell, George, 5
Rushing, Jimmy, 94, 114
"Rusty Dusty Blues," 72, 79

St Martin-in-the-Fields, 159
St Paul's Cathedral, 102
St Peter's Church, 1, 163
Sahl, Mort, 62
"Salt Peanuts," 32, 33, 88
Salud! João Gilberto, 76–77, 107
San Francisco Chronicle, 88, 92, 109
San Francisco Jazz Festival, 121
Santamaria, Mongo, 88, 97
"Saturday Night Fish Fry," 77
"Saudade da Bahia," 77
Sausalito, CA, 90
Savitt, Jan, 169
Scott, Bruce, 120
Scott High School, 21, 22
Scott, Ray, 123
Scott, Ronnie, 97, 99, 102, 107
Sebastian, John, 121
"See See Rider," 75
"September of My Years," 140, 154, 156
September Songs – see Times of Love
"Sermonette," 69, 79

SHAEF, 28
"Shake, Rattle and Roll," 62
Shakespeare, William, 82, 173, 180, 187
Shanghai Jazz, 144
Shank, Bud, 77
Shavers, Charlie, 106
Shearing, George, 62, 143
Shéherazade, 149
Shelley, Percy Bysshe, 175
"Shiny (Silk) Stockings," 85, 87, 91, 104, 137
Shore, Dinah, 53
Short, Jack and Mary, 53
Shorter, Wayne, 112
"Shorty George," 179
Sides, Doug, 124
"Sidewinder, The," 140
Sidran, Ben, 4, 5, 51, 109–112, 165
Siegel, Janis, 118–119
Sigman, Carl, 71
Silver, Horace, 61, 62, 75, 84, 94, 153, 191
Sims, Zoot, 44, 57, 61, 94
Sinatra, Frank, 60, 72, 92, 100, 140, 143, 167, 169, 185
"Since I Fell for You," 143
Sing a Song of Basie, 55–59, 71, 87, 123, 129, 130, 148, 159, 172, 194
Sing Along with Basie, 58, 89, 179
Sing Ellington, 68, 70, 75
Sing Me a Jazz Song, 112
"Singing the Blues," 172
"Sister Sadie," 89
Sloane, Carol, 76, 82
"Slow Train," 107
Smith, Jimmy, 87, 100
Smith, Keely, 41, 62
Smith, Marvin "Smitty", 124
Smith, Willie "The Lion", 19
Smithsonian, The, 160
"So What," 174
"Social Call," 59, 137
"Some Stopped on de Way," 74
"Sometimes I Feel Like a Motherless Child," 75
"Somewhere to Lay My Weary Head," 124
"Song is You, The," 4, 36
Sons and Daughters, 92

Sorbonne, The, 149
Soundstage, 112
Speckled Red, 16
"Spirit Feel," 59, 70, 72
Springfield, Dusty, 105
"Springsville," 160
Stanyan label, 107
"Stardust," 39, 189
Staton, Dakota, 102
Steps Ahead, 123
Stewart, Buddy, 42–43
Sticky Mack, 132
Storyville, 60
Stott, Wally, 107
Strayhorn, Billy, 196
"Sufferin' Blues," 75
"Sugar," 135
"Summertime," 69, 160
"Sun Gonna Shine in My Door," 75
Swift, Veronica, 1
Swing Buddies, The, 22, 23
"Swing Low Sweet Chariot," 74
"Swing That Music," 135
Swingers!, The, 61, 62, 72, 107, 171
"Swingin' Till the Girls Come Home," 61, 72, 78, 79, 85, 153, 159, 163, 171
Swingle Singers, The, 188
Symphony Hall, 144

"Take the 'A' Train," 153
Talk of the Town, The, 105
Tate Gallery, 82
Tatum, Art, 2, 17–22, 32, 36, 61, 170, 190
Tatum family, 17
Taylor, Creed, 51–57
Taylor, James, 185
Telarc label, 142
Telesforo, Gegé, 142
Tell Me the Truth (album), 109, 111, 142, 159
Tell Me the Truth (film), 25, 153, 155
"Tell Me the Truth" (song), 112, 123, 153
Territory bands, 15
Terry, Clark, 87, 88, 91, 94, 142, 144
"That Old Black Magic," 62
Thelma (girlfriend), 23
Thelonious Music Corp., 136

Theosophical Society, 82
"This Could Be the Start of Something,"
    85, 87, 91
"This Here," 78
Thomas, Hywel, 106
Thomas, Leon, 112
"Three Blind Mice," 89
Three Musketeers, The, 197
Thriller, 129
"Tickle Toe," 59
Tiedtke's, 16
Times, The, 189
Times of Love, 107, 111, 123
Timmons, Bobby, 68, 84, 137
Tinseley, Dave, 28–29
Tolbert, Fred "Freeloader", 135
Toledo, OH, 4, 13, 19–24, 145–158
Toledo Free Press, 157
Toledo Jazz Festival, 152
Toledo Jazz Society, 4
Tomkins, Les, 57
Tormé, Mel, 93, 99, 125, 143, 167, 169, 170
Tracey, Stan, 99
Tralfamadore, The, 125
Travis, Mike, 103
"Trem de Ferro," 77
Trianon Ballroom, 16
Trident, The, 90
"Trinkle Tinkle," 135, 158
Tucker, George, 87
Tunnell, George "Bon Bon", 169
Turner, Big Joe, 143
Turrentine, Stanley, 133, 135
Twain, Mark, 187
"Twist City," 78, 79
"Twisted," 51, 53, 68, 70, 127, 176
"Two for the Blues," 56

Ukegwo, Ugonna, 137
Umbria Jazz Festival, 130
Underground, 98
Union College, Schenectady, 84
United Artists, 61, 70
United Future Organisation, 142
United World Federalists, 34
University of California, Berkeley, 109
University of Toledo, 4, 34, 36, 73, 145,
    146, 155, 157, 158, 187, 198

"Until I Met You" – see "Corner Pocket"
"Upa Neguinho," 91
USO, 26
US Supreme Court, 65
Utah Beach, 26

Vance, Joel, 123
Vaughan, Sarah, 80, 83, 121, 122, 143
Venice Beach Boys, 140
Victor Records, 169
Village Gate, 94
Village Vanguard, 60, 90, 107, 118
Village Voice, 87
Vine Street Bar and Grill, 126
Vitro, Roseanna, 171
Vocalese, 129, 133
"Voce e Eu," 77
Voice of Annie Ross, The, 53
Vuckovich, Larry, 93, 99, 100, 112, 114, 149

Waiters and Bellmen's Club, 21–24
"Walkin'," 78, 87
Wall, Murray, 124, 127
Waller, Edward, 10, 15
Waller, Thomas "Fats", 15, 19, 39
Wally Heider studio, 109
Walsh, Ellis, 77
Wardell, Anita, 159, 160, 161, 163
Warlocks, The – see The Grateful Dead
Warner Bros, 71
Warren AME Church, 14
Water Music, 156
"Watermelon Man," 87, 91
Waters, Muddy, 16
Watkins, Doug, 23
Watson, Andy, 137, 140, 153, 154, 165, 168
Watson, Leo, 169
WBAI, 94
WBKB, 70
WTTW, 112
Webster, Ben, 15, 74, 169, 171, 193
Weinstock, Bob, 53
"Well Alright, OK, You Win," 62
"Well You Needn't," 91
Welles, Orson, 196
Wenner, Jan, 109
Werber, Frank, 90
West Side Story, 59, 101

Weston, Randy, 59, 61, 70, 107, 123, 176
Westport, CT, 94
Westwood Playhouse, 115
"What Am I Here For?," 70
Wheeler, Kenny, 99
"Where," 61
"Where?," 107
White, Josh, 15
White Men Can't Jump, 140
Whitman Red, 14
Wilberforce University, 10
"Wildwood," 70, 156
Williams, Andy, 167
Williams, Joe, 58, 60, 62, 63, 70, 72, 83, 92,
    100, 114, 140, 141, 144, 167, 185
Williams, Mary-Lou, 102
Williamson, Nicol, 102
"Willie's Tune," 123
Wilmer, Val, 105
Wilson, Nancy, 150
Wilson, Teddy, 21, 185
Wiltshire, George "Teacho", 42, 44, 53
Winehouse, Amy, 157
Winstone, Norma, 105
Winterland Ballroom, 109
"With Malice Towards None," 75

"With 'er 'ead Tucked Underneath 'er
    Arm," 89
Witherspoon, Jimmy, 73, 74, 75, 93, 100,
    114
Wolf, Don, 122
Woods, Phil, 59, 99
World Pacific Records, 70
World, Take a Holiday – see *The Real
    Ambassadors*
World War II, 2, 23, 24, 43, 185, 186
Wormsworth, Jimmy, 61, 67, 70
"WPA Blues," 75
WSPD, 22
Wythe County, VA, 8

"Yeh Yeh," 88, 91
Yes, 102
"You Baby," 48
"You'll See," 155
Young Generation, The, 105
Young, Lester "Prez", 5, 22, 59, 71, 74, 75,
    178
Young, Trummy, 78

Zawinul, Joe, 118
Zimmerman, James, 20, 140, 188

www.ingramcontent.com/pod-product-compliance
Lightning Source LLC
Chambersburg PA
CBHW070842100426
42813CB00003B/712